25-

D0076972

28 DAY BOOK

B Smith J
Jeansonne, Glen
Gerald L.K. Smith,
minister of hate.

GERALD L. K. SMITH

‡

GERALD L. K. SMITH

Minister of Hate

Glen Jeansonne

YALE UNIVERSITY PRESS

NEW HAVEN AND LONDON

Designed by Jo Aerne and set in Melior type by
Keystone Typesetting, Orwigsburg, Pennsylvania.
Printed in the United States of America by Murray
Printing Co., Westford, Massachusetts.

Library of Congress Cataloging-in-Publication Data
Jeansonne, Glen, 1946–
Gerald L. K. Smith, minister of hate / Glen
Jeansonne.
   p. cm.
Bibliography: p.
Includes index.
ISBN 0–300–04148–9 (alk. paper)
1. Smith, Gerald L. K. (Gerald Lyman Kenneth),
1898– . 2. Politicians—United States—Biography.
3. Protestants—United States—Biography.
4. United States—Politics and government—1933–
1945. 5. Conservatism—United States—History—
20th century. I. Title.
E748.S66J43 1988
973.91′092′4—dc19
[B]   88–814
        CIP

The paper in this book meets the guidelines for
permanence and durability of the Committee on
Production Guidelines for Book Longevity of the
Council on Library Resources.

10 9 8 7 6 5 4 3 2 1

To Sharon Pace Jeansonne
whose love inspires me

Contents

Illustrations

frontispiece

Gerald L. K. Smith addressing a meeting of his Christian Nationalist Crusade in the 1940s. (Courtesy of the Bentley Historical Library, University of Michigan)

following page 100

Gerald L. K. Smith in the 1930s. (Courtesy of the Bentley Historical Library, University of Michigan)

Gerald L. K. Smith poses with church members outside the "Azusa" Pentecostal Temple. (Courtesy of the Bentley Historical Library, University of Michigan)

Huey P. Long addressing a rally of farmers. (Courtesy of the Louisiana State Museum, New Orleans)

Huey P. Long marching in support of bonuses for veterans in 1932. (Courtesy of the Louisiana State Museum, New Orleans)

Huey P. Long. (Courtesy of Louisiana State University Libraries)

Huey P. Long escorted by bodyguards at the Louisiana State Capitol. (Courtesy of the Louisiana State Museum, New Orleans)

The body of Huey P. Long lying in state. (Courtesy of Louisiana State University Libraries)

Gerald L. K. Smith campaigning for the U.S. Senate in 1942. (Courtesy of the Bentley Historical Library, University of Michigan)

Gerald L. K. Smith at an America First Party rally during World War II. (Courtesy of the Bentley Historical Library, University of Michigan)

ix

The cover of the first issue of Smith's *The Cross and the Flag*. (Courtesy of the Bentley Historical Library, University of Michigan)

Gerald L. K. Smith and Elna M. Smith at the foot of a monument to Huey P. Long (1940s). (Courtesy of the Bentley Historical Library, University of Michigan)

A meeting of Smith's Christian Nationalist Crusade in the 1940s. (Courtesy of the Bentley Historical Library, University of Michigan)

Gerald L. K. Smith addressing a meeting of his Christian Nationalist Crusade in the 1940s. (Courtesy of the Bentley Historical Library, University of Michigan)

Gerald L. K. Smith in his office at Penn Castle, Eureka Springs, Arkansas (1974).

The Christ of the Ozarks, Eureka Springs, Arkansas. (Courtesy of the Bentley Historical Library, University of Michigan)

Acknowledgments

Many hands in addition to my own have gone into making this book. Some of them have contributed large portions of their time with no more reward than the knowledge that they had helped a friend. The most difficult favor one can ask fellow scholars is to put aside their work to help with mine; these people have done that. Some read and edited chapters through many revisions and suggested chapter titles. Some wrote dozens of letters of recommendation for me which contributed to my receiving fellowships and grants that aided my research and writing. Some furnished advice on directions my study might take; others gave their time for interviews. In addition to my academic friends people not normally concerned with academic publishing have helped me. Some of them photocopied materials in places too distant for me to travel to. Some furnished the intellectual sustenance that all writers need. My wife, Sharon, provided inspiration and moral support, as did my parents. The work and any mistakes are mine, but I could not have written the book alone.

Juanita Terry provided research assistance. Susan Sarrow photocopied the voluminous files of the Eureka Springs *Times-Echo* and Ginger Shiras did the same for the Little Rock *Arkansas Gazette*. Stephen A. Webre read and edited the entire manuscript and Steve Bhaerman provided many stylistic revisions. Herbert M. Levine provided assistance at all stages of the manuscript. James Barros provided sound counsel about publishing.

During the year I spent in Ann Arbor the staff of the Bentley Historical Library at the University of Michigan became my surrogate family. I especially want to thank Director Francis X. Blouin, and William K. Wallach, Thomas E. Powers, Nancy R. Bartlett, Diane L. Hatfield, and Kenneth P. Scheffel. Robert M. Warner brought the Smith Papers to Michigan and wrote letters of recommendation for grants. It was a pleasure to be a colleague of Sidney Fine, who helped acclimate me to the University of Michigan and also wrote letters.

The staff at the Louisiana State University Archives also provided assistance beyond the call of duty: Robert Martin, Gisela Lozada, Myrna Whitley, and Stone Miller. Lee Dalzell did yeoman work for me at the Williams College Library. James MacGregor Burns of Williams College took time from his own work to support mine.

I wish to thank Jerome Bakst, Gail Gans, and Alan M. Schwartz of the Anti-Defamation League of B'nai B'rith; Milton Ellerin and Harold Applebaum of the American Jewish Committee; Leon Schur of the Milwaukee American Jewish Committee; and Judy Mann of the Milwaukee Jewish Council for providing information.

Leo P. Ribuffo, Alan Brinkley, and Michael Bouton shared their research with me. Hubert Humphreys of Louisiana State University-Shreveport arranged oral interviews for me. Ed Jeffords consented to a taped interview and suggested other interview subjects in Eureka Springs, Arkansas. Gordon Hall provided me with substantial information from his files on political extremism. I wish to thank Charles Grench of the Yale University Press for his steadfast interest and prompt consideration of my manuscript.

My mentors, William Ivy Hair, and Richard A. Bartlett, encouraged my work and gave valuable suggestions. My colleagues at the University of Wisconsin–Milwaukee—among them Bill Roselle, Bruce Fetter, Reginald Horsman, Roland Stromberg, Walter Weare, James Jablonowski, and Frank Cassell—were generous with their time and assistance.

In addition to those above, the following friends read all or part of the manuscript: Edward F. Haas, Wendy Bousfield, Milton Bates, Mathé Allain, James Cortada, Margaret Fisher Dalrymple, Michael Beschloss, and Dimitri Lazo. My students at the University of Southwestern Louisiana, Williams College, the University of Wisconsin–Milwaukee, and the University of Michigan stimulated my interest in the far right, particularly Alan Aides at Williams College.

I wish to acknowledge grants from the following granting institutions: the American Council of Learned Societies, Earhart Foundation, American Philosophical Society (2), Williams College, University of Wisconsin-Milwaukee, American Historical Association (Beveridge), and National Endowment for the Humanities.

I can never repay my friends and colleagues for their generous giving except perhaps someday to do the same for someone else.

Prologue

‡

*Those who crusade not for God in themselves, but against the
devil in others, never succeed in making the world better but
leave it either as it was, or sometimes even perceptibly worse
than it was before the crusade began.*

—Aldous Huxley

It is June 1979. I am driving for the third time to Eureka Springs, a once-sleepy hamlet perched high in the Arkansas Ozarks. Here I plan to continue my research on Gerald L. K. Smith, who altered the community by constructing a complex of religious shrines and who is buried nearby. Route 23 snakes its way over and around the mountains, through verdant pines and oaks dotted with bursts of azaleas and violets. The rocky terrain is only sparsely settled, but it is sprinkled with real estate developments, lakes, and golf courses. The narrow mountain road is treacherous for one like me, reared in the flat Mississippi delta of South Louisiana—particularly because I am tempted to snatch glimpses of the breathtaking mountaintop views.

As I near the town limits, motels, restaurants, gas stations, nightclubs, and gift shops suddenly appear, crammed together, clinging to the craggy peak. Eureka Springs is literally built into the side of a mountain. As dusk settles I can hear foot-stomping, hand-clapping music emanating from the Pine Mountain Jamboree, a large, orange, corrugated metal building that features country music and comedy. Closer to town there is a water slide for children, then a series of motels: Pine Cone, Pine Top Lodge, Land of Nod Motel, Swiss Village, Le Roi, Eureka Springs Motel. I turn onto the winding little main street, barely wide enough for two cars. The downtown area is bustling with gift and curio shops selling hand-made jewelry, leather goods, and postcards featuring the projects that are the objects of my research.

1

Fifteen years ago, on a summer vacation, I visited what was then a tiny community. It was charming, but utterly devoid of any activity of interest to an energetic high-school senior. I stayed in the old Basin Hotel in the heart of Eureka Springs, run-down, rickety, unsafe, and nearly empty.

In 1974 I again drove to Eureka Springs, this time to interview Gerald L. K. Smith. The old, shabby homes I remembered from my earlier trip had been repaired and refurbished with new coats of paint. In Basin Square, beside the renovated Basin Hotel, a country and folk group was filling the street with music. I even saw a few coffee houses for rock-and-roll enthusiasts. Now, in 1979, it is livelier still. Smith has transformed the face of the town.

Gerald L. K. Smith came to Eureka Springs as an elderly entrepreneur of religious tourist attractions. He constructed a seven-story cross-like statue of Christ in 1965, followed it in 1969 by a Passion Play depicting the Crucifixion and Ascension of Christ, and still later by a religious art gallery and Bible museum. While some of the older retired folk were unhappy about their community's new business and congestion, the majority accepted Smith as an economic godsend.

To most Eureka Springs residents, Smith seemed a gentle, kindly patriarch whose work had rejuvenated his adopted community. Few of them knew about Smith's notorious past—that he was a political organizer for Louisiana's Huey Long, a brilliant, demagogic orator in the 1930s, a traveling speaker against Communism in the 1940s, and a visceral anti-Semite for much of his adult life. Since 1942 he published *The Cross and the Flag*, a hate-sheet of limited circulation but of substantial influence on the racist ultra-right. He ran for president and for the U.S. Senate. He knew generals, politicians, journalists, and high-level businessmen. He conducted direct-mail campaigns (before contemporary political action committees adopted such tactics), which brought him a comfortable income. He was described as "the Horatio Alger of the American fifth column"[1] during World War II and in 1971 was labeled "probably the most vicious of the rabble-rousing and sensational hate-mongers operating today."[2] H. L. Mencken said of him: "Gerald L. K. Smith is the greatest orator of them all, not the greatest by an inch or a foot or a yard or a mile, but the greatest by at least two light years. He begins where the next best leaves off. He is the master of masters, the champion boob-bumper of all epochs, the Aristotle and Johann Sebastian Bach of all known ear-splitters, dead or alive."[3] Herbert Harris, comparing Smith to another spellbinder of the 1930s, wrote that "before a live audience he makes Father Coughlin seem somewhat less articulate than a wax-works."[4] Smith's utilization of his golden voice in the service of bigotry, however, had led the *Arkansas Gazette* to editorialize, on hearing that

Smith planned to move to Eureka Springs: "Smith is no garden variety racist or hate monger. He is worse, by any objective standard, than Robert Welch, and far worse than any of the lesser bigots."[5]

Such thoughts flicker through my mind as I register at the Eureka Inn, a fashionable new motel featuring a Gazebo dining room and a heated pool. I am sharing the inn with a group of girls from the Bossier City, Louisiana, Baptist Church, one of many church groups bused in to see Smith's towering *Christ of the Ozarks* and to attend his *Great Passion Play.*

The following morning I drive south along Route 62 to the site of the *Christ of the Ozarks,* the Passion Play, the Christ Only Art Gallery, and the Bible Museum. The winding road, full of potholes, is flanked on either side by real estate developments I did not see in 1974. There are also mobile home parks and dozens of garish signs, neon and painted. Turning off Route 62 onto a dirt road leading to the *Christ of the Ozarks,* I see lush pastures on both sides and as many as two dozen Lilliputian horses, smaller than Shetland ponies when full-grown, which Smith had raised. I am tempted to stop and pet them. Raising miniature horses was Smith's hobby; when living in Los Angeles he rented a number of stalls for them at a private stable.

A quarter of a mile down the dirt road is the *Christ of the Ozarks.* It is a simple, white, plaster-and-cement depiction of Christ with arms extended, appearing as a cross at a distance. Nearby is a small living quarter for a security guard. A sign beneath the statue reads: "Free, But Please Register." Tourists who sign their names and addresses become entries on the mailing list of the Elna M. Smith Foundation, a nonprofit religious corporation organized by Smith and now run by his chief surviving assistant, Charles F. Robertson.

The statue has no inscription. Some local people I talk with believe that within fifty years it will be crumbling. There are already cracks at the base. Directly behind the statue is a marker honoring the sculptor and his assistant. To the right, as I face the statue, is a double tomb marked "Smith," where Gerald and his wife are buried. There is no inscription on the tomb other than the name and their dates of birth and death. Smith died in 1976; his wife outlived him by four years.

About a hundred yards beyond the *Christ of the Ozarks* is the Passion Play ticket office and the Christ Only Art Gallery, both housed in a single-story white stucco building. Directly across the road is a smaller, circular structure, also white—the Smith Memorial Chapel and the Bible Museum.

When I visited the art gallery in 1974 there were, just inside, large portraits of the Smiths, but they were removed after an unkind magazine article pointed out that Smith's advertisements claim only portraits of

Christ, his family, and his disciples are housed in the gallery.[6] However, the museum still contains a small wooden bust of Emmett Sullivan, sculptor of the *Christ of the Ozarks*, and a similar bust of Robert Hyde, who plays Christ in the Passion Play.

The building is small for an art gallery and its contents are arranged haphazardly. Many of the paintings and other objects are unlabeled, and even those labeled usually give only the artist's name. These pieces were collected by someone who knew little about art; besides works of substantial value are trinkets and trivia, including many small replicas of the *Christ of the Ozarks*. Assembling this collection must have taken hundreds of thousands of dollars, perhaps millions. Smith claimed that the money came from an inheritance of Mrs. Smith, but more likely it was diverted from donations to his Christian Nationalist Crusade.

The collections depict Christ in every form imaginable. There are oil paintings, watercolors, tapestries, jewelry, candelabra, cups and mugs, pottery, and small figures in bronze, wood, porcelain, gold, silver, and brass. Aspects of Christ's life are also portrayed: most prominent are Madonnas, Mary and Joseph, the disciples, and scenes of the Annunciation, the Last Supper, the Crucifixion, and the Resurrection. Included are pieces from the seventeenth, eighteenth, nineteenth, and twentieth centuries, along with a few earlier items, such as a 1492 bronze bust of Christ. Perhaps the most intricate effort is a miniature wood carving of the Hague Cathedral, made during the nineteenth century by an unknown priest who devoted fifteen years to the project. My favorite is a work entitled *The Last Supper*, by Mrs. Wesley Whitson, a bright mosaic made entirely of butterfly and moth wings. It must have taken years of painstaking effort and hundreds of moths and butterflies to construct.

Across the street from the Christ Only Art Gallery, in a smaller, domed building painted white like the others, are the Smith Memorial Chapel and Bible Museum. The upper floor houses the chapel; the basement, the Bible collection. After inspecting the chapel, where I see no one praying but several tourists gawking at the garish interior, I descend to the Bible Museum. The Smiths began collecting Bibles shortly after their marriage and continued for fifty-four years until Gerald's death. I enter as one of the two attendants is beginning a tour. The room is small, so I can hear the guide while looking on my own. After the tour concludes, a matronly woman approaches me and tells me intimate details of the Smiths and their collection. She is quite proud of her knowledge.

The Bibles are grouped according to their origins. Lining the walls of one section of the circular room are hundreds of foreign Bibles. There is a Martin Luther collection, an Egyptian and Hebrew collection, a Quaker collection, and a collection of American Indian Bibles, including a rare Cherokee Indian Bible. There are Bibles owned by such prominent Americans as George Washington and Thomas Jefferson, and a Gideon Bible signed by each of the founders of the Gideon Society. There are wedding Bibles. Smith must have had a sense of humor, for one collection consists entirely of misprints, including one that reads, "Thou shalt commit adultery." There is a handwritten eleventh-century Bible written on vellum and a 420-year-old Bible in five languages. The oldest artifact is a cornerstone from a pagan temple before the time of Christ. More recent is a "Space Bible" taken aloft and later donated to the Smiths by an astronaut. There is also a hieroglyphic Bible depicting the Gospel in pictures for nonreaders.

Most interesting to the historian is a collection of Bibles and artifacts given to the Smith family by friends. Included is Smith's silver communion set, a Bible that belonged to his parents, and one he used in his preaching. I am fascinated by a Bible given to Smith by a rabbi, containing the following handwritten inscription: "May 2, 1930. Property of B'nai Zion Congregation. Presented to our dear brother Dr. Gerald Smith on the day he preached a beautiful Jewish sermon out of his genuinely true Christian heart. Rabbi Abr. Brill."

After viewing the art gallery and Bible Museum, I stroll about a quarter of a mile along a dirt path to the site of the main attraction, the *Great Passion Play*. The outdoor set of the Passion Play is a four-hundred-foot street scene of Old Jerusalem, located in a hollow between two mountains. The amphitheater, which seats forty-two hundred viewers, is built into the side of one mountain, the set is in the valley, and the Christ of the Ozarks is atop the other peak, Magnetic Mountain. Smith has named the site of the Passion Play Mount Oberammergau, after the village in Germany that stages a Passion Play every ten years.

Smith insisted that the complex of religious constructions was not commercial, but was rather the Smith family's "gift to humanity." This was largely true while he was still alive. However, since his death and since my previous visit in 1974, numerous commercial activities have been added. A gift shop sells postcards, T-shirts emblazoned with "Christ of the Ozarks" (for six dollars), cups, saucers, jewelry, copies of Smith's autobiography (modestly entitled *Besieged Patriot*), and some of his pamphlets and religious books. Outside the amphitheater are machines offering coffee, soft drinks, sandwiches, ice cream, potato chips, popcorn, and other junk food.

There are several large parking lots in the complex, but there is a major traffic jam after each performance of the Passion Play, since the only access to the amphitheater is by a single one-lane highway. Security is tight. Uniformed men direct parking. When Mrs. Smith was still alive, a deputy sheriff wearing a pistol would stand beside her as she autographed programs.

The play starts at eight-thirty because it must be dark for the performance. Smith's taped voice asks the members of the audience to tell their relatives about the play, because the performance is something they shall never forget and should be shared by all Christians.

The Passion Play is impressive, but I come away from it troubled. Most of the people who have seen it seem to have enjoyed it, and, I must admit, so have I. Smith made a remarkable comeback in his twilight years, and the image of him that lingers among people who know little about him is not that of a bigot. He is remembered instead as a benign, grandfatherly builder of Christian shrines. This is not as it should be.

Though not a great man, Smith was an important and interesting one. As a biographer, I believe that individuals like Smith influence the course of history even if they do not determine it in the manner of the "great man theory." After all, it has been written that he was "the most persistently successful of America's anti-Jewish propagandists," that he was "the most infamous American fascist," and that his mouthpiece, The Cross and the Flag, was one of a handful of periodicals that had "influence out of all proportion to their circulations."[7]

However, much of a person's impact on his or her era depends upon chance and timing. An individual is nothing without fortune, the accident of birth, the manner of upbringing, his or her social and ethnic identity and origins; even ability is something of an accident. There is still another element, at once easily perceived and difficult to define. When charisma and social conditions converge, their chemistry may produce a reaction without which either alone would remain inert. Bert Cochran, in his biography of Harry S Truman, explains:

> In political leadership there is a romantic aspect. All leadership partakes of the element of magic, whether supplied by the leader through personal elan, or by the machinery of government through institutionalized ritual. . . . It matters little that the phenomenon is an optical illusion, that without the social environment selecting the great man who is enabled to speak with the voice of multitudes, Bonaparte would have ended up a staff officer in the service of some foreign prince, and Hitler would have achieved the status of a Teutonic Gerald L. K. Smith.[8]

Only by understanding individuals can we comprehend social movements. Only by studying a leader can we determine the mind of his or her followers. Some individuals have an influence entirely disproportionate to the intellectual validity of their doctrines. They may begin as irritants and become movements. Eventually they may become parties and governments. Fortunately, this was not the case with Smith. But there are points at which he could have become a major leader. One opportunity was missed when his mentor, Huey Long, was murdered. Smith and Long together could have moved masses, perhaps mountains! His relationship with Henry Ford culminated in another missed opportunity when Ford, after some initial encouragement, refused further support. With Ford's open support and financial patronage, Smith could have become a formidable national figure.

Smith was convinced of his own importance, and if history relegates him to a lesser status, he is nonetheless a significant figure. He represents a strain that has been present in America since the Puritans hanged witches. Smith is no mere aberration, but part of a singularly pervasive American tradition defined by Richard Hofstadter as the "paranoid style" and "anti-intellectualism."[9] Threaded through our history is this theme of scapegoating, dealing with real issues in an unrealistic manner, equating personal failure with conspiracy, simplifying complex problems, and using the forum offered in a free society to preach hatred and to exorcise one's personal demons in the public arena. It is also important to examine Smith's constituency. The disturbing facts are that there were twenty-five thousand subscribers to *The Cross and the Flag* and that Smith had substantial financial support. Moreover, for more than forty years he was teacher, mentor, and associate of some of the most vituperative bigots in the United States. If Smith's career can be adequately chronicled and his philosophy objectively analyzed, we should learn something about the nature of demagoguery, the mentality of people who support extremists such as Smith, and the most effective way to combat their vicious propaganda.

Smith's demagoguery probably peaked in 1935 and 1936, when he won an audience of millions by promoting Huey Long's gospel of sharing the wealth and the equally chimerical proposals of Dr. Francis E. Townsend and Father Charles E. Coughlin. Smith fancied himself a mass leader, and he was able to move vast audiences better than any other man of his generation. He had the ability to sway and temporarily persuade, but these led to few tangible results beyond the stirring of passions and aggravation of hatred. Moreover, Smith's crusade was short-lived and, although some historians believe that it forced President Roosevelt toward the left, its overall impact was not great.

For the remainder of his life Smith's audience was rather small, but he managed with their help to accumulate a personal fortune that enabled him to indulge his taste in Bibles, jewelry, and Victorian art and artifacts.

His supporters also enabled him to employ a small staff, mail out millions of pieces of propaganda, publicize such anti-Jewish propaganda as *The International Jew* and *The Protocols of the Learned Elders of Zion*, and publish his own rabidly reactionary hate-sheet, *The Cross and the Flag*. But his printed material was not the only source of his impact. He maintained surreptitious correspondence and contacts with congressmen, senators, governors, southern segregationists, isolationists, religious leaders, and several dozen commentators and journalists who would have cringed to hear their names associated publicly with that of Gerald Smith.

Smith's limited following in the 1950s and 1960s was more intense than his audiences in the 1930s and 1940s. In a certain sense, he thrived on misery. During the Great Depression desperate problems seemed to call forth desperate solutions, and Smith's ranks swelled. But it was difficult to sustain this level of support over time, particularly when prosperity returned. In a sense, Smith's later anti-Semitic crusades were more successful than the mass movements he inspired because his later followers remained more consistently loyal over many years. Smith's hopes of gaining political power depended ultimately upon fair-weather supporters, but his movement owed its continuity and financial base to a cadre of zealots who supported him from the time he first began espousing anti-Semitism in the 1940s until his death in 1976.

The influence of these zealots was not inconsiderable in their own communities. Smith claimed that his followers constituted a balance of power in Michigan in the 1940s and in Southern California in the 1950s and 1960s. Though certainly an exaggeration, the claim is not entirely without foundation. Smith benefited from a backlash of middle-class whites, stemming from their antipathy to the violence and chaos of the late 1960s. The relationship between Smith and his times was symbiotic. Earlier he profited from the isolationism of the early 1940s and the McCarthyism of the 1950s. He exploited such issues, churning out propaganda around them, spinning conspiracy theories. He knew the chords to play to tap the discontent of those ideologically and psychologically disposed to take his message seriously. Smith's sheer longevity distinguished him from the collection of other shrill voices on the right, and in addition, he was a source of much propaganda utilized by other extremists.

Smith did not have to invent a constituency. It had been there all along, and it is still there, waiting to be exploited by some mass leader who emerges at the juncture of a national crisis. It is not necessary to prove that the Populists were anti-Semitic or that the Know-Nothing Party was the source of Smith's antipathy to foreigners. The truth is that adherents to these groups and to Smith's movement were motivated by a variety of subjective and objective conditions, including discontent with the prevailing system and a personal sense of inferiority. Some people supported Smith merely because they hated the same people he hated. Some supported him because of only one aspect of his crusade. And probably many accepted the bulk of his program uncritically because it seemed to explain conditions that were otherwise incomprehensible to them. Confusion, frustration, and dissatisfaction were the cornerstones of Smith's movement.

Smith consummated a contract with these alienated people who followed him. Certainly he would have been impotent without them; but it is equally true that such factions are ineffective without a champion to articulate their views. From the earliest days of the Republic it has been the organized who have been heard and heeded. In American politics it is not numbers alone that count. A relatively small group, if intensely committed, may achieve at least some of its objectives in spite of its size. Moreover, majorities are comprised of shifting coalitions united by demography, ethnicity, and political objectives. Thus one period's minority may be another era's majority.

It was not necessarily Smith's ideas that attracted his followers: more important was his ability to communicate on an elementary level with his constituents, usually middle- and lower-class people of modest means and limited education. Few of his ideas were original. He borrowed from many sources, some reputable, many questionable, some the product of diseased minds. He frequently quoted respectable sources—Washington, Franklin, Jefferson, and especially Christ—but molded their thoughts to his purposes or, more precisely, twisted them. For Smith words were weapons of combat rather than tools of communication.

Smith went one step further than Emerson, who dismissed "foolish consistency" as the product of small minds. He supported the confiscation of millionaire fortunes yet later opposed the income tax. He opposed the United Nations as a tool of Communists and Zionists, then supported it when Arab nations gained the upper hand in the General Assembly. He denounced General Eisenhower as a "Swedish Jew" during Eisenhower's campaign for president in 1952, then applauded his stand in the Suez Crisis, declaring that Eisenhower was the first president to recognize the full danger of the Zionist threat. He opposed Richard Nixon as vice president, later defended him against impeachment, and finally concluded that Nixon had been compelled to resign by Zionists, who realized that he sought to abort their plot to rule the world.

An intense man who could not control his emotions, Smith fed his voracious ego by belittling others. He wanted to channel his compulsive work into politics but could not be elected. He wanted to dominate hand-picked candidates, but the ciphers he selected as figureheads were too obviously ciphers. He liked strong men, respected and admired them, but they did not feel the same way about him. Smith had to dominate or be dominated—he could not maintain a partnership of equals. Thus Smith dominated Dr. Townsend until Townsend saw his movement slipping away and repudiated Smith. Father Coughlin declared Smith unwelcome in his movement. The only people Smith influenced for any length of time were those who were easily swayed.

Smith told me two years before his death that he would not die a bitter old man. He protested too much in saying that. He would have preferred a panegyric, but what he wanted to avoid at all costs was oblivion; he became a master showman because to him, notoriety was far better than anonymity. When I interviewed him, he was still a compulsive talker. Though he disliked journalists and suspected historians, he was always willing to talk to me. Complaining that he disliked reminiscing about the past, he launched into a half-hour monologue on his relationship with Huey Long.

A man of considerable talents, Smith had a flawed character. His life illustrates that the career of a person of remarkable talents can be tragic if it is guided by a lust for power and fueled by a bigotry that appeals to latent hatred. The *Arkansas Gazette*, in its obituary of Smith, offered the best verdict on his career: "To have the power to touch men's hearts with glory or with bigotry, and to choose the latter, is a saddening thing."[10]

one

A Superabundance of Wind

‡

As befitted a future "man of God," Gerald Lyman Kenneth Smith was born on a bright, crisp, Sunday morning, February 27, 1898, at Pardeeville, a hamlet in south-central Wisconsin thirty-five miles north of Madison. This was dairy country, rolling hills and grassy meadows, a place where the winters were cold and the people hardy.[1]

Among the hardiest were Smith's ancestors. He came from four generations of rock-ribbed Republicans and three generations of fire-and-brimstone, circuit-riding, fundamentalist preachers. A descendant of English pioneers, his paternal grandfather, Zechariah S. Smith, emigrated from Virginia to southern Wisconsin, a sparsely settled, rural region peopled principally by Danes and Norwegians. Zechariah brought five hundred dollars in gold along with tools and supplies in his Conestoga wagon and bought up much of Columbia County. There he established a large farm, where he tamed and fattened wild horses from the Montana prairie and sold them to wealthy buyers in Milwaukee and Minneapolis. A devout man renowned as an orator, Zechariah preached in several communities each Sunday. His Bible-thumping sermons impressed his own children, who in turn passed along to Gerald's generation a pride in oratory. Grandfather Zechariah had ten offspring, who divided his large estate into modest individual inheritances. The youngest child was Gerald's father, Lyman Z. Smith, known as L. Z.[2]

With only a small portion of Zechariah's large farm, L. Z. was forced to

11

hustle for a living. A stocky, intense, hardworking man, he traveled in Wisconsin, Minnesota, and Illinois by horse, train, and bus, peddling salves, liniments, and patent medicines for the W. T. Rawleigh Medical Company of Freeport, Illinois. He was on the road Monday through Saturday, spending nights in the homes of clients and in cheap hotels. On Sundays he made efforts to return to his family because he preached in several small churches in neighboring villages.[3]

Despite his fragile health, L. Z. traveled dozens of miles to sell only a few cents worth of liniments. He seldom sold more than two dollars worth at any single home. Each month he mailed in his sales to W. T. Rawleigh, who deducted his expenses and returned to him a commission. L. Z. kept meticulous account books, written in a cramped, painfully lettered hand. In 1916, he grossed $1185.92 and his profit for the year, after expenses, was $222.75. He sold medicines only 174 days that year; the other days he worked on his farm or was too sick to travel.[4]

A popular speaker, L. Z. was called upon to deliver orations on the Fourth of July and on other patriotic occasions. He taught love of God to his son, Gerald, and his daughter, Barbara, ten years older than Gerald. Family life revolved around God and country. Gerald explained, "We took it for granted that the word 'Christian' was the companion for the word 'American.' We assumed that if there had been no Christ, there would have been no America as we know it. . . . We were taught to believe that the Constitution of the United States was the Bible of patriotism and that in this Constitution and in the Bible was everything necessary for the development of Christian character and American statesmanship."[5] It seems only natural, then, that when Smith founded a journal more than forty years later, he called it *The Cross and the Flag*.

In the tiny town of Smith's birth and in the rural Wisconsin villages where he spent his boyhood, the values of church, country, and family prevailed. Although the Populist Party was never large in Wisconsin, populist sentiment reached a high point during Smith's childhood. An impressionable child like Gerald could hardly have escaped that influence.

Like many mass political movements, populism was rife with contradictions. On one hand was a populism with a propensity toward industrial regulation, cooperative agricultural marketing, and humanitarian social legislation. On the other was a more romantic, Jeffersonian strain of populism that sought to restore the idealized past of the yeoman farmer. Many of those living on the edge of poverty, as did L. Z. Smith, blamed their difficulties on a conspiratorial alliance of Jewish bankers, railroad barons, business monopolists, and politicians who had sold out to these interests. This conspiracy theory was prevalent among people of limited education in rural areas of the Protestant South and Midwest. The solution these populists proposed was to cut the conspirators down to size—to whittle their fortunes and reduce their political power. Smith's early exposure to this brand of populism may help to explain his later enthusiasm for Huey P. Long's plan to redistribute wealth by confiscating large fortunes. From populism Smith also developed his preference for rural life and family farming. He disliked the chaos and complexity of twentieth-century urban industrial society and longed for something simpler and purer.[6]

Although populist thought indirectly influenced Smith, the source for some of his ideas can be traced more directly to progressivism. A person of Smith's intelligence and inclination could hardly have grown up in Wisconsin in the early 1900s without being influenced to some extent by the ideas of Robert M. La Follette. La Follette, first as governor of Wisconsin and later as a U.S. senator, made his reputation by fighting for the survival of the family farmer and the corner grocer against monopolists who controlled much of the nation's wealth. He and his fellow progressives shared with populists the belief that monopolists were conspiring to exploit the nation's resources.[7] Through his governmental and economic reforms and devotion to principle, La Follette earned the unwavering support of Smith's father and many other working-class heads of families. The elder Smith introduced his son to La Follette's speeches, and Gerald heard much about the progressive philosophy at home. Smith avidly read his father's copies of *La Follette's Weekly*. Sixty years later his memory of L. Z.'s attachment to Robert La Follette was undimmed. He told an interviewer, "My father was a great admirer of Robert La Follette. We were taught to admire his freedom from the status quo political thinking of the time."[8]

L. Z. Smith's influence on his son's thought and character was, of course, more than political. According to Gerald, L. Z. was a sensitive man who loved his family and was loved in return. Smith called his father "the best Christian I have ever known," adding, "I never experienced any disenchantment with the behavior of my father."[9]

L. Z. Smith's handling of adversity was an inspiration to his young son. When Smith was just two years old, his father became seriously ill with what Gerald called "pernicious anemia." The prolonged illness compelled him to give up his sales work, and the family moved to a small farm Smith owned in Richland County. At first, L. Z. could hardly sit up in bed. He improved very slowly and did not recover completely for ten years. In the meantime, his wife and children raised horses and cows and worked a large garden, storing home-grown potatoes and apples to subsist on when other food ran out.[10] Smith explained later that he considered his father's illness a blessing in disguise because it brought them closer together. He said that his father taught him to think for himself, to be independent, and never to substitute the advice of experts for his own judgment.[11]

More immediately, his father's illness forced Gerald to cope with poverty. The family lived in an isolated part of Richland County. The one weekly train brought in salesmen and waited for them while they made their calls. It was a slow-paced life, and in some respects a dismal one.[12] Smith was later defensive about his early poverty. He said that his family would never have accepted a handout and considered the offer of one an insult. He bristled at suggestions that their poverty meant that his people were culturally crude: "My mother and father were not the proverbial hillbillies. They were high-toned, proud people."[13] Although they all worked hard, he said, they were also refined. His resentment at being labeled lower-class flared when he said, "We had nothing in common with the illiterates that were in that area."[14]

The family's Christian faith guided them through the hard times. His mother loved to sing to him: "My Father is rich in houses and land. He holdeth the wealth of the world in his hands. . . . I'm a child of the King."[15] Gerald accepted Christ at the age of seven and was baptized in his father's small church in Richland Center. Five years later he decided to become a minister and never seriously considered any other profession. His grandmother delighted young Gerald by giving him a Bible on his twelfth birthday. He remembered that he opened it, "elevated myself" and "preached a small sermon to my father and mother."[16]

Smith's parents were gratified to learn that their son intended to carry on the family tradition. Smith himself, scarred by poverty, had no use for ivory-tower intellectual ministers who became rich and insensitive. He was quick to point out that his family's attachment to God had nothing to do with money. "I come from three generations of country preachers," he explained, "the kind that earned an honest living in the week and preached on Sunday and didn't sit around and do nothing but eat chicken dinners."[17] According to him, a man who took money for serving God was like a woman who took money for making love. "The most dangerous thing that we have in this country is paid preachers," he warned.[18] Nor did Smith believe that ministers needed advanced university degrees. "Christianity is as simple as a Western Union telegram," he said. "Suppose you inherited a hundred thousand dollars. It wouldn't take an intellectual to bring a telegram to your door. Jesus said everything that needed to be said about Christianity."[19]

Smith's parents taught him to interpret the Bible as the literal word of God; anything that contradicted it was a tool of Satan. "If it is more than the Bible it is too much," his father told him; "if it is less than the Bible, it is not enough; if it is the same as the Bible we don't need it."[20]

Every evening after dinner, the Smiths opened their Bible and each member of the family read a few verses. After L. Z. closed the reading he would ask, "Does anyone in this family have aught against another?" If there had been a quarrel or misunderstanding during the day, family members would ask each other for forgiveness, kneel and pray together, then go to bed content that they were at peace with themselves and with God. Smith never forgot this "family altar" custom; he spoke of it frequently and wrote about it in *The Cross and the Flag*.[21]

His father's overlapping interests in religion and politics also shaped Smith's future vocation. In the rustic environment of Gerald's boyhood it was common for a minister such as his father to be a political leader as well. L. Z. saw nothing wrong with admonishing his congregation not to sin and urging them at the same time to vote for La Follette. Throughout his mature life Smith also fused spiritual and political interests, a union that did not seem at all unusual in the small-town Wisconsin he knew as a boy.[22]

Smith was fortunate that he learned from his father and at church, because he learned little at school, in fact receiving only a rudimentary formal education in his early years. He enrolled at a one-room schoolhouse, a weather-beaten wooden building without indoor plumbing, which was constructed by his father near their farm. The poorly paid teaching job there attracted young women who themselves had only a minimal education—usually eight years of school and a certificate earned by six weeks of instruction at a teachers' institute. The little school operated during the winter and spring for small children; older boys attended during the winter and spent the spring harvesting corn and cutting hay. Many of the working boys—Smith called them "muscular ignoramuses"—were older and bigger than the teacher and enjoyed teasing her.

All the grades were taught in a single room; each student in turn recited by rote. Smith claimed that by the time he was nine, he had memorized all the lessons for all the grades, but in other respects he was not a particularly diligent student. He let his mind drift and giggled at the antics of his classmates. This irritated one teacher, a firm disciplinarian who carried a hard white oak rod. One day she whacked Smith several times and sent him home in pain with three marble-sized knots on his head.

Eleven-year-old Gerald decided that he had had enough of rote learning and corporal punishment. He asked his parents if he could attend the larger school in the village of Viola. There were two obstacles—transportation and his chores at home—but Smith persuaded his parents to let him go. The Viola school, seven miles away, was reached by a bumpy, seldom-traveled dirt road that wound among the hills. Smith rode the fourteen-mile round trip bareback astride a spirited little bronco named "Pet," barely broken in from the Montana prairies. He arose every morning at four, fed the horses and cattle, and milked five cows before leaving home.

In Viola, Gerald had to accommodate his horse while he was in class. He proposed to the local livery stable, which rented horses and buggies to traveling salesmen, to work for his horse's food. Every day on his lunch hour he went to the stable and put down hay for all the horses quartered there; in return he received hay and a stall for Pet. This left Smith little time for lunch, but he ate little anyway. His mother packed the same lunch for him every day: several hard-boiled eggs, an apple, and a piece of bread and butter.

Smith enjoyed school in Viola much more than in the country and he finished the seventh, eighth, and ninth grades there. He had a special fondness for one teacher, a vivacious young woman named Mabel Bennett, who took a special interest in the young boy who got up so early and came so far to attend school. They corresponded for the rest of her life, and Smith never forgot her.

By the time Smith was ready for high school, his father's health had improved sufficiently for him to resume his work selling salves and liniments. The family moved to Viroqua, a few miles northwest of Viola, where Smith enrolled in high school. High school opened new vistas for the boy who had spent his early years in isolation in the hills. A nervous, inquisitive extrovert, he admitted that he was "not a goody-goody," boasting, "I knew my way around with the high school girls." He plunged into extracurricular activities, overcoming his indigence with imagination. For example, he wanted to play in the high school band so that he could attend football and basketball games, but he could not afford most instruments. Studying the Sears-Roebuck catalogue, he found out that he could buy a piccolo for $1.98. Although he had never seen a piccolo before, he learned to play it.[23]

Smith also continued the family tradition of speaking eloquence by joining the debating society and winning prizes for oratory. He once recited William Jennings Bryan's "Cross of Gold" speech for a contest; sixty years later he still had it committed to memory.[24]

The young Smith was amazingly energetic. He starred in *Twelfth Night*, edited the yearbook, became a First Class Boy Scout, and taught a boys' Sunday School class. He was statistician for the track and basketball teams and won his first newsworthy attention in track. The Viroqua team, participating in a district track meet at La Crosse, was losing every event;

late in the day it appeared that the team would not win a single medal. Gerald had an idea. He approached the coach and asked to enter the mile race, explaining that he ran home for lunch every day—a distance of about a mile each way. Although Smith had never run competitively, the coach agreed. They could not obtain a pair of running shorts for him, so Smith borrowed a swimsuit and gained third place—the only medal Viroqua won. The next day the local newspaper carried an article about Smith's achievement. It was the first time he had seen his name in print. He kept the clipping for the rest of his life.[25] Beneath his photo in the school yearbook, the caption read: "He possesses a superabundance of wind, ergo, he delves into track and oratory."[26]

One cold winter night Smith accompanied the Viroqua basketball team to the village of Soldiers Grove for a game. The high school there had no gymnasium, so they played at the local movie theater, moving chairs and setting up baskets after the last show ended at ten P.M. At midnight, when the game ended, the temperature outside was 48 degrees below zero and, worse yet, the only way to get back to Viroqua was to walk. Smith bundled up in two pairs of underwear, heavy socks, boots, a sweater, and a thick coat and started the fifteen-mile trek home. He arrived at five A.M., shivering and exhausted, and collapsed into bed. He had just fallen asleep when his mother shook him and said, "Gerald, it's time to get ready for Sunday school." She never considered letting her weary son sleep through services.[27]

This was not the only instance in which Smith's mother seemed insensitive to his feelings. He wrote that "she had a strong mind and did not hesitate to give me a good scolding when I needed it."[28] Smith pretended to appreciate such discipline as character-building, but it is impossible to miss the undertone of resentment in his reminiscences of his mother. He said that she refused to pamper him; he was never a "Momma's boy." In his autobiographical account he wrote, "One of the great advantages of my life was being raised by a Mother who was not foolish enough to think that I was the only perfect child in the world. She was not a son worshipper. She never hesitated to criticize me and point out my mistakes."[29]

Smith was eager to attend college; one senses he wanted to get away from home. After graduating from high school in 1915, he spent the summer harvesting tobacco, a hot and dirty job, but one that paid well.[30] He wrote to colleges, but all of them seemed too expensive. Finally he applied to Valparaiso University, a school in Indiana specifically for indigent students. A no-frills institution, it allowed time off from classes for part-time work and cost only about a hundred dollars per year for room, board, and tuition. In Smith's day Valparaiso educated thousands of children from poor families.[31]

Smith earned enough money in the tobacco fields to buy two Sears-

Roebuck suits and a train ticket to Valparaiso. It was the longest railroad trip he had taken in his life; passing through the metropolis of Chicago, he was awestruck. Arriving in Valparaiso after the semester had begun, he paid the twenty-dollar tuition, bought his books, and found himself with only ten dollars to last him the rest of the year. All the dormitories were full and he could not afford an apartment. At a towering old Victorian home which served as a boarding house for some two hundred students, a large, forceful, no-nonsense matron offered Smith board if he would serve as a dishwasher. He agreed, and asked for a room as well, promising to sweep the ground floor every morning. There were no vacant rooms, so she put him in a large linen closet, where he slept on a sanitary cot. The accommodations delighted Smith. He had a room, a cot, meals, books, and enough clothes to last all winter. The industrious youngster rose at five-thirty every morning to sweep the dining room, in time to see the housemistress's husband water down the milk before serving it to the students. He washed dishes for two hundred students three times a day for only $2.10 a week, the price of board. He so pleased his employers that within a few weeks they promoted him to waiter. When spring came he found extra jobs mowing lawns and working gardens.[32]

At Valparaiso there was no limit to the number of courses a student could take and no attendance regulations; the sole requirement for course credit was to pass the final exam. Smith took overloads each semester, once receiving credit for forty hours in a single session. Most of his courses were in literature, biblical history, and dramatics.[33] He studied rhetoric with Professor Rollo Anson Talcott, who he claimed was "considered the greatest public speaking coach in America."[34]

Smith's various activities—working at the boarding house, attending classes, cutting lawns, and running errands—did not entirely consume his energy. He also became active in the First Christian Church, where the pastor, Reverend Claude Hill, a personal friend of his father, taught him Bible courses at night and found him part-time preaching jobs. One such job had Smith preaching Wednesday nights to a little congregation of about fifteen stalwart believers who met in a schoolhouse because they could not afford to build a church. Before his first effort, Smith carefully wrote out his sermon word-for-word. It looked longer to him written than spoken; he finished in eight minutes flat. Nonetheless, the worshipers were pleased. They gave Smith a collection amounting to $1.80, which left him a one-dollar profit after he deducted his bus fare. He perfected his speaking skills on these people and soon he was ready for something more challenging.[35]

One weekend during Smith's sophomore year, Hill took him to a little church in the countryside where he frequently preached. The church, called Deep River, stood on the banks of a stream shaded by a grove of tall elms. Smith preached a guest sermon which so delighted the congregation that they hired him to preach on alternate weekends for a salary of twenty-five dollars a month—more money than Smith had ever earned. Soon he was earning another twelve dollars a month preaching at a church in Gary, Indiana, on the weekends he did not go to Deep River. Unlike Deep River, industrial Gary was far from pastoral. The city and the church had grown up in a hurry and the congregation had hastily constructed a rough building. (They ran out of money after painting only one side and left the others bare.)

Always with an eye for opportunity, Smith had discovered that his oratorical talent provided a path to wealth and fame. He continued to preach while in college and his financial problems vanished. The congregation at Deep River "adopted" him, buying him clothes and other necessities. Smith organized activities such as spelling bees to increase attendance. One Sunday he held a contest to reward the church member with the biggest feet, and he himself won. Shortly before graduating he preached at a week-long revival, gaining twenty-eight converts, whom he baptized in the river.[36]

Smith's cramming enabled him to graduate in just two-and-a-half years. He did not even remain at Valparaiso long enough to attend commencement; his diploma had to be mailed to him. In the fall of 1918, Gerald began applying to graduate schools in the hope of earning a master's in theology. He volunteered for the army in November, but World War I ended before he could report for duty. Then an attack of nephritis, a serious kidney infection, forced him to return to Viroqua to live with his parents while he recuperated.[37]

Early in 1919, as soon as he could get out of bed, Smith began preaching as temporary pastor at the Christian Church in Soldiers Grove, a Wisconsin town of about eight hundred. His energy and enthusiasm for recruiting souls astounded and gratified the congregation. On Saturdays he prowled local pool halls seeking sinners, sometimes leaping onto pool tables to preach spontaneous sermons. In a few months he had converted the struggling church into a prospering one, with the pews filled every Sunday. He even raised enough money to pay off a four-thousand-dollar mortgage on the church building.[38]

Clearly, destiny meant Smith for bigger things. Before the year was out, he accepted a call to a larger church in Footville, Wisconsin. Once again his energy, industry, and extraordinary speaking ability impressed his congregation and church attendance soared. In May 1921, Smith staged an "Auto Sunday," offering to photograph all the cars brought to the church and to give a copy of the New Testament to the driver who brought the most people—the winner brought fifteen! People arrived at church in the morning for this all-day affair. After Smith delivered his sermon there was music, a basket dinner, and an automobile tour of the countryside. The congregation returned to church for another sermon that night.[39]

Smith's mother had once said that "Gerald was born to be a preacher," and he was rapidly proving her correct. A Footville woman called him "an outstanding man—the greatest idealist I have ever known." But even at this early stage in his career a few people who knew Smith well began to express doubts about his methods and his raw ambition. One member of the Footville church said later, "Smith was a promoter, not a preacher. He tried to build a new church here when it wasn't needed and he talked people into giving money when they didn't have it to give."[40]

Less than a year after taking over at Footville, Smith organized a church in the larger community of Beloit. He was rapidly earning a reputation as a sensationally effective minister, but he was still quite provincial, with little experience outside the rural Midwest. Once he accompanied a member of his congregation to Chicago for a few days. When he returned to Beloit, he wrote to his parents:

> We also visited some of the underworld districts and saw many shocking things. I wish I had the time to tell you some of the things we saw. One of the worst was the dancing in dance halls. People who tolerate the dance should have been with us. Its [sic] a shame to society. We were out to one of the midnight frolics in the colored districts. Rather amusing in some ways but when you see the white and black mixing it is terrible. White girls dancing cheek to cheek with black men. And of the uncanny motions they make. It sickens one.[41]

Smith's prominence and popularity made him a highly eligible bachelor in the eyes of every parent who had a marriageable daughter—or at least that's the way he remembered it. One Sunday he attended a dedication ceremony for a building renovated to house the Footville Methodist Church, where a friend of his was pastor. The Sorenson sisters of nearby Janesville—Nan, Elna, and Belva, a popular trio who performed for local churches and civic groups—provided the music. Smith found the middle sister, a contralto, "the most beautiful young woman I have ever seen" and vowed, "God willing, some day she will be my wife."[42] Despite Smith's inveterate exaggeration, Elna was in fact a strikingly beautiful woman, even sixty years later.

Smith wondered how he could discreetly arrange to meet the lovely contralto. Deciding to stage a fundraising benefit at his own church, he invited the Sorenson sisters to perform. Afterward he met the woman he had already decided to marry. Although in his excitement he failed to learn her first name, he did learn that she worked as a private secretary for a gas company executive in Janesville. Writing a letter addressed simply to "Miss Sorenson" in care of the gas company, he stated that if his presumption did not offend her, he would like to spend an evening with her. She replied in equally formal language that she would be pleased to see him. She later claimed that during her visit to his church she had noticed the young minister and found him highly attractive.[43]

Smith arrived in Janesville for his first date with Elna in October 1921 and proudly showed her his new Model T. He developed a weekly ritual, driving every Wednesday evening to see her and spending the night with Reverend Leland L. Marion, a Janesville minister. Marion was best man at Smith's wedding and later he became his pastor when Smith lived in Detroit.[44]

Soon Smith began seeing Elna twice a week. He proposed just a few weeks after meeting her and she accepted. There was one major disagreement between Smith and Elna's family: he was a minister in the Christian Church (later the Disciples of Christ) while the Sorensons were Methodists. Elna's mother planned to have the wedding in a Methodist church, but Smith adamantly insisted on being married in a church of his denomination. He wrote his parents, "Mrs. Sorenson was also taking for granted that the wedding was to be in the Methodist Church. I said, 'Now Mrs. Sorenson, to be married in the Methodist Church is just as far from me as not being married at all. That is one thing I will not do. I will compromise on colors of decorations, food for the wedding supper and such things but in matters of religion the whole thing will have to be completely *one sided.*'"[45] He described an argument he had with Mrs. Sorenson: "Then after a forenoon's talk I got her mother to admit that we were the nearest right." She had begged him at least to let a Methodist minister offer a prayer, but he had refused. "If you have a Methodist minister that you would like to invite all right, but he shall have no part in the services." He concluded, "It was kind of hard but they will have to get used to it and they are."[46]

Gerald and Elna were married on June 22, 1922. After the ceremony, Gerald's Grandmother Henthorn whispered in his ear, "Gerald, the woman doesn't live that has ever been loved too much." It was advice he never forgot. He could hardly have selected a more compatible mate. Elna was a completely dedicated wife who supported him in adversity, never disagreed with him publicly, and accompanied him on all his travels. She managed the family finances and nursed him back to health when he fell ill.[47] Within a few months Smith realized that he had found a remarkably agreeable mate. As he wrote to his parents, "I shall never cease being thankful for such a wonderful Christian wife. I have never seen her say or do a think [sic] that even bordered on being dishonorable. She is loved by the entire congregation. She listens much and talks little but is always ready to do her duty. She keeps the house tidy, is an excellent cook and is just as nice in the home as she is out."[48]

Elna was twenty-four at their marriage, the same age as her husband, and the daughter of first-generation Danish immigrants. Her father, a buggy- and harness-maker and a blacksmith who later became super-intendent of a large concern that marketed sugar beets, died when Elna was only eight, but he provided a comfortable living for his two sons and three daughters. From her teenage years, Elna took music lessons and sang in area churches. She attended business school, then worked as a bookkeeper, a telephone operator, and finally at the gas company, where she was when she met Smith. Elna knew little about politics, but she seemed to share her husband's views about everything. Later, he used her as a front by placing her on the boards of his enterprises, even creating a foundation in her name. Elna seemed never to question the career her husband had chosen, nor his change from the ministry to politics. In 1974 she described her marriage as a "fifty-two-year honeymoon."[49]

By the time he married Elna, Gerald had moved from the Footville church to a larger one in Beloit. In his third year there his compulsive work caught up with him: he suffered a complete breakdown brought on by fatigue and nervous exhaustion. He explained to his parents, "I love Him so and am so anxious to do his mighty will. The only trouble is that I want to do more than I am able."[50]

Bedridden for three-and-a-half months, Smith resigned as minister. Almost immediately after his recovery, however, he accepted a call to a larger church in the cattletown of Kansas, Illinois. This church, like the others, was only a step in his climb to success—since graduating from college he had remained at each small church he pastored an average of less than two years. Clearly this peripatetic, restless minister had limit-less potential and ambition. In 1922, Smith attended a ministerial con-vention in St. Louis, where his rousing "Come to Jesus" sermon brought the crowd to its feet. This resulted in a call from a still larger church, the prestigious Seventh Christian Church in Indianapolis, with two thousand members. The homespun rustic who had ridden a bronco to school, washed dishes in a boarding house, and ordered suits from the Sears-Roebuck catalog had already come a long way.[51]

Smith's performance at the Seventh Christian Church was extraordi-nary. He organized youth groups, served as an officer in several minis-terial organizations, and found time to take night courses in theology at Butler University. Still, the young minister was restless and sought new challenges. He left the established church to reorganize the University

Place Christian Church, a declining institution that appealed to college students. He quickly rebuilt the membership and the congregation adopted his twenty-five-year plan proposing a new sanctuary. In a single year he was thus responsible for sixteen hundred converts at the two churches. Smith described his promising career years later: "I was going like a house afire. I was influential in the community, I was respected in the city, in fact I was one of the book reviewers for the big daily."[52] His congregation was proud of him. At the conclusion of a revival at University Place, members delivered tributes to Smith. One said, "The Reverend Mr. Smith came to the church two years ago when it was about to discontinue and through his courage, zeal and hard work he has more than quadrupled the membership. He has remarkable ability. I am at a loss for words to express the deep feelings of love which the congregation and officials of the church have for him."[53]

Despite the acclaim and adulation he received, some people had misgivings about Smith. Rumors circulated that he belonged to Indiana's flourishing Ku Klux Klan. Smith denied it, stating that his father had warned him to avoid all secret organizations. Membership in the Klan would have been consistent with his subsequent career, but his accusers never produced verifiable evidence.[54]

In 1929 Smith left Indianapolis, not for a larger church, but because of his wife's health. Elna developed tuberculosis and remained bedridden for three months. Her doctor warned that the smoky, sooty air of Indianapolis might aggravate her condition. If she were to recover, the Smiths would have to move to a milder climate. "Indianapolis was poison anyway," Smith later complained. "You had to change your shirt three times a day because the place was so full of coal smoke and it was really a T.B. manufacturing plant."[55]

Smith's congregation hated to lose him. Some members worried that the youth work and the plans to build a new church would languish if he departed, and one of the church elders suggested that he send Elna to the southwest while he remained in Indianapolis to continue his work. Smith bristled at the suggestion: "I looked at him and said I wouldn't send that woman any place. I said if I have to sleep with her in a tent in Arizona I'm going to do what it takes to get her well."[56]

After Smith advertised his imminent departure, he received offers from several churches in warmer climates. One, from the First Christian Church in Honolulu, Hawaii, conjured visions of beaches, swimming, and sailing. Another came from the Kings Highway Christian Church in Shreveport, Louisiana, the largest of Smith's faith in that state. In his work as a fundraiser for Chatauqua lectures, Smith had befriended a man who lectured on public health; now he sought his advice. Which place would be the more hospitable for his wife's recovery? The answer surprised him. Although Louisiana had a reputation for swamps and alligators, his friend wrote, Shreveport, a city located in the pine hills of North Louisiana, was one of the most healthful places in the country for a tubercular convalescent. That settled it. Smith accepted the call to the Kings Highway Christian Church. He planned to remain only long enough for Elna to recover, but his stay there changed his life.[57]

The young minister struck the staid Kings Highway Church like a cyclone. The conservative, wealthy institution, which included among its members the mayor of Shreveport, two bank presidents, and the president of the Chamber of Commerce, had never known a minister even remotely similar to Smith. In his first two years he added 356 members to the congregation. He spoke at banquets and meetings of the Chamber of Commerce, at Kiwanis, Elks, and Rotary Clubs, did youth work with the Boy Scouts and the YMCA, and preached at revivals. He collected more contributions than any previous minister, despite the crash of the stock market three months after he arrived in Shreveport.[58]

Smith was ecumenical, popular among clergymen of different faiths. A Rabbi Brill of B'nai Zion Temple invited him to fill his pulpit and in return spoke at Smith's church. Following the exchange, Rabbi Brill wrote that Smith's guest sermon had appealed to his congregation. In a thank-you note to Smith, he asserted, "We are co-religionists, worshipers at the same shrine."[59]

Smith also participated in the labor movement. He became a friend of E. H. ("Lige") Williams, president of the Louisiana American Federation of Labor (AFL), who made him chaplain, invited him to speak at the state convention, and arranged for national president William Green to issue him an honorary membership card. Smith helped the pulp workers organize a union. But he was not one-sided: the same year he spoke to the state labor convention, he also delivered the keynote address at the Louisiana chapter meeting of the American Bankers' Association.[60]

Smith began broadcasting radio sermons over a powerful station owned by W. K. Henderson, a local millionaire who was a large contributor to Huey P. Long. Smith was as effective on radio as he was in person. He preached a message of social reform, attacking conditions in sweatshops and mines and denouncing Louisiana's largest newspapers and its biggest corporation, the Standard Oil Company. His style approached demagoguery; he told one meeting of labor men that "you who toil are nailed to the Cross . . . but remember the Resurrection followed the Crucifixion."[61] His reputation began to spread beyond Shreveport. Smith's work with the Shreveport Recreation Department came to the attention of the National Recreation Association, which invited him to tour southern cities urging them to set aside land for parks and recreation. The United States Olympic Committee invited him to attend the 1932 games in Los Angeles. Smith spent several weeks in California, then made an extensive tour of the East Coast before returning to Shreveport.[62]

Some of Smith's parishioners worried that he was beginning to neglect his own church and that all the publicity was making him arrogant. Upon his return, members of the board of directors insisted that he pay more attention to his church, accusing him of meddling in affairs outside of the proper interests of a minister.[63] For example, Smith was applying intense pressure to local people to contribute to charity. As head of the Community Chest campaign, he insisted that the wealthy individuals who owned 72 percent of the property in Shreveport, many of them members of his church, contribute a proportionate share to the charitable goal—a total quota of two hundred thousand dollars. And Smith angered one church member by accusing him of piping oil in excess of federal quotas and selling it illegally.[64]

Those who knew Smith during these years have quite varied impressions of him. Some remember him as kindly and ingratiating, others as impulsive and arrogant. In fact, he was all of these; different situations brought out different traits.

No one denied that Smith was a brilliant speaker. One church member recalled, "He had a wonderful flow of the English language. Oh, he was an eloquent speaker. His language, his choice of words, was superb."[65] A man who did not like Smith said, "He was a convincing speaker. I don't think everybody knew what he was talking about, and he didn't either. But it sounded right."[66] An incident related by another churchgoer reinforces the impression that Smith was a brilliant improviser. He described overhearing his father talking with Smith before church one Sunday morning. Smith was tired from nightclubbing the evening before. As he walked into church he asked, "What shall I preach on today?" The man's father replied, "John 3:16." Smith proceeded to preach a moving sermon on precisely that verse. According to this source, Smith had sermons memorized and could preach them spontaneously.[67] A close woman friend of his admitted, "I think I've heard it said that he did a lot of preaching just from the cuff. He didn't have to really [prepare]. That may have been part of what got him in trouble. He was spending time with other things. But he was smart enough to get up there and preach that sermon on Sunday mornings without a lot of preparation."[68] Smith's later tendency to recite stock answers to controversial questions and to dictate dozens of pages daily without any preparation reinforces this testimony. He was always clever but rarely thoughtful; his reliance on his quickness kept him from developing depth.

Many of his parishioners saw Smith as a brilliant, energetic, popular young minister. One churchgoer called him "dynamic" and "lovable": "you couldn't help but like him."[69] Another remembered that he was an effective proselytizer who "filled our sanctuary all the time."[70] He could also be unselfish—sometimes flamboyantly so. During the days of the Great Depression, he fed and sheltered schoolteachers whom the city could not afford to pay.[71]

One church member thought Smith unprincipled and crudely ambitious: "Kings Highway Church was too small to hold him." He remembers Smith barhopping and "living it up."[72] Smith did not deny that he drank, but insisted that he used alcohol in moderation. "Early in my life," he said, "when I thought I was more sophisticated than I was, Mrs. Smith and I would indulge occasionally in cocktails with good friends." But once he saw drink ruined men, Smith explained, he became a teetotler.[73] Not particularly proud of his years as an aggressive young minister, he later described himself as "a smart aleck big shot."[74]

One of Smith's harshest critics was Dr. Willis P. Butler, the parish coroner, who told an interviewer, "But I think he was a typical Judas or hypocrite if I have ever known one. I don't believe that man had the slightest bit of real religion in him, yet he was the pastor of a fine church here."[75] Dr. Butler remembered that Smith had a morbid curiosity about cadavers. One day while Butler was on call he encountered Smith. Learning that Butler was going to see a young woman who had been murdered, Smith asked to go along. He took a keen interest in the examination and afterward wanted to accompany the coroner on all his calls. Butler concluded, "I thought it was a genuine interest of a human being wanting to know about such things. But what he was looking for, it seemed to me, was a contact of some kind. Whether it was sexual or medicines, or what, I don't know."[76]

Inevitably, Smith's social activism conflicted with his duties as minister. The rich members of his congregation were suspicious of his relationship with U.S. Senator Huey P. Long, the virtual dictator of Louisiana, who had risen to prominence as an enemy of vested wealth and corporate power. Smith met Long shortly after moving to Shreveport, where Long, then governor, maintained a law office. Mayor George Hardy, a member of Smith's congregation, was a leading anti-Long figure in Louisiana, and some of Smith's other members felt equal antipathy toward the brash young governor. Smith met Long through his friends in the labor movement; it was "Lige" Williams who introduced them. Although Smith knew of Long's reputation as an uncouth demagogue, he was attracted to Long's forceful personality. This was Smith's first acquaintance with a man of substantial power. Throughout his life such strong personalities attracted him; he vicariously enjoyed their fame and power.[77]

Smith's relationship with Long was casual until he asked Long to rescue some of his indigent church members. One Sunday morning as Smith was greeting his congregants on the church steps, one of them approached him in tears, explaining that he was going to lose his home. He owed less than a thousand dollars on the mortgage, but foreclosure was imminent. Smith knew that Congress was considering a federal mortgage guarantee bill that would make money available to small property owners. If the congregant could hold on just a few more months, he might save his home. Smith did some checking and found that his was not an isolated case: many of the church members stood in danger of losing their homes. Ironically, the concern that held the mortgages, the Shreveport Mutual Building Association, was partly owned by other members of his own church!

Smith thought perhaps he could reason with the mortgage holders. But when he met with them they told him to stick to being minister; this financial affair was none of his business. Moreover, the church was also mortgaged; they implied that his actions might place the building itself in jeopardy and result in the denial of loans for future expansion. Smith pounded a table in rage and told the bankers that they were no better than criminals! He might not know banking, he thundered, but he knew the Bible and it said "Thou shalt not steal."[78]

The director and controlling partner of the Mutual Building Association was a wealthy Jewish businessman named Philip Lieber. In later discussions of the foreclosure incident, Smith never failed to mention that Lieber was Jewish. In later years he said that the first time he was accused of being anti-Semitic was when he opposed Lieber.[79]

In desperation Smith turned to his acquaintance, Huey P. Long, by now a U.S. Senator, although he continued to control Louisiana. Long was just as angry as Smith when he heard the story, and he told Smith to wait by his phone; he would act immediately. Half an hour later a shaken Lieber telephoned Smith and said that he had received a terrible phone call from Huey Long, who had threatened to destroy his business unless he cancelled the mortgages. Lieber knew that Long's threats were not idle, so he asked for an appointment with Smith. Smith responded that there was no need for an appointment; all the banker had to do was to walk across the street to the courthouse and cancel the mortgages. Lieber did.[80]

The mortgage foreclosure episode became common knowledge in Shreveport. While it encouraged some of Smith's congregation, others saw it as one more example of the minister's meddling in affairs beyond his calling. They were suspicious of his friendship with Huey Long. Coming soon after Smith's extended travels and in the midst of his increasing neglect of his ministerial duties, the incident raised doubts about whether he should continue as pastor.

Shortly afterward another incident occurred that brought the issue to a head. In Washington, photographers caught him elbowing his way through reporters as he emerged from Huey Long's hotel suite, and the *Washington Post* identified him as one of Long's bodyguards. Smith sued the *Post*, claiming that the story jeopardized his job. (He later dropped the suit.)[81] The publicity identifying Smith as a lieutenant of Long, coming after all the earlier incidents, divided the church. Long was highly controversial and was disliked by some of the rich members of the church's board of directors. The board demanded Smith's resignation. He refused, appealing to the congregation, who supported him. But pressure continued to mount as rumors circulated about Smith's relationship with Senator Long. Smith finally summoned a general meeting of the church and announced his resignation; he admitted later that he was on the verge of dismissal.[82] He was quitting the ministry to devote his time to humanitarian work and to preserve his self-respect. "I am resigning not to become a whiskey-drinking ex-preacher," he added, "but in order to save my soul because I want to go to Heaven."[83] He later claimed that he became a better Christian after he left the church.[84]

Without a job in the midst of the Great Depression, Smith began searching for something to do. There was an interval of several months between his resignation from the Kings Highway Christian Church and his joining Huey Long's political organization. Jewish organizations and a variety of journalists have claimed that at this point in his career, Smith briefly joined William Dudley Pelley's pro-Nazi Silver Shirts. Pelley, a minister, publisher, and mystic who claimed that he had died and gone to Heaven for seven minutes, and that he was in contact with the spirit world, assembled in North Carolina a motley crew of recruits who marched and drilled and planned somehow to seize control of the U.S. government.[85]

There is strong evidence that Smith at least considered forging an alliance with Pelley. Avedis Derounian, for his exposé *Under Cover*, examined the files of Reverend Leon M. Birkhead, whose Peoples' Institute of Applied Religion investigated Smith. Birkhead wrote Pelley directly, asking if Smith had ever been connected with his movement. On August 5, 1936, H. E. Martin, then executive director of *Pelley's Weekly*, sent the following letter on Pelley's stationery:

> Answering your letter of the 3rd regarding Mr. Gerald L. K. Smith's connection with the Silver Shirts, which you say he denies, we have on file certain letters and telegrams from him received during July and August of 1933. The letters are all written on Silver Shirts of America letterheads and signed by him. His registration number as a member of the Silver Shirts was 3223 and his wife's number was 3220.

The enclosed extracts from these letters will undoubtedly serve your purpose.

(Signed) H. E. Martin
Executive Director
The Pelley Publishers[86]

Among the extracts was one from a letter Martin claimed Smith sent to Pelley on August 15, 1933: "By the time you receive this letter I shall be on the road to St. Louis and points north together with a uniformed squad of young men composing what I believe will be the first Silver Shirt storm troop in America."[87]

According to Martin, Smith wrote Pelley two days later from Hot Springs, Arkansas: "We have held three mass meetings, two street meetings, and appointed key men for literature in six towns; no, seven towns."[88]

Clearly, Smith had some contact with Pelley. There are, however, some discrepancies. Derounian's account of Martin's letters to Birkhead places Smith in Pelley's employ in August 1933. However, an article by Pelley himself in the *Weekly*, in the files of the American Jewish Committee, indicates that Smith did not appear at his General Headquarters in Asheville, North Carolina, until August 1934.[89] This date appears more likely: Smith had by this date recently left the Kings Highway Church, whereas the Derounian account puts him with Pelley prior to his resignation from the church.

In the article in his *Weekly*, Pelley describes his relationship with Smith in some detail. According to him, Smith appeared uninvited and asked to become a Silver Shirt leader, claiming the sponsorship of a prominent Shreveport man, Major Luther Powell. Elna also applied for membership, as did her brother. Major Powell and a mutual friend from Dallas served as character witnesses, and Pelley issued membership cards to Smith, his wife, and her brother.

Smith signed an agreement that, in return for an advance on expenses, he would proselytize in Louisiana, Arkansas, Missouri, and Iowa for the Silver Legion. He would hold open-air recruitment meetings throughout the Midwest and would keep the money he collected by passing the hat. Smith started from Shreveport and soon sent Pelley several telegrams advising him of his progress. After only a few days, however, Smith became discouraged and returned to Shreveport, abandoning the followers he had recruited. Pelley swore that this account was true and could not understand why Smith denied it.[90]

Smith gave different accounts at different times. In 1946 he told the House Un-American Activities Committee that the Silver Shirts had issued him an unrequested "complimentary" membership card, which he had returned within six weeks.[91] In 1942, however, Smith wrote former U.S. Senator Robert R. Reynolds the following account: "In 1933 William Dudley Pelley made overtures to Huey Long and me. At the suggestion of Huey Long, I investigated Pelley for about six weeks, at the end of which time I repudiated his organization and shortly after that he wrote an article repudiating me. That was about nine years ago. I have not seen the man from that day to this."[92]

In 1950, when both men were middle-aged, Smith and Pelley reconciled. Pelley wrote that he was over any ill feeling and understood that Smith had left him because he had seen better opportunities with Huey Long. This seems to verify that a relationship existed. Pelley wrote in response to a letter from Smith stating that he was happy Pelley had been paroled after spending time in prison for sedition. Pelley invited Smith to visit him and to discuss how they could support their common cause. He specified, however, that he did not want Smith to publish anything linking them publicly.[93]

The most reasonable conclusion is that Smith flirted briefly with Pelley after resigning the pulpit, developed grandiose plans, grew disillusioned quickly, and then denied any alliance. Smith had just experienced his first encounter with a formidable Jewish opponent, the banker Philip Lieber, but it is unlikely that Pelley's anti-Semitism alone attracted him: Smith did not become a full-fledged anti-Semite until later. But Pelley fits into the pattern of Smith's activity. Smith dreamed of political power, was attracted to strong, unconventional personalities, and sought in the Silver Shirts a movement in which he could conveniently utilize his oratorical talents. The Pelley episode became an embarrassment, however, and Smith denied that it had occurred for the rest of his life.

But it is clear that in the early 1930s Smith was beginning to manifest the traits that characterized his later career. His FBI file includes a letter dated January 8, 1933, that he apparently wrote to a Dr. Hugo Fack, who had visited Germany and knew personally some of the officials in the Nazi hierarchy. Later, Fack was accused of spying for Germany and his personal correspondence was confiscated. Among the documents was the following letter from Smith:

Dear Sir:
    I write to you concerning a very confidential matter based on the confidence that some of my friends have in you.
    I am anxious to get in touch with his Honor, Adolf Hitler, but, knowing that you are recently removed from Germany, before doing so I desire your opinion of conditions in that country. They look good to me. Can you give me a code for getting in touch with Herr Hitler or one of his representatives in America?

The Semitic propaganda in America is growing more serious every day. I enclose herewith a bulletin that was put out on the streets of our city as the result of an attempt on the part of a Jew to take hundreds of homes away from the people. I am convinced that the Jews are trying to rob American people just as they attempted to do in Germany and Germany and America will be closer together than any two nations in the world.

You will be interested to know that my grandfather's name was Herr Schmidt, and that I was reared in the state of Wisconsin. You may feel free to write me directly or through any one of your friends in Shreveport. Surely there must be an organization now existing in America to overcome the terrible anti-German propaganda being promoted by the Jews. Please enlighten me.

Guten tag,
(signed) Gerald L. K. Schmidt[94]

The letter seems heavy-handed, even for Smith. Moreover, it is not true that his grandfather's name was Schmidt. On the other hand, the letter is written on authentic letterhead paper of the Kings Highway Christian Church; it is in the rhythms of Smith's language; and the signature resembles Smith's. Some of the facts in it were not widely known. Finally, the letter is consistent with Smith's later career, when he expressed the opinion that Hitler had been "misunderstood." Fack's reply, also among the documents seized, stated that he had written to Hitler and Goebbels on behalf of Smith and advised Smith to write to Hitler in care of Goebbels. He also told him that Nazis in New York might have the ear of Hitler.[95]

The authenticity of the Fack letters is dubious, but it is evident that Smith was changing. He was beginning to focus on more secular and political ambitions, seeming to envision himself more as a leader of the masses, less as a minister. It is also clear that he craved power and was attracted to men of power, which soon led him to begin active political organizing in the service of Senator Huey P. Long. Mesmerized by Long's personality, charisma, and brilliant political instincts, Smith left the ministry permanently for politics. The taste of political power was irresistible.

two

The Savonarola of the Swamps

‡

*There may be smarter guys than Huey Long, but they ain't in
Louisiana.*

—Huey P. Long

Gerald Smith described Louisiana in the 1920s as a backward, oppressive oligarchy, dominated by planters who, allied with the New Orleans city machine, ran the state like feudal lords. Education was poor, state services inadequate, and the aristocrats who dominated the legislature and governor's mansion had no sympathy for the common people. They could make or break men by hiring or firing, by selective taxation, or by false conviction on criminal charges. They controlled the major newspapers and thus repressed all dissent.

Then, according to Smith, Huey P. Long appeared upon the scene and shifted the power from the aristocrats to the people. Long was an altruistic statesman who constructed roads and bridges, furnished free schoolbooks, provided cheap natural gas for New Orleans, and completely overturned the ruling oligarchy. Long was a strong leader, Smith explained, but not a dictator or a demagogue. Rather, he dominated Louisiana as a surgeon dominates a complicated medical operation; others deferred to him because of his knowledge, expertise, and ability.[1]

The truth was a bit more complicated. Louisiana was a complex state divided by class, ethnic, religious, geographical, and rural–urban differences. Race was a potential issue, but in the 1920s there was little race-baiting because the subservient place of blacks in the state's political and social hierarchy was virtually unchallenged. Louisiana's governors generally favored low taxes and opposed incurring governmental debts to finance capital construction. There was a mild progressive movement characterized by educational reforms under Luther Hall and Superintendent of Education T. H. Harris, and there were further improvements in

33

education, bureaucratic reforms, and a movement toward more progressive taxation under Governor John M. Parker.

There can be no doubt, however, that Huey P. Long revolutionized state politics. Reared in a poor parish, he had little formal education but possessed superb intelligence, awesome energy, and a prodigious memory. While still a young man he was elected public service commissioner and then governor. In 1930, midway through his term as governor, he was elected to the United States Senate. Long constructed his power base by uniting the poor of all ethnic groups and religious persuasions. His forte was not theory but ruthless pragmatism. He wielded every weapon at his disposal: patronage, isolation and demoralization of opponents via overwhelming coalitions, demagogic appeals to the masses using radio and sound trucks, manipulation of elections and law enforcement via the machinery of the state government, selective taxation, extravagant publicity, and even physical intimidation. His was a movement that exploited fear, bewilderment, and hopelessness and replaced these apprehensions with a utopian dream. His program was mildly progressive but hardly original or innovative. He built roads, bridges, and such public buildings as the new capitol and governor's mansion at Baton Rouge—all designed to be showpieces of his administration. He improved the state university but neglected other state schools and did nothing for labor or the elderly. Long's motives were mixed. He had some sympathy for the poor and uneducated but was never carried away by it. He shrewdly directed his appeal to the masses, whom he could then mobilize to sustain himself in power.

Gerald Smith was attracted by Long's program, by his charisma, and by the opportunities the Long organization afforded a neophyte with speaking skills. Long saw in Smith a brilliant speaker whose status as a clergyman could also provide some religious credibility to his movement. Shortly after resigning from the Kings Highway Christian Church, Smith went to work for Long. An ambitious gladhander who relished publicity and harbored great ambitions, Smith believed that Long was headed straight to the top, and Smith wanted to go along. "Huey Long," Smith said, "is a superman. I actually believe he can do as much as any ten men."[2]

Smith described Long as a demigod, the smartest, most noble, most humane man in America, who was no demagogue because he kept his promises to the common people while conquering the feudal lords of Louisiana. He ascribed to Long virtues the Kingfish did not have, such as religious conviction and a genius for football strategy,[3] while largely oblivious to the man's faults. Although he admitted that at one time Long was a heavy drinker and womanizer, he blamed the latter vice on Long's

Jewish adviser, Seymour Weiss, who Smith claimed served Long as a pimp.[4] Smith was uncharacteristically deferential to Long, bragged about wearing his clothes, and pretended to be closer to the man than he actually was. He boasted on one occasion, "I've slept with him, eaten with him, talked with him, prayed with him and I know he is a man of God."[5] There was also a practical aspect to Smith's adulation. "No great movement has ever succeeded," he said, "unless it has deified some one man. The Share the Wealth movement consciously deified Huey Long."[6]

Long hired Smith for the job of national organizer for Huey's Share Our Wealth Society, based upon a utopian scheme devised by Long to confiscate and redistribute the great fortunes of America. No individual was to be permitted to earn more than a million dollars a year or to possess a fortune in excess of five million. With the money confiscated Long would provide a home, an automobile, a radio, and a guaranteed annual income of two to three thousand dollars for each family. Qualified students would receive free college educations; there would be a veteran's bonus, old age pensions, public works (including highways), and more time for pleasure and recreation. Long's government would buy farmers' excess production, store it in warehouses and elevators, and employ farmers on public service projects when they were not needed on the farm. This would be done without compulsion: millionaires were to inventory their goods, decide what they wanted to keep, and hand over the surplus.[7]

The Great Depression, Long believed, was caused by the accumulation of capital resources in the hands of the very rich, who selfishly hogged wealth beyond their needs. Of course, Long's scheme was wildly impractical: there were too few millionaires and not enough money to go around; much wealth was not easily liquefiable; and enforcement would require a police state. It had, however, a classical political appeal—something for nothing, the political equivalent of a perpetual motion machine. Long was well aware of the plan's impracticality, but Smith seems to have been naive enough to believe in it. If he did, such a belief was inconsistent with his later views in defense of property and even in opposition to the graduated income tax.

In his own mind, of course, Smith was consistent, although he did employ some convoluted reasoning. "At heart Huey Long was a Conservative," Smith claimed.[8] Long, he explained, only wanted a decent living for poor people: "You're not radical if you don't want a man to starve to death."[9] Smith's share-the-wealth sentiments were also consistent with his religious beliefs. The Bible, in its own way, is a revolutionary document, exalting the humble and disparaging the wealthy. The meek will inherit the earth, and Jesus advised the rich man who wanted to get into heaven to give his material possessions to the poor.

Smith's revolution would not herald a new order but rather restore an idyllic past. In the early days of the republic, land had been widely distributed and the gap between rich and poor less pronounced. What Smith really desired was a return to the Arcadian past before society had been warped by wicked urbanism. He seemed to favor a vision of medieval days in which decisions were supposedly made not on the basis of economic gain but on ethical and religious principles. He believed America's problems resulted from a moral breakdown, not from evils inherent in the capitalist system. To Smith, even the most complex issues could be reduced to a contest between good and evil. Whatever the problem, villainy was to blame, a theme that became even more pronounced later in Smith's career.

Smith wanted to streamline rather than enlarge the government and manifestly wanted to preserve the capitalist system. His utopia required a static middle class that would have little upward mobility yet would be protected from indigence. Moreover, the role of the family was crucial. The family as an economic institution was central to the plan: each *family* was to receive a car, home, and radio. It was unclear where single adults, widows, and divorced people fit into this scheme.

Smith was only one among millions of Americans mesmerized by Long's finesse in converting a utopian idea into a vehicle for political power. Long's ability to isolate, synthesize, focus, compress, and intensify issues had broad appeal. The appeal was psychological, personal, and intuitive, rooted in genuine need and embellished with simple eloquence. The plan was attractive to everyone except millionaires and economists. In the prosperous 1920s Long may have been laughed off as a buffoon with a curiously preposterous program, but in 1934 the masses responded enthusiastically. People who would never have thought of embracing communism or socialism hopefully turned to Huey. The timing of his pronouncements was critical: they came at a time of economic unrest resulting from the Depression, low wages for laborers and farmers, and the urban blight that followed the closing of the frontier. Yet Long's proposals remained in the American utopian tradition—advancing the idea that problems could be solved by tinkering with the machinery of democracy. Although Long made the established social and political elites uneasy, he offered comfort to those he addressed—and part of the appeal for them was precisely the discomfort he evoked in the rich and powerful.

Gerald Smith, the apostle who converted masses to Longism, had keen insight into the appeal of political movements. "Every great movement must have a superficial appeal," he explained; "it must be philosophically sound, absolutely dramatic and politically practical." He likened this appeal to the marquee of a movie theater, which attracts people to see the show inside. Long, Smith, and their followers were convinced of the philosophical soundness of their plan. While Roosevelt erred in compromising, Smith explained that in his mind, "there can be no compromise—Hell or Heaven with no alternative." As for political practicality (as opposed to economic feasibility), Smith boasted, "Movements are usually managed by impractical idealists. We have the most practical politician in the country at our head. Senator Long knows how to trade a cat for a cow, the cow for an elephant, and the elephant for a farm."[10]

Smith's technique for promoting the program was to talk simple and promise big. He admitted he and Long believed that "the average voter runs an I.Q. of about eleven to twelve years of age."[11] Smith claimed that he advised Huey to make elections seem like Christmas day to these poor, simple-minded voters. They should give the voter something tangible, like a "red bicycle under a Christmas tree," as a reward for having voted on the right side.[12] The opposition underestimated the voracity of the voters, Smith believed. "If we who are responsible to the great unschooled masses cannot learn how to make elections as interesting to the voter as Christmas is to the child, then we had better prepare to be defeated by someone who does know how."[13] Smith and Long were buying affection, or more bluntly, buying votes. This was not unusual, but it had seldom been done on so grand a scale or so blatantly. Demagogues, Smith claimed, flattered voters by praising their intelligence, but he and Long knew better.[14]

Smith was an effective advocate with a bull-like drive, sustained by idealism, tempered by practicality, and fueled by a passion for adventure. Smith combined frankness with lofty idealism and selfish ambition. A zealot in the mold of Robespierre or Hitler, his words were simple, direct, blunt, repetitious, self-serving, and cleverly obscure on specifics. Using fundamentalist techniques, brandishing a Bible, he could whip audiences to a fever pitch, exhorting them to "pull down those huge piles of gold until there shall be a real job, not a little old sow-belly, black-eyed pea job but a real spending money, beefsteak and gravy, Chevrolet, Ford in the garage, new suit, Thomas Jefferson, Jesus Christ, red, white and blue job for every man."[15]

At first Huey used Smith as a substitute when he was unable to address a meeting. The Kingfish soon discovered, however, that Smith was a far more effective and captivating orator than he had realized. Smith launched his speaking and organizational activities in early 1934 in Louisiana. He had spoken to more than a million people by the end of the year, addressing crowds wherever he could round them up, in pastures, in fields, in courthouse squares, and on city street corners. Denied an indoor arena in New Orleans, he addressed a large audience at the foot of Canal Street, on the bank of the Mississippi. Removing his coat and flinging it on a chair, he led his listeners in prayer for Huey Long and then commented that he, like Christ, was launching his ministry on a river bank. He spoke for two hours while the audience grew in size, becoming increasingly boisterous until the emotion-charged crowd turned rowdy.[16]

Smith emphasized that he was no "pantywaist" preacher in his organizational exertions—in fact, his proselytizing for Long required both physical courage and lung power. In the strongly anti-Long West Feliciana parish Smith was not permitted to speak at all; he was escorted to the parish line by the sheriff and a group of citizens, who warned him not to return. At Independence, Louisiana, his denunciations of two anti-Long women prompted a man to shout, "You can't talk about women like that!" and brandish a pistol. The man was disarmed, but soon afterward a firecracker exploded near the platform. Without a pause, Smith turned the incident to his advantage by screaming, "They've tried to kill me before, but if they ever did and I went down in a pool of blood, there would be a thousand to rise in my stead!"[17] In Lake Charles a man approached Smith one night and pressed an automatic pistol to his ribs, but Smith disarmed the elderly assailant and turned him over to the man's son, who apologized for the incident.[18]

Smith usually spoke to large crowds, even in rural areas, but his efforts sometimes provoked animosity rather than support. Hecklers disrupted his early efforts in Louisiana. Once a skeptic started down the aisle toward Smith. According to Smith, when the angry man was right beneath him, he hoisted the heckler by the collar and shook him to make a point.[19]

Smith traveled beyond Louisiana and toured Georgia and South Carolina that year, making more than a hundred speeches in each state, starting at daybreak and ending with torchlit rallies. He was one of the first men to tour the rural South attacking an incumbent Democratic president. In one small Georgia town he was heckled badly; when the sheriff sided with the hecklers, Smith's followers hauled him away.[20] In McRae, Georgia, one of his opponents turned on an ambulance siren every time Smith tried to speak. His supporters were infuriated and gained revenge by turning in false ambulance alarms for months afterward.[21] A more ominous incident occurred in Swainsboro. Opponents released the brake on Smith's sound truck and the truck rolled down a hill. They took the cable, looped it over a tree branch, and threatened to lynch him. Smith shouted that God would slay any man who touched him. In the end, no one was hanged or slain.[22]

Smith was egged in several small towns. In one he set up his sound truck in front of the town's largest store so that eggs missing him would hit the establishment. Sometimes he set up his platform on the top of a sound truck in an open area and gathered the crowd around the truck. When the egg-throwing began, the eggs that missed Smith hit local citizens on the other side. One egg hit a local constable.[23]

Such incidents only aided in gaining Smith's tours publicity. They were not really organizational tours because he rarely spoke with local leaders or left behind any formal apparatus. Rather, he would appear in town, deliver a bombastic speech, and hurry on. Smith loved the publicity he was receiving and granted dozens of interviews. He was so accommodating that he once conducted an interview from a bathtub while the journalist sat on the commode.[24]

Smith was a compelling orator, described once as "a combination of Savonarola and Elmer Gantry."[25] He was particularly effective at attracting rural people through his use of biblical analogies and the rousing entertainment he provided. He was a superb showman, "next to me the greatest rabble rouser in the country," Huey Long said.[26] For once Huey may have been guilty of understatement. Smith was, in fact, even more impressive in his flamboyant rhetoric than the Kingfish himself. H. L. Mencken considered him superior to William Jennings Bryan, describing Smith as "the greatest rabble-rouser seen on earth since Apostolic times."[27] Smith himself believed he was the third most powerful person in the nation, just behind Roosevelt and Long.[28] He boasted to a reporter in 1935 that he might enflame the entire country and "duplicate the feat of Adolph [sic] Hitler in Germany."[29]

Smith presented a dramatic appearance. Husky of voice and grown stout and muscular, his deep blue eyes flashing, sweat pouring down his brow, his sandy brown hair falling over his face, he would jab and flail his arms in the air to make a point. Sometimes he would tell his listeners when to applaud, and they never failed to respond. Square-shouldered, beak-nosed, his handsome face set in a smile, he instinctively drew people from almost deserted streets to gather and listen to him. His eloquence was such that a two-hour oration seemed like a twenty-minute pep talk. His voice was deep, mellow, and reassuring, then suddenly rough, terrifying, emotional. He flaunted his opinions, challenging, "If I'm not speaking the truth, shoot me while I stand here helpless!"[30]

Smith had a repertoire of surefire gimmicks. "All of you that ain't got four suits of clothes, raise your two hands," he would shout to his listeners. As hundreds of hands shot up he would continue: "Three suits. Two suits. Not even two suits of clothes. Oh my brethen, J. P. Morgan has two suits of clothes. He has a hundred times two suits of clothes."[31]

Sometimes he asked about undergarments, items even more luxurious than coats and pants. Afterward, hundreds of grim farmers would file by Smith's sound truck to receive cards and sign the roll for Share Our Wealth Society. But Smith's appeal was not limited to farmers; his versatile talent also allowed him to deliver successful speeches in New York City and to the Minnesota State Legislature. He captivated these more sophisticated audiences by telling them about his "secret" meetings with Harry Hopkins, Frances Perkins, and William Green.[32]

After just four weeks of speaking in 1934, Smith had added 207,000 members to the mailing list of the Share Our Wealth Society. By February 1935, after a year of organizing, the society claimed 4.5 million members; by July, 7 million. Clubs were created in every state. Louisiana had the most members, followed by Arkansas, Mississippi, and other southern states, but there were strong contingents in New York, California, and the Midwest as well. In the sparsely populated Great Plains and mountain states, thousands listened to Long and Smith on the radio and wrote to them.[33]

Smith basked in his mission. He believed that Huey Long was a man of destiny and that, through him, Smith would share that destiny. Fueled by this belief, Smith redoubled his energy. "When you're right and know you're right, you should now be ruthless," he said.[34] He even found protégés among Louisiana State University students. He trained them in oratory, infected them with his zeal, and dispatched them to college campuses across the nation to organize the Share Our Wealth clubs there.[35]

Everyone wanted to know what Long and Smith would do in 1936. Would Long run for president or would he handpick some candidate? If Long himself ran, would Smith be his campaign manager? The answer to this question was yes. Smith was gathering momentum and looked forward to organizing the nation as he had Louisiana. Roosevelt's pollster, sampling twenty-one thousand voters, found that Long was the first choice of 7.8 percent. That percentage was troubling to the Roosevelt campaign, especially since the election was still a year away.[36]

Long was not certain that he wanted to run, but Smith encouraged him. In flights of fantasy Long wrote a book explaining what he would do as president. At times he claimed he might back a progressive candidate from a major party. He also sometimes stated that there would definitely be a Share Our Wealth candidate in the race, but it would not be him. The most likely scenario was this: Long would run as a third-party candidate in 1936 and take enough votes from Roosevelt to engineer a Republican victory. Four years later, exasperated by ineffectual Republican leadership and still languishing in a depression, voters would demand Huey. If the Democrats refused his ultimatum for the nomination he would run as an independent again and either win himself or prevent any Democrat from winning. Smith would be at his side, making speeches, signing people up for the mailing list, and exerting his charm on potential allies. Smith later claimed that some conservative businessmen who wanted to defeat Roosevelt promised Long their support. Huey would accept their money, he explained, but he could not promise to lose.[37]

President Roosevelt was concerned. Long had been far more effective campaigning for him in 1932 than anyone had predicted. He had also almost single-handedly elected the meek widow Hattie Caraway of Arkansas to a full term in the U.S. Senate. Long was smart; he was a brilliant strategist and speaker, and he would get enough money. He was a genuine threat.[38] Coincidentally or deliberately, Roosevelt moved to the left in 1934 and enacted progressive taxes and social welfare legislation far milder than what Long demanded, but sufficient to appeal to his constituency. It is doubtful that he did so solely because of Long: some of the laws had been researched and drafted before Long became an issue, and Roosevelt had advocated several of the programs while he was still governor of New York. Long, sensitive about being preempted, voted against most of the reforms.

All of Long's and Smith's ambitious plans collapsed on a hot September evening when Long was assassinated in the hallway near the governor's office in the Louisiana capitol building at Baton Rouge. Father Charles E. Coughlin, who was with Franklin Roosevelt when they both heard the news, called it "the most regrettable thing in modern history."[39] Roosevelt doubtless disagreed privately; the assassin had removed an irritant and a strong dissenting voice from the Senate.

Rising politicians who die at the apogee of their careers inevitably become martyrs to their followers. Martyrs are eulogized, and Gerald Smith was Long's principal eulogist. He preached Long's funeral on the grounds of Louisiana's skyscraper capitol building to 150,000 mourners who covered six acres with flowers. Smith moved them. He proclaimed that Long's voice could not be stilled while children were hungry and families poor. Long's movement would not die with him; his successors would build upon Huey's legacy. Smith thundered, "This tragedy fires the souls of us who adored him. . . . He has been the wounded victim of the green goddess; to use the figure, he was the Stradivarius whose notes rose in competition with jealous drums, envious tomtoms. He was the unfinished symphony."[40]

Smith exaggerated, as most eulogists do, but even people who disliked him admitted that he was sincere and eloquent. At this moment, Smith realized his calling. He thrived on oratory, and he had never found it more rewarding than that September afternoon. The other survivors of the Long machine later regretted that Smith had been given the opportunity.[41] Some believed that he was glorifying himself rather than Long, but that was only partly true. Smith could be truly inspirational when speaking for a cause he believed in; and he loved Huey Long—that day and for the rest of his life. For a brief moment he could see himself picking up Long's fallen scepter and becoming his successor.

Long's assassin, Carl Austin Weiss, was a physician. His motives were never learned because he was killed instantly by Long's bodyguards. Rumors circulated that a ricochet from a bodyguard's gun, not Weiss, had killed Long. Some witnesses said that Weiss never even fired. Although no autopsy was done on Long and no formal state investigation of his death mounted, there was an inquest into Weiss's death. Smith was to be the star witness, but when called to testify, he denounced the hearing, accused the district attorney of complicity in Long's death, and stalked out. The hearing was never completed because Smith and other Longites refused to participate. The pro-Long governor, O. K. Allen, scuttled the investigation.[42]

Long's death left politics in Louisiana in chaos. His surviving followers were political hacks and no logical successor emerged. Smith asserted himself boldly. He quickly organized a ticket for the Democratic primaries, to be held in January 1936: for governor, James A. Noe, the incumbent lieutenant governor; for U.S. Senator, Wade O. Martin, chairman of the state public service commission. Smith planned to become Martin's executive assistant in the Senate and utilize his free mailing privilege and Long's mailing list to take over the Share Our Wealth Society. He wanted Earle Christenberry, Huey Long's personal secretary, to keep the records and answer the correspondence, while he handled public relations and speechmaking. If they needed money, they could levy dues of ten cents per week on the seven million persons on the mailing list.[43]

Smith's preemptive coup angered some of Long's cronies. Seymour Weiss, a New Orleans hotel tycoon and Long's chief fundraiser, and Robert Maestri, another millionaire, who was Long's principal financier, distrusted Smith. Weiss and Maestri announced a rival ticket: obscure district judge Richard Leche for governor—they claimed Huey had personally selected him—and Louisiana House Speaker Allen J. Ellender for Long's Senate seat.[44]

Realizing that he could not muster enough support or money to defeat the Weiss–Maestri ticket, Smith deserted his own candidates, announcing that upon reconsideration, he would not only back Leche and Ellender but would campaign for them. This opportunistic maneuver isolated

Noe, but he refused to quit the race. He grew bitter because Smith had abandoned him and charged that Smith had offered to stick with him in return for a bribe. Noe and Smith nearly came to blows on several occasions and Noe warned Smith that if he caught him at a meeting in Monroe he personally would thrash the former minister.[45]

Smith now turned his speechmaking prowess to devising effective gimmicks to elect the Leche ticket. He would cry about the blood of Huey and then dip his hands in red dye and hold them aloft. He would summon down the voice of Huey from heaven, and Long would "speak" from a loudspeaker planted in a nearby tree. Smith knew the memory of Huey Long was more potent than any issue Long's opponents could raise. The Leche ticket was elected with more votes than Huey himself had ever polled.[46]

When the election was over, however, Smith's usefulness to the Maestri—Weiss faction ended. His only political experience was operating the Share Our Wealth Society, which they intended to abolish: as millionaires themselves, Weiss and Maestri were not interesting in sharing the wealth. More ominously, Weiss and several other Longites faced federal prosecution on charges of income tax evasion. It was in their interest to end Huey's feud with Roosevelt; in return the Justice Department might drop the charges. Nor did they have ambitions beyond Louisiana. They hoped only to receive federal money earmarked for relief efforts in Louisiana but withheld while Huey was alive. They wanted to regain a voice in federal patronage by making peace with President Roosevelt. The president wanted Louisiana's vote at the Democratic nominating convention, and he wanted the annoying Share Our Wealth Society dismantled and its nettlesome spokesman, Gerald Smith, silenced. So a deal was struck, a deal Smith described as the "Second Louisiana Purchase." Louisiana seconded Roosevelt's nomination, and the charges against Weiss were dropped. Federal money flowed and patronage bloomed.[47]

There was still the matter of the Share Our Wealth Society. It had become a burden and Smith a nuisance. Smith knew that the Society's continuation depended upon Long's massive mailing list. Whoever controlled it would dominate the organization. But Weiss and Maestri, as part of the deal with Roosevelt, melted down Long's addressograph plates and fired Smith. If Smith wanted a movement, he would have to search beyond Louisiana.[48]

Smith's expulsion from the Louisiana machine was a watershed in his career. He headed for New York City, where he began to raise funds for his own organization. Then he heard that Earle Christenberry, who had a copy of Long's mailing list, had gone to work for Dr. Francis E. Town-send, advocate of a depression panacea based upon helping the elderly. Perhaps Christenberry had given Townsend his copy of Huey's mailing list. Smith eventually learned that Townsend did not have Long's list, but by then he had inserted himself into Townsend's movement.[49]

Forty years after he left Louisiana an embittered Longite, Smith erected a nine-foot bronze statue to Huey near the Kingfish's birthplace. Smith returned to Louisiana a few times through the years, but he was never again an effective political force there. He became, however, a part of the folklore surrounding Huey Long. Every Louisianian since infancy has become acquainted with the story of Huey Long. For almost thirty years after his death Louisiana was still divided into Long and anti-Long fac-tions. Many Louisianians believe that the Kingfish could have become president. No governor since then has overshadowed Long; he became the standard by which the state's residents measure their governors. It has been said that he did both more good and more evil than any other individual in the history of his state.[50]

Historians still debate Long's place in history. On the one hand, he awakened the needy, invigorated an apathetic electorate, and jolted the existing power structure. On the other, he was a corrupt dictator, ruth-lessly vindictive and motivated more by his ambition for absolute power than by concern for the welfare of the people.

Huey's grandiose ambitions probably were not achievable. It is highly unlikely that he could have become a productive senator, much less president. Impatient, impetuous, too nervous for civil argument or sus-tained work, he would more likely have ended up in the penitentiary than the White House. Federal prosecutors were planning to summon a grand jury to indict him at the time of his death.[51]

It can be argued that Long left Louisiana worse than he found it, that the tyranny of his personal dictatorship was too high a price to pay for change. Certainly he left a different Louisiana. On both the state and the national levels, he directed attention to needs that were genuine, but by linking economic reform with demagogic excess, he tainted the concept of reform.

Gerald Smith was cast adrift by Long's death. During Huey's brief but meteoric career Smith had become something of a national figure. It was now up to him to work his magic without his mentor. He was talented, aggressive, and energetic. As a spokesman for Long, he had earned a reputation for spellbinding oratory and had acquired as well a bitter per-sonal hatred for President Franklin D. Roosevelt. In fact, Smith maligned Roosevelt during the coming years more than he did any other individual. As long as Roosevelt lived, Smith worked to drive him from office. With the election of 1936 approaching he began to formulate plans to oppose the president. These plans led him initially to Dr. Townsend and soon afterward to another raucous voice of the depression era, Father Charles E. Coughlin.

three

Smith, Coughlin, and Townsend:

Three Merchants of Discontent

‡

When he left Louisiana in 1935, Gerald Smith had two objectives: to wreak revenge on President Roosevelt, who he believed had master-minded the death of his mentor, Huey Long; and to attach himself to some movement in which he could apply his organizational and oratori-cal talents. Smith's plans for achieving those objectives were muddled even in his own mind. At first he considered running for president himself; but he decided that it would be more realistic to construct an alliance with some politician who could challenge the incumbent presi-dent. His odyssey took him first to Georgia, where he lent his support to the state's governor, Eugene Talmadge, a reactionary politician far re-moved from Huey Long's economic liberalism but, like Long, an adamant opponent of Roosevelt. Smith claimed to control 110,000 votes in Georgia and boasted, "I'm the balance of power in Georgia between Roosevelt and Talmadge and I am going to support Talmadge."[1] Smith's intense hatred of Roosevelt and his bitterness over Long's assassination ultimately warped his judgment and led him into an alliance of conve-nience that proved destructive to both him and his allies.

Eugene Talmadge, like Huey Long, was a champion of the rural poor, an experienced politician, and a successful demagogue. Unlike Long, he opposed deficit spending and bridled at the suggestion of confiscatory taxes and redistribution of wealth. Although he had no real power base outside Georgia, some powerful Southerners flattered him into believing that he was a power broker who could negotiate concessions from the major party leaders, and they offered to finance a Talmadge campaign for the presidency.[2]

Ironically, Talmadge's ambitions were fired and financed by some of the very moguls Huey Long had sought to destroy. Pierre Du Pont contributed five thousand dollars to defray the cost of a Talmadge "grassroots convention" at Macon, Georgia; and Alfred P. Sloan, head of General Motors, gave a thousand; other magnates gave smaller amounts. Smith, no stickler for ideological consistency, offered his support to these fiscal conservatives.[3]

Most of the delegates who came to Talmadge's convention on January 27, 1936, were from Georgia; almost all were Southerners. Since there was no credentials committee and anyone who showed up was admitted, it was impossible to determine exact attendance. The setting was straight out of the movie *Gone With the Wind*. A huge Confederate flag decorated the speakers' platform, and each delegate was given a copy of the *Georgia Woman's World* featuring a large photograph of Eleanor Roosevelt, whom the caption described as "going to some nigger meeting, with two escorts, niggers, on each arm." The article further stated that since the Roosevelts had occupied the White House blacks had been invited to eat in the executive mansion and even to sleep in beds there.[4]

Thomas L. Dixon, author of *The Clansman* (basis for the movie *Birth of a Nation*) and *Leopard's Spots*, both of which glorified the Ku Klux Klan, delivered a resounding address in which he warned the white people that anti-lynching bills favored by the president might prevent the meting out of Southern justice to blacks.[5]

None of the speakers, however, could rival Gerald Smith. He labeled Eleanor Roosevelt "that female Rasputin in the White House," and denounced the president in terms that were extreme even for him.[6] He called Roosevelt a Communist, an atheist, and a cripple. "Roosevelt is rapidly becoming the most despised President in the history of the country," Smith bellowed. "He gave us the Russian primer and cursed the Bible. . . . He and his gang are in the death rattle. We have only to put the cloth of the ballot over his dead mouth."[7] When he asked people to kneel and pray for the defeat of the Roosevelt administration, every man and woman dropped to the ground and prayed audibly.[8] At the conclusion of Smith's vituperative speech, a tobacco-stained man dashed to the platform and planted a kiss on his sweaty face.[9]

Talmadge's speech followed Smith's but could not match his theatrics. Angry at being upstaged, he never invited Smith back to Georgia. Talmadge's brief campaign faltered, and in June he withdrew from the Georgia presidential primary. In September 1936, he was trounced by Richard Russell in the Democratic primary for the U.S. Senate.[10]

Smith knew that in order to gain political prominence outside the South, he needed to ingratiate himself with some national figure, a politician or the leader of a mass movement. He had no following of his own and lacked the finances, support staff, and mailing list to perpetuate Huey Long's Share Our Wealth crusade. He returned empty-handed from an attempt to raise money in New York City, haunted by his failure to procure Long's elusive mailing list. However, Smith knew that Earle Christenberry, personal secretary to the late senator, had recently been hired by an elderly physician named Francis E. Townsend. Townsend had attracted millions of followers with his plan to use public funds to pay generous pensions to the elderly, which he claimed would end the Depression. Smith mistakenly believed that the mailing list he was doggedly and opportunistically pursuing had been turned over to Townsend. This, more than any inherent affinity for the Townsend plan, explains why Smith selected Townsend from among the many mass leaders the Depression had spawned.[11]

Townsend lacked the charisma of Huey Long; he was old, feeble, perhaps almost senile. But he was also guileless and susceptible to exploitation by an oratorical magician like Smith. Even without Long's lists, Townsend had a large following. By gaining Townsend's trust Smith hoped to merge the Long and Townsend movements and thus to wield considerable power in the 1936 election.

Smith stalked Townsend for weeks, seeking an opportunity to win his confidence. His chance came when Townsend testified before a congressional committee investigating his movement. The committee treated him to rough, unfriendly questioning. At Smith's suggestion Townsend suddenly walked out of the hearing. Smith then took the role of Townsend's protector, making a path through the crowd and herding the doctor into a waiting taxi. (Smith paused long enough to pose for a newspaper photographer.) They drove to Baltimore, where journalist H. L. Mencken took them into his home until they could settle in at the local Townsend headquarters. Townsend was later cited and convicted for contempt of Congress, but he was pardoned by President Roosevelt.[12]

Superficially, Smith and Townsend appeared unlikely allies. Townsend was old, Smith young; Townsend was a dry and dull speaker, Smith oozed charisma; Townsend believed wholeheartedly in his plan, while Smith opportunistically viewed it as a vehicle to establish a movement of his own. Smith in fact was fuzzy about details of the Townsend plan and sometimes made errors in discussing it with the press.

Townsend's concept was simple: each retiree sixty years of age or older would be given two hundred dollars per month by the government, with the stipulation that he or she must spend it all before receiving the next check. This would encourage retirement, opening jobs for younger workers, Townsend believed, and the spending provision would stimulate buying, thus increasing profits and then wages. The pensions would be financed by a 2-percent "transaction tax" each time a product was sold.[13] Townsend had conceived the scheme in 1933, and within two years it had grown to be the largest single panacea movement in the nation. He possessed few attributes of a demagogue: he was small and shy and a weak speaker. Nevertheless, the movement caught on among destitute and desperate elderly people, who had been denied economic and political power and who often found themselves bored with retirement. It was these aged zealots who committed themselves to unstinting support of the Townsend program. Although the plan was impractical, it became an important political issue that publicized the plight of the elderly.

Smith had little of tangible value to contribute to the Townsend movement, although he persuaded Townsend to change the name of his organization from the cumbersome "Old Age Revolving Pensions, Ltd." to the catchier "Townsend Recovery Plan." Smith's other idea for "reform" was to mobilize youth for the Townsend movement, a plan that smacked of Hitler's youth movement.

> I am going before the Youth Committee of this organization within ten days and ask them to set out on a program to enlist an average of twelve young men picked for their fitness, picked for their appreciation of this Plan, picked for their physical alertness, and in thirty days from that date we shall enroll an army of one hundred thousand Townsend youths in America who will constitute a great movement of youth. We are going to have young men who think straight, young men who think honestly, young men who think fearlessly, young men with strong bodies to watch these polls so that the Townsend votes will not be counted out by the thieving politicians in November.[14]

Smith began appearing with Townsend at rallies and interviews and telling the old man what to say. Townsend seemed overwhelmed by the younger man's aggressive personality. Smith told the press in Philadelphia that he and Townsend "stood under the historic arch in Valley Forge and vowed to take over the government."[15] Within a few weeks Smith had made himself Townsend's closest adviser, and Townsend had appointed him to his board of directors.[16] In Townsend's presence Smith was relatively circumspect; in his absence he was arrogant and boastful. He accommodated himself to the doctor's ideas only because he knew the subordination was temporary: he really wanted neither Townsend's ideas, his leadership, nor his friendship, but his following. Together with his own contacts, a few influential friends, and the name identification he had gained as a Share Our Wealth organizer, he hoped to consolidate the popular discontent upon which all of the Depression demagogues preyed.

Smith used his personal relationship with the old doctor to gain influence in the Townsend movement. Most of Townsend's assistants viewed him with alarm, seeing him as a rival for their leader's affection, a formidable figure determined not only to dominate the doctor but eventually to supplant him. But Townsend was slower to recognize that Smith was stealing his movement.

During 1936, Smith and Townsend shared the spotlight with a third merchant of discontent, Father Charles E. Coughlin of Royal Oak, Michigan, a suburb of Detroit. A Roman Catholic priest, Coughlin may be the most popular radio speaker of all time. He had begun his broadcasting career in 1926; his topics concerned religion, philosophy, and occasionally economics. During the early years of the Great Depression, however, he turned his attention more and more to politics, and his audience multiplied to the point where he employed 220 workers simply to cull contributions from his mail. At the height of his influence in 1935 and 1936 he received more mail than the president, more than Huey Long, in fact more than any other individual in the nation. Along with the letters came thousands of dollars in contributions. Young children who lived near his church regularly combed his garbage for discarded envelopes containing small amounts of money that his sorters, in their haste, had overlooked.[17] Coughlin's radio audience may have been the largest in broadcasting history. He had more regular listeners than *Amos 'n' Andy*; and when listeners had the option of hearing Coughlin or the New York Philharmonic, 187,000 favored Coughlin while a mere 12,000 preferred the orchestra. One public opinion poll voted him the most admired American—a judgment that had less to do with the content of his broadcasts than with his rich, resonant voice, his beguiling charm, and his simplistic approach. Early in the Depression years, Coughlin became a harsh critic of President Hoover. Later, when Roosevelt failed to adopt his nostrums of inflation backed by silver currency, he turned against him too. He was incensed when the administration revealed that he had been using contributions from his followers to speculate in silver.[18]

Coughlin was easily the most controversial Roman Catholic priest of his time. His lifestyle was flamboyant, his morals questionable, his ambition enormous. President Roosevelt was so concerned about having Coughlin for an enemy that he ordered a thorough investigation of the cleric's affairs. Various unconfirmed rumors were reported to the FBI: that he was sleeping with his secretary, or with the wife of a prominent Detroit man; that he was sleeping with a maid; that he had a mistress named Babe with whom he was seeing an analyst for sexual problems; that he visited Europe incognito; that he had nine hundred thousand dollars on deposit in a London bank; and that he had paid an irate husband fifty thousand dollars of church money to keep quiet about an affair the priest had had with the man's wife.[19] Treasury Secretary Henry Morgenthau seriously considered indicting Coughlin for income tax evasion but decided that the political repercussions of a Jewish cabinet officer's prosecuting a Catholic priest might be too damaging.[20]

Father Coughlin wanted to select personally a candidate to challenge President Roosevelt in 1936. He distrusted Huey Long, whose ego clashed with Coughlin's, but they might have pooled their resources in 1936, had Long lived. Long had dispatched Gerald Smith as his emissary to Coughlin and certain other potentially powerful allies in 1935, and Coughlin was intrigued by the possibility of union. He agreed to remain neutral, at least, if Long campaigned for president. After Long's death, Smith realized he could be instrumental in fusing the Coughlin and Townsend movements because he was strategically known to both of them. Although Townsend had some anti-Catholic prejudice, Smith was able to convince him that cooperation would be mutually advantageous.[21]

The choice of a candidate for the proposed alliance came from Coughlin. In 1935, he worked with Congressman William Lemke of North Dakota in support of his bill for refinancing farm mortgages (this would have indirectly produced some of the inflation Coughlin desired). In May, Lemke addressed a mass meeting of Coughlin's political pressure group, the National Union for Social Justice, and endorsed its membership drive. The bill's defeat in spite of their efforts further alienated Lemke and Coughlin from the Roosevelt administration, and Coughlin resolved to organize a third party.[22]

In September 1935, Coughlin turned his parish over to an assistant in order to devote more time to politics. Two months later, he opened negotiations with Townsend and Smith to back Lemke as the candidate of the new party. Smith decided to support Lemke because he believed that Huey Long had planned to select Lemke as his running mate.[23] Convincing Townsend was more difficult. He insisted that Lemke commit himself to unequivocal support of his pension scheme, but the most Lemke would say was that he would sign the bill if passed by Congress. He would work for some form of aid for the elderly, he said, but not necessarily the Townsend plan.[24] Finally Townsend agreed to support Lemke personally, but he refused to make him the official candidate of his pension organization. He did, however, invite Lemke, along with Coughlin and Smith, to speak at his national convention of Townsend clubs in Cleveland. It was agreed that Lemke would announce himself as the candidate of the new Union Party, with endorsements to follow. Three days prior to Lemke's announcement, Gerald Smith told the press that he, Townsend, and Coughlin would back Lemke in common opposition to "the communistic philosophy of Frankfurter, Ickes, Hopkins and Wallace."[25] Coughlin was furious at being upstaged, but he respected the original timetable and announced his support of Lemke six hours after Lemke's own announcement, three days after Smith had made the premature endorsement.[26]

The Democrats and Republicans met before the conventions planned by Townsend and Coughlin. The Democrats renominated President Roosevelt and the Republicans nominated Alf Landon, the governor of Kansas. A social liberal and fiscal conservative, Landon supported much of the New Deal program and was a personal friend of the president. A charming, ingratiating man socially, his prepared speeches consisted mainly of ambiguous platitudes. (In one speech he actually said, "Wherever I have gone in this country, I have found Americans.")[27] Landon was so ineffective as a campaigner that Smith came to believe that the governor's nomination was part of a plot to guarantee a second term for Roosevelt. Smith later wrote, "Alf Landon, who was offered in 1936 by the Republicans, was an insipid weakling selected by the Eastern Establishment to take the fall and accept defeat, thus facilitating the merger between the secret Establishment posing as Republican and the Roosevelt dictatorship."[28] As for Roosevelt, Smith believed he was an unprincipled scoundrel. He chuckled in agreement when he read H. L. Mencken's characterization of the president's opportunism: "If he became convinced tomorrow that coming out for cannibalism would get him votes he so sorely needs, he would begin fattening a missionary in the White House back yard come Wednesday."[29]

On July 15, some twelve thousand delegates assembled in Cleveland for the Townsend convention. Most were idealistic, elderly people who had made substantial financial sacrifices to attend. Many were staying in rooms without baths and in tourist courts; some camped on the outskirts of Cleveland and rode buses or trolley cars into the city, bringing bag lunches with them. The Smiths and the Townsends shared a large hotel suite near convention headquarters.[30]

The delegates were bewildered by the mixed message offered by their leaders. On the morning of the opening day, Congressman Martin E. Smith of Washington and Otto A. Case, Townsend treasurer for the same state, delivered pro-Roosevelt and anti-Lemke speeches, to hearty cheering.[31] On Wednesday afternoon Townsend and Smith had their turn. Two hours of national radio coverage had been allotted them. Townsend spoke first, giving a dry speech packed with statistics that had some delegates nodding off in their seats. Nonetheless, he was such a beloved figure that his speech inspired affection if not excitement. After Townsend's half-hour speech, Smith appeared. He took the remaining ninety minutes of air time and then continued for another ninety, pushing several other scheduled speakers completely off the convention program. He began by stating that he had discovered a conspiracy to deny him the opportunity to speak. When he asked his audience how many would "hang" anyone who attempted to prevent him from speaking, every hand shot up. Smith then poured it on, pausing occasionally to say "give that a hand," which the crowd did enthusiastically. Brandishing a Bible, he pounded on the rostrum and whipped off his coat, revealing a sweat-soaked blue shirt. A number of times during his three-hour marathon, he gulped ice water, lofting the entire pitcher instead of pouring the water into a glass. He proclaimed that if it was rabble-rousing to defend the Constitution, quote the Bible, praise the flag, and advocate the Townsend plan, then he wanted to be the best rabble-rouser in the nation.[32] He utilized meaningless platitudes and irrelevant references to work his audience to a fever pitch of excitement:

> You give me Santa Claus and the Bible and the Constitution and the Flag and the Townsend Plan, and I will do ten thousand times as much as you will with the Russian primer, no Santa Claus, and the Lenin communistic Marx plan. We are going to continue in America having Santa Claus, Christmas trees, Easter Bunny, Holy Bible, and we are going to sing hymns, have meetin's, go to church, and if you want to know what is going to happen between now and November, I can tell you we are going to seize the government of the United States.[33]

Old people squirmed in their seats, applauded, and shouted "Amen" ecstatically, screaming for Smith to pour it on. H. L. Mencken, who watched in fascination from the press gallery, wrote of Smith's speech: "It ran the keyboard from the softest sobs and gurgles to the most ear-splitting whoops and howls, and when it was over, the 9,000 delegates simply lay back in their pews and yelled." Even journalists hardened to political oratory were carried away. Like most of Smith's appeals, the speech was almost all emotion and little substance: few people left the meeting with more than a visceral hatred of Roosevelt and a gut feeling that Smith had the answers. In fact, Mencken observed that, although they applauded Smith to the point of exhaustion, a few minutes after he sat down no one in the audience could remember what he had said.[34]

The next day Father Coughlin addressed the convention, knowing he faced a challenge in following Smith. Coughlin's speech was equally vituperative and emotional, but he was less charismatic in person than he was on radio. He stood only a few inches from the microphone, and remained motionless except for rocking back on his feet with motions that reminded one observer of the bumps and grinds of a professional stripper. Nonetheless, Coughlin too got caught up in the spirit of the event. Overheated and soaked with sweat, he took off his coat and even removed his clerical collar. Denouncing Roosevelt, he claimed that those Townsendites who still supported the president had sold out to the Rothschilds and the international money changers.[35] FDR, he proclaimed, stood for "Franklin Double-crossing Roosevelt." When a few people booed this remark they were removed by the sergeant-at-arms. The rest of the crowd roared; they had come for a show and were getting one.[36]

Despite the inflammatory speeches of Smith and Coughlin, the Townsend convention chose to remain neutral toward the election, although Townsend said that he personally would back Lemke. However, some loyal Democratic Townsendites also spoke. Gomer Smith, a part-Cherokee from Oklahoma who had narrowly lost the Democratic nomination for the U.S. Senate, defended Roosevelt and attacked Gerald Smith. He claimed that fighting the president would only weaken the movement and diminish the chances of enacting the Townsend plan into law. When he demanded, "Shall this great Townsend organization debauch itself and go off on a windmill fighting expedition?" the audience responded with a thunderous "No!"[37] He ridiculed Smith's claim to six million followers and predicted that if one sought Smith's followers in the swamps of Louisiana, "they would turn out to be bullfrogs." As an orator, the Oklahoman was nearly the equal of Smith and Coughlin, and the old people cheered him loudly, much to the embarrassment of the preceding speakers. The elderly Townsendites seemed more responsive to the decibel level than to the content of the orations.[38]

Candidate William Lemke spoke on the final day, but his monotonous voice evoked little enthusiasm, even when he praised Huey Long and announced that his administration would "bring about a condition where every man is a king" and "every woman . . . a queen." He did not directly endorse the Townsend plan but promised, "As President I will sign any bill that Congress enacts which will give an honest and fair compensation to old people."[39]

Three weeks after the Townsend convention, eight thousand Coughlin supporters assembled in the same auditorium in Cleveland for the convention of Father Coughlin's National Union for Social Justice. Smith later claimed that Father Coughlin had begged him to address his convention; but Coughlin was actually quite reluctant to invite Smith, and some of his supporters vigorously objected to Smith's appearance. Coughlin arranged a compromise: Smith would speak, but not until late on the last day, after the convention had technically adjourned, and after many delegates had departed or were exhausted and listless. Upon his arrival in Cleveland, Smith told reporters that he knew of a plot to assassinate him but promised that he would speak anyway, regardless of the danger to his life. When the time finally came for him to deliver his speech, the delegates appeared weary after an entire day on the floor without even a recess for lunch. But Smith quickly roused them to a frenzy with a theatrical speech that was even more effective than his previous address to the Townsendites. He stripped to his shirt, sweating profusely and thundering:

> A nursing baby, they say, is content while it's taking milk; you set in your places and take it while I pour it on, and I'll tell you when to clap. I come to you 210 pounds of fighting Louisiana flesh, with the blood memory of Huey Long who died for the poor people of this country still hot in my eyes . . . and I'll show you the most historic and contemptible betrayal ever put over on the American people. . . . our people were starving and they burned the wheat . . . hungry and they killed the pigs . . . led by Mr. Henry Wallace, secretary of Swine Assassination . . . and by a slimy group of men culled from the pink campuses of America with friendly gaze fixed on Russia.[40]

Coughlin, upstaged by Smith for the second time in three weeks, swore that he would never again share a platform with him. He considered Smith a ruthless opportunist who sought to steal his followers just as Smith had come to dominate the Townsend movement. Coughlin was demoralized by his aggressive, forceful personality.

While Smith overshadowed Coughlin, the candidate William Lemke was eclipsed by all three of his principal sponsors. Amidst all the extravagant oratory Lemke was almost mute; a bland, unexciting speaker who preferred logic and statistical evidence to fiery rhetoric, he was no match for either Smith or Coughlin. Would-be supporters were disappointed by his shabby appearance—his baggy pants, his dusty and unpolished shoes, and his ubiquitous tan tweed cap. His face was scarred from smallpox, he had a glass eye, and sometimes there was stubble on his chin because he disliked shaving. Smith later described him as "a complete composite of unattractiveness. He looked like a hayseed. He was not eloquent and all he could talk about was money and agriculture."[41]

Neither Smith nor Coughlin had much respect for Lemke's intellectual or speaking ability, but he was nevertheless the type of candidate they wanted, someone who would not compete with them for attention. Lemke's running mate, Thomas C. O'Brien, a Boston Irish Catholic, Harvard graduate, railroad labor attorney, and Coughlin organizer in Massachusetts, added geographical balance to the ticket, but he was little known outside of New England.[42]

The Union Party platform followed the principles of Coughlin's National Union for Social Justice more than the Townsend plan or the Share Our Wealth scheme. It advocated inflation, aid to farmers, a protective tariff, an isolationist foreign policy, and free college education. It endorsed help for the aged and limitations on incomes, but only in general terms. The platform was ignored during the campaign.[43]

Lemke campaigned valiantly but conceded that his cause was hopeless by standing for reelection to Congress at the same time that he ran for president. Traveling by air from his Chicago headquarters, he made the most extensive third-party campaign tour since the Bull Moose effort of Theodore Roosevelt. Lemke waged write-in campaigns in states where he could not get on the ballot.[44] While Lemke campaigned alone, Smith, Coughlin, and Townsend decided against campaigning together, ostensibly because it would be an inefficient duplication of effort, but actually because Smith and Coughlin refused to share the spotlight. Dr. Townsend made several appearances with Smith, but his advanced age prevented him from traveling much. When the two did appear together, it was clear that Smith, who spoke longer and more noisily, was the chief attraction.

Townsend was less interested in electing Lemke than he was in promoting his plan. "I would vote for a native-born Chinaman if he was for the plan," he confessed.[45] Townsend was not enthusiastic about Lemke and admitted that he supported him only because both Landon and Roosevelt were hostile to his proposition. He was more interested in defeating Roosevelt than in electing Lemke, and near the end of the campaign he advised his followers to vote for Landon in states where Lemke was not on the ballot.[46]

Father Coughlin's enthusiasm also waned because he saw that it was impossible to combine his following with Dr. Townsend's without getting Gerald Smith in the bargain. After hearing Smith arouse the rabble at his own and Townsend's convention, Coughlin developed an aversion to the former minister that hardened into outright hatred. "I was frightened by Smith," he told one interviewer.[47]

Smith brought out the worst in Coughlin, who was driven to excess as he tried to compete with him. His speeches became increasingly demagogic and his credibility declined. Moreover, by associating with Smith he linked his own organization with a man who was widely believed to be a dangerous extremist. Some people who had previously considered

Coughlin a voice of reason, if not of moderation, were repelled by his association with Smith. Had Coughlin backed down from this increasingly strident crusade, he would have lost face. On the other hand, the increasingly extremist nature of the movement could only hurt his prestige in the long run. So Coughlin oscillated between enthusiasm and dismay, between hard campaigning and despondent indolence.

The 1936 campaign was a crossroad for Coughlin. Previously his movement had been large and strong but directionless. By giving it more definite direction, he risked alienating those who might be repelled by his associations or the specifics of his program, and he faced abandonment by his "fair-weather" friends who had no stomach for losing. Coughlin could not sustain his movement without the enthusiasm derived from emotional oratory; but he could not keep escalating his pronouncements in competition with Smith without draining himself and his followers of emotion. When emotionalism receded in the face of reality, the heart went out of his movement.

Gerald Smith, on the other hand, had no movement of his own and thus little to lose from the campaign, even if it failed. Smith lacked detailed knowledge about Townsend's and Coughlin's programs and was not entirely committed to either. What he did want—what *they* had—was public attention and a dedicated following. Smith had admired Huey Long as a master politician, but he had contempt for Lemke and distrusted Coughlin, and he befriended Townsend only because he knew he could dominate the aged physician. Smith's goal was to keep himself in the national limelight while building a following of his own based on some gimmickry which he had not quite figured out. What he needed was a platform for his oratory. It was always questionable whether Smith's oratory was a means or an end. He clearly enjoyed speaking for itself—it made his own adrenaline flow and stimulated his listeners. But Smith also craved power, and during the 1930s his chief opportunity to achieve it seemed to be through oratory. For this he needed the forums that Townsend and Coughlin provided.

Smith was more active than either Coughlin or Townsend in the Lemke campaign. From August to November he toured the nation, sometimes with Townsend, but usually alone, denouncing Roosevelt, dismissing Landon as a nonentity, telling jokes, and claiming that if Roosevelt were reelected it would be the last free election in America. Smith promised that if Roosevelt did win, he would personally lead a campaign to impeach the president. He linked Roosevelt with Communists on one hand and international bankers on the other, oblivious to the irony of such a pronouncement. He asserted that Lemke would win the election because he permitted "the Rev. Charles E. Coughlin to define his money plank—

Dr. Townsend to define his old age security plan—Gerald Smith to define his plank on labor, education and homesteads."[48]

Even if Lemke lost, Smith continued, many Smith-endorsed congressmen would win, and they would hold the balance of power in Congress. He made absurd claims, asserting that Roosevelt had offered him a cabinet position or "everything from the Goddess of Liberty to Catalina Island" if he would drop the Lemke crusade and support the president.[49] Roosevelt might try to put Dr. Townsend in the penitentiary, Smith claimed, but the burly ex-minister promised to thwart physically any such effort. Indeed, the threat of physical force underlay many of Smith's statements.[50] At times he seemed to be a fanatic, at others a self-conscious rogue. In a moment of candor he revealed his basic approach: "Religion and patriotism, keep going on that. It's the only way you can get them really 'het up.'"[51]

Smith predicted a revolution if Roosevelt won. The only thing that held the Democrats together, he claimed, was money. When Roosevelt ran out of money, chaos would ensue. Smith would then capitalize on the situation: "When the politicians overplay their hand, certain nerve centers of the population will begin to twitch. The people will start fomenting and fermenting and then a fellow like myself, someone with courage enough to capture the people, will get on the radio, make three or four speeches, and have them in his hand. I'll teach 'em how to hate."[52]

Smith's flamboyant oratory quickly eclipsed the program of the Union Party. Even among the party's more serious advocates rhetoric took the place of grassroots organization. Speechmaking appealed to Smith and Coughlin but precinct organization and creation of a party infrastructure did not; it was hard work that could not be expected to yield immediate dividends. The party did not make much of an effort to get Lemke on the ballot in every state. In fourteen states he was not on the ballot at all, and in six others he was listed under a different label or as an independent, not as a Union Party candidate.[53]

Without any rational basis for his optimism Smith promised to deliver six million votes to Lemke, while Coughlin vowed that if he could not deliver nine million he would retire from politics. Townsend claimed the allegiance of ten million voters. Even fundraising, something at which all three excelled, languished in favor of boasts. The Union Party spent only about ninety-five thousand dollars, compared to fourteen million for the Republicans and the Democrats' nine million. Of the small sum expended, two-thirds was used merely to get on the ballot.[54]

At first Gerald Smith was intoxicated by the movement and by the power he sensed flowing into his hands. Roosevelt was doomed, he claimed. The president might try to stop Smith the way he had stopped

Huey Long, by killing him, but even that would fail: "They can kill me if they want to, but I warn them I'll still keep on fighting Roosevelt, dead or alive."[55]

Even before the election, however, Smith began to believe that he was outgrowing the Union Party and that he could achieve power on his own, without the coattails of Townsend and Coughlin. Although a sober analysis would have revealed no grounds for such arrogant optimism, Smith began to conceive of himself as bigger and more important than his chief allies. The Union Party crusade had had a therapeutic effect on him. After Huey Long's death Smith had questioned his own ability to succeed as a mass leader, but now he knew that he had not lost his power to move listeners. He recognized that the crusade in behalf of Lemke was a lost cause; he wanted his own movement, so that when the chaos he expected came, he would not have to share power. On October 20, 1936, he announced from New York that he was creating an independent movement for the purpose of fighting Communism, one that would "seize the government of the United States."[56] He claimed to have "a following of ten million patriots" willing to sacrifice their lives to save the country from "an international plot to collectivize it." He had four hundred rich friends in twenty-two key cities who would give him 1 percent of their incomes "to make America vigorously nationalistic."[57]

When Townsend read reports of Smith's remarks, he promptly disowned him. "If the press reports concerning the fascist action of Gerald L. K. Smith are true," he stated, "then I hereby disavow any connection that Mr. Smith may claim in the organization of the Townsend National Recovery Plan. I am against fascism."[58] Smith was a gifted speaker, he admitted, but extreme nationalism was anathema to him and had no place in his movement.[59] Lemke's campaign manager likewise expelled Smith from the Union Party.[60] Smith protested that Lemke and Townsend had been misled about his intentions and that he had been misquoted in the press. Besides, he bristled, he could not be fired by Townsend because he had never been on the payroll of his organization. Coughlin chose to ignore both Smith and Lemke: he did not mention either of them in his last radio addresses.[61]

Smith's campaigning ended with several bizarre incidents. On October 22 he was punched in the face by an unknown assailant after delivering a radio talk in New Orleans.[62] And on election eve he was arrested in the Crescent City on trumped-up charges of disturbing the peace, reviling the police, and using obscene language after he had attacked the Louisiana Leche–Maestri machine on statewide radio and at a mass rally.[63]

The election itself was anticlimactic because by then *each* of the trio of Union Party crusaders had given up, either ignoring his candidate

entirely or treating him unenthusiastically. Franklin Roosevelt overwhelmed his opponents by winning all but two states and polling a huge
majority in the popular vote. Lemke received only 891,858 votes, less
than 2 percent of the total. He won no electoral votes, nor did he affect the
outcome in any state.[64] Lemke did best in heavily Catholic precincts
where Coughlin's influence was greatest. He polled fewer than 5,000
votes in the entire South, where Coughlin's broadcasts were not heard
and where Roosevelt captured 94 percent of the popular vote.[65] Smith
delivered few votes to Lemke and may have lost more votes than he
attracted because "many of the farmer-laborites of the Midwest were
scared away by Smith's campaign statements."[66] Lemke barely retained
his seat in Congress and was stripped of seniority by his Republican
colleagues. He attempted to continue the Union Party, but within two
years it disbanded due to lack of funds.[67]

To historians familiar with third-party failures since 1936, it seems a
foregone conclusion that the Union Party would fail. But it was not so evident at the time. They were tempestuous times, and desperate schemes
were the order of the day. From the beginning, however, the coalition of
Smith, Coughlin, and Townsend was unstable. Their only unifying factor
was hatred of President Roosevelt, who was a politician far superior to
any of them. The poor and elderly victims of the Depression—the very
people the Union Party was trying to attract—were most likely to vote for
FDR, because his humanitarian program had given them what little hope
they still possessed. In making Roosevelt their chief target of attack the
trio of crusaders erred badly. It would have been better to identify Wall
Street or big business as the enemy—but these too were the opponents
of Roosevelt and thus aligned with Townsend, Smith, and Coughlin.
(Smith later learned the importance of identifying acceptable scapegoats.)

Even more important, the Union Party failed to attract the support of
labor and thus had no mass base. The movement depended too heavily
on the public relations skills of the leaders. It had little tangible organization: instead of a well-organized fund-raising program, the party relied
on mailing lists and small contributions inspired by emotional reactions
to their oratory. But their supporters were zealots, and while zealots do
not lack enthusiasm, they are not known for their ability to sustain day-
to-day involvement. Moving a mass audience to cheer may be gratifying,
but it is also transitory. Moving people to enact programs requires consistency, hard work, and dedication. The weakness of the trio of crusaders
was the weakness of all insurgent movements from the Populists of the
1890s to the George Wallace crusades of the 1960s. They relied upon
discontent, in this case economic discontent. As the economy improved

their following dwindled. While negativism as expressed in opposition to Roosevelt may have had temporary appeal, it proved ineffectual when Roosevelt's program mitigated hardship. These various panaceas appealed only to desperate people.

The Union Party's dismal showing also reflected the limitations of its leadership. These leaders were essentially special-interest advocates, supreme egotists who were more interested in adulation than in enacting a program. Their credibility suffered when they proved to be poor prophets: neither Smith's Communist takeover nor Coughlin's apocalypse ever materialized. Their power depended upon the continued gullibility of their supporters, but the faith of their followers in the unseen and the undelivered finally diminished, leaving the leaders with obsolete programs and fleeting constituencies.

Finally, the Townsend Plan and Share Our Wealth leaders failed because they found it necessary to enter the political fray while their movements were still in infancy. Huey Long had intended merely to lay the foundation for a serious effort in 1940 by campaigning in 1936. But Lemke's electoral disaster effectively destroyed any plans for 1940. In a fundamental sense, the schemes advocated by Smith, Coughlin, and Townsend were passing fads, though they had some impact. Townsend took credit for the old-age provisions of the Social Security Act and Smith for the soak-the-rich tax policy of 1936. Roosevelt may have had these reforms in mind all along, but in any case he was skilled in political expediency.

That Smith was able, even temporarily, to gain such a high position in Townsend's movement can be attributed to his charm and persuasiveness. But he was unable to restrain himself long enough to derive maximum benefit from his position. Consequently, when he did launch his own movement even before the election in November, although he had a cadre of wealthy contacts in the East, he lacked the mass base of support he desired. Although he managed to conceal his ambition for a while, he ultimately revealed himself to be self-serving, concerned more with personal power than with political goals. Smith was susceptible to the influence of another strong personality, but neither Townsend nor Coughlin was a Huey Long, and neither possessed the personal magnetism that could subdue Smith.

Coughlin was the senior partner in the triumvirate because his movement was the largest and most volatile. Smith was the junior partner because he relied on the others for forums and mailing lists. But while Smith was temporarily weak, he had assets which made him potentially the strongest of the three: he was bold and fearless, unlike the aged and infirm Townsend, and he was better at speaking to a live audience than either Townsend or Coughlin. Smith was also the most ambitious and the most likely to use demagoguery and even violence to achieve his nebulous goals. Coughlin and Townsend were slow to realize this, but it eventually became clear to them that Smith was a parasite: he brought them no additional followers of his own, and he threatened to steal the allegiance of their own supporters. Smith, however, overplayed his hand. Had he remained in the background, deferring to his allies, particularly to Townsend, he might have slowly built a personal mass following, perhaps even merging and taking over the movements of his less vigorous allies. But Smith could not resist soapbox oratory, and he frightened and alienated first Coughlin and then Townsend, so he was unable to absorb their movements by boring from within.

Some observers believe that Smith was merely a genial cynic, because he was candid with journalists about his own opportunism. Indeed, the Union Party effort was the most purely opportunistic phase of Smith's career. The historian Arthur Schlesinger, Jr., argues that Smith failed in his later crusades not because he lacked principle, but because he was too principled. In support of this argument Schlesinger wrote, "Whatever may be said for Gerald Smith's subsequent career, it certainly represented a triumph of principle over success."[68]

Smith always loved to speak before large crowds, and the 1936 campaign was the last opportunity he had to make speeches to so many people. He was caught up in the frenzy of the moment; there was a kind of electricity between him and his audiences. In 1936 barnstorming was still a very important component of political campaigning. The electricity and frenzy Smith was able to create in his audience was a less important factor in future campaigns, which relied on radio or television.

A third party in America, to be "successful," does not have to elect a president or a majority in Congress; it merely has to have its program absorbed and implemented by one of the major parties. Smith, Coughlin, and Townsend liked to claim credit for some of the more progressive features of the New Deal, such as the Social Security Act, the sharply progressive income tax of 1936, and some social welfare programs. These reforms, however, were enacted not only without their support, but against their active opposition. These zealots were so convinced of their own infallibility that they would accept nothing less than total fulfillment of their programs. They shirked their moral responsibilities to help the needy people they tried to appeal to, opting instead for partisan opposition. Townsend was probably an exception, but what Smith and Coughlin wanted was not some abstract program, however salutary; they wanted political power. Smith was the most incessant, the most driven of the three. He thrived on popular discontent—implementation of his program, however unlikely, would have dissipated the very sentiment he fed on. Best on the attack, he could work only outside the establishment, and only oratorically, not tangibly.

Father Coughlin became the most embittered of the triumvirate. After the campaign he resigned as editor of his journal, *Social Justice*, and ceased his radio broadcasts. When he returned to political activism, he became increasingly shrill and anti-Semitic. He hated Gerald Smith for the rest of his life, even denying that he had known him well. He told one biographer: "Smith was a viper . . . a leech . . . who was anti-Christian, anti-Semitic, and anti-God. I had no more of a relationship to him than I had with Spartacus and the gladiators."[69] Coughlin's bitterness in his old age was reflected in his answer to the question, "If you had your life to live over again, is there anything you would do differently?" Coughlin replied, "There is nothing I would do the same."[70]

Looking back on his association with Coughlin, Townsend, and Lemke in the Union Party crusade, Smith wrote to H. L. Mencken, "No man knows better than you how I opportunized on all forms available in order to develop a personal acquaintance across the nation. This strategy had its liabilities and its assets, but inasmuch as my man had been killed and I had no money with which to organize independently, I had the choice between dropping back into obscurity or pursuing the course I followed."[71] It is notable that Smith's major fear was obscurity. For the next six years he groped for an ideology, seeking a movement to which he could commit himself wholeheartedly. He craved publicity; without a movement he was nothing, his life was empty. Smith never shrank from controversy. What he really feared was being ignored.

four

A Run for the Senate

‡

The reelection of President Franklin Roosevelt and the gubernatorial victory of Richard Leche in Louisiana in 1936 irrevocably changed the direction of Gerald Smith's career. Although Smith appealed to his former allies in Louisiana to revive the Share Our Wealth Society, they permitted it to die of "planned malnutrition."[1] Following the Union Party debacle, Smith left Louisiana for New York City, the nerve center of the nation's financial and communications networks. He rented a four-room suite in the Hotel Pennsylvania, where he employed a staff of two stenographers, two bodyguards, a secretary, and a few part-time helpers.[2]

Once in New York, Smith turned his considerable energies to the creation of a mass political organization to "save America," placing himself at the helm. He set about the task of raising money and recruiting members for an anti-Communist and anti-New Deal Organization which he originally called the Committee of Ten Thousand. Later, he changed the name to the Committee of One Million, claiming that a million of his friends had asked him to create it. The name was particularly ironic, considering that the organization boasted a grand total of nine charter members.[3] *The Detroit News* greeted Smith's latest brainchild with derision: "Mixed in its concoction will be nearly every brand of hooey and hokum calculated to appeal to fanaticism."[4]

Membership in the Committee was supposed to be secret, but members were authorized to wear badges entitling them to investigate Communist activity.[5] With the Share Our Wealth program in shambles, Smith redirected his crusade toward obliterating Communism. In place of redistributing wealth he now emphasized preserving the sanctity of private property, promoting patriotism, and repelling threats to "Christian civilization." In his Shreveport days Smith had condemned exploitations of labor, but now he opposed the CIO, calling it a "Trojan Horse" for Communism.[6]

Smith's Committee of One Million did not rely on grassroots financing, as the name implied. Instead, Smith sought funding from rich business-men and bankers who feared a Communist takeover. At the time he launched his anti-Communist crusade he claimed he had been given 1.5 million dollars by four hundred individuals who had pledged 1 percent of their incomes for one year.[7] Smith's biggest contributors included Wil-liam Brown Bell, president of American Cyanamid; Lewis H. Brown, president of the Johns-Manville Company; James A. Noe, ex-governor of Louisiana and a self-made millionaire from oil and radio broadcasting; Charles Costa of Costa Trucking, who wanted Smith to get him business; Horace Dodge, the auto magnate; some of the female heirs to the Pullman fortune; and the Pew family of the Sun Oil Company.[8] An FBI informer reported to his superiors that Smith was receiving fifteen hundred dollars a week from a donor whom he would not identify. Smith carried about large sums of cash because he distrusted federally backed banks.[9]

Smith admitted that he even accepted money from the underworld. "I was fighting a battle; I had to have money to fight it; and I accepted support from anybody who offered it to me," he explained. "If I am standing in a pulpit and Al Capone comes in and drops a thousand dollars in the collection plate, I'm not going to refuse to take it."[10] He also received money from supporters of Fritz Kuhn, leader of the German-American Bund. Smith invited Bund members to his meetings and many of them attended. He collected cash and sped it to headquarters where it was already locked in a safe by the time the meeting ended. Donors were asked to include their names and addresses, which wound up on Smith's mailing list.[11]

Smith promoted his movement wherever he could find an audience. He talked to Rotary and Kiwanis clubs, chambers of commerce, American Legion posts, and private gatherings. He spoke at the Executives Club of Chicago and the National Press Club of Washington. He even spoke to organizations whose memberships were largely Jewish. Arthur Hays Sulzberger invited him to deliver a talk to executives of the *New York Times*, and Lowell Thomas introduced him to members of the Advertis-ing Club of New York. He hammered away at his apocalyptic theme: the United States was in imminent danger of a Communist revolution. He told a New York audience that Communists planned to seal off the island of Manhattan by dynamiting bridges and tunnels. When a young woman hissed at this outburst, Smith leaned forward and dared, "Come on, you Reds, you shall not pass!"[12]

Smith collected fifty to seventy-five thousand dollars from a few wealthy sponsors as "seed money" to test his effectiveness. He tried union-busting at the Johns-Manville Company in New Jersey, where organizers canceled an election after Smith incited anti-union prejudice. In Akron, Ohio, which was already unionized, he turned public opinion against the workers. He also claimed credit for electing a Republican ticket in Toledo for the first time in twenty years.[13]

Smith's promising career as a political organizer in New York was ruined by the defection of Pat Powers, his partner in the Committee of One Million. Smith and Powers had divided the work of the organization: Smith made speeches and wrote promotional tracts for the Committee, while Powers raised money, kept the books, paid bills, and supervised the office staff. Powers devised organizational schemes that Smith approved and then returned to Powers for implementation. Powers, not Smith, had coined the name and devised the emblem of the Committee of One Million, and he zealously set about the task of establishing the organization, working initially without pay. He was not above cutting legal and ethical corners in his quest for support. To this, Smith voiced no objection. However, when Powers began challenging Smith's judgment and demanded to be paid, Smith expelled him from the movement. Powers sued. Although he agreed to a modest settlement, the publicity wrecked Smith's fundraising efforts, which relied upon confidentiality. Some donors demanded their money back; others balked at giving more. Reluctantly, Smith canceled his plans for radio broadcasts.[14]

The months following the Powers controversy were among the bleakest in Smith's career. Unable to pay his bill at the Pennsylvania Hotel, he was evicted. His files were seized and turned over to the Internal Revenue Service. He contracted more bad debts at other hotels and could not pay a bill from Jefferson Military Academy in Natchez, Mississippi, where his son was enrolled.[15]

Smith's fundraising efforts were further thwarted by a *March of Time* newsreel entitled "The Lunatic Fringe," which compared him to Hitler and Mussolini. Flattered when Time, Inc., requested his help in making a feature about him, Smith permitted them to film him orating in the shower and while shaving and practicing facial gestures before a bedroom mirror. But the final version of the film enraged him. The narrator called Smith "a national figure with the making of a fascist dictator" and a "self-anointed messiah of the so-called lunatic fringes of the United States electorate," and wondered whether Smith was "a man of destiny or merely a political windbag."[16]

Smith filed a five-million dollar lawsuit, stating that the slanderous newsreel had caused clubs to cancel speaking invitations, thus depriving him of income. Time replied that the film was factual and that Smith himself had helped to make it. Smith later boasted that he obtained monetary compensation from Time; in fact, they settled out of court for one dollar.[17]

With dwindling financial support from New York, Smith decided to move to a more receptive environment in the Midwest. He had grown up in Wisconsin and felt at home in that part of the country. In early 1938 he established headquarters in Cleveland but received little money; the *Cleveland News* editorialized against him. He took his act to other cities where there was labor trouble and spoke out against the CIO for employers who paid him to break strikes.[18] When there were no strikebreaking opportunities Smith spoke in churches, schools, and even synagogues. He addressed Democrats, Republicans, Townsendites, and Coughlinites—anyone who would listen. He spoke in the open air, in snow and rain. Often he could not afford a good hotel room and went without a bath. He had to shout at his audiences because he had no sound equipment. Finishing the day hoarse, he drove all night to the next city. He got a variety of responses, friendly and hostile, indifferent and enthusiastic.[19]

In February 1939, Smith moved to Detroit, which was centrally located and strongly unionized and had good broadcasting facilities. Horace Dodge and other Detroit businessmen had promised him money, and Henry Ford also expressed interest. If not for the move to Detroit, Smith's movement might have collapsed totally. Once there, his talent for self-promotion and his oratorical skill kept his cause alive, and before long he had more speaking invitations than he could accept. To be sure, they were usually before small groups that paid him little, but he acquired a reputation as an entertaining and patriotic orator. His emotional paeans to Christianity and patriotism were received much better there than on the East Coast.[20]

In addition to his talks to small groups, he held mass rallies which he carefully stage-managed. A song leader would "warm up" the audience by leading them in "God Bless America," "The Star-Spangled Banner," "Battle Hymn of the Republic," and other patriotic songs. After a local minister led the invocation, one of Smith's cronies or employees would read a flowery introduction that Smith had written about himself. By the time he began to speak, the audience was primed and his bombastic rhetoric incited them to frenzy.

Although these meetings appeared spontaneous, they were exceedingly well-planned. Smith always invited twice as many people as there were seats and then boasted that many had been turned away. Although no admission was charged, tickets were required. Smith took collections and the silver and currency he received provided a moderate income. He also sold literature and collected names and addresses for his mailing list. Everywhere he went the crowds were enthusiastic. In the winter and spring of 1940–41 Smith held twenty-five mass meetings in midsize cities in the Midwest. With the nation still deep in the Great Depression, his successful tour convinced him that his speaking ability and ministerial experience gave him the makings of a political power broker.[21]

Smith was as effective on radio as he was at meetings. In 1937 wealthy backers bought him twenty-six weeks of broadcasting time in Cleveland.[22] When he moved to Detroit he took over the forty-eight-station network that had carried Father Coughlin's program.[23] Smith even had some of his addresses translated into Polish and broadcast, although they proved unpopular with Polish Catholics in Michigan.[24] At the conclusion of each broadcast Smith urged listeners to write. He promised everyone who wrote an anti-Communist pamphlet entitled "101 Facts" and a copy of his talk. Truckloads of letters poured in, many with contributions enclosed. Smith asked contributors to give their addresses so that he could add them to his mailing list. Within months Smith had 250,000 names in his files. He still accepted money from businessmen, but with growing grassroots support he was becoming self-sufficient.[25]

Smith used his organizing talents to create a hierarchy under him. Rank was determined by the number of members recruited and amount of literature sold. Participants received pins and certificates as they climbed the ranks of Recruiter, Key Man, Unit Leader, and Degree of Service No. 4. A supporter became a Recruiter once he collected ten or more signatures on a petition for one of Smith's causes. A Key Man (or woman) had sold a dollar's worth of literature and collected signatures for five petitions. (The literature had to be sold to at least five people, at ten cents per tract, no more than two pieces per individual.) A Unit Leader organized a group of assistants and dispatched them to do field work. Those who reached Degree of Service No. 4 were given confidential assignments directly by Smith.[26]

Smith organized his own activities into four areas: direct mail, radio, book distribution, and personal appearances. Direct mail focused on local issues and was targeted at particular constituencies; the radio appeals were more comprehensive. Smith also organized mass meetings where many voters could be influenced. Direct mail cost 10 cents per letter; radio coverage $1,000 to $4,000 per week; books mailed to individuals, $3,000 per thousand copies; and mass meetings about $1,000 each. Smith trained and coached fifty volunteer speakers, each of whom was instructed to make ten appearances within the next thirty days. Smith's talent for organization would have made him even more successful had he possessed modern technology such as computers to generate form letters.[27]

In January 1942, Smith created an elite group of especially generous contributors, which he called the Inner Circle. In return for their substantial support, he offered them positions on a special advisory board that would receive confidential reports. Those who sent contributions received a newsletter containing information too sensitive to use on radio. They also received a manuscript entitled "The Undelivered Speech"—about a plot to make the United States a part of the British Empire—and a calendar featuring photographs of Smith and his wife. Smith explained that this Inner Circle could be considered a "wheel" of key advisers within the larger "wheel" of the Committee of One Million. He signed up five thousand for the Inner Circle. Even some congressional leaders endorsed the group, including Senator Robert R. Reynolds (North Carolina), head of the Senate Committee on Military Affairs; senators Arthur Vandenberg (Michigan) and Burton K. Wheeler (Montana); ex-senator Rush Holt (West Virginia); and Representative Clare E. Hoffman (Michigan). Smith continually warned that unless his most trusted supporters responded with money, he would be compelled to cease his broadcasts.[28]

Smith's recruiting was effective, and his movement grew rapidly between 1939 and 1942. By 1942 he claimed three million members in the Committee of One Million and boasted that he was adding between three and six thousand per week. A more accurate estimate would be slightly fewer than one million, still a substantial following. Some verifiable figures were impressive. He collected 420,000 signatures on a petition supporting continuation of the Dies Committee investigating un-American activities. His radio speeches, broadcast to a population area of 30 to 40 million potential listeners, cost eighteen hundred dollars per week. His offices occupied an entire floor in the large Industrial Bank building in Detroit, where Smith employed twenty-five to fifty helpers to sort his mail. A journalist writing in Colliers in 1944 estimated that Smith grossed an average of five thousand dollars a week. This enabled him to rent a suite at the Statler Hotel and to maintain a private residence in suburban Detroit.[29]

Smith's public activities veiled the shadowy internal machinery of the Committee of One Million. It was incorporated in Delaware and its purpose was "educational." Smith himself was chairman, his wife vice-chairman, and Bernard A. Doman of Detroit, a Smith employee, was secretary-treasurer. It was not generally known that the fiscal agent of the Committee of One Million was something called the Federation of Ameri-

canization of Michigan. This nonprofit corporation paid no taxes and
Smith never mentioned it. According to the Michigan Corporation and
Securities Commission, the federation was incorporated by H. H. Lucker
of Detroit, who was president; Elna Smith, secretary; and Bernard A.
Doman, treasurer. Lucker, like Doman, was a Smith employee; but he later
broke with Smith, whereupon Doman replaced him as president, with
Elna Smith becoming treasurer. The total assets of the federation in 1939
were listed as nine hundred dollars.[30]

Some of Smith's associates in this enterprise were unsavory opportunists who operated on the fringes of the law. Smith hired a defrocked
clergyman, E. S. Bramble, to raise money for the Committee of One
Million. Bramble was notorious for high-pressure selling activities promoting hospitalization insurance and whiskey certificates, and he operated anti-Semitic groups for profit. Smith hired other professional solicitors who utilized hard-sell tactics. Solicitors went out with ten prospect
cards and reported back on alternate days; they received no more cards
until they returned the ten. Contributors who gave more than five dollars
went into a special prospect file. Few wealthy men and women openly
admitted their support of Smith, but Mrs. Horace Dodge, wife of the
millionaire auto magnate, testified in her divorce case that her husband
bankrolled Smith's work.[31] Smith's home and headquarters were
shrouded in secrecy. All four of his telephone numbers were unlisted.
Radio station WJR, which carried his broadcasts, could not call Smith,
nor could his own followers. They mailed contributions and letters to a
post office box. Neither were Smith's headquarters nor his residence
listed in the Detroit city directory. Journalists thus could interview him
only at his convenience. His staff was instructed to refuse to answer
questions from anyone who showed up at headquarters. Callers were to
write down their questions for Smith's attention. The staff told reporters
that they only handled printed matter and knew nothing about the operations of the organization.[32]

Smith's activities were supposed to combat Communism, Fascism,
and Nazism, and to rebuild a moral America based upon Christian principles, good citizenship, and patriotism—but with an authoritarian leader.
Smith was certain that only his leadership could save Christian America,
and he openly admitted that he wanted to control the nation. He expected
a revolution, and when it occurred he would be ready to seize power. The
Committee of One Million was the vehicle that would propel Smith into
power, perhaps by election, perhaps by force. He had little idea what he
would do with power; all he knew was that he would be ready to lead
when the time came.[33]

Though his goals were vague, Smith knew whom he hated and what he opposed, although his reasoning—and motives—were questionable. With the war underway in Europe, Smith took pains to equate Communism with Nazism. Communism and Fascism—the extreme left and the extreme right—were all the same to him. "It is no longer necessary for us to separate the words 'nazi' and 'communist.' Whether a man be a member of Hitler's bund under Fritz Kuhn or the Communist Party under Earl Browder, we can just as well refer to him as a 'nazi-communist.'" "The communism of Stalin and the socialism of Hitler spring from the same root," Smith elaborated: "conceived in atheism, hatched in hate—they thrive only under the shelter of God-less paganism."[34]

Smith also disliked militant labor unions. Although he professed to be a friend of labor, he devoted many of his broadcasts to labor-baiting. He rationalized his antipathy to unions by claiming that he opposed only those infiltrated by Communists—but Smith considered even moderate labor leaders communistic. Sidney Hillman, John L. Lewis, and Walter Reuther were Reds out to cripple production. In one radio broadcast he proclaimed, "in discussing this problem of communism and radicalism and collectivism; socialism and CIO-ism and New Deal-ism, there is no way to isolate one particular phase of the problem."[35] "People joining the CIO are following a program devised by Josef Stalin," he insisted.[36] Hillman "was an obnoxious, atheistic, Communist Jew" who had been born in Russia and could not even speak English without an accent.[37] It was preposterous that such a man should order around a good American like Henry Ford.

Smith passionately hated UAW president Walter Reuther. Reuther, Smith claimed, did not want higher wages for workers; he wanted to place disciplined Communists in strategic positions in the automotive industry so that the assembly line could be shut down at his command. Furthermore, Smith claimed, Reuther plotted with President Roosevelt to nationalize American industry. Under the alleged plan, they would open idle factories under government control. These factories would underbid privately owned businesses until they bankrupted them, and then these too would be taken over. Reuther and Roosevelt had devised an even more nefarious scheme during the war, Smith asserted. Reuther recommended to Roosevelt that members of the CIO be armed for civilian and coastal defense. But, Smith said, this group would actually be used "as the nucleus of a revolutionary army which can move in and seize the communities of our country after the war army has been demobilized."[38]

Smith even produced a letter he alleged was sent home to America by Walter Reuther and his brother Victor while they were in Russia for "indoctrination": "Carry on the fight for a Soviet America," it said. The letter was a forgery, but Smith promoted it so effectively that it was published by other far-right propagandists including Gerald B. Winrod, Upton Close, and Dan Smoot. It was difficult for responsible publishers to discredit such propaganda, because Smith manufactured incidents more rapidly than they could be disproved and he repeated his fabrications so often that they were commonly accepted. But Smith did not limit his activities to fabricating stories about Communism: he also hired detectives to investigate labor leaders, their backgrounds, their finances, and their domestic lives.[39]

Smith was often successful in undermining support for unions. Although workers booed and hissed at Smith, he invariably won some over by the end of his speech, and he always ended up with a bigger crowd than he started with. He knew that American workers, despite their desire for higher wages and improved working conditions, were fundamentally anti-Communist, and he played on this relentlessly, realizing that if he could convince the workers that the CIO was a Communist organization they would reject it. Smith was particularly adept at exploiting the differences between the AFL and the more militant CIO. To many Americans, particularly in rural areas, the CIO seemed menacing. Smith exploited this fear, attempting to drive a wedge between the union organizers and the masses. The degree to which he succeeded is difficult to judge, but certainly some industrialists considered him effective enough to pay him.[40]

Even in the midst of the Depression, Smith had no sympathy for the unemployed. "Anyone without a visible means of support who refuses to work should be rounded up and put into a compound," he recommended, to work or starve. If these "refuseniks" worked, their wages were to be placed in an escrow fund that they could utilize only if they proved themselves productive members of society after their release.[41] Communist workers were to be given one-way tickets to Russia.[42]

Smith had influential friends whom he expected to introduce bills implementing his ideas. His closest political ally in the U.S. Senate was Arthur H. Vandenberg of Michigan. Their friendship was the product of similar views on labor and foreign policy; both were isolationists and both fought to cripple the pro-labor Wagner Act. Vandenberg and Michigan congressman Clare Hoffman sometimes inserted Smith's speeches in the *Congressional Record*.[43]

Smith also collaborated with Texas senator W. Lee ("Pappy") O'Daniel to enact so-called "anti-violence" acts, modeled on a Texas statute which practically outlawed strikes and picketing. He supported Ohio governor Martin L. Davey, who used troops to break a steel strike, and renegade union leader Homer Martin, who led back-to-work movements at Chrysler and Dodge plants. Smith cooperated with a Detroit organization, the

Society of Sentinels, and a Chicago group, the Citizens U.S.A. Committee, in an effort to repeal the Wagner Act. He fought union organizing along with the notorious anti-Semite Joseph P. Kamp and Dr. Edward Rumely, director of the reactionary Committee for Constitutional Government. Rumely, who had been convicted of concealing the German government's million-dollar investment in his newspaper, published anti-black and anti-Jewish diatribes.[44]

Henry Ford was Smith's most valuable ally in the war on labor. Smith practically worshipped Ford's wealth and success. Both men were racists, nativists, and anti-Communists who hated organized labor. Ford, seemingly a simple-minded man, was in fact a complex individual with highly unusual and inconsistent beliefs. One of the greatest mechanical geniuses America has produced, Ford was by 1920 the richest man in the world. He introduced the movable assembly line to American industry, paid his employees decent wages, and produced cheap but durable cars. The crusty automobile magnate so fascinated Americans that a poll of college students in 1920 voted Ford the third greatest figure in recorded history, behind Jesus Christ and Napoleon. There was even a grassroots movement to promote him for president—and one observer believed that he was just a Dale Carnegie course away from political office.[45]

But Ford, though kindly, was poorly informed, eccentric, and insensitive in his dealings with people. He so disliked intellectuals that he refused to let his son Edsel attend college. "I don't like to read books," he once said; "they muss up my mind."[46] Ford was interested only in tangible and practical things. He knew little about history; asked to identify Benedict Arnold, he replied that he must have been a writer.[47] Ford opposed divorce and repeatedly tried to patch up family quarrels among his workers.[48] He was puritanical in sexual matters and fanatically opposed to both alcohol and tobacco. Curiously enough, he believed in the possibility of reincarnation. For example, he told an employee about how chickens react to automobiles: "When the automobile was new, and one of them came down the road, a chicken would run straight for home—and usually get killed. But today when a car comes along, a chicken will run for the nearest side of the road. That chicken has been hit in the ass in a previous life."[49]

Ford so worried about his personal safety that he always carried a gun; he hired a former boxer named Harry Bennett as a bodyguard. Bennett organized a department of thugs to protect Ford's person and property, investigate employees, and spy on union leaders. His personal friendship with Ford enabled Bennett to become one of the most influential individuals in the Ford Motor Company.[50]

Because Ford was a brilliant mechanical engineer and industrial planner, people respected his views on social and political issues. Unfortunately, he was as ignorant of politics and race as he was gifted in making cars. Though not a malicious man, he was a misguided racist and anti-Semite.[51] In the early 1920s Ford published a series of anti-Semitic articles in the *Dearborn Independent,* later collected under the title *The International Jew.* He also distributed the notorious anti-Jewish forgery, *The Protocols of the Learned Elders of Zion.* Ford believed that Jewish moneylenders caused wars and manipulated the stock market and that Jewish intellectuals had created Communism.[52] He thought Jews "lewd" and "erotic" and accused them of corrupting the morals of Gentiles by promoting chorus girls, liquor, and jazz.[53]

Ford's anti-Semitic publications even inspired Adolf Hitler. Hitler paraphrased Ford's anti-Jewish articles in *Mein Kampf,* hung a portrait of the automaker on his wall, and awarded Ford a medal which Ford unwisely accepted. Ford lost his enthusiasm for Hitler when he began to gobble up small nations, but he thought he knew how to handle the dictator. "Do you really want to get rid of Hitler?" he told a friend. "I'll send Harry [Bennett] over there with six of his men. They'll get rid of Hitler for you in no time."[54]

Gerald Smith considered Henry Ford, like Huey Long, a superman. He idealized Ford as representing the best in America: Christian faith, hard work, and patriotism. Ford inspired young Americans, and Smith resented Ford's critics, calling them "these cantankerous, repulsive, un-American agitators, these Communists, these racketeers, these rats, these reds, who conspire against the spirit of America."[55]

Smith loved to regale visitors with stories about his friendship with Ford, which grew more intimate each time he told a story. The Smith–Ford friendship, however, was one-sided. Ford once invited Smith to his home to show him his memorabilia and his first automobile, but that was their only social contact. Afterward, Smith wrote fawning letters to Ford and his wife, Clara. He boasted that he and his wife had received handwritten responses from Clara, but these were actually no more than polite acknowledgments. Smith hung a large portrait of Henry Ford in his home, and later he created a Henry Ford I Memorial Award which he bestowed on reactionary "patriots."[56]

It was Ernest Liebold, Ford's private secretary, who introduced Smith to Ford after hearing Smith speak at the Detroit Advertising Club. Smith was much closer to Liebold than to Ford, and Liebold convinced Ford to contribute money to Smith's cause. Smith's memory of meeting Ford was faulty: "I met Henry Ford because he sought me out and his personal secretary took me to meet him," he said in an interview. "He was a great admirer of Huey Long and became a great admirer of mine."[57]

Ford gave Smith two thousand dollars for three radio broadcasts[58] and loaned him several "investigators," who helped Smith compile index cards listing alleged Communists. Smith called this collection of cards the Ford Company Red File.[59] The "flivver king" also at times provided Smith with bodyguards. But Ford later grew disillusioned with Smith. He disliked being linked to Smith publicly and winced every time he heard Smith boast of their friendship. Before he knew Smith very well, Ford had rashly commented that he wished Smith were president. Smith repeated this remark continually in his tracts, magazines, and speeches, much to the industrialist's embarrassment. The more Ford learned about Smith the less he liked him, and after the early 1940s he would have nothing more to do with him. Smith, however, continued to solicit contributions until finally Harry Bennett threatened him physically. Smith told people that Ford broke with him on orders from President Roosevelt and because of a Jewish boycott of Ford cars.[60]

Smith claimed that Ford was the one who taught him the connection between Jews and Communism. When they met in 1937, Smith said, he was less anti-Semitic than Ford. Ford gained "insight" into the "Jewish question" because of an attempt by Jews to take over the Ford Motor Company, Smith explained. A "brilliant adviser" had told Ford that "the New York Jews are trying to get hold of your business and they are going to try to do everything they can to destroy you until you will be forced to sell." Ford doubted this "brilliant" advice, although according to Smith he did invest five million dollars in an investigation of Jews that confirmed a plot.[61]

Smith claimed that Ford once asked him when he would recognize the real enemy of America. Smith asked Ford what he meant and Ford replied: "No one can understand the issues of this hour unless he understands the Jewish question." Smith then read The International Jew and concluded, "The day came when I embraced the research of Mr. Ford and his associates and became courageous enough and honest enough and informed enough to use the words: 'Communism is Jewish.'"[62]

Ford employed some crackpot anti-Semites, including Elizabeth Dilling and Fritz Kuhn; it is unlikely, however, that Ford influenced Smith as much as the latter claimed. Smith exaggerated the relationship because he enjoyed name-dropping. Ford may have encouraged Smith's anti-Semitism because Smith idolized him and was gullible, but he hardly "converted" him.

Smith hoped that Ford would finance his ambition to seek the Republican nomination for U.S. senator in 1942, but Ford declined. In typical fashion, Smith pretended that he had been reluctant to run but had been drafted by his supporters. At a mass meeting in Detroit, he stated that it was necessary to remove the incumbent Democratic senator, Prentiss Brown, and elect a good Christian Republican who would oppose the New Deal. But who could defeat Senator Brown? According to Smith's account, the audience spontaneously began to murmur "Smith." Smith then took a straw ballot. All but 40 of the 475 ballots favored Gerald Smith![63] He pretended surprise. Before accepting, he said, he would have to "get the consent of my Christian mother and father, because years ago I had promised them that I would not seek office."[64] Smith also had to consult his Inner Circle friends, he explained; he needed time to consider this "draft." He mailed coupons to Inner Circle members, asking them to indicate if he should run for the Senate, and including a request for money.[65] He soon reported that more than 90 percent of them wanted him to run. His mother, he explained, told him to seek office in order to save "this glorious republic from ruin." She counseled him, "Yes, son, The Lord knows best. Go and follow Him."[66]

Observers who remember Smith's later career find it ludicrous that he expected to be elected to the U.S. Senate. But this was not apparent in 1942. Smith was not yet as bigoted as he became in the years after World War II, and he had support among some of the most respected members of Congress. He had a network of allies throughout the Midwest and was known as a brilliant orator. Lacking a strong opponent, it was conceivable that he could win.

Smith needed a petition with twenty thousand signatures to earn a place on the ballot. He collected more than thirty thousand. Former football star Jim Thorpe solicited signatures for Smith at the Ford Motor Company. Smith promised to make each person who obtained ten names on a petition a Primary Campaign Adviser. After he won the primary, he would make each of them an Election Campaign Adviser, and when he went to the Senate each would become a Senatorial Adviser. As an added inducement he gave his Advisers an 8″ × 10″ photograph of himself.[67]

Smith seized upon issues he hoped would arouse the public. He advocated support for Father Coughlin, the Townsend plan, "a farm program based upon the teachings of the Bible, a 'hoop of military steel around America,' food before whiskey, protection for the tourist industry and the small businessman, and Christ First in America."[68] His most inflammatory issue, however, was his stand against rubber rationing, which had gone into effect after the Japanese captured the sources of raw rubber in Asia. Drivers were not permitted to carry spare tires; replacements were difficult to obtain and involved bureaucratic delays. Smith claimed that synthetic tires could be manufactured by the Ford Motor Company or the Dow Chemical Company from potatoes, grain, or vegetables if President Roosevelt would permit it. The president, however, was more interested in protecting the "rubber trust" than in providing tires. Smith's charges were groundless, but there was much opposition to tire rationing and Smith exploited the issue in every speech. He obtained what he claimed was a synthetic tire manufactured by Henry Ford and used it as a prop at his rallies. He said that Ford had constructed a new synthetic rubber plant which had been shipped to Russia.[69]

At first Smith was the only Republican candidate, but several weeks after he announced, Elton R. Eaton, a newspaper publisher and former state senator, entered the race. Eaton was a weak opponent and many Republicans feared that Smith would defeat him, embarrass the party, and assure the reelection of Brown. Republican leaders therefore persuaded Circuit Judge Homer Ferguson to enter the race. Ferguson, who had a reputation for racket-busting as a special prosecutor in Detroit, was a moderate.[70]

While Eaton waged an active campaign attacking Smith, Ferguson relied on his reputation, campaigned little, and never mentioned Smith. Smith's campaign was by far the most aggressive and expensive of the three. He spent more than $10,600 to Ferguson's $6,000; Eaton, who did not accept contributions, spent only $2,000 of his own money. Smith received $1,500 from an anonymous group of industrial workers whom he said he could not identify, and $5,800 in lesser contributions, the largest of which was $105. He claimed that Charles A. Lindbergh had made a generous contribution, but Lindbergh would not confirm this. Smith raised the remainder of his money by "passing the hat" at political rallies, just as he had once done at evangelistic revivals.[71]

Smith had a genius for eliciting contributions from his audiences. After each speech he introduced his wife, who collected the money. A shy but attractive woman, she stood to the side while supporters filed by and gave her coins and currency. Smith asked those not ashamed to give to raise their hands; others invariably "followed the herd" and came forward.[72] Smith urged them to give as much as they could. "If you can't give more than a nickel, don't bother," he said. "If you are that hard up, just come up after the meeting and I'll give you the nickel."[73] He explained that advertisers paid for newspaper publicity, but not for his campaigning. "When you pay three cents for a newspaper, that doesn't cover the cost of the paper it's printed on. But I can't do that. How would it sound for me to say in my speeches: 'Down with war. Up with Ex-Lax?' "[74]

Smith emulated Huey Long by campaigning in rural areas that conventional candidates neglected. He was best at speaking to farmers and merchants in small towns. Smith was preceded by an advance man who drove a sound truck blaring Sousa marches. He invited curious passersby to come closer, luring them with promises that the "dynamic," "fear-less," "courageous" candidate would be there soon. Then, when their curiosity peaked, he shouted: "Here he comes now—Mr. Gerald L. K. Smith—that great crusader, all six feet and two hundred and twenty-five pounds of him."[75]

Smith lived up to his billing; he was utterly uninhibited and disarm-ingly candid. "Now I know some of you folks out there don't like what I've been saying. We'll stop right here for just a minute to let you go home if you don't like it, because I warn you, it's going to get hotter as I go along." The audience chuckled. Then, turning to the press table: "All right, you fellows get out your asbestos paper now because I want you to get this down. It's going to be hot stuff."[76] He charged that his opponents wanted to kill him, but snorted, "I am perfectly willing to burn that the bonfire of my bones may light the way for future generations."[77] Crouch-ing at the microphone, grinning slyly, he whispered, "They say I am insane." Then, rising to his full height, he shouted: "Maybe I am insane, and I will continue to be insane—insane enough to believe in the Bible and America First."[78]

Smith campaigned in city parks, on farm roads, and on street corners in rural hamlets. He campaigned at county fairs, in churches, and at larger meetings which had the fervor of tent revivals. He attempted to duplicate in a northern, industrial state the success he had enjoyed with Southern fundamentalists. Pounding the rostrum, thrusting his hands above his head, he flourished the Bible and oratorically wrapped himself in the flag. He also campaigned on the radio, where he was more restrained but equally effective.

No one could predict the effect of Smith's tactics. Many expected light voter turnouts because of the absence of soldiers, restrictions on travel necessitated by the war, the limited time people could devote to politics, and Judge Ferguson's passive campaign. Smith's fanatical supporters seemed more motivated than Ferguson's followers. There was no provi-sion for a runoff, so a plurality in the three-way primary race could win the nomination. In the final days of the campaign, Ferguson's leading backers warned against apathy.[79]

Ferguson need not have worried. He defeated Smith by a two-to-one margin, winning a majority of the vote. Ferguson polled 195,000 votes to Smith's 109,000 and Eaton's 43,000. Despite all Smith's publicity, Fer-guson had defeated him without waging a spirited campaign. The great crowds Smith attracted had come to see an entertaining curiosity, not to support a legitimate senatorial candidate. However, Smith's vote was not dismissed altogether. He had been in Michigan only three years and this was his first campaign for public office, yet he had made himself known throughout the state. It was possible that he might run again, perhaps for a lesser office, and win.[80]

But instead of accepting the gains he had made, Smith was embittered by defeat. He believed that he had been robbed of victory and explained his loss by writing that "they pass the word down the line for all the Jews to vote, and they had a holiday, so they, the Jews, stepped in the last minute and they beat me. But all the white people voted for me."[81] More than thirty years later Smith wrote in his autobiography, "it was generally believed that I did win, because I carried a majority of the votes in the State outside of Detroit and certain metropolitan areas. But suddenly the reports quit coming through, and it was generally believed that the Democrats, and the Republicans under arm-twisting pressure from the Jews, stole my votes and declared me defeated."[82]

Smith was furious that the Republican Party chairman did not permit him to speak at the state convention that followed the primary, and that Ferguson did not seek his support. He rashly decided to run in the general election as a write-in candidate. This only alienated the Republican leaders who still respected Smith. They feared that he might take enough votes away from Ferguson to elect Brown.[83] Smith, however, proved more of a nuisance than a serious contender. Although he outspent his opponents again, he received only 32,000 votes to Ferguson's 590,000 and Brown's 561,000.[84]

Smith's defeats in the elections of 1942 permanently damaged his credibility, and this was his last attempt to gain power within the two-party system. He knew now that he could not be elected to public office. If he did run for office again it would be to make a point, not to win. He would become a crusader, not a pragmatic politician. Since it was no longer necessary to curb himself for the sake of the system, what he said and wrote became increasingly extreme. Smith never recovered from the pain of rejection and used the defeat to further portray himself as a martyr. His frustration boiled to the surface. His rhetoric grew strident. For the remainder of his life he operated on the fringes of the political far right. If he could not win by the rules of the game, he would invent his own rules. If he was condemned as an extremist, now there was no reason to pretend that he was not one. He would stand on principle and defy his critics. He would be true to his cause and scorn popularity.

five

War and Postwar Crusades

‡

Two years before his defeat in the U.S. senatorial election, Smith shifted his focus from opposing organized labor to promoting isolation. He believed World War II was being fought to protect European Jews and preserve the British Empire. Smith also opposed America's involvement in the war because he feared it would increase the power of President Roosevelt, whom he compared to Hitler. "The only reason Roosevelt has not Hitlerized America is because he is not as smart as Hitler," he said.[1]

Roosevelt, Smith told a congressional committee, was a Fascist, a Communist dupe, maybe even a Jew. Smith circulated thousands of copies of a spurious genealogy tracing the Roosevelt family to Jewish ancestors.[2] "When a man like Roosevelt is elevated to the position of leadership in a Country," he wrote, "his chromosomes become a matter of public concern."[3] Even if Roosevelt were not a Jew, which Smith was not willing to concede, he surrounded himself with Jewish advisers: Frankfurter, Rosenman, and especially Baruch. Bernard Baruch, he wrote, was a "Jewish Warmonger" and "Public Enemy Number One."[4] In order to force Roosevelt out of the White House, he advocated a constitutional amendment to allow the people to recall the president.[5]

Smith worried that obsessive fear of Hitler might drive America into the clutches of Stalin. As far as he was concerned there was no difference between Communism and Fascism. "Hitler brown and Stalin red join together to lift the brown-red flag of paganism, atheism, and tyranny," he insisted.[6] After Germany attacked Russia, Smith promoted via his radio broadcasts a petition calling for America to avoid a military alliance with the Soviet Union.[7] When Stalin began an offensive Smith claimed that Russian soldiers were raping every German woman between the ages of fourteen and sixty-seven, and that twenty million Christians in Russia were being slaughtered.[8]

Although Smith's views might seem eccentric or comical to modern readers, millions of Americans shared them. *The Nation* estimated that Smith and others who rationalized Hitler's atrocities influenced more than fifteen million people.[9] Sentiment favoring appeasement was not limited to the far right. Respected politicians such as Robert LaFollette, Jr., of Wisconsin, George Norris of Nebraska, William E. Borah of Idaho, and Burton K. Wheeler of Montana, the historian Charles A. Beard, and the Reverend Harry Emerson Fosdick all advocated isolationism and were apologists for Hitler. The anti-Semitism implicit in such a position was muted by patriotic nationalism on one hand and internationalist pacifism on the other. Smith's assertion that America was God's chosen country, not to be tainted by Old World militarism, found support among college students, women's clubs, and veterans.

Smith carried on his crusade to keep America out of the war by delivering radio addresses, holding public meetings, circulating petitions, and testifying before congressional committees. He broadcast weekly in the Midwest, and between October and December of 1941 he made twelve speeches on a Washington, D.C., radio station advising Congress and the president how to handle the war crisis. He even wrote President Roosevelt, telling him to listen to the broadcasts. Although Smith drew large crowds to his meetings, he sometimes had to create fictitious organizations in order to rent halls because most managers of public meeting places refused to rent facilities to him.[10]

Smith's mass petitions impressed politicians and provided his supporters with an opportunity to participate in the antiwar movement. In July 1940, Senator Arthur H. Vandenberg presented to the Senate a Smith petition to outlaw Communism and to avoid American entry into the war. Smith claimed that his petition contained more than a million names. Vandenberg praised Smith and his movement on the Senate floor, and Senator Robert R. Reynolds inserted the text of the petition in the *Congressional Record*.[11]

Smith devoted his most aggressive efforts in 1940 and 1941 to opposing passage of the Lend-Lease bill to permit Britain to buy on credit or borrow war materials. Smith asserted that the bill would give the president the power to declare war, a power Roosevelt would doubtless invoke. Our first line of defense, Smith insisted, should be the western hemisphere. Concentrating our forces here will make us invulnerable, but if we dissipate our forces, we will be helpless.[12] The British, he charged, were interested only in money and empire. Smith was invited to testify before the Senate Foreign Relations Committee's hearings on Lend-Lease because the committee believed he represented a large constituency. He was one of only ten witnesses selected by the committee to testify against the bill. Smith spoke for an hour and his testimony was widely publicized, but he had little impact on the committee.[13]

Smith advocated withdrawing all American forces to the boundaries of the continental United States, ending trade with the rest of the world, and constructing a "hoop of steel" around America. Smith also urged President Roosevelt to appoint a new cabinet to include isolationists Gerald P. Nye as secretary of state, David I. Walsh as secretary of the Navy, and Charles A. Lindbergh as secretary of the Air Force, a new position.[14]

Despite Smith's almost fawning support of isolationists in Congress, some of them demurred at his attempts to claim them as friends and allies. Senator Burton K. Wheeler, for example, declined an invitation to speak at a meeting sponsored by Smith, and leaders of the America First Committee refused to permit Smith to join. After Pearl Harbor, the committee, which had existed for the sole purpose of keeping America out of war, disbanded.[15] Pearl Harbor also necessitated a change in Smith's approach. After the Japanese attack, he pledged himself to support the war and converted his antiwar rallies to "victory rallies." He promised to criticize President Roosevelt only as a politician, not as commander-in-chief, but he added that the war could be won expeditiously only if Roosevelt did not politicize it. Smith wrote to the Office of Civilian Defense to offer his support and that of his "3,000,000 supporters"; he was hurt when Attorney General Francis J. Biddle responded with nothing more than a form to complete.[16]

Smith boasted of his son's heroics in the war as proof of his own loyalty. Gerry Smith fought with Merrill's Marauders in Burma, where he was wounded in both arms and legs and survived a mission from which only nine hundred of three thousand volunteers returned. He received the Silver Star, the Presidential Citation, and the Purple Heart. Smith complained privately in 1944 that "our son is back in the jungles again helping to save Burma for the British."[17]

Smith capitalized on discontent and suffering to create a new political party critical of President Roosevelt's handling of the war. On January 10, 1943, he summoned five hundred of his supporters to a "political convention" in Detroit where he proclaimed the creation of the America First Party. Although his party had no formal connection with the defunct America First Committee, Smith promised to continue in its spirit. He explained that this was a contingency party that would dissolve if either major party nominated a "nationalist." He announced that The Cross and the Flag, which he had begun to publish in 1942 (see chap. 8), would be the official journal of the new party and said that he would appoint a "working committee" of a thousand nationalists to organize at the grass roots.[18]

Smith took his party's program literally from its name. He advocated bonuses for veterans, deporting foreigners to create jobs, raising the standard of living for Americans before aiding other nations, protecting white Americans from "abuse" by minorities, putting a halt to immigration, raising tariffs, investigating Lend-Lease, avoiding entangling alliances, and fighting Communism and "bureaucratic fascism."[19] He called for the impeachment of Vice President Henry Wallace and denounced Bernard Baruch, who was supervising rubber procurement.[20]

Smith took his America First crusade across the Midwest. In St. Louis, he spoke to an audience of about 650, many of them members of the old America First Committee, and proposed nominating Charles A. Lindbergh for president. His voice resonated to the balconies, grew soft as a whisper, and then exploded in indignation. "You are not dealing with an amateur," Smith shouted; "you are dealing with an old battle-scarred veteran. But you cannot squelch the truth. If they put me in a concentration camp the blood of the martyrs is the seed of the church and freedom will not die."[21] At the end of his two-hour spiel he was soaked in sweat, his hair tousled, and his coat unbuttoned.[22]

Smith pounded home the theme of "America First." "What's wrong with the idea of America First?" he shouted during a return appearance in St. Louis. "Churchill puts England first, Stalin puts Russia first, let's us put America first in war as well as peace."[23] Smith's supporting cast on his Midwest tour included Mrs. Ernest Lundeen, widow of an isolationist U.S. senator from Minnesota; Charles Madden, commander of an American Legion post and president of the organization Friends of George Washington's Principles; and the Rev. L. L. Marion of Pontiac, Michigan, who frequently accompanied Smith to rallies. Madden recited the Declaration of Independence from memory, and women belonging to the National Blue Star Mothers of Pennsylvania sold literature.[24] In Chicago, Smith was sponsored by isolationist Earl Southard's Citizen's U.S.A. Committee, known before Pearl Harbor as the Citizen's Keep America Out of War Committee. From Chicago he went to Minneapolis–St. Paul, where he was sponsored by two evangelists, the Rev. C. O. Stadsklev and the Rev. W. D. Herrstrom, as well as right-wing groups that included the Mothers of Minnesota, Royal Oak clubs, and Townsend clubs.[25]

Smith claimed that Jewish and New Deal smear artists had persecuted thirty good Americans by indicting them for sedition and staging an unfair trial. Some of the major figures of the extreme right were indicted, including Gerald B. Winrod, William Dudley Pelley, and Elizabeth Dilling. Smith, a close friend of Winrod and Dilling, also knew personally many of the other defendants. Smith himself was investigated by the FBI, the Internal Revenue Service, and Army Intelligence; the Justice Department concluded that while he had hindered the war effort, he had committed no crime. But the indictment did cite *The Cross and the Flag* as one of the organs through which the defendants disseminated their propaganda, and the Canadian government banned it from the mail.[26] Smith raised money for the defendants but later broke with Winrod and Dilling, who claimed he kept the money for himself. Eventually a mistrial was declared because of the death of the presiding judge.[27]

Smith hoped that his support of the sedition defendants would win their gratitude and the goodwill of their followers. His ambition was to unite all the factions of the fragmented isolationist, anti-Communist, anti-Semitic movement under his own leadership. He was energetic and bold enough to do this. But the nationalists were a vain, jealous, stubborn group, and their petty differences were difficult to reconcile.[28]

Smith's troubles started with the intimate allies working on his staff. His office manager, Bernard Doman, who joined him part-time in 1938, had become his chief assistant by 1940. Doman supervised a staff of thirty to fifty women who sorted correspondence and mailed out five to eight thousand letters a day. He also rented halls, planned meetings, and made travel arrangements. Smith's irascibility and constant demands drove Doman to the verge of a nervous breakdown. He was a mild-mannered man who became disillusioned with Smith's movement and the controversy it generated. Doman quit in 1944, ostensibly because of his health—actually, he could no longer stand Smith's domineering personality and increasingly virulent hate-mongering.[29]

During the war, Smith hired Renata Legant as his personal secretary, along with Don Lohbeck and Opal M. Tanner. The three became his most trusted assistants. Lohbeck, twenty-seven, was a concert pianist who had studied in Paris and traveled in Mexico, but he gave up his career because he believed only Jewish pianists got recognition. He worked as an organizer for the America First Committee before the war and when he joined Smith in the fall of 1944, he brought with him a fifteen-thousand-name mailing list. Lohbeck was energetic, aggressive, and eager to learn anti-Semitism from a master. Smith treated him like a son and also hired his wife to work in the office. Lohbeck, a terse writer and shrill speaker, was nervous, hot-tempered, unstable, and consumed by bitterness. An agnostic, he believed that history was the struggle of the Caucasian race against the Orientals and the Africans, who, inspired by Jews, plotted to divide the spoils.[30]

Lohbeck replaced Doman as office manager, but within a month he was drafted. A conscientious objector on philosophic rather than religious grounds, he was assigned to a work camp near Elmira, New York. He hated the regimentation of the camp and sought medical release. A psychiatrist and several medical doctors declared him unfit for work and he was released briefly. When Lohbeck returned to work as Smith's office manager, however, the army concluded that anyone fit to work at a demanding full-time job was sufficiently healthy to do war work and recalled him. Smith complained that Lohbeck was being persecuted because of his relationship to Smith. Lohbeck engaged in political organizing at the camp, sold copies of *The Cross and the Flag*, and wrote bitter letters to Smith. "So help me," he concluded one of them, "when I get out of this damned place it will be with a ruthlessness that I never would have acquired in 100 years living in the way that I have lived. Bloodthirstily yours."[31]

Opal M. Tanner (White) and Renata Legant (Martz) remained with Smith to his death in 1976. Women, in fact, constituted more than half of his followers and did most of his volunteer work. Nonetheless, Smith believed that women belonged in the home and was never comfortable with women who wanted to be treated as equals. The most prominent of Smith's female allies during the 1930s and 1940s was Elizabeth Dilling, a Chicago woman who had studied music and traveled in Europe and Russia. She returned to write a series of anti-Communist books: *The Red Network, The Roosevelt Red Record,* and *The Octopus*. Smith praised Dilling as one of the most "fearless Americans" he knew, and Charles B. Hudson, a sedition trial defendant, called her "America's Joan of Arc." Smith bought and resold thousands of copies of Dilling's books, corresponded with her regularly, and the two spoke together at rallies. Dilling, however, was a strong-willed, independent woman; after the war she and Smith broke and became arch enemies.[32]

Dilling attracted recruits from among the Mothers groups that flourished prior to and during the Second World War. Before America's entry into the war thousands of isolationist women, many of them mothers with draft-age sons or husbands, had organized to oppose selective service and Lend-Lease. Fervently anti-Communist, anti-Semitic, and anti-Roosevelt, they sold material published by Smith and Father Coughlin.[33] There were sharp divisions among the women antiwar crusaders. Smith, with his huge ego, aggravated them by insisting on controlling the movement. He collected mailing lists from some of the groups and used them in his own organizing efforts.[34] He would not tolerate any rivals who competed for leadership. Smith considered himself above these smaller groups, viewing them merely as potential recruits to absorb, control, and manipulate.

Smith's relationship with male leaders on the extreme right paralleled his experience with the Mothers: initial enthusiasm followed by disillusionment. This was true of his relationship with the well-known bigot

Gerald B. Winrod, an anti-Semitic, anti-Catholic, and anti-Communist crusader and publisher who was among those indicted for sedition. Winrod and Smith cooperated in the 1930s, broke in the 1940s, and reconciled in the 1950s. When Smith was starting out, Winrod, a more experienced writer, composed fundraising letters for him, polished Smith's own prose, and permitted Smith to reprint essays from his *Defender*. "*Plagiarisms don't count between friends*," Smith wrote Winrod, who replied, "If we are able to clothe your thoughts with words sufficient to make them of value in your literature, they are yours."[35] "We've often had prayers together," Winrod said of Smith; "he's one of my closest friends." He described Smith as "an absolute altruist."[36]

Smith and Winrod also exchanged views about other figures on the extreme right. Shortly after Smith met Joseph McWilliams and Frederick Kister he wrote Winrod: "Neither of these young men in any sense give the impression of being buffoons. On the contrary, they give a definite impression of intelligence, integrity and capacity."[37] Winrod, the more established figure, introduced Smith to his friends on the extreme right, including Harvey H. Springer, a six-foot, six-inch "cowboy evangelist" who ministered the largest Baptist church in Colorado.[38]

Smith served as an inspiration for Captain Earl Southard, a veteran who organized the America First Party in Chicago. Southard, along with William J. Grace, organized the Citizens Keep America Out of War Committee, which before Pearl Harbor advocated repeal of the Lend-Lease Act and impeachment of President Roosevelt. Southard was a friend of Charles Lindbergh and William Dudley Pelley, and he participated in secret conferences with Lawrence Dennis, the chief of intellectual fascism in the United States and one of the defendants in the aborted sedition trial.

Smith's temporary alliances with isolationist politicians, publishers, and other public figures were more tenuous than his partnerships with fellow extremists. In some cases the "friendships" existed chiefly in his own imagination. One of Smith's most exaggerated claims for friendship was with Charles A. Lindbergh. Lindbergh was convinced that Germany was the wave of the future and would doubtless defeat Britain; therefore, he claimed, it was in America's interest to come to terms with Hitler. He believed that Britain was a greater danger to America than Germany because it might lure America into the war. Lindbergh was not a fervent anti-Semite but he was insensitive to the plight of German Jews. If America made war on Germany, he stated, it would only worsen the persecution of Jews in Germany.[39]

After failing to obtain a commission in the U.S. Air Corps, Lindbergh moved to Detroit to work for Henry Ford.[40] While there, Lindbergh met

Smith for dinner at the Dearborn Inn. This was their only meeting, but Smith magnified it into a personal friendship. Lindbergh seldom replied to Smith's many letters and refused to speak at any of Smith's meetings.[41]

Senator Gerald P. Nye of North Dakota, who claimed that "those of the Jewish faith are contributing to the cause of intervention,"[42] was misled into cooperating with Smith to advocate isolation. He spoke at a Smith rally in Detroit on March 2, 1941, and permitted himself to be exploited for Smith's cause. Nye corresponded with Smith regularly and did not object when Smith boasted, "The best man in the United States Senate is Gerald Nye. I love Nye. We have exchanged many long, personal letters."[43]

Nye shared Smith's isolationism but not his anti-Semitism. Senator Robert Rice Reynolds of North Carolina, however, shared Smith's bigotry as well as his opposition to internationalism. In 1938, Reynolds organized the Vindicators Association, Inc., and founded his own newspaper, the *American Vindicator*, which had thirty thousand subscribers in its heyday (it folded in 1939). Reynolds advocated the registration and fingerprinting of all aliens and deportation of "undesirables."[44] "Hitler and Mussolini have a date with Destiny," he said in a Senate speech in 1938. "It's foolish to oppose them, so why not play ball with them?"[45]

Reynolds furnished anti-immigration speeches in franked envelopes to George Deatherage, who headed the American Nationalist Confederation, a group that used the swastika on the masthead of its bulletins. Reynolds inserted a speech by Gerald Winrod in the *Congressional Record* in 1939, and his own speeches and essays were reprinted and distributed by Father Coughlin and Elizabeth Dilling.[46] Reynolds's closest friend on the far right, however, was Gerald Smith. He wrote a letter to Smith praising the first issue of *The Cross and the Flag* and Smith published it as an endorsement.[47] Reynolds wrote to a woman who asked him about Smith, "Mr. Smith, insofar as I know, is a real, genuine American who loves his country better than any other country in the world, and I do not believe I could pay a man a higher compliment than that."[48]

During his days as a leading isolationist, Smith also came to consider himself a personal friend of Michigan's isolationist senator Arthur H. Vandenberg, who praised his "inspiring chairmanship" of the Committee of One Million, and called him "the Voice of America."[49] Vandenberg also praised Smith's testimony against Lend-Lease and wrote, "It certainly is comforting and helpful to have you 'in my corner' when the bell rings for these big battles."[50] The cordial correspondence continued after Pearl Harbor. Smith's fawning admiration for Vandenberg flattered the senator, who carefully answered each letter. When people in Michigan having trouble with the federal bureaucracy wrote to Smith, he sometimes referred them to Vandenberg, who obtained results.[51]

Smith's closest friend in the House of Representatives was Michigan representative Clare E. Hoffman. Hoffman spoke at meetings of Smith's America First Party, subscribed to *The Cross and the Flag* for himself and ten friends, and inserted Smith's propaganda in the *Congressional Record*. Smith called Hoffman "one of the most courageous men in the United States Congress"[52] and circulated thousands of copies of Hoffman's "Roosevelt Is a Judas" speech. Despite their common enmity toward Roosevelt, however, Smith's racism troubled Hoffman. The two remained allies through the war, but broke in 1949 when Hoffman introduced legislation prohibiting racial discrimination in employment. Smith attributed his action to senility.[53]

Smith also had close ties with Roy O. Woodruff, another Roosevelt-hating, isolationist congressman from Michigan, whom he characterized as "a patriot beyond reproach." In August 1941, Woodruff inserted a letter from Smith in the *Congressional Record*, terming him a "great leader,"[54] and the following year he inserted the featured editorial from the first issue of Smith's *The Cross and the Flag*. Smith appropriated from Woodruff the issue of rubber rationing and the alleged conspiracy to prevent the production of synthetic rubber from farm products.[55]

Smith claimed Congressman Hamilton Fish, a close friend of Woodruff's, as his friend, but Fish never evinced any propensity for cooperation with Smith. Smith wrote long letters to Fish, praised his work against Lend-Lease, and told Fish that he deserved to be president of the United States. After America entered the war, Fish took pains to distance himself from Smith.[56]

Smith was never as close to these senators and congressmen as he claimed, but some politicians were misled into supporting him in the prewar and early war years. Almost all of them later regretted it and found Smith's fawning endorsements embarrassing. Most of the prewar isolationists joined the bipartisan effort to win the war, but the war brought no respite to Smith's criticism of the New Deal and President Roosevelt's foreign policy. Smith favored a negotiated peace with Germany but not with Japan. He claimed that the president would use the war to make himself dictator of America and "President of the World"; he insisted that Roosevelt was going to cancel the election in 1944 and install his relatives in key positions of power. Smith also felt certain that the president was manipulated by Jewish advisers.

Smith's descent from principled antiwar crusading to anti-Semitism cost him much respectability and eventually the friendship of political figures such as Nye, Vandenberg, Hoffman, and Woodruff. Smith should have been aware of this, but he was following his emotions and instincts, not rationally planning his activities. He was so blindly angry that he elicited almost universal condemnation. He was sincere in the positions he took. However, it was one thing to be a principled isolationist or even a principled pacifist; it was another to be an anti-Semite.

Smith's activities continued to generate headlines and his magazine reached many readers who responded to his appeals for money. Although he received as much financial support as he had during his Union Party campaign in 1936, his sources had shifted. Smith now relied upon thousands of small contributors rather than on a handful of corporate backers. Some religious people, former followers of Coughlin and Winrod, supported him, as well as some German sympathizers who were followers of Pelley and George Sylvester Viereck.

During the waning days of World War II, Gerald Smith continued to identify and sympathize with Adolf Hitler. He believed that Hitler, like himself, was a misunderstood man, persecuted by the Jews and maligned by the Jew-dominated media. He saw Hitler as the innocent victim of a Jewish conspiracy to destroy the German race. As "evidence" he stated, "Hitler's servants speak of him with the deepest regard."[57] The Jews hated Hitler, Smith argued, because Hitler was a Bible-believing Christian. He reprinted an address in which Hitler used biblical references to justify his Jewish policy and asked, "What good Christian American can find any fault with the above quotations? Could it be that the same Jew-controlled newspapers that lied to us about Father Coughlin and Gerald Smith failed to tell us the truth about Hitler?"[58]

Smith believed the charge that Hitler had killed six million Jews to be preposterous. The Jews had not been slaughtered, he said, but illegally admitted to the United States to keep Roosevelt in power.[59] He claimed that there were more Jews after the war than before. "Most of the dead Jews whom 'Hitler killed' are now walking the streets of American cities," he wrote.[60] This was only natural, he continued, because "the big purpose of World War II was to create supremacy for the Jew machine."[61] When, many years later, Jewish Nazi-hunters captured and tried Adolf Eichmann for his role in the Holocaust, Smith concluded that his arrest was a clever ploy to gain sympathy and money for Israel. "Eichmann looks like a Jew to me," he wrote; "I wouldn't be a bit surprised to find out that the whole thing was a Jewish conspiracy with Eichmann's collaboration."[62]

Smith argued that Franklin D. Roosevelt was a far more menacing figure than Hitler. Roosevelt's demand for unconditional surrender, he maintained, lengthened the war and permitted the plunder of Germany.[63] Roosevelt got drunk at Yalta and gave away Eastern Europe;[64] worse yet, he accepted a Torah from a rabbi.[65] Those who believed Roosevelt had died a natural death were simpletons, Smith said. He had several theories about the president's death—he even dictated a book about it while driving from Denver to Salt Lake City in 1945.[66]

According to one of his theories, FDR had not died at all but was being kept in seclusion at a mental institution by Jews who planned to return him as "President of the World."[67] Stalin, for one, did not believe Roosevelt had died—rather, he had feigned death to escape his Yalta commitments. Stalin asked to see the body, but Roosevelt's family declined.[68] If Roosevelt had indeed died, he may have been struck down by God for plotting with Wendell Willkie to abandon conservatives in the Democratic and Republican parties in order to create a liberal party.[69]

Smith had an alternate theory that Roosevelt became conscience-stricken as he sat alone in Warm Springs and committed suicide when he realized the havoc he had wrought upon the nation. "If ghosts could tempt a man to suicide," Smith wrote, "if the ghastly reminders of guilt could tempt a man to reach for the fatal weapon or drink the deadly potion, then surely this man Franklin D. Roosevelt had all the temptations necessary to encourage him to retire from the scene in advance even of Nature's call."[70]

Even after the president's death Smith and his followers continued to malign Roosevelt. At a meeting in Chicago a few months after Roosevelt had died, one of Smith's supporters remarked, "the real reason why they wouldn't open the casket was that they were afraid he would jump out and run again!" The audience roared with laughter. Another Smith backer handed out toilet paper with pictures of Franklin and Eleanor Roosevelt printed on each sheet over the captions "Dead?" and "Living?"[71]

Smith believed that amidst the postwar chaos the line would be drawn between Roosevelts, Communists, and Zionists on one side and on the other true Americans like himself. "My time will come in the postwar period," he wrote. "The candidate will not be me; it will be a young veteran of this war, but I'll be behind him. If business conditions are bad—inflation, widespread unemployment, farm foreclosures—then my candidate will be elected. . . . Then the flame will spread and the extreme nationalists will come to power. . . . When chaos comes, I'll be the leader."[72]

Satisfied that he had exposed the Roosevelts' plot, Smith turned his attention to preventing the nation from becoming a pawn of Communists and imperialists under the auspices of the United Nations. Smith's first sally against the internationalist infidels was his attempt to attend the Dumbarton Oaks conference as an uninvited guest in August 1944. He rode in a taxi to the Dumbarton Oaks estate in suburban Washington, where an armed guard prevented him from entering. He gave the guard a letter to the State Department and orated to him for five minutes while awaiting a reply that never came, complaining that an American citizen could not enter where Britons and Russians were permitted.[73]

Smith also turned up in San Francisco when the conference to create the United Nations convened there on April 25, 1945. Accompanied by his secretaries and bodyguards, he could not obtain press credentials despite his claim to represent "81 periodicals, 21 organizations, 6 members of the Senate, and 17 members of the Lower House." But then what could be expected of a conference "where the Prince of Peace could not be mentioned by name"?[74] To term Smith's boasts "exaggerations" would be an understatement. The periodicals he claimed to represent were his own; the organizations existed only on letterheads he had printed. He represented no congressmen or senators. He did, however, have fourteen suitcases bulging with nationalist propaganda.[75] Smith savored encounters where he could employ his renowned persuasive powers. "Just let me at the delegates when they are drunk," he begged.[76]

Smith was chagrined to find that the only room available was at a second-class hotel; but after bribing a clerk he obtained more commodious quarters. Smith and his self-appointed watchdogs sat in on conferences, buttonholed delegates in lobbies, and interviewed participants who believed them to be bona fide journalists. He exploited every disagreement. Any chance remark, a word said in anger or jest, could end up in *The Cross and the Flag*.[77]

Smith found San Francisco a virtual Sodom. "I knew that Reds, mostly Jews, had been the instigators," he wrote, "but when I got to San Francisco . . . it became increasingly obvious that the whole thing was a dreadful scheme to loot America's wealth, drain the blood from our sons, and destroy our national sovereignty."[78] Turning to historical metaphor, he asserted that "Tallyrand [sic], Ivan the Terrible and the historic conspirators of the past fade into insignificance compared to the gang that is now operating in San Francisco."[79]

Smith issued a press release from his hotel on May 12, stating that he would hold a mass meeting in the ballroom of the Mark Hopkins Hotel, and he mailed invitations to every foreign delegation at the conference except that of the Russians. The foreigners were puzzled by the invitations; they had never heard of Smith, who promised to speak on "Liberty in the Balance." Minutes before the meeting, the manager of the Mark Hopkins canceled Smith's lease for the ballroom on the grounds that it had been rented under an assumed name, a ministers' organization that Smith had created only a few days earlier. Undaunted, Smith decided to hold his meeting in the hotel lobby. He climbed atop a table and began speaking. Confusion ensued as Smith's followers and reporters gathered around him while flashbulbs popped. The hotel manager called the police, who ejected Smith from the building, but Smith was not yet ready to give up. He crossed the street to another hotel, followed by the crowd, and delivered a red-baiting speech from the steps of the building. Police officers led him away from that forum after a few minutes, and he returned to his own hotel in a taxi, having achieved the enormous publicity he had sought.[80]

Smith boasted that he had succeeded in his major goal in San Francisco—masterminding an amendment to the United Nations charter, the Connally Resolution, that reserved to the U.S. Congress the right to confirm any foreign policy commitments and ensured that the United States would have veto authority over proposed economic or military sanctions. Smith claimed, probably erroneously, that he had accomplished this by exerting pressure on Senator Arthur H. Vandenberg. Vandenberg had pushed the resolution, Smith boasted, because he could not be reelected without Smith's support.[81]

Smith wrote of his role in directing adoption of the Connally Resolution, "If I had dropped dead after the passing of that resolution, I would have considered this one function in my life worth my whole life. At the risk even of being accused of boasting," he continued, "I will say that without the general public realizing it at the time, this strategic effort on the part of two or three of us saved the independence of the United States of America from the threat of a world government."[82] But Smith's support only jeopardized passage of the resolution, if it had any effect at all.

Smith did not cease fighting the "Jew-infested" United Nations after his trip to San Francisco. Although he had "saved" American sovereignty, he still found much objectionable in the United Nations. For one thing, it was headquartered in evil New York City. "New York City is really the Jew capital of the world, and the Zionist machine, through the United Nations, wants to make it the ruling capital of the world by way of Palestine," he explained.[83] Smith created the Citizens Congressional Committee for the explicit purpose of withdrawing the United States from the United Nations and expelling the United Nations from New York. He often traveled to the city to observe the organization in action. There he and his associates interviewed delegates, sometimes assuming false identities. Smith claimed to have learned much "inside information," which he reported to his readers in *The Cross and the Flag*.[84]

Smith was outraged by conditions he found at the U.N. headquarters. He learned that Russian flags were sold at its souvenir shop, and he saw statues of naked men and women in the lobby. He heard delegates speaking Yiddish and criticizing the Bible. The U.N. flag, he charged, was the same color as the "Jew flag" and somewhat resembled the hammer and sickle of the Soviet Union. Any good American would find the whole scene repulsive.[85]

Smith continued to oppose the United Nations throughout the 1940s and 1950s. He circulated petitions, testified before congressional committees, published "exposés" in *The Cross and the Flag*, staged rallies, and held conferences at which his followers adopted anti-U.N. resolutions.[86] Smith gave delegates certificates bearing gold seals, promising that they would become collectors' items, and likened his conferences to the Boston Tea Party.[87]

Later that year Smith wrote to friends, "it might interest you to know that Mrs. Smith and I flew to New York City and served an ultimatum on Ambassador Lodge, urging him to lead a campaign to withdraw from the United Nations."[88] Smith warned the American ambassador that if he did not veto the admission of Red China into the United Nations, Smith would help defeat Republican congressional candidates. He challenged Lodge to denounce the U.N., resign as ambassador, and call for expulsion of the world organization from New York. Lodge ignored his threats.[89]

Smith particularly resented the role of the United Nations in the Korean War. He complained that American boys were being compelled to fight an undeclared war under the flag of the United Nations instead of "Old Glory." The war was undeclared, Smith explained, because a formal declaration would make American Communists subject to incarceration as enemy aliens. Since 90 percent of Jews were Communists, this would mean the imprisonment of one hundred to five hundred thousand Jews.[90]

Smith vehemently opposed the U.N. treaty outlawing genocide, claiming that it was a plot to prevent him from criticizing Jews.[91] In an essay in *The Cross and the Flag* Smith stated that U.N. armed forces had taken military possession of six cities in California and had expelled the mayors. He asserted that "the United Nations is the greatest subversive plot and plan in the history of the world for the destruction of the Constitution of the United States and its substitution by a World Government with all our citizens slaves."[92]

Smith relentlessly sought to uncover plans for "world government." From the right-wing National Economic Council he obtained, and later published, a map that showed the world divided into regions, each to be occupied by an international police force. The United States was to be policed by Russians, Colombians, Venezuelans, Belgians, Irishmen, and

Mongolians. According to Smith, no American forces would be permitted to supervise the United States and American citizens would be tried in world courts.[93]

Smith's postwar opposition to the United Nations coincided with his effort to organize returning war veterans into a formidable political movement under his command. He and other extreme nationalists hoped to forge in America a coalition of jobless malcontents and innocent dupes, much as Hitler had begun his movement with disillusioned veterans of World War I. They appealed to recently discharged men who were accustomed to violence, inciting them to "clean out" the internationalists. Some two hundred nationalist veteran groups had been created by mid-1945.[94] Special groups proliferated. There were organizations for wounded, deaf, and amputee veterans. There were regional, labor, and religious groups, and branch groups such as the Seabees. Some organizers sought to appeal to veterans by advocating benefits such as bonuses, mustering-out pay, and special pensions.[95] They flourished on white supremacy, hatred of Britain and Russia, Protestant fundamentalism, superpatriotism, hatred for Roosevelt, and opposition to the United Nations. Many of the groups blamed Jews for the war; all thrived on chaos.[96] Among the heralds of the right were the Protestant War Veterans of Edward J. Smythe; the St. Sebastian Brigade of Father Coughlin; the Servicemen's Reconstruction Plan, sponsored by Joseph McWilliams; the George Washington Bodyguards, led by George Deatherage; and the United Veterans Political Party, headed by ex-Congressman John H. Hoeppel of California, who had been impeached for selling appointments to West Point.[97]

Right-wing extremists advocated a return to isolationism and support of Germany as a bulwark against Russia. Above all, they favored "Americanism" and hated anything foreign—except the gallant Germans, who were being punished for having waged war to save the world from Communism. The various groups quoted the *Chicago Tribune*, the Hearst papers, and the radio commentaries of Upton Close. At the nerve center of the nationalist press was the Nationalist News Service, created by Smith in 1945 to furnish nationalist bile culled from obscure sources and distributed to anyone who might print it.[98]

This situation allowed Smith to expand his sphere of influence. He compiled material for his Nationalist News Service, started a weekly called *The Letter*, and created a nationalist lobby on Capitol Hill. His aspirations were still more grandiose: a book-of-the-month club, a publishing company, and a chain of radio stations. Smith envisioned training schools for speakers, a network of nationalist attorneys who would bring libel suits to stop the "character assassination" of right-wingers, and a thousand letter-writers, each of whom would promise to send ten letters to Congress on notice. He planned to put together an organization of a hundred amputee vets to produce literature and to speak for his cause, and he wanted to advertise on billboards.[99]

Smith's program for transition to a peacetime economy was borrowed from Huey Long, Father Coughlin, and Dr. Townsend, with additional benefits for veterans. Each family would be guaranteed an annual income of twenty-five hundred dollars and workers could earn more through free competition. There would be a home for every family, good prices for farm products, and freedom from bureaucracy for businessmen. Veterans would receive a thousand dollar bonus when they became civilians. All this would be done without raising taxes.[100]

Smith called his program The Plan. It was advocated by his Postwar Recovery Commission, which listed only a post office box in Detroit. Readers were urged to form local societies and send the addresses of their members to the central headquarters. When the first thousand societies had been formed there would be a national convention with all the local presidents as delegates.[101] "Plutocratic industrialists are feudal lords who laugh at me today," Smith warned; "unless some such plan as this is carried out, [they] will have their throats slit tomorrow by the bloody disciples of Joe Stalin, and rue the day they laughed at Gerald Smith."[102]

Smith created two organizations, the Nationalist Veterans of World War II and the Committee of Veterans of World War II. The first objective of both groups was to circulate petitions requiring the armed services to increase pay for enlisted men and to pay each veteran a bonus. The Mothers groups of Mrs. David Stanley and Mrs. Katherine V. Brown provided the womanpower to circulate petitions. Stacks of them piled up in Smith's office, and each name was added to his mailing list. These veterans' organizations were a cruel hoax: their chief purpose was to provide names and addresses to Smith.[103]

Smith's figurehead organizers were not people to inspire confidence. Frederick Kister, who headed the Nationalist Veterans of World War II, was a vicious anti-Semite who had graduated near the bottom of his high school class; he had worked for the hate-sheet *Scribner's Commentator* before World War II. Kister's commitment to the cause was dubious; when Avedis Derounian asked him why he engaged in hate work, Kister replied, "I gotta make a living, don't I?"[104] Kister lost a steady job when he became a propaganda agent for Smith. Embittered by his lack of success, he disbanded the Nationalist Veterans in 1947. In the 1950s he became a police informant in Chicago. Later he married a Jewish woman.[105]

George Vose headed Smith's other group, the Christian Veterans of America. Vose left high school without a diploma and became a lecturer for Dr. Townsend. He ran unsuccessfully for Congress in 1942. He enlisted in the army, was convicted of selling army shirts and passes, and was sentenced to six months' hard labor.[106] While digging ditches he developed ulcers on his left leg, lost the use of it, and was medically discharged. Smith exploited Vose's bitterness. "He is mad at the Army and that's the way I like my people to be, angry," he said.[107] Vose was Smith's America First Party candidate for lieutenant governor of Michigan in 1944. After polling very few votes, he began traveling to cities in the Midwest, where he set up "central committees" of veterans to promote Smith's organization.[108]

Vose was a paragon of moderation compared to another Smith organizer, Lorence Asman. Born in Russia, where his mother perished in the Bolshevik Revolution, Asman emigrated to the United States and became a passionate anti-Communist and anti-Semitic agitator while still in high school. In 1941, at the age of seventeen, he became a cartoonist for nationalist journals and an organizer for the America First Committee. After graduating in 1942, he campaigned for Smith's Senate race throughout Michigan. He worshipped Smith, who treated him like a son. During this time he wrote long letters to congressmen, senators and newspaper editors, condemning Communism and Zionism. He became so angry and depressed that in 1943 he wrote President Roosevelt a vitriolic nine-page letter denouncing him, the New Deal, and the war:

> Just as Judas betrayed Christ, so you have betrayed America, and just as Judas went out and hanged himself, so you should have done many years ago. If you continue to destroy our wealth and our treasury, and if you continue to promote Jewish Communism, and if you continue to shed the innocent blood of our sons on foreign battlefields, then we the 100,000,000 Christians of America will rise up in righteous anger and tear down your tower of Babel and get you.[109]

Another Smith organizer and speaker, Homer Maertz, called for the deportation of Jews and sterilization of those who refused to leave. Maertz claimed that Jews had instigated the war, that they had created the United Nations, and that they engaged in ritual murder of Gentiles. Maertz, at one time a member of the Silver Shirt League, had been convicted in 1939 of smashing windows and painting swastikas on Jewish-owned buildings.[110]

Smith's efforts to organize veterans also received support from Elizabeth Dilling, Earl Southard, Mrs. Lyrl Clark Van Hyning, Colonel Eugene Sanctuary, and Ernest Elmhurst. None of Smith's organizations wielded much political clout, however, and they deceived few veterans. One important reason was that veterans received aid from the government, including free college education, mustering-out pay, and accumulated-leave pay for enlisted men. Despite predictions of another depression following the war, most veterans were able to find jobs and relative security.[111]

Smith's grand scheme for postwar America included young people as well as veterans. Early in 1944, he staged a "convention" hosted by Reverend Harvey Springer to create the Christian Youth for America and to establish committees for circulating propaganda among soldiers and high school students. Kenneth Goff, a former Communist, was selected national chairman. Goff had written for *The Cross and the Flag* and for other ultra-right journals, had spoken to Earl Southard's Citizens U.S.A. Committee, and had assisted Smith in combating the United Nations.[112]

Smith sought out young fundamentalist Christians who were militant about their cause. He was less concerned with what they believed in than with their commitment to following orders. Smith planned to establish throughout the nation branches of a "Commonwealth University" to educate students who passed rigorous mental and physical tests. He was greatly concerned with physical education, believing that America's strength would diminish if her people became "soft."[113]

None of Smith's organizers, for all their zeal, could match the man himself in lungpower, stamina, and organizational skill. During the latter half of the 1940s, Smith spoke to more and larger audiences than any other American of that time. No longer dependent upon wealthy patrons, no longer subordinate to other leaders, he traversed the nation, speaking in stadiums, auditoriums, and schools. He traveled chiefly by car and did most of his own driving. Smith's wife and Renata Legant, his secretary, always accompanied him; Miss Legant took dictation from her boss while he drove, and slept in the back seat. When they arrived at a hotel she would stay up all night typing. The next morning she would have letters ready for Smith's signature and tracts and essays ready for the printer.

Smith's travels in 1945 took him from coast to coast and included speaking tours in the South and Midwest as well. He spoke against Reds, fascists, labor radicals, Wall Street, "racketeering Jews," and such "dangerous" Hollywood personalities as Orson Welles. He called for an investigation of Pearl Harbor to smoke out that arch-conspirator, Franklin Roosevelt.[114] His strenuous schedule left him little time to prepare his talks. He spoke extemporaneously, unless he was broadcasting over the radio, but he delivered the same speech in each city, using his stock heroes and villains and repeating the same religious and self-glorifying statements. He varied the speeches only slightly, rearranging the material to suit the audience.

At first Smith stayed in shabby hotels and ate at cheap restaurants. At one hotel he was plagued by bedbugs. In Flagstaff, Arizona, he was served watered-down milk, and he convinced the waitress that she would go to hell for cheating customers. Sometimes he could not drink from the tap and had to buy bottled water. Smith concluded from these experiences that, if possible, he would travel first class and reside at the best hotels. "I would rather travel half as far and have quality service than to make a long trip and practice the false economy that brings food poisoning and bed-room filth," he reminisced in his autobiography.[115]

Wherever he spoke, Smith attracted large crowds and generated extensive publicity. Sometimes he needed police protection; a few times he was arrested, usually for disorderly conduct, disturbing the peace, or inciting to riot. He occasionally lost his temper, baiting hecklers and defying threats. Many cities and private concerns would not rent facilities to him, so he had assistants engage them under the names of fictitious organizations. He usually traveled incognito, registering as Stephen Goodyear, a young Californian who let Smith use his name as an alias. His wife kept twelve thousand dollars in emergency money rolled up in a necklace in case they were robbed. Theirs was an adventurous life; Smith gloried in it. His wife tolerated the traveling and never complained.[116]

Smith did not find at home in Detroit the same satisfaction he enjoyed on the road. His home city was becoming increasingly hostile: he had trouble finding auditoriums in which to speak; his audiences were small and consisted largely of hecklers; and his property was vandalized. In December 1947, Smith announced that he was moving his headquarters to St. Louis. The Missouri city, more centrally located than Detroit, was the home of Smith's office manager, Don Lohbeck.[117]

Some people in St. Louis viewed Smith with concern. His first land-lady, a Jewish woman, evicted him from the building he leased, and other realtors refused to rent to him. Finally, Opal Tanner, his trusted assistant, used an inheritance from the estate of her former boss, Carl H. Mote, to purchase a building, which she leased to Smith for a nominal sum.[118]

Smith had not been welcome in St. Louis in 1944 when he spoke there: veterans, labor unions, and Communists had fought to deny him use of Kiel Auditorium, a city facility. "Any appearance Smith makes in St. Louis should not be in the auditorium, or even in the city jail, but in a cage at the zoo," one of his opponents claimed.[119] Nonetheless, Smith held his two-day convention in Kiel Auditorium, and some four hundred followers heard him deliver the usual stem-winding speeches in which he blamed his opposition on "Moscow gold."[120]

In fact, while many of the citizens of St. Louis detested Smith, thousands were responsive to his blend of racism and superpatriotism. Smith's meetings succeeded in gaining him publicity, which attracted the curious as well as the committed to his rallies. Missouri was a border state and St. Louis had a large black population, resented by working-class families to whom Smith appealed.

Smith and his assistants, particularly Don Lohbeck, became active in local politics. The Christian Nationalist Party (which replaced the America First Party in 1946) ran tickets for both state and national offices. Although the candidates fared poorly, they received radio and television time to deliver racist diatribes. Don Lohbeck circulated petitions demanding compulsory racial segregation in St. Louis, but he failed to obtain enough signatures to place a referendum on the ballot.[121]

St. Louis was Lohbeck's birthplace and he continued to live there; but Smith stayed in St. Louis only a few months before moving to Tulsa, Oklahoma. From then on, Smith lived in cities distant from his headquarters and ran the office by mail and telephone.[122]

Smith described Tulsa to a friend as a city "free from coal smoke, free from alienism, with a population of only 2,800 Jews, with 35,000 Negroes thoroughly in their place." There he could "breathe an atmosphere of Americanism which you smoke-besmirched vassals of a Jew-dominated, mongrelized East can hardly imagine."[123] Tulsa was conservative; neither threats nor hecklers would bother him there. He and Elna bought a house, the first they had ever owned, and took pride in furnishing it with antiques and in landscaping the lawn. He joined the First Christian Church, where his Valparaiso mentor, Rev. Claude Hill, was pastor. He even taught a men's Sunday school class. Smith liked Tulsa so much that later he circulated nationally a petition demanding transfer of the national capital from Washington to Tulsa.[124]

But the city that held the greatest attraction for Smith—and to which he also evinced the most hostility—was Los Angeles. Smith found the rapidly growing sunbelt city exciting. Returning from a speaking tour on the West Coast, he wrote a friend: "Tulsa is more naive. My audiences receive me with warm and receptive appreciation, but there isn't the live, tense cheering and emotional demonstrations that we get in Los Angeles."[125] Smith first visited California in 1943, and after experiencing its lure he returned there every year. After his 1945 crusade against the United Nations in San Francisco, he toured California to deliver speeches. In 1946 he made a series of talks in Southern California advocating a pension program proposed by brothers Will and Lawrence Allen.[126]

Everywhere he went in California Smith attracted both fanatical supporters and hostile pickets—tens of thousands of pickets. He found many public auditoriums closed to him, but he usually won when he sued for the right to speak. He ran up against his strongest opposition in Los Angeles when he announced plans to hold meetings in a city high school. Thousands of students, socialists, and labor union activists marched against him. Hollywood stars teamed with California's attorney general, Robert W. Kenney, to oppose him. Kenney created an anti-Smith organization that attracted dozens of luminaries and raised hundreds of thousands of dollars to keep Smith out of California.[127] Kenney condemned Smith as a "political patent medicine man" who exploited the gullible.[128]

Smith often needed hundreds of police officers to protect him at mass meetings, and at one rally he showed up with a dozen bodyguards of his own. He was front-page news for weeks and he collected thousands of dollars at his rallies. Smith also attracted devoted political and religious allies. Los Angeles city councilman Meade McClanahan defended Smith's right to speak, sat on the platform with him, and introduced him to audiences; subsequently, his constituents voted him out of office.[129]

In 1953, Smith moved his headquarters from St. Louis to Los Angeles. Don Lohbeck broke with Smith and remained in St. Louis; a new recruit, Charles F. Robertson, replaced him. Smith bought a lavish Victorian home in Glendale and furnished it with antiques. He retained his home in Tulsa, but spent most of his time in Los Angeles, opening a headquarters nearby but continuing his habit of working at home. He liked the climate, the topography, and the politics. He was also able to save money by using fifty to one hundred volunteers to stuff envelopes.[130]

As he moved into middle age, Smith grew increasingly bitter and felt more and more alienated from the America he championed. Although he lost none of his appetite for power, he became more realistic about achieving it. He turned his attention away from public speaking, sharpening his skills as a writer and becoming a master of direct-mail solicitation.

During the 1950s Smith evolved from a fire-eating orator to a sort of political patent medicine man (in the words of Robert Kenney), hawking his wares of anti-Semitic and anti-black prejudice to a nation exhausted by war, eager to find scapegoats, and suspicious of nonconformists. He appealed to the weak and vulnerable and offered a heady elixir for aimless people: a cause to join to save Christianity and America. Although his medicine brought short-term catharsis to the gullible, it offered little in the way of cure for deep-rooted problems. Like the classic patent medicine man, his elixir was one part cure, nine parts hokum.

Gerald L. K. Smith in the 1930s.

Gerald L. K. Smith (*back row, center*) poses with church members outside the "Azusa" Pentecostal Temple in Wisconsin (c. 1917).

Huey P. Long addressing a rally of farmers.

Huey P. Long marching in support of bonuses for veterans in 1932.

Huey P. Long.

Huey P. Long escorted by bodyguards at the Louisiana State Capitol.

The body of Huey P. Long lay in state on September 11 and 12, 1935.

Gerald L. K. Smith campaigning for the U.S. Senate in 1942.

Gerald L. K. Smith (*center*) at an America First Party rally during World War II.

THE CROSS AND THE FLAG

25c

Year: Two Dollars

VOLUME I • NUMBER 1

APRIL 1942

WE TAKE OUR STAND

— *An Editorial*

(Pages 8-9)

FOUNDED BY GERALD L. K. SMITH

The cover of the first issue of Smith's *The Cross and the Flag.*

Gerald L. K. Smith and
Elna M. Smith at the foot
of a monument to Huey P.
Long (1940s).

A meeting of Smith's Christian Nationalist Crusade in the 1940s.

Gerald L. K. Smith addressing a meeting of his Christian Nationalist Crusade in the 1940s.

Gerald L. K. Smith in his office at Penn Castle, Eureka Springs, Arkansas (1974).

The Christ of the Ozarks, Eureka Springs, Arkansas.

six

High Priest of Prejudice

‡

Gerald Smith campaigned for president because he lusted for power, but his hatred of the Jews and his relentless crusade against them had no such "rational" motivation. He defended his anti-Semitism by claiming the Jews were persecuting *him*. In fact, any "persecution" that did occur at the hands of Jews was strictly in response to Smith's own vicious attacks.

Smith's bigotry was not unusual for his time. Yet while his contemporaries learned to temper their views, Smith's bias grew stronger with age. He learned nothing from exposure to more cosmopolitan and tolerant views. His education, his political experience, and his associations with people who opposed racism had no effect. Long after his views became outdated, after most others had shed their racism or at least repressed it, Smith remained a bigot. He could be kind to friends and to his family, but his bigotry persisted, immune to criticism, impervious to evidence. He rejected as "biased" any views that contradicted his own, never admitting that he himself might be biased. It was this inability to moderate his views that ultimately led to his rejection as a national political figure. Although any theory about how Smith's anti-Semitism developed is pure conjecture, there is evidence that the rigidity of his upbringing could have led to development of a classic authoritarian personality. His parents instructed him in a stoic Protestant ethic; they taught him to value discipline and conformity above tolerance and imagination, hard work above relaxation. There was no middle ground between good and evil. The Bible was literally true and it was the only guide one needed. Discipline in the Smith household was swift and severe. Gerald could neither contradict his parents nor keep a secret from them; they placed a premium on obedience and conformity. This stern upbringing likely imparted in Smith a respect for authority, a belief in absolutes, and a repressed hatred that later emerged as violent anti-Semitism.

There is evidence that Smith acquired specific prejudices from his parents as well as a propensity to think in rigidly categorical terms. His mother wrote him in 1950, "I remember too how your Father talked against Socialism when you were still in the grades."[1] A few weeks later she wrote, "Am glad I feel like I had a *little* to do with the good work you are doing. Your father should always receive much credit for being *firm* in what he *believed*."[2] Her letters to him reek with anti-Semitic, anti-black, isolationist, anti-Roosevelt, and anti-labor attitudes.[3]

The evangelical Protestantism that Smith grew up with, based on a literal interpretation of scripture and belief in the damnation of those who rejected Christ, was another element that likely contributed to his anti-Semitism. He learned to reduce all things to New Testament fundamentals, to view human society as a basic struggle between the forces of good and evil, between God and the Devil. The Jewish religion, which rejected the Messiah, thus represented to Smith the forces of the Devil. He once stated, "According to my Bible the two greatest sins in the world are to deny Jesus Christ is the Son of God and to collect usury."[4] Smith claimed that the concept of "brotherhood" had been perverted by Christ-hating Jews. He criticized church groups that invoked prayers without mentioning the name of Christ in order to "please the Jews." Christianity, he maintained, was the only true basis of brotherhood. There was no such thing as love for one's fellow man without love for Christ. Smith tried to exclude from brotherhood all those of different origins and beliefs, rather than to assume the responsibility of being his brother's keeper. He believed that the only way Jews could become brothers of believers was to renounce their religion and accept Christ. He warned Christians against mixing with Jews, quoting scripture: "Be not yoked with unbelievers." Smith's narrow view of theology reinforced his narrow view of ethics. He thought it was perfectly natural to accuse Jews of evil conspiracies, but any Jewish suggestions that he might suffer from paranoia Smith denounced as "smears" and "character assassinations."[5] If Jesus himself returned to earth, Smith said, he would be persecuted by the Anti-Defamation League.[6]

Smith rationalized his hatred of the Jewish people by claiming that they had crucified the Son of God. The Jews, not Pilate or the Romans, were solely responsible for the Crucifixion. Smith liked to cite from the New Testament the Jewish mob's reply to Pilate's statement that he found Jesus innocent: "His blood be on us and on our children" (Matt. 27:25).[7]

Smith's use of the Jewish people as a scapegoat for the Crucifixion was ironic because, according to Christian teaching, Christ, by shedding his blood for the sins of the world, became a divine scapegoat who made redemption possible. Christ's death for mankind is the basis of Christianity; it had been predicted by the prophets and is commemorated by communion. Christ prayed for his killers rather than condemning them: "Father, forgive them; for they know not what they do."[8]

Despite this oft-quoted passage from the Scriptures, Smith sought to justify his hatred of Jews via reference to the Bible. "There is not one word in the Bible which condemns hate itself," he wrote. "Hate can be evil; hate can be righteous. It all depends upon the object hated."[9] Smith wrote a British friend in 1949, "Why can't men of understanding grasp the fact that if Christianity is the greatest thing humanity has ever known, then its destroyers must be the vilest things humanity has ever known?"[10]

Jews lied when they claimed to be the "chosen people" of God, Smith charged. "The crucifiers of Christ were not God's chosen people," he wrote. "They were a throng of devil-possessed agents of the anti-Christ."[11] Nor were Israelites, the chosen people, necessarily Jews, Smith argued. A tract he published claimed that the present-day Jews were descendants of "pagan phallic worshippers" called Khazars, a Ukrainian tribe transplanted to Judea and forcibly converted to the Jewish religion.[12]

Smith supported a small sect whose adherents called themselves Anglo-Israelites and believed that Anglo-Saxons, rather than Jews, were the chosen people of God. He preached at the churches of Anglo-Israelite ministers Wesley Swift of California and C. O. Stadsklev of Minneapolis, and he published the tracts of Howard B. Rand. Smith claimed that Anglo-Israelism was biblical. "I warn you in studying the Bible not to confuse the Israel of the Old Testament with the people we now call Jews," he wrote. "The true Israel which grew out of the seed of Abraham was lost and absorbed in the personality of Jesus Christ and their tribes were scattered across the earth. The tribe of Dan was developed in the tradition of the Danube and Denmark. The tribe of Isaac developed into the races known as the sons of Isaac, or Isaac's son. Later the word was contracted to mean Saxon."[13] Thus the "real" Israelites, the chosen people, were Gentiles who accepted the Messiah and became Christians. "As a believer in Jesus Christ, born of water and the spirit, I am of the seed of Abraham, circumcised by faith," Smith wrote.[14]

It was difficult for Smith to believe that Christ was a Jew, so he blithely changed history to suit his fancy. Jesus was not a Jew, he claimed, but a blue-eyed blond with a golden beard. Smith said that modern Jews did not look anything like Jesus and offered pictures to his readers as proof.[15] "It is a matter of common knowledge," he wrote, "that the physical Jesus was fair and blond and of open countenance and bore no resemblance whatsoever to the modern hook nose shop keeper, money changer, brothel owner and whiskey peddler."[16] Christ's disciples were not Jews either; they were "Galileans"—except for Judas Iscariot, who was a Jew.[17]

Smith argued that he was not prejudiced against Jews; rather, he opposed them because he had studied them carefully and objectively. Since his antipathy was "objective," he was not anti-Semitic. Anti-Semites were ignorant; he claimed, whereas he disliked Jews for valid reasons. Besides, Smith said, he hated only ideologies and vices, not people. He hated Communism, atheism, alcoholism, banditry, and treason, not individual Communists, atheists, alcoholics, bandits, and traitors.[18]

Like other classic anti-Semites, Smith projected his own hatred onto the object of his scorn, the Jews. It was they who were to blame for anti-Semitism, not he. "The promoter of anti-Semitism is not Gerald Smith," he wrote. "It's the people who call me an anti-Semite. They cry to the world that I am against the Jews. Then my people say—'Well, if Gerald Smith is against the Jews, there must be something wrong with the Jews.' "[19] Smith claimed that the Anti-Defamation League used trumped-up charges that he was an anti-Semite to gain sympathy and raise money.[20]

No one is more prone to believe in conspiracies than those who conspire themselves. If Smith thought night and day about his enemies, they must think constantly about him. When someone asked him why more people did not recognize the Jewish threat, he replied that they might be part of the conspiracy themselves; they might be ignorant dupes; or they might lack the courage to reveal unpopular truths. The fact that so few people "knew" the truth made it all the more imperative for him to spread the word by orating, publishing, exposing, and financing.

Smith's own vices were reflected in the evils he saw in Jews. Jews wanted world conquest; Smith wanted power. He denounced Jews for being wealthy, yet he lived in luxury and collected antiques, Bibles, and paintings. He was blind to the inconsistencies in his accusations: the Jew was a wealthy manipulator and at the same time a parasitic indigent; they were the originators of capitalism and also the hidden hand behind Communism. Smith damned Jews for clannishness and social assertiveness, for apostasy and religious fanaticism. All of these were vices apparent in Smith.

Smith complained that he was smeared for revealing that Jews were behind Communism, when all he was doing was fighting Communism.[21] Jews would rue the day they had persecuted him: "I prophesy that the day will come in America when Jewish leadership will say to themselves, 'Oh, if we could have but understood and appreciated the temperance of a Gerald Smith. How could we have so abused a man who suffered so much rather than yield to the extremities of intolerance.' "[22]

Whether Smith actually believed he was the model of tolerance, no one can say. It appears that his prejudice came first, and then he began to amass "evidence" to rationalize and reinforce his beliefs. His research and writing were not scientific but the product of a kind of chemistry: he responded emotionally to what he read and heard and expressed it in his writing. He did not hate Jews because he actually knew bad Jews: he knew very few Jews personally and there is no evidence that any Jew tried to harm him personally before he began attacking them.

Smith had been mildly prejudiced against Jews since adolescence, but his hatred did not manifest itself until he moved to Shreveport, thwarted what he called a Jewish banker's attempt to steal homes, and subsequently joined Huey Long. Although most members of Long's entourage did not think of Smith as conspicuously anti-Semitic, he was latently hostile. He once claimed that there were too many Jews in Long's organization, a remark that Seymour Weiss, Jules Fisher, and Abe Shushan resented.[23]

Smith's anti-Semitism did not become a prominent force in his life, however, until after Huey Long's assassination, the most traumatic experience of Smith's life. He worshipped Long; the politician symbolized for him a strong, robust replacement for his natural father, who had been weak and ill. Smith, who had seen his father slowly sapped of energy by disease, feared that he too might become weak; thus he was attracted to men of strength and power: Long, Father Coughlin, Henry Ford, and General Douglas MacArthur. Smith was only a few feet from Long when his father figure was killed; in an instant he lost his symbol of security and stability. He developed the belief that Long's (Catholic) assassin was Jewish, and he could never forgive Jews for perpetrating this crime. He imagined that Long's murder was the product of a conspiracy of Jews and New Dealers, which further reinforced his belief that conspiracies determined history.

Smith's propensity to imagine conspiracies led by Jews was strengthened by his theory that the Jewish banker he fought was responsible for the loss of his church, a loss which deprived him of respect and prestige. He associated losing his church with becoming weak and helpless like his father. Smith's prejudice was further exacerbated when Long's Jewish lieutenants, Seymour Weiss and Abe Shushan, fired Smith and abolished the Share Our Wealth Society. Hungry for power but gnawed by failure, Smith's bitterness simmered and later erupted as hostility toward Jews.

At about the time he went to work for Long, Smith experienced an emotional "call" which revealed to him that Jews were an evil force. He did not become an outright anti-Semite immediately, but after Long's death the call became more important. He began publicly espousing anti-

Semitism after a second call in 1942. Smith explained his emotional and spiritual experiences to readers of The Cross and the Flag: "One day I experienced a call. It was more definite, it was more real, it was more vivid than any spiritual experience that I had ever had. Even when I was ordained to the ministry I was not overwhelmed as I was when this call came to me late in 1933. It was reconfirmed and emphasized in 1942."[24] These experiences changed his life: "The call in 1933 and the confirmation of the call in 1942 were not accompanied by any strange manifestations, but I received the definite impression that I was being commissioned to do a special job for my Master. And what was it? It was to save Christian America from the invasion of the enemies of Christ."[25]

Smith told his friends of the experience; they called him an alarmist and told him that the issue was too controversial to make public. But Smith felt so strongly about the calling that he could not let it rest, even though he knew that he would be condemned as a fanatic and a bigot. Smith thought of himself as a prophet with a special relationship with Christ. He received revelations; he could predict and interpret the future. The more Jews hated him, the closer he walked with Jesus. He had discovered a Divine Purpose for his life.

With the creation of the State of Israel in 1948, Smith had an entire nation to hate, and his propaganda became not only increasingly strident but better organized and more fully integrated. Smith usually tried to equivocate his anti-Semitism by claiming that he only opposed "Zionists," not all Jews. He wrote that Zionists had fomented both world wars in order to create a homeland in Israel. Armed by the United States, they had driven innocent Arabs into the desert to die and had stolen their homes. Jews could have settled in an uninhabited part of Africa or Asia, but they had demanded Palestine because of the "super" mineral wealth of the Dead Sea.[26]

Smith asserted that Jews in the United States constituted a "fifth column" loyal to Israel rather than to America, who planned to involve the United States in a war in the Middle East in order to make Israel the fifty-first state. These disloyal Jews should be expelled from America, insisted Smith, but they should not be permitted to go to Palestine. They belonged in Russia because, after all, they were Communists. If Russia would not take them they should be sent to Poland: if four million Jews actually had been killed there, there ought to be room for them.[27]

Smith manipulated reality to make it conform to his stereotypes. He lived in a fantasy world of plots, secret meetings, confidential communications, spies, agents provocateurs, evil geniuses, and assassins. It was his mind that concocted the conspiracies: against Christianity, against Gerald Smith, by atheist Communists, by international bankers, and by

Zionists who controlled the media. Smith did not admit mistakes, failures, or coincidences. History might appear random and accidental, but in fact there was a cunning and deceptive hidden hand behind all events.

The hidden hand was responsible for the French Revolution, Freemasonry, Liberalism, Socialism, Communism, Modernism, abstract art, and all wars. Jews worshipped the Devil; they worshipped snakes and goats; they participated in sexual orgies, infanticide, and cannibalism as part of their religious ceremonies. Jewish physicians murdered Christian patients. Jews manipulated Stalin and Roosevelt. The Holocaust was invented or staged by Jews to elicit sympathy.[28]

Smith published and distributed a classic hoax, *The Protocols of the Learned Elders of Zion*, describing a meeting of Jewish elders at Basel, Switzerland, in 1897, where they outlined plans to undermine Gentile civilization and make themselves rulers of the world. Actually *Protocols* originated in an obscure French novel that attacked Napoleon III. It was later plagiarized by a Russian cleric who made Jews into villains in order to justify pogroms in czarist Russia. The story of *Protocols* is replete with inconsistencies, botched translations, and contradictory accounts about how it was obtained. After appearing in Russia, *Protocols* was smuggled to America, where it was published by Henry Ford and endorsed by Father Coughlin. Historians branded the book a forgery and ninety-three leading Americans, including President Woodrow Wilson, issued a statement repudiating it. American and British newspapers discredited it, and courts of law in Switzerland and South Africa pronounced it false. Entire books were devoted to proving *Protocols* spurious, but this did not stop anti-Semites from peddling it. Smith insisted that it had to be true, regardless of its origin, because it described events that were actually taking place. He also claimed that he had been marked for "liquidation" for publishing it.[29]

The transparent fraudulence of *Protocols* was reminiscent of another hoax that Smith and his fellow anti-Semites concocted. They claimed that the Order of the Illuminati, a secret society founded at a Bavarian university in 1776, was responsible for a plot to destroy Christian civilization. Its founder, Adam Weishaupt, a former Jesuit and humanist described by Smith as a Jew, had hoped that the Illuminati would replace religious dogma with reason. The order, which did not advocate violence, was secret because Weishaupt feared persecution by the church; it was dissolved after a few years. Smith claimed, however, that Weishaupt, not Karl Marx, was the inventor of Communism and charged that the Illuminati had arranged the assassinations of Abraham Lincoln and John F. Kennedy. Robert Welch, founder of the John Birch Society, also traced Communism to the Illuminati. They provided no evidence, but the mysterious order intrigued individuals inclined to believe in conspiracies. According to Smith, it took experts like Welch and him to identify these enigmatic plotters.[30]

Smith also believed that Jewish bankers manipulated history. The Rothschilds, for example, wanted to place the United States in debt to them by financing the Civil War; and when President Lincoln sought to thwart their conspiracy by printing greenbacks rather than borrowing from them, they had him assassinated.[31]

Smith used alleged anti-Semitic statements by famous people to enhance his own credibility. He claimed that George Washington once called Jews a threat to patriots during the American Revolution.[32] He published a genuine order issued by General Ulysses S. Grant to expel Jews from the Department of Tennessee.[33] Smith even speculated about Napoleon: "Could it be that Napoleon was destroyed and banished and died in exile because of a statement which he issued at one time concerning the Jews?"[34] Smith defended the anti-Semitic poet Ezra Pound, terming him "one of the greatest poets of this century" who was "known to be intelligently alert to the Jewish problem." He said that Pound had been confined to a mental institution because of his candor.[35]

Smith liked to quote Martin Luther, who had despaired in his efforts to convert Jews to Christianity and had written some attacks against them. Smith collected these statements, added others that were probably spurious, and published them in a tract entitled "The Jews and Their Lies." "If Martin Luther were alive today and would speak and write as he did in this sensational book, he would easily be the victim of an assassin's bullet within 48 hours after his utterances," Smith wrote.[36] He also published a collection of anti-Semitic statements he attributed to Roman Catholic popes.[37] He wrote his assistant, Don Lohbeck, "If we can demonstrate that the Jew was the big problem to the Popes, to Luther, to St. Paul, and to Jesus, those four themes of observation should constitute four cornerstones on which we might build a movement and remove once and for all the silly theory that to manifest annoyance over the devilish behavior of the Jews is a sign that one has lost his mind or descended into the pit of hate to feed on venom."[38]

The most controversial quotation Smith published was one he attributed to Benjamin Franklin at the constitutional convention. Franklin purportedly proposed banning Jews from the United States, warning that if they were permitted to enter, they would dominate the nation within two hundred years. Franklin allegedly termed them "vampires" and told the delegates, "I warn you, gentlemen, if you do not exclude the Jews for all time, your children will curse you in your graves."[39] Smith's source was a woman who said she had seen Franklin's statement in the diary of

Charles Coatsworth Pinckney at the Franklin Museum in Philadelphia in 1892. She and her daughter were the only people to have seen the diary, although prominent historians had searched for it. Smith charged that the Pinckney diary had been stolen by Jews and asserted, "Its absence now only strengthens the case."[40]

No information about Jews reached Smith that he did not utilize in the most invidious manner. He interpreted accounts flattering to Jews as lies, Jewish propaganda, or the work of Gentile dupes. When he could not locate real Jews Smith manufactured them. He speculated that Gentiles he disliked might really be Jews who had changed their names. Even when there was no hard evidence that a criminal or bad character might be Jewish, Smith would observe that he had "the Jewish nose." He and his office staff sometimes labeled Gentiles Jews, based on wild rumors. Thus Pope Paul VI, Franklin D. Roosevelt, and Dwight D. Eisenhower became Jews. Smith made some individuals "honorary" Jews on the basis that they behaved so badly they deserved to be called Jews even if they were not.

Nor would Smith admit that any Jew did anything useful. He hated Albert Einstein and published in *The Cross and the Flag* a photograph of him with his hair on end and his tongue hanging out. He charged that Stalin counted Einstein "as one of Russia's seven best friends in the U.S.A."[41] Smith asserted that Einstein had plagiarized his theory of relativity from a Gentile scientist. He cited as his authority one Gaston Burridge, who claimed that an Austrian physicist named Friedrick Hasenohrl had discovered the equation a year before Einstein. Smith concluded, "If Mr. Burridge is right, it means that Mr. Hasenohrl was ahead of the much publicized Marxist Jew by about one year. In fact, it could be even worse than that. It could be that Hasenohrl was ahead of him completely and that Einstein merely copied the formula."[42] Smith concluded that tougher immigration laws would have barred Einstein from the United States.[43]

Smith described a United States ruled by Jews. Revolutionary blacks would confiscate homes; money would be abolished; the state would take over production; permanent identification numbers would be stamped on each baby; old people would be put out to starve; and the masses would be subdued with tranquilizers, marijuana, and "nullifying potions." Only a patriotic elite could save America—Smith invited his readers to become a part of it. "Civilizations are not saved by the masses. They are saved by the little handful that blocks the road of the tyrant and by the grace of God I shall be part of that handful."[44]

Smith lured readers with sensational headlines, including "Jewish War Crimes in Palestine: Genocide"; "Jews Eradicating Christianity from

the Holy Land"; and "Zionist Leaders Conspire to Railroad the United
States into a Third World War." He published "A Secret Interview" he
had conducted with "a world figure that cannot be named for strategic
reasons" and a "White Paper" entitled "Super Secret" after he had "had
the unusual opportunity of being in contact with the most important
individual having to do with the future of the nations in the Middle East,
a man who would be page-one news if he revealed his name."[45] Smith
always seemed miraculously to penetrate to the nerve center of the
enemy organization. He revealed not secrets, but the existence of secrets.
Behind each such statement was the implication that he knew more than
he could say and that ultimately nothing could remain hidden from him.
Because he did not reveal his informants he commanded dependence
from his followers.

The perplexing and threatening nature of Smith's fantasies demanded
his complete attention and stimulated his crusading spirit. He lived in
constant fear; no refuge was safe because enemies were out to "get" him.
He was ceaselessly excited, apprehensive, and keenly alert, finding the
most contorted plots in the most innocent conversations. He could not
afford to waste time. Every minute he rested, conspirators were at work.
Smith admitted that he might not triumph in his lifetime, but he predicted that some day God would intervene to bring victory. One could
not argue rationally with him because he claimed to receive his instruc-
tions from God; to contradict Smith was to contradict God.

Although Smith's anti-Semitism frequently seemed to cross the line
into hysteria, his followers did not always reflect his personality. One
problem with defining the origin of anti-Semitic prejudice, and to a lesser
extent anti-black and anti-Communist beliefs, is that most studies do not
distinguish between leaders and followers, between those who embrace,
disseminate and proselytize and those who silently assent and perhaps
give money. It is an important issue to settle, because it can help determine what tactics society should use to deal with bigots and demagogues.
Smith probably appealed to people who were already ripe for hating; his
contribution was to identify the enemy and direct the hatred toward a
specific object. Smith provided not only an object to hate, but the opportunity to belong to a movement in which one could submerge one's own
personality.

Individually, Smith's followers were frustrated, embittered, and impotent; together they constituted a force to be reckoned with. They believed
that they alone recognized the enemy and therefore were responsible not
only for their own fate, but for that of other Gentiles who were ignorant of
the conspiracy. Smith's movement had the thrill of secrecy, the excitement of mystery, and the adventure of a crusade. It brought prestige

through devotion to a cause and direction to meaningless lives. Part of Smith's appeal was the camaraderie his followers enjoyed through association with like-minded zealots. Together they could express their own values in a manner approved by others. Expression of hostility was cathartic; belief in a conspiracy dispelled confusion and provided a neat ordering of events otherwise impossible to understand.

Some of Smith's followers were anti-Semitic for the same reasons he was, but most were not driven by Smith's volcanic energy, and not all were authoritarian personalities. In order to grow, the movement did not have to vanquish its enemies; it merely had to feed the neuroses of Smith's followers. Indeed, the more defeats they incurred, the more menacing the enemy appeared, and the more dependent they were on Smith.

Individual involvement varied. Some people only read Smith's material or listened to him on the radio. Others contributed money, attended meetings regularly, and volunteered to stuff envelopes for mailing. These people had in common their alienation from society; most were rebels against urbanism, modernism, internationalism, and secular humanism. Joining Smith's movement might compensate for lack of education or for a menial occupation. Few of Smith's followers had attended major universities and a Smith supporter with a postgraduate degree was rare.

Smith's propaganda was particularly appealing to religious fundamentalists. Fundamentalism varies according to denomination, but its basic doctrines include biblical inerrancy and salvation by faith and conversion. Fundamentalists demand purity of doctrine and condemn pragmatism and compromise. This refusal to dilute their beliefs or compromise their principles leads them to view the world in sharply delineated, apocalyptic terms; the world is divided between the saved and the damned, between the forces of good and those of evil. Fundamentalists generally view the conflict with Communism as part of the struggle between God and Satan. Sometimes superpatriots, they view America as the last bastion of Christians besieged by godless Communists. To fundamentalists, the threat of Communism is not so much its military power as its ideology, which they believe is creeping into American life.[46]

But Smith's appeal was not limited to fundamentalists. He attracted people for many reasons: bigots opposed to Jews, blacks, and other minorities; reactionary industrialists; small capitalists; and those who responded to Smith's charisma and their own neuroses. He attracted nativists, militarists, crusaders, and people who feared that America was losing its status as the world's premier state because it was abandoning religion. Smith appealed to some who believed that the indigent were getting a free ride from the welfare state; to those appalled at the spread of

Communism in Asia and Eastern Europe; to those who repudiated our wartime alliance with the Soviet Union as evil pragmatism; and to those who favored capitalism unfettered by government regulation.[47]

Smith's followers cherished traditional truths. Viewed by intellectuals as fanatical extremists, they resented not being taken seriously. They believed that secular society was abandoning values that had made America a strong, democratic, Christian nation. America was rejecting God's plan to serve as an example and a model for the world. Its leaders were not pious; young people were openly agnostic; sexual purity was scorned; and such arbiters of society as ministers and teachers were ridiculed. Some nonreligious people were attracted to Smith because he provided scapegoats for their frustration. Some of these were white supremacists, but others cared little about the identity of the scapegoats. Conspiracy was to them a philosophy to explain anxiety, to rationalize failure, or to define dissatisfaction. If they were asked if they suffered anxiety, delusion, or fear, they might deny it. They would not justify hatred of individuals because of their religion or race, but once these persons were labeled threats to the American way of life it was intellectually permissible to hate them. They did not think of themselves as bigots but rationalized their hatred as a defense of Christianity and America.[48]

Those who were attracted to Smith's movement reveled in having "inside" knowledge. They read his books, pamphlets, tracts, and magazines and attended meetings and study groups where they learned secret information; they proceeded to spread these "truths" to others, delighting in parading their "knowledge." They no longer felt helpless; their knowledge was a weapon. There was an element of self-satisfaction in the idea that everyone else was ignorant and wrong.

Smith's followers were influential in state and local governments, where a minimum of pressure could exert influence. Because they did not hold national power and benefited from the apathy of their local opponents, their zeal was not tempered by the pragmatism required to forge coalitions. Smith's followers were disproportionately white, Protestant, and female. More than half of the attendees at his meetings were women, especially elderly women, perhaps because they had few social outlets. Most of the volunteers who worked in Smith's print shop were women and retired men. Many of his followers had grown up in small towns; few streetwise young people were attracted to him.[49]

It is clear that distinct personality styles cluster in the radical right, but not all individuals with those kinds of personality become radical rightists. What makes some embrace this dogma while others remain immune? The chief factors seem to be education and intelligence. People believe radical right dogma only if they lack the analytical tools to see through its intellectual pretensions.[50]

If education is the key, one might ask why the uneducated do not become attached to some other cause equally fulfilling to their needs. The answer is that this does happen. The type of personality attracted to a cause may find its content incidental or accidental. It depends on what one is exposed to; what one's friends espouse; one's geographic location, or the beliefs of those one seeks to emulate.

Although the shock troops are relatively poor in analytical ability, this is not necessarily true of their leaders, who possess manipulative skill. They may be no more sophisticated intellectually than their followers (although they often are), but they have the ability to build a movement around a prejudice or a set of ideas. They may be charismatic and skilled writers and speakers. Smith did not rise above analytical simplifications, but he had the personality and, even more important, the iron will to mold a movement.

Smith and his followers were symbiotic. The followers needed leadership and purpose; he needed attention and acclaim. Both were insecure. Smith was compulsive, unsatisfied unless he was acting as a leader. He had many of the qualities of a leader: he was tireless, passionate, resolute, and indomitable. But his imagination was overactive, he was ruthless, and his egocentricity led him to exaggerate and fabricate. In Smith, the attributes of an extremist were grafted onto a diligent and persistent personality. He might have become an extremist for another cause had he been exposed to a different ideology. Although not psychotic, Smith was not mentally healthy; he so closely approximates a textbook description of an authoritarian personality that there can be little doubt that his bigotry was a basic element in his personality structure.

Smith had the conviction of a fanatic. His faith was like that of a child who believes in Santa Claus; he was naive and prepared to believe whatever he imagined. But unlike a child, he never grew up—even when contrary evidence was introduced he stubbornly clung to his original beliefs. His dogma was simple and definitive. Smith was so positive of his own righteousness that he invited the Dies Committee and the California Un-American Activities Committee to investigate him. There were incidents in Smith's background that might have embarrassed any minister or politician, but Smith was oblivious to his faults.[51]

Despite his glowing self-image, Smith seethed with hostility. He did not merely disagree with people who held views different from his, he loathed them and called them anti-Christian. He did not argue, he fulminated; he did not persuade, he frightened. "The gastric juices of my mental curiosity are flowing at a high rate and my crusading saliva keeps my mouth wet constantly," he once wrote to Don Lohbeck.[52] Smith was obsessively concerned with his enemies. He could lose a friend and rationalize it—and he lost many through the years—but he could not stand to lose an enemy. Thus, he was tied inextricably to the objects of his hatred.

Smith was neither a cynic nor a hypocrite, but a twisted idealist. He gave away millions of dollars, rejected offers for lucrative positions in industry and public relations, and worked himself to exhaustion every night. He was compulsive; if he did not work for a few days, or even for a few hours, he felt nervous and guilty.

If Smith had been interested primarily in money, he would have found it more profitable to moderate some of his extreme statements and to concentrate more on anti-labor and anti-Communist issues than on cathartic but less profitable anti-Semitism. He could have become a popular crusader had he continued to emphasize opposition to Communism, but once he had "learned" that Jews were behind Communism he felt compelled to crusade. It was not easy, he conceded self-importantly: along that path lay only "hot coals, thorny paths, torrential storms, mocking voices," but then, he recalled, "I lifted my eyes to the horizon of spiritual reality and I sensed the joy that must be akin to the experience of our Lord after he resisted temptation."[53] Smith deliberately chose unpopularity. "I labor under no illusions or delusions," he wrote. "I expect to live and die a misunderstood man by millions of my compatriots."[54] And in the final analysis, his slavish devotion to anti-Semitism caused his somber prediction to come true.

seven

Fighting Reds and Blacks—
and Every Shade in Between

‡

Gerald Smith's world was populated by villains who tirelessly plotted mischief against white, Christian America and against its champion, Gerald Smith. If largely imaginary, this world provided Smith with endless challenge and constant work. It demanded every ounce of his wit and will. He was in a high-stake game with world domination the prize, and he knew his enemies would not tip their hands. So he carefully plotted his strategy, planning for the moment when he would trump his enemies as soon as they played their cards.

Smith simplified his task by lumping all his enemies into one master conspiracy. Communists were "international bankers" and "One-Worlders" were Jews; liberals were socialists; blacks were Communists. The presidents he hated were Jew-Communist-dominated. He painted and tainted everyone he despised with Jewishness, a catchall category that encompassed everything wrong with the world.

To hear Smith tell it, Jews plotted every day in every country to arrange a Zionist takeover; they never rested or slept. Jews had organized and financed the Bolshevik Revolution, set up the Iron Curtain, stolen our atomic bomb secrets, financed the American Communist Party, and promoted the Communist-dominated United Nations; they ruled the Soviet Union and served as a "fifth column" in democratic countries. Marx, Lenin, and "more than 290 of the 300 commissars" were Jews who revolted against the Czar and slaughtered millions of Christians. Jews masterminded the Second World War. After the war, they became the vanguard of Communism in Eastern Europe. Jews in America led the National Association for the Advancement of Colored People, manipulated presidents, and controlled the State Department.[1]

Smith worked particularly hard to link Jews and Communism. He circulated a fabrication he attributed to Rabbi Stephen Wise: "Some call it communism, I call it Judaism."[2] Smith countered reports of Stalinist purges of the Jews in Russia with elaborate falsehoods. The Soviet government, he claimed, was run by Jews. After Stalin's death, Smith wrote, Jews were "still in command" in Russia. "Stalin's widow is a Jew. His son is married to a Jew. His daughter is married to a Jew. The second in command is a Jew—Beria. And the third in command is a Jew—Kaganovitch."[3]

These Jews concealed their control of Russia by changing their names, promoting Jews "who do not look Jewish," using Jews in minor positions to dictate to their puppet supervisors, and placing Russians married to Jews in high offices.[4] Smith even made up a theory to explain why Jews tried to leave Russia: they were trying to flee before an anti-Communist revolution in which they would be the first to die.[5]

Smith also used his vivid imagination to explain the enmity between the Soviet Union and the state of Israel. Israel, he wrote, "has posed for political and opportunistic reasons as an enemy of Russia," but actually, he pointed out, "Israel is the only state in the Middle East where the Communist Party is legal."[6] Smith predicted that after war in the Middle East, "Israel and Russia will have put on a squeeze play against the Arabs, and when it is all over they will have divided the loot."[7] As part of this Israeli–Soviet pact, Israel planned to lure the United States into a Middle East war. America would then have to withdraw its troops from Vietnam, which would surrender to the Communists.[8]

Like his crusade against the Jews, Smith's anti-Communism was an opportunist attempt to represent himself as a patriot determined to save America from its enemies. Unlike many other anti-Communists of the 40s and 50s, Smith took no pains to distinguish Communism from liberalism or progressivism. He used *Communist* as a catchall epithet, which he flung around with the same abandon as he did *Jew*. Smith never read Marx and did not know the theoretical basis of Communism. *Communist* described anyone he considered a threat—a labor leader who called for higher wages, an advocate of the graduated income tax, a liberal intellectual, one who professed an "exotic" religion or believed in international brotherhood, or one who advocated a stronger federal government. To Smith Communism was not merely a threat in faraway Russia; it menaced U.S. schools, factories, government, labor unions, and churches. Smith accused not only Communists but all left-wingers of planning treason. Anyone who advocated an objective view of Communism, praised the military feats of Communist allies of the United States in World War

II, or just sympathized with the working class, was according to Smith a "Communist atheist."

Smith's anti-Communism predated Senator Joseph R. McCarthy's by more than ten years. In 1939 he argued that it did no good to defeat Hitler if we strengthened Communists in the process. These views were not well received during the war, and Smith's lack of patriotism resulted in a poor showing during his 1944 and 1948 presidential bids. However, as the Cold War developed and anti-Communism gained credibility, Smith's influence grew among respected conservatives. His warnings appeared prophetic as more people came to believe that President Roosevelt had underestimated the threat of Communism.

The threat from international Communism was real enough, but not in the way Smith imagined. He used the strong feeling against foreign Communists to sow hatred against Americans. Smith's irrational anti-Communism was animated by displaced emotion, distorted by rash judgment, fueled by stereotypes, and exaggerated by an overactive imagination. He told reporters in 1947, when America still had a nuclear monopoly, that the United States should suspend an atomic bomb over Moscow and detonate it if Stalin did not follow our orders.[9] He professed to fear Communism more than nuclear war: "As far as Mrs. Smith and myself are concerned, we would rather die under twenty feet of nuclear rubble than to bow our knees to the Christ-hating Moscovites."[10]

While Senator McCarthy was content to find his Communists within the government, Smith found them everywhere—even in the Boy Scouts. Communists, he said, used sex as bait to lure Americans into spy rings.[11] Scarcely could his readers absorb one sensational charge before more were announced; and Smith claimed that those who denied the conspiracy must be party to it.[12] Historian Michael Parenti summarized his interpretation: "If the communists act belligerently, this demonstrates their wickedness; and if they act moderately, even threatening to become downright friendly, this in turn proves their duplicity, mendacity, and again, their wickedness."[13]

The Chinese Communists were especially crafty. According to Smith, impressment gangs roamed China, seizing homeless men. They put them in the holds of ships and pumped them full of heroin. Once addicted, they were shipped to America, dumped ashore, and told that they could not have another "fix" until they had gotten an American addicted.[14]

Within the United States, Smith believed, there were half a million Communists. "One of these oriented inside traitors can accomplish five times the damage of a paratrooper landed from Stalin's plane," he wrote.[15] He advocated imprisonment of American Communists and deportation of alien ones. Most of our politicians and diplomats, he insisted, were Communist traitors or dupes who consciously or unwittingly were selling out our national interests and our way of life.[16]

The traitors in our government had engineered the "fall" of China. Chinese nationalist leader Chiang Kai-Shek "could have won if he had been loyally supported by the Americans, but he was disarmed under orders from General George Marshall, who not only did it, but boasted about it." Traitors arranged that "supplies intended for Chiang Kai-Shek from the United States were dumped into the sea under military superiors acting under orders from Washington, D.C." Chiang was banished to Formosa and prohibited from attacking the mainland, although "on numerous occasions Chiang Kai-Shek and his brilliant army could have reinvaded the homeland if they had had the encouragement of the Washington Administration, which down through the years has pandered to Moscow and Peiping."[17] Smith fought diplomatic recognition of Red China and its admission to the United Nations. In December 1958, he announced that he was "organizing a nationwide campaign operating through 10,000 key committeemen for the purpose of fighting and opposing the recognition of the Peiping savages."[18]

Smith resented the lack of appreciation for his work. While treacherous Americans escaped blame for losing China, Smith did not receive due credit for saving America from Communism: "The pioneers in fighting communism in the United States were, among others, Hamilton Fish, Martin Dies, Elizabeth Dilling, Jack B. Tenney, John Rankin, Rev. Charles E. Coughlin and Gerald L. K. Smith." Denying ambition for money or fame, he wrote in self-pity, "A materialist would be bitter over this circumstance. He could easily say, 'Why was I compelled to do the foundation work while someone else gets the credit?' "[19]

Smith saw himself as personally responsible for a miracle that would save America from Communism. "I believe that when one, in faith, resists the impossible by hard work, sacrificial endeavor and complete devotion to principle that then and only then does the miracle happen."[20]

Smith made an industry of fighting Communism to trigger the miracle. He provided material for textbooks and for church seminars and study groups. He told his supporters to pray, read patriotic literature, and contribute money to the Christian Nationalist Crusade.[21] He circulated a petition to sign up "Minute Men and Women" to report Communists, to inform themselves about Communist activity, to distribute literature against Communism, to campaign to outlaw Communism, and to work to fire Communist teachers.[22] Smith also utilized reformed Communists to combat Communism. He hired a repentent black Communist, William Nowell, as his "advisor on Negro affairs" and used him to make speeches and to testify before congressional committees.[23]

Smith employed another former Communist, Kenneth Goff, to organize youths and veterans. Goff, who had a wooden leg, claimed that a Communist had pushed him under a train. An unstable man with a checkered past, Goff had once been arrested for writing a bad check and had been fined for hurling stink bombs and for charging rent in excess of federal regulations.[24] Goff and two Smith supporters were convicted of placing on the lawn of the Soviet Embassy signs that read: "BEWARE! SPIES AT WORK; MURDER INCORPORATED; CLOSED, RAT INFESTED" and "FOR SALE, OWNERS LEAVING SOON."[25]

Some anti-Communist leaders disapproved of Smith and ostracized him. Rev. Billy James Hargis, founder of the Christian Crusade, refused to speak to Smith, and Meyer G. Lowman of the Circuit Riders, Inc., would not sell him literature.[26] Robert Welch considered Smith a bigot and refused to let him join the John Birch society, nor would he send Smith a copy of *The Politician*, in which Welch argued that President Eisenhower was a Communist dupe; Welch threatened to sue Smith if he sold the books without permission.[27] Later Smith called Welch an atheist, adding, "he is a hypocrite and a liar and he is afraid of the Jews."[28]

Smith fawned on Senator Joseph R. McCarthy. "Among intelligent patriots," he wrote, "it is now a settled fact that McCarthy, the fearless statesman, has done as much or more than any member of the United States Senate to uncover treason and expose traitors." "United States Senator Joseph McCarthy might easily go down in history as the man who saved America."[29] Smith bragged, "For four years I maintained a liaison and confidential contact with Senator McCarthy by way of an individual whose name I shall not mention."[30] His boast was a fabrication: McCarthy avoided Smith.[31] Smith blamed McCarthy's snub on two young Jews on the senator's staff, Roy Cohn and G. David Schine.[32] Cohn said about Smith, "Of all the attacks on me, the two which I value most highly are those by the *Daily Worker* and by Gerald L. K. Smith. To me, they are both in the same class. I am glad they disapprove of me. As I have said time and time again, I want no part and will have no part of either of them."[33]

Despite the snub, Smith did all he could to prevent censure of Joe McCarthy. When the Senate considered a censure resolution in November 1954, Smith checked into the Mayflower Hotel (registering as Stephen Goodyear) and mobilized support for the Wisconsin senator. He packed the galleries with demonstrators, who later trooped to senators' offices and called them at home late at night.[34] In December Smith attended a meeting in Madison Square Garden of "Ten Million Americans Mobilizing for Justice" to save McCarthy. Spotted sitting in the Kansas section wearing a ten-gallon hat, he told a reporter that he was "Mr. Phillips" from California; then he ran out of the building.[35]

Smith insisted that McCarthy's reprimand was a Jew-Communist idea. After the censure he collected hundreds of thousands of signatures calling upon the U.S. Senate to apologize to McCarthy, and he demanded that Senator Ralph Flanders, who had introduced the motion to censure, apologize to God.[36] McCarthy should be memorialized: "God hasten the day when a tower or a monument or a memorial for Joe McCarthy shall rise in our Nation's Capitol built with the gifts which shall come from the humble patriotic citizens of our Nation who still believe that eternal vigilance is the price of liberty," Smith wrote. After the censure, Smith urged McCarthy to continue his fight against Communism. He should create a national committee and launch a direct mail campaign, emulating Huey Long, who had set up his own propaganda machine because the conventional press was hostile. McCarthy should not, however, hire Jews and must address the "Jewish issue," Smith warned.[38]

Privately, Smith despaired because McCarthy spurned him and called him an anti-Semite. "We have had some experiences with McCarthy which would make you sick to your stomach if we were to review them," he wrote a follower in 1956.[39] Nonetheless, Smith never attacked McCarthy publicly, even after the senator's death in 1957.

Smith accused Jew-Communists of murdering McCarthy. "Left-wing preachers, Marxist-influenced intellectuals, Jewish-manipulated editors, spineless opportunists, Communist-influenced manipulators on radio and television all joined the lynch mob to worry this man to death."[40] They studied McCarthy's constitution; then they directed their lies, rumors, and innuendos so as to overstimulate certain glands, producing "glandular murder."[41] The plot was orchestrated by Bernard Baruch. "*Anyone who doubts that the destruction of Joseph McCarthy was a Jew-inspired plot confesses his naiveté and immaturity*," Smith cried.[42] After McCarthy's death Smith organized a national committee to present yearly a McCarthy Memorial Plaque to some "outstanding individual" who "has sought to perpetuate the ideals of this fearless and martyred statesman."[43]

Smith also championed the House Un-American Activities Committee (HUAC), boasting that he and four other "patriots" had inspired Congress to create the committee in 1939. Smith knew its chairman, Texas Democrat Martin Dies, whom he had met when Dies taught Sunday school at a Texas church Smith visited.[44] Smith and his allies praised Dies and his successors and explained Dies's attacks on the right as expediencies. William Dudley Pelley told his Silver Shirt followers that Dies "for

propaganda reasons must rant and roar against race prejudice and religious intolerance but behind the scenes . . . a different trend is apparent." In 1940, when Dies sought appropriations to continue the committee, Smith collected four hundred thousand signatures on a petition in
support of it.[45]

Smith provided HUAC with lists of alleged Communists to investigate.[46] His friendship with HUAC chairmen induced Congressman Frank
E. Hook of Michigan to label the committee "a sounding board for the un-
American Fascist groups" and to charge that "Gerald L. K. Smith is not
only the Committee's advisor on un-Americanism, he is also the confi-
dant of the Committee's plans." Congressman Charles R. Savage of Washington, even more concerned, wrote: "It seems to me that all Gerald L. K.
Smith has to do is yell 'sic em,' and the Committee's Counsel takes after
whatever party Mr. Smith is peeved at."[47] Smith's close ties with the
committee spurred a dozen congressmen to demand that the committee
investigate "Native Fascists." The committee questioned Smith in 1944,
1946, and 1948, but Smith turned each hearing to his advantage, using
the opportunity in 1944 to talk about his son's heroism in battle.[48]

Called back in 1946, Smith claimed he was persecuted by a "left-wing
cabal" seeking to destroy all enemies of Communism.[49] The cabal included Frank Sinatra, Orson Welles, Eddie Cantor, Edward G. Robinson,
and Walter Winchell, as well as tax-exempt liberal groups: the Anti-
Defamation League, Friends of Democracy, and Non-Sectarian Anti-Nazi
League. Friendly congressmen "fed" Smith questions and some even
prompted him when he could not recall details. Congressman John E.
Rankin of Mississippi asked, "Would you say that [the New Deal] was
more fascist or communist?"[50] Granted fifteen minutes to read a prepared
statement, Smith spoke for two hours. He lost his poise only once—when
Representative J. Parnell Thomas of New Jersey asked Smith if he was
anti-Semitic. Smith snapped, "Is it un-American to criticize a Jew?"[51]
Questioned about the sources of his money, Smith said that his contributors also gave money to congressmen on the committee. Smith claimed
that while he had nothing to conceal, to reveal his sources might cause
Communists to harass them.[52]

Smith took credit for persuading HUAC to investigate Communist
subversion in the motion picture industry. He assembled a huge petition,
pasting together sheets with hundreds of thousands of signatures calling
for the Committee to examine Hollywood. Smith presented the petition
to Congressman Rankin, who unrolled it in the aisles of the House Chamber.[53] Smith also staged a sensational meeting in Hollywood that was
even more dramatic than the petition. He obtained a list of alleged Communists from "one of the great scenario writers of Hollywood who has

the lowdown information on every phase of the motion picture colony from unimpeachable sources," and he hired a young actor he called Mr. X to read it to an audience. Wearing a black hood, Mr. X drove up to the exclusive El Patio Theater in a black limousine protected by six bodyguards in tuxedos. After the affair made headlines, Smith wrote Don Lohbeck, "The whole community is agog. We have actually upset something."[54]

The meeting featuring Mr. X led to the creation of the anti-Communist Cinema Educational Guild by Smith and Myron C. Fagan. Fagan, a successful Broadway playwright and producer, had moved to Hollywood to produce anti-Communist plays. Smith funded the Cinema Educational Guild and promised to subsidize and distribute Fagan's book, *Red Treason Over Hollywood*. Both men agreed that Smith's involvement should remain secret. But Smith could not resist boasting about his role in Fagan's activities. When the press published his remarks, Fagan denied knowing him. Hurt, Smith withdrew his backing for Fagan's book and called him a Jew.[55]

Just as Smith's anti-Semitism spilled into anti-Communism, his obsession with Communism led him to condemn blacks. He wrote his parents in 1947 that "a vicious and diabolical attempt has been made to communize the Negroes and they are becoming unruly, and nothing but Christian Americanism can turn back this tide, in my opinion."[56] He published a map showing how Communists intended to carve a black republic from the Southern states.[57] Blacks, however, were only naive puppets controlled by clever Jew-Communists:

> The South will never free itself from the bondage of the political mongrelizers until it realizes that behind the mongrelizers stand the Jews. . . . Even brilliant statesmen like Talmadge and Eastland are slow to see the point. . . . Anyone knows that the poor Negro is not smart enough or natively evil enough to be victorious over us. A Southern politician will vibrate even to the point of screaming about the "Nigger," but after the meeting he will go right down and have a drink of whiskey or a cup of coffee with the worst Jew in town.[58]

Smith offered a free one-year subscription to *The Cross and the Flag* to "any citizen of the United States who can name one Jewish Rabbi opposed to integration, race-mixing and such."[59] (Why anyone associated with Jewish rabbis would want a subscription to *The Cross and the Flag* escapes logic, but Smith had made his point.)

Smith's prejudice against blacks derived from his belief that they were racially inferior as well as pawns of Jew-Communists. Blacks were a "child race only 200 years out of cannibalism"[60] who, without whites,

would never have "got past the loin cloth or the G-string."[61] Smith said
he loved the "good, simple plantation niggers" of Louisiana and wanted
to protect them from militant blacks who fomented trouble.[62]

Blacks were corrupted by Yankee demagogues who promised them
welfare in return for their votes. "Literally millions of blacks refuse to
work. They won't pick strawberries, they won't mow hay, they won't cut
a lawn, they won't do common labor, they won't do anything except
stand in front of the welfare office," Smith complained. He had seen
blacks take food stamps and buy steaks while hardworking, taxpaying
whites had to get hot dogs and hamburgers.[63]

Smith knew few blacks other than those he saw buying steaks at
supermarkets. There were few blacks in rural Wisconsin, none in the
schools and churches Smith attended as a boy. His Shreveport church
was strictly segregated. Smith's first encounter with black masses occurred in racially troubled Detroit during World War II. He wrote his son
from Detroit in 1944, "The Negro situation is especially bad as they are all
full of money and gin, and since they also have lots of syphilis they are
not in the army."[64] But after he condemned blacks to his mother, she
wrote, "Watch your words, Gerald, don't cheapen yourself by saying
rough things about the colored citizens."[65]

Smith had black cooks and housekeepers, whom he got along with only
so long as they were submissive. He advised his relatives and their
children visiting him in Tulsa not to fraternize with the black help
because "this is a custom which, when violated, might spoil a good
person."[66] In another letter he said, "no matter how good a Negro is, they
have to have white supervision."[67] Writing a letter of recommendation
for his Tulsa maid, he concluded, "She keeps herself immaculately clean
at all times and represents the type of Negro which, if duplicated, would
solve all our racial problems."[68]

Not surprisingly, few blacks attended Smith's political rallies, and in
his races for U.S. senator and president he received few black votes. Not
many subscribed to *The Cross and the Flag*, few contributed to his
crusades, and there were almost no black pilgrims to his Sacred Projects
in Eureka Springs. On many nights there is not a single black in the
Passion Play amphitheater that seats four thousand.

While Smith had no black friends, he did include among his close
friends some of the most vicious racists in America. He admired U.S.
senator Theodore G. Bilbo, wrote flattering letters to him, and sold Bilbo's
book, *Segregation or Mongrelization?* "By this book you have made
yourself immortal," he told the senator.[69] Smith also supported another
Mississippi senator, James O. Eastland, a segregationist and arch-conser-
vative. Eastland, however, spurned Smith's offer to help him fight racial

integration.[70] Smith fawned on Judge Thomas P. Brady, author of the racist book *Black Monday,* in which Brady vowed, "We will die before we will mix."[71]

Smith peddled William H. ("Alfalfa Bill") Murray's *The Negro's Place in the Call of Race,* a bestseller among racists, and he tried, without much success, to strike up a personal friendship with the Oklahoma senator.[72] When Georgia's anti-black governor Eugene Talmadge died in 1946, Smith eulogized him as "one of the greatest men America ever produced" and blamed "mongrelizers" for hounding Talmadge to death.[73] He praised Arkansas governor Orval Faubus for fighting racial integration in Little Rock, even staging a Faubus for President rally at the Democratic National Convention in 1960. Privately, however, Smith criticized Faubus for using too little force to oppose federal troops sent to Little Rock to enforce desegregation of the all-white Central High School and for failing to recognize the Jew-Communist conspiracy behind the civil rights movement.[74]

As lavishly as Smith praised his allies in his fight against integration, he saved his most extravagant rhetoric for condemning his enemies. Supreme Court chief justice Earl Warren, he said, was a puppet of Jews and Communists. Many segregationists advocated impeaching Warren, but that was not enough for Smith: he wanted to impeach all nine justices and put them in prison. He delivered a fifteen-hundred-foot-long petition to Congress to demonstrate popular support for this draconian solution.[75]

Smith detested Rev. Martin Luther King even more than he hated the Supreme Court justices. He termed King "one of the greatest frauds of the century"[76] and charged that he had attended a Communist training school in Tennessee.[77] "God save us from the tradition of Martin Luther King," he prayed, "who was a Communist, a traitor, a revolutionist and an atheist while posing as a Baptist preacher."[78] Smith protested the lowering of American flags to half staff after King's murder; he condemned Robert F. Kennedy, Eugene McCarthy, and Richard Nixon for attending King's funeral. They might have been justified, he explained, "if Martin Luther King had been a truly great Negro like George Washington Carver or Booker T. Washington."[79]

Smith's racist activities were not limited to talk. In 1949, St. Louis, where Smith's headquarters were located, voted on a new city charter that would eliminate Jim Crow buses. Smith mobilized a Racial Purity Committee that sent volunteers house to house to obtain the twenty thousand signatures required to place a countermeasure on the ballot. Smith's bill called for separate entrances to buildings for blacks and segregated seating at restaurants, night clubs, and athletic contests. Blacks would be required to sit in the rear of streetcars and buses.[80] Smith failed to obtain enough signatures, however, and the *St. Louis Post-Dispatch* concluded, "the thing that makes Gerald L. K. Smith's doctrine of white supremacy hardest to swallow is that Gerald L. K. Smith is supposed to be some sort of example of it."[81]

At the heart of Smith's fear of blacks was the image of interracial sex. Sex, he believed, is the ultimate leveler: to engage in sex with someone of another race would be to make him or her an equal. Smith cited no less an authority than God to condemn interracial sex: "When the Scripture says: 'Thou shalt not commit adultery,' it is reasonable to believe that we must not adulterate the blood line which God Almighty established in the identity of the races."[82] Smith believed that every black man lusted for white women and claimed that black men had been photographed having sex openly with white women in Martin Luther King's civil rights marches.[83] Black children were libertines who matured sexually at the age of nine or ten.[84] Once they were permitted to mix with whites, interracial dating and sex were inevitable. This in turn would lead to mixed marriages and "mongrelization" of the white race. The adulterated, weakened mongrels would surrender to Communists. Smith advocated a constitutional amendment prohibiting interracial sex and marriage, justifying the measure as a defense against Communism.[85]

Smith's prejudice was not limited to Jews, Communists, and blacks; it permeated every aspect of his life: his friendships, the types of art objects he bought, the kinds of books he read, the places he chose to live, his relationships with the people who worked for him, and his views of other nations. Intuitive rather than intellectual, he never made any decision entirely rationally.

Smith's emotional crusades encompassed numerous issues, including most of the causes espoused by the extreme right. He charged, for example, that fluoridation of water to prevent tooth decay was really a Communist plot to poison Americans with a chemical that alter our mood and weaken our will to resist Communism. Smith claimed that he drank only bottled water. He published a tract entitled "Poison Water Red Plot" and created the National Pure Water Committee to fight fluoridation,[86] against which he published a little rhyme in *The Cross and the Flag*:

> Aye, pass the brimming cup around
>   Though it be fluoridated,
> For old-time liberties and rights
>   Are strictly antiquated.
>
> What matters now if kidneys rot
>   Or blood and brain go dry?
> We'll have a lovely set of teeth
>   To grin with when we die![87]

Smith also opposed alcohol, tobacco, and marijuana. Jews, who he claimed monopolized the manufacture of whiskey in the United States, utilized it to weaken Gentile resistance to their domination. "They not only took it over, but they corrupted the whiskey beyond its original poisonous condition with all sorts of neutral spirits and dope-like dilutions."[88] Smith wanted to outlaw liquor advertising and to limit its sale to special stores whose addresses would be available only in a directory.[89] He also wanted to ban advertisements of tobacco; he thought that Jews encouraged addiction to nicotine to facilitate Communist conquest.[90] Marijuana was worse—a "treacherous, benumbing narcotic" promoted by "perverted sociological sadists."[91] Of course, many ordinary, reasonable people also oppose these vices, but Smith's positions lose credibility when seen in the context of his delusional web.

Smith was highly sensitive to issues involving sex, opposing immodest dress, premarital intercourse, birth control, sex education, homosexuality, pornography, and abortion. He abhorred miniskirts. "Women," he wrote in 1969, "actually attend church garbed in a manner that would have effected their arrest even five years ago." Topless and bottomless bars and restaurants, he said, encourage depravity. "Thousands of restaurants have opened up in America where the waitresses are serving their customers in the nude." Illicit sex permeated society, encouraged by the Supreme Court and winked at by the clergy.[92] "One white girl brought down by the beatniks experienced sexual intercourse not less than 15 times in one night from Negroes," he told a correspondent.[93]

Teenagers were taught to commit depraved acts in sex education classes, or "academic pornography," as Smith called them. In one such class in Fort Worth, Texas, several young women fainted from shock at what they were being taught. Smith argued that these classes constituted "a program of perverted education which, if allowed to continue, could destroy our nation in the tradition of Sodom and Gomorrah."[94]

Any kind of sex angered Smith, but homosexuality made him apoplectic. He claimed that this "deviancy" pervaded the journalism, motion picture, and music industries, and that perverts and marijuana addicts had become a political bloc. A healthy heterosexual could not be employed unless he tolerated deviants. According to Smith's figures, there were 250,000 homosexuals employed by the federal government![95]

Pornography, he said, had been invented by Jews to undermine Gentile civilization. "Invariably the publishing is done by Jews and the distribution is done by Jews, and the organized financed sympathy comes from the Jews." Rock music, television, and Broadway—all were controlled by Jews, and all glamorized sex.[96] Abortion, however, was the ultimate evil. It was perpetrated by "sadists who are attempting to murder people before they are born."[97] Smith launched a campaign for a constitutional amendment outlawing abortion, urging his supporters to circulate petitions, write their congressmen, and give him money.[98]

Smith blamed the women's liberation movement for popularizing abortion and birth control. "The so called Women's Liberation Movement," he wrote, "is led by sex perverts, lesbians, women disappointed in love, masculine-minded felines and usually they are pro-Communist and take a treasonable attitude toward the basic qualities of American life."[99] These women leered at photos of naked men in magazines and made obscene phone calls. Better to remain single than to marry a "women's libber," he counseled. His own wife returned unopened any envelope addressed to her as "Ms.," he claimed.[100]

Smith also traced moral decay to the nation's welfare system. Contemptuous of anyone who received welfare, he reported that "a Puerto Rican can land in New York at 10 o'clock in the morning and be on the relief rolls by 4 o'clock in the afternoon."[101] He inveighed against "welfare loafers that are sucking billions of dollars out of our public treasury" and proposed that "these loafers should be rounded up and given employment on great compounds and made to earn their bread by the sweat of their brow."[102] Smith called for a three-million-man secret police force to arrest vagrants and suspicious characters. We should impeach "corrupt, spongy, soft, unrealistic" judges, investigate "alien agitation, native dupes, treasonable organizers, instigators of violence," and use force to protect white Americans from black savages. He threatened defeat to any congressman who did not endorse "law and order."[103]

Smith opposed gun control, believing it a Communist plot to help criminals by disarming Christian Americans. "The campaign is on," he wrote, "to force us to surrender our protection while savages are being trained to slaughter us."[104] Only "the sentimentalists and the nuts, the traitors and the criminals" favored gun control.[105] Smith contributed money to the National Rifle Association and urged it to continue its crusade against disarming honest Americans.[106]

He accused the press of encouraging criminals and supporting the enemy in Vietnam. He was unrestrained in criticizing "the treason machine, which is my name for the Jew-controlled radio and television networks as well as the left wing news media in general."[107] "There is not a fraternity of people in this country that is more contemptible and spoiled than the representatives of the news media," he wrote. "They are mean, cantankerous, dishonest and in many cases positively criminal."[108] Smith blamed his own bad press on his courageous criticism of the media, particularly of television. "I am not so sure but what television has completely hypnotized our nation," he wrote. "It is the curse of mankind."[109] Unfortunately, American politicians did not have the courage to stand up to the press, especially on the issue of Vietnam. "The commentators on the Jew-controlled television are free to refer to the Vietnam war as a bad war as though we did the wrong thing in going in. We did the right thing, and we could have won the war in three weeks if it hadn't been for the yellow compromising cowardice of Kennedy and Johnson."[110]

Smith called for a jingoist military policy like that Andrew Jackson or Teddy Roosevelt practiced. The president should "call on our Congress to give our Pentagon . . . the strongest military machinery on the face of the earth so we don't have to take sass, back talk or abuse from anybody."[111] Instead of vacillating, President Johnson "should have sent our great bombers over there and blown hell out of the capital of North Vietnam." He condemned student demonstrators against the war as traitors, asserting that "in better days they would have all been shot." But Lyndon Johnson, the "yellow demagogue from Texas," had surrendered to the antiwar protestors. "Instead of calling out the troops and shooting a few people and running another 10,000 or 20,000 of them into concentration camps, he wilted like Ferdinand the Bull."[112] Then a spineless Congress "made up of fools, demagogues, traitors, hypocrites, nitwits, homosexuals, sodomists and grafters" failed to provide President Nixon with supplies to arm the South Vietnamese and consummate our victory. In 1975 the "treasonable Congress" denied President Ford's request for emergency money to arm the South Vietnamese, "and the Communists from North Vietnam came in to overcome an army with empty guns and there was nothing to do but surrender."[113]

The greatest scandal of the war, according to Smith, was the prosecution of Lieutenant William L. Calley, who had ordered his men to slay Vietnamese civilians at My Lai. In Smith's mind Calley not only was innocent, but deserved to be decorated for protecting his men. "He fought like a he-man and attacked a community where every man, woman and child was armed with hand grenades designed to slaughter our soldiers."[114] His only crime was valuing the lives of his men more than the lives of the enemy. "Word went down the line to fight a 'No Win' war, but Calley didn't seem to get the message and he made the criminal mistake of fighting to win."[115] Calley had been "framed" because Zionists wanted to discredit the honorable American commitment to Vietnam so that American troops would be dispatched "to fight a war to slaughter the Arabs in the Middle East and enthrone the Zionist imperialists."[116]

Behind every new, liberal, or progressive idea or movement, Smith found Jews, Communists, or both plotting against the national interest. He charged that the energy crisis of the 1970s was perpetrated by Jews who wanted the United States to blame the Arab nations. If the United

States invaded the Middle East to seize Arab oil, a nuclear war would provoke Armageddon. The irony was that the United States did not even need Arab oil. "There are 2,000,000,000 barrels of oil off the coast of Los Angeles and San Diego, far enough out to hurt nobody, that would have been producing now had it not been for the ecological nuts and the saboteurs."[117] Thus, Armageddon would result from an alliance of Zionists and the Sierra Club! Despite impending Armageddon, Smith was heartened because most of the world blamed Israel for the Arab oil embargo, and other nations were urging policies he had advocated for years. "Now they stand alone and the world is on my side," he gloated.[118]

Smith considered every alien and nonconformist a threat to America. He never conceded that people who differed with him might be patriots. Any support for Israel was equivalent to treason. Peaceful overtures to Moscow were "sell-outs" to Communism. Aid to the needy was robbery of everyone else. Tolerance of ethnic diversity was aggression against native whites like him.

Taken in isolation, some of Smith's positions had some merit. His opposition to alcohol, drugs, and tobacco, his concerns about the threat of Communism and the spread of pornography have all been at one time or another mainstream political attitudes. But when seen in the constellation of Smith's racism, anti-Semitism, and opposition to anything progressive, all of these positions add up to a rather sad view of the world. While some crusaders are motivated by a genuine desire to create a better society, Smith was motivated by anger and hatred. He seized upon every shred of information that came his way as evidence that the forces of evil were at work, using this to fuel his anger. His hatred of reds, blacks, yellows, and just about any other shade different from his own ultimately poisoned his relationships even with his allies—and destroyed whatever potential he may have had for contributing positively to the world.

eight

A Glib Tongue, Acid Pen,

and Hard Cash

‡

For over four decades, as public speaker and writer, Gerald L. K. Smith was one of the most prolific and influential spokesmen for the far right. His emotional, pungent, earthy rhetoric captivated audiences and amazed journalists.[1]

H. L. Mencken wrote in 1936 that although he had been paid to listen to speakers for thirty-seven years, he had heard none who equaled Smith. Mencken explained that he had heard William Jennings Bryan, Chauncey M. Depew, "Uncle Joe" Cannon, and Robert M. LaFollette; he had sat through ten successive sermons of the evangelist Billy Sunday, and he had heard Huey Long, Tom Heflin, Cole Blease, and Teddy and Franklin Roosevelt. Smith was better and more versatile than any of them. Mencken described Smith's speeches as "a magnificent amalgam of each and every species of rabble-rousing, with embellishments borrowed from the Algonquin Indians and the Cossacks of the Don."[2]

Mencken enjoyed a good show—the more bizarre the better—and his description might be dismissed as characteristic hyperbole, except that almost everyone else who heard Smith agreed. Huey Long described him as "the only man I ever saw who is a better rabble-rouser than I am."[3] Smith did not mind being called a rabble-rouser—he referred to himself as one. He even asked the faculty of Harvard University to create a "chair of rabble-rousing" and hire him.[4] Smith would say:

> They tell me that I mustn't refer to our sacred flag. That would be
> rabble-rousing. They tell me I must not speak of our glorious Consti-
> tution. That would be rabble-rousing. They say to me that I mustn't
> quote from the Holy Book, our Christian Bible. But let me tell you

friends, that if it is rabble-rousing to praise the flag and the Constitution and to love the Bible, then I can only pray to God that in His infinite wisdom He will make me the greatest rabble-rouser in the United States.[5]

According to eyewitnesses, Smith's reputation as the nation's premier rabble-rouser was deserved. Following Smith's address to the Washington Press Club in 1936, feature writer Mark Sullivan of the *New York Herald Tribune* wrote that he was "a combination of the late William Jennings Bryan, the Rev. William Sunday, and the late Senator LaFollette, the elder." He was "as good as Bryan except that he has not Bryan's range of voice," was "better in his art than Billy Sunday," and "has much of the late Senator LaFollette's intensity of passion, and he has humor, which the late Senator never had."[6] Another journalist, William Bradford Huie, wrote, "The man has the passion of Billy Sunday. He has the fire of Adolf Hitler. . . . He is the stuff of which Fuehrers are made."[7]

Smith said that his speaking ability was a talent which came from God because his parents had prayed for a son who would be a great speaker. "My gift of speech is nothing for which I should boast. It came to me from the loins of a consecrated and devoted father and from the womb of a praying and Christ-loving mother. Through the years both my mother and father confessed to me that while I was being borne prior to birth, they both desired and prayed that I be endowed with a gift of speech dedicated to the Lord Jesus Christ and His high principles."[8] Smith claimed he had cultivated his oratory by listening to his father. "My father was a good speaker, my father was an eloquent speaker for the environment that he grew up in," he told an interviewer. "I mean he could always stand up on the Fourth of July, or at a political meeting, or at a church meeting and hold the people's rapt attention. And they always were interested in what he had to say. So he wanted me to learn how to speak, and so I took interest."[9]

His schedule left Smith little time to read, reflect, or plan and so he repeated essentially the same speech at every meeting. This enabled him to deliver remarks extemporaneously with little preparation. He usually did not campaign for political candidates or try to set up local organizations. It was talk and travel, talk and travel. At each stop he collected names and addresses from his audience. He also collected money, but his primary purpose was to compile a mailing list.

Smith's meetings capitalized on the theme of ultrapatriotism. Flags, bunting, and paintings of the Founding Fathers decorated the auditorium. An "advance man" warmed up the audience with patriotic songs, followed by a prayer and the pledge of allegiance. The chairman next introduced a secondary speaker, who delivered a fifteen- to twenty-minute talk. By the time Smith spoke, the audience was ripe for the plucking. They squirmed with anticipation, gossiping about Communism, liquor, and Jews. Then Smith appeared and whipped them into hysteria for an hour or two.

Tickets were required for admittance to the meetings, which made people who received them feel favored, although anyone who asked could get tickets. Several weeks before his appearance in a city, Smith would send tickets to people on his mailing list there, instructing the recipients to distribute the tickets among friends. People entering a meeting were screened at the door. If they were known to Smith's staff, they were usually admitted with or without tickets. Those who seemed to be Jews or Smith opponents were barred. The ticket system made it difficult for Smith's adversaries to pack the meetings and excluded hecklers in large numbers.

Those who got in were seldom disappointed. Smith had a crisp, mellifluous voice, filled with expression, rising to a crescendo of indignation, falling to appeals to love Christ and America, frightening and reassuring in turn. His inflection was measured; he never hesitated; his pauses were always deliberate; he never groped for a word. He had a precise sense of timing and sprinkled his sentences with the names of important Americans. Words gushed out like a waterfall, clear and clean, rushing to a dramatic conclusion. He feasted on feedback, responding to his own emotions and to those of his audience.

His speeches were a combination of a high school pep rally and a Klan cross burning. He held up a hand, waggled it, then smashed it into his palm. Although he really did not need a microphone, he used one to surround and envelop the audience with noise. Some became hysterical, rising, waving their arms, sobbing and screaming. Smith boomed into the loudspeaker: "The nicest fair grounds, the best restaurants, they all belong to us. Why shouldn't we enjoy them? Who enjoys them now?"

"The Jews," the crowd yelled back.

"Yes, and if the Jews don't like our country they can go back where they came from! We'll even buy 'em a one-way ticket!" Smith responded.[10]

Smith's appeal was based on simplicity and a nursery rhyme rhythm directed at the uneducated and built around a few short phrases: "The Cross and the Flag," "America First," and "The Christian Nationalist Crusade." He contrasted his stock villains with his own Christianity, patriotism, and persecution. He personalized conflict. If there was a strike, it was instigated by Communists; if there was unemployment, it was because immigrants were getting all the jobs.

Smith's analogies and metaphors were vivid. He knew a biblical story for every occasion: "If Al Capone had lived in those days, he would have been the king. Al Capone is a Sunday School teacher compared to Herod."[11] For sheer entertainment he outdid anything Cecil B. deMille ever staged. Get out and fight for the Stars-and-Stripes, he told his audiences. Bow your head in prayer, lift up your voice in song, salute the flag. He was angry and outlandish, but what spewed from him in speech after speech welled from the depths of his troubled soul.

Smith's listeners would follow him anywhere, applauding, "amen-ing," "ayeing," urging him to pour it on. Then, for a moment, he would step back, look at his audience, and ask them how they liked what he said. If his remarks provoked only mild applause he would stop and say, "All right, if you like that give it a good hand!" A roar would result.[12]

Brenda Ueland attended a Smith meeting in Minneapolis, the topic of which was "Christ First in America," and wrote in her *Minneapolis Daily News* column: "But he is so singularly unchristlike himself, as when he'd yell something frightful about widely loved people like Stassen, Roose-velt, Beveridge, and the audience would boo faintly, and he'd rive the air with a yell: 'Yes, come on—BOO! Give them a BOO!' Like a horrible cheer leader in reverse. He led them in hatred."[13]

Smith gained sympathy from his audiences by telling them that both he and they were in danger. He told them of threats on his life and efforts to break up his meetings. "I have just received information that our enemies have planted a lot of toughs in this audience who are going to try to break up this meeting," he warned a Detroit audience. "Now I want 100 of you men to volunteer to throw out the first man into the street who tries to break up this meeting." Immediately two or three hundred men jumped to their feet, while the audience howled.[14]

Once in Alabama Smith attracted only two or three hundred support-ers to hear a speech. After speaking to them for half an hour, he told them to go out and find friends to attend a second meeting in forty-five min-utes. The crowd for the second meeting was double or triple the size of the first, but Smith wasn't finished. He sent them away to gather people for a third meeting; five thousand enthusiastic listeners returned. On another occasion, after speaking for hours beneath a southern sun, Smith abruptly left the platform for fifteen minutes, returning clad in a fresh suit of white linen. His audience never abandoned him. In Kansas City, after a heckler set his revival tent on fire, the audience remained to listen to Smith while aides extinguished the flames.[15]

Smith's radio addresses were dictated to a secretary. Although tran-scribed, they had much of the spontaneity of his extemporaneous speeches. His radio talks, loosely organized and rambling, sounded much better than they read. Smith was more effective in person because he could project passion through body language as well as words.[16]

Although Smith's oratory before mass audiences won plaudits, it was not always appropriate and its effect, though intoxicating, was transient. His rhetoric was crude, unsophisticated, and bombastic, entertaining rather than enlightening. His audiences were hand-picked to respond favorably; he seldom converted opponents to his cause. He talked too loudly and too long, and his lack of dignity was sometimes embarrassing to supporters. He was a publicity monger who shamelessly promoted himself and his meetings.[17]

The chief weakness of Smith's oratory, however, was its vaporous content. He did not focus discontent on some program, he merely manipulated the discontented, thus aggravating social problems rather than helping solve them. He blamed scapegoats rather than exploring complex issues. He appealed to the irrational, exploiting his audience's frustrations and projecting their collective antipathy onto Jews, blacks, and Communists, while mouthing patriotic platitudes.[18] He said little that was original; his magic was in his delivery. One journalist concluded: "He says nothing at all and says it very emphatically."[19]

Smith possessed great vitality, but he so taxed himself physically and mentally that he finally began to lose his stamina and enthusiasm. An American Jewish Committee informant who heard Smith speak in Tulsa in 1952 wrote, "Five, ten and fifteen years ago he was rated by competent observers as one of the nation's spell-binders. But, to be sure, he was the kind who inevitably must some day wear out. The long, terrific harangues he delivered required the expenditure of enormous energy and the man is now in his mid-fifties. Maybe he has burned himself out as far as the platform is concerned."[20] Smith's audiences too changed. In his younger days he could instruct people to applaud and they responded. By the 1950s, people were better educated and less credulous and they did not always react as he wished. Smith's type of oratory was out of date. Years later, reflecting on his career, Smith deplored the death of mass oratory. Speakers could no longer enthrall audiences of tens of thousands for hours. Such rallies had been displaced by television. "It saddens my heart to think that these great dramatic assemblies have about disappeared in our national life," Smith concluded.[21]

But for his vanity and obstinacy, Smith might have become an effective television crusader on the scale of Jerry Falwell, Oral Roberts, or Jimmy Swaggart. He believed that a middle-aged man like him should not be seen on television because he was not "slick" and "pretty." He thought television permitted little margin for error and magnified every mistake.

In retrospect, Smith's fear of television was a strategic mistake; the medium could have arrested his decline.

Faced with the declining popularity of his rallies and his unwillingness to utilize television, Smith felt that he could reach people most efficiently by writing tracts. After the early 1950s he rarely spoke publicly. "Meetings as such, are not a fundamental part of our Movement," he wrote to his mother, "because there is no way for a person to get around the country and talk to everyone. It is too slow. The way to meet people is with millions of tracts, and that is what we are doing."[22] "For the cost of one meeting I can get out a million pieces of literature," he explained. He already had a large mailing list, and the number of new supporters he could add through public rallies was not large enough to justify a major investment of time and energy.[23]

Smith became one of the most prolific polemicists in America. He claimed to have written over five hundred books, tracts, and pamphlets, 90 percent of each issue of *The Cross and the Flag*, and collected works that surpassed in length the *Encyclopedia Britannica*.[24] In sheer output, Smith ranked with Toynbee and the Durants. Quality was another matter. Few writers with so little literary skill have made such an indelible mark on so many people. Smith's style was sensational and simplistic, whether he was writing a paragraph for a hurried reader or a letter to President Roosevelt. His sentences were either short and choppy or verbose, tangled, and lacking in transitions. He made grammatical errors, misspelled proper names, omitted details such as places and dates, and quoted out of context. His words were like hordes of lemmings plunging over a cliff into the sea. If he wrote enough, Smith thought, he could fill up the ocean.

Smith condensed complicated issues into small tracts. Some were only lists; others were unconnected paragraphs bunched together. He relied on boldface type, large print, and color type as well as shocking headlines to entice readers to purchase his tracts. They were crude and heavy-handed, lacking erudition and overloaded with adjectives. Drew Pearson, for example, was described as "a low-grade, highly paid renegade, hypocrite, liar, blackmailer, character assassin working for the Jewish Anti-Defamation League."[25] There was little room for equivocation in Smith's writing. Congressman Francis Walter, chair of the Un-American Activities Committee, was called "one of the three most important men in America today," while a Jewish plan to divert the Jordan River was "one of the ten most immoral acts in human history."[26]

Smith's frequent exaggeration and use of such adjectives as *super*, *great, terrific, sensational*, and *colossal* detracted from his style. He used a few favorite phrases repeatedly: *sappy, illogical, insipid sentimentalist*. Sometimes Smith used words he did not understand. He called everyone he opposed an "enigma," apparently believing the word had pejorative connotations. "Harry Golden of Charlotte, North Carolina, is a Jewish enigma,"[27] he wrote; "the late Albert Einstein was an enigma and his memory is an enigma."[28] Smith could not sustain a thought without resorting to clichés; he recycled the same ideas in every issue of *The Cross and the Flag*. He was an agitator, not a scholar; a propagandist, not a journalist.

Smith cranked out his autobiography, *Besieged Patriot*, his tracts, and his magazine essays with a methodical, assembly-line consistency. Most of his writing referred to current events that he read about and regurgitated, with his own embellishment and interpretation. His essays were compilations of rumors he had heard or read in both respectable news magazines and lunatic-fringe publications, stirred together then poured out like a witch's brew.[29]

Smith's writing was sophomoric and subjective, his proposed solutions ludicrous. His answer to racial hatred was suppression of blacks; to poverty, ignoring the impoverished; to unemployment, forced labor camps; to poor education, segregated schools; to terrorism, counterterror; to crime, locking up every suspicious person; to corruption, ferreting out conspiracies. The villains were always the same, only the details of their crimes and their insidious alliances changed.

Smith's credibility was further damaged by his tendency to believe anything said by an ally, but nothing said by a foe. He refused to believe *The New York Times*, while accepting "facts" that appeared in Conde McGinley's *Common Sense*. He seldom checked sources, claiming that he had developed a "sixth sense" that could intuitively distinguish truth from falsehood. He conveniently invented "bridges" between accurate and spurious sources and filled in the gaps with imagination.

Smith did not confine his exaggerations to attacks on his enemies. After Robert Warner, director of the Bentley Historical Library, visited Smith in Eureka Springs and perfunctorily complimented his "Sacred Projects" there, Smith wrote his relatives, "The head of the historical department of the University of Michigan, together with his wife, visited us shortly before we left Eureka Springs the last time. They were so carried away with the Art Gallery as well as the Passion Play and the Statue that they pronounced all three of them as positively the greatest things of their kind in the world and impressive beyond imagination."[30] But Smith did not always have to exaggerate what he heard or read, since many of his sources were highly sensational and inaccurate to begin with. He used material from the files of J. B. Matthews and Allan Zoll, collectors of right-wing publications, and utilized the large library Carl Mote bequeathed to Opal Tanner, who in turn gave it to Smith.[31] Smith confined his reading on current events to *The Chicago Sun, The Chicago Tribune, PM,* and *Time* and *Life* magazines.[32] He also gleaned material from government publications, particularly those of the House Un-American Activities Committee, the Senate Internal Security Committee, and the Attorney General's list of subversive organizations. He used the files of the California State Un-American Activities Committee and the Louisiana Joint Legislative Committee on Segregation. Sometimes he had friendly politicians insert his "research" in the *Congressional Record*: then, when he was asked to document a statement, he cited the *Congressional Record*.[33]

Smith often evaded requests for sources. "Every sentence that appears in *The Cross and the Flag* is documented and you can gamble on its accuracy," he told one reader, "but I cannot afford the research staff required to peruse the files and dig out materials such as requested by you in your letter of March 22."[34] He wrote fellow bigot Joseph Kamp, who asked Smith to confirm a source, "I do these things on the run and sometimes I forget where I put them; but I know it was documented."[35] If Smith did have files documenting everything he wrote, they do not survive in the comprehensive collection of his papers bequeathed to the Bentley Historical Library.

Some readers wanted Smith at least to footnote sources that were not confidential, but Smith never footnoted anything. He explained to a reader in 1970, "We would be only too happy to quote newspapers and periodicals whose material we use in footnotes, but the Jews have arranged a formula to have me sued every time I quote a metropolitan newspaper for copyright infringement. In our files, however, we have background evidence to support everything I say."[36] Smith occasionally used research assistants, but they were no less prejudiced than he. They undertook research not with an open mind but to confirm their prejudices. When Smith wanted information, he wanted it immediately. He wrote his researcher Ralph Baerman in 1947: "Rush, rush, rush any kind of a picture of Langston Hughes, especially if the picture makes him obviously a Negro."[37] He made an equally brusque request of Don Lohbeck: "I am preparing a tract on the subject COMMUNISM IS JEWISH. I want a profile of Karl Marx, Trotsky, Felix Frankfurter, and Bela Kun."[38]

Other than the few newspapers and magazines he read consistently, Smith's reading was serendipitous. He liked short, easy-to-read books with large print and few footnotes or statistics; he rarely read books cover to cover. He never read for pleasure—only a handful of novels in his entire life. He was not much of a student of the Bible: he lacked the patience to read it regularly, and most of his biblical quotes were acquired secondhand. Smith was most interested in sensational and unscientific books that attacked Jews and their Gentile allies. His favorites were Henry Ford's *The International Jew* and *The Protocols of the Learned Elders of Zion*.[39]

Smith also read some books dealing with blacks and segregation of the races. He preferred outdated works by Southern scientists that described the inferiority of Negroes. When asked for an authority on race, Smith suggested the 1930 edition of the *Encyclopedia Britannica*, commenting that later editions had been "tainted" by leftist writers.[40] Smith's favorite books about blacks included *You and Segregation* by Herman E. Talmadge; *Color, Communism, and Common Sense*, sold at American Opinion bookstores, which argued that racial integration was a Communist plot; Wesley C. George's *The Biology of the Race Problem*, which argued that blacks were genetically inferior to whites; and Carleton Putnam, *Race and Reality: A Search for Solutions*, which contended that race-mixing would destroy the white race. He also liked *God, the Original Segregationist*, written by a Southern Baptist minister who was also president of the Citizens' Council of America for Segregation.

Smith had a small collection of books about Communism. He recommended W. Cleon Skousen's *The Naked Communist* to readers of *The Cross and the Flag*. His favorite book on the subject, because it also discussed the "Jewish question," was John Beaty's *The Iron Curtain over America*. He liked Beaty's book because the author pretended to be a scholar. Smith sold more copies of *Iron Curtain* than any book he peddled other than *Protocols* and *The International Jew*.

Much of Smith's "research" consisted of clippings he received from readers. "I have the best research staff on earth," he once said: "I have people who send me clippings and materials from every nation on earth and every state in the nation."[41] He expressed his gratitude to one supporter by claiming, "If I had to hire people to do the research that is done for me by my friends, it would cost thousands and thousands of dollars."[42]

Some of Smith's "researchers" were crackpots. The letters that accompanied the clippings were often written by angry, bitter people. Many did not include the sources of their clippings, but Smith never questioned the clippings' veracity. Sometimes he did not even read the entire clipping, only passages underlined by his staff.

In 1942, Smith began publishing *The Cross and the Flag*, to which he subsequently devoted most of his literary efforts. He started the magazine because his radio talks were being censored and the conventional press was hostile. He wrote U.S. Senator Rush Holt that his magazine would be more aggressive than his Sunday night broadcasts. "I will praise Heaven on Sunday night and cuss Hell in the magazine," he explained.[43]

Smith chose the title *The Cross and the Flag* because these two objects symbolized the most important values in his life and also, he said, because he had been "inspired" by an angel. While he was agonizing over a title, "one morning in my den, as though an angel had whispered in my ear, the words came: 'The Cross and the Flag.' " "In my imagination and mind's eye the words 'Cross and Flag' emblazoned themselves in the sky," he continued; "they reproduced themselves on the ceiling of my room through the instrumentality of a visionary eye. They burned like fire. They symbolized the battle cry of victory."[44]

The Cross and the Flag was a family project. In the first issue Smith listed himself as editor and Bernard Doman, his office manager, as an associate editor. Smith's wife, Elna, Doman's wife, and Smith's teenage son, Gerry, were also associate editors. Smith wrote in the first person, including homilies about himself and his family. He devoted page 2 of each issue to an editorial celebrating his faith in Christ.[45]

The Cross and the Flag was slightly smaller than a tabloid, with enormous headlines. Published on the fifteenth of each month, it was mailed out on the twentieth. At first Smith planned a number of departments: a quiz, a section on biblical prophecy, a survey of current events, letters, and announcements of his speaking engagements. Soon he found this format overly structured, however, and abandoned the departments in favor of short editorials and reprints of speeches.[46]

Smith's first issue was violently isolationist, but not blatantly anti-Semitic like later issues. Printed on cheap pulp because of the paper shortage, the magazine was sixteen pages long; later it would be twice that length. It sold for twenty-five cents.[47] Smith experienced difficulty finding printers for his magazine during the war. For his first issue he used a commercial printer, who was intimidated out of printing the next issue. The second printer he engaged also published only one issue; and the third refused to deliver an issue already completed until he was physically threatened by Smith. Smith finally found a Jewish printer who accepted his business but demanded a kickback and used black market paper.[48]

After the war Smith hired a new printer, E. E. Manney of Fort Worth, Texas. Manney, who also printed *The Defender* for Gerald Winrod, printed *The Cross and the Flag* until the early 1950s. In 1951 Don Lohbeck and Opal Tanner created a private company to handle printing, but the venture failed and they sold their equipment at a loss. After moving his headquarters to California, Smith employed Britta N. Robertson, who printed Christian literature. She was the most reliable printer he used; her son, Charles F. Robertson, went to work for Smith and remained his loyal assistant until Smith died. But the Robertsons' capacity was limited, so in 1962 Smith bought his own equipment. He purchased twenty-five machines, each capable of turning out from two to ten thousand printed pages per hour, and he operated them around the clock every day, including Sundays. Until Smith purchased an envelope-stuffing machine a few years later, his mailing was done by a crew of volunteers who worked for three to five hours at a stretch, one to three times a month.[49]

From its birth in 1942 until its demise in 1977 The Cross and the Flag operated at a loss. Subscriptions cost only two dollars per year until 1974, when Smith raised the price to three dollars. The magazine cost between four and six dollars per copy to print and mail. Smith refused to accept paid advertisements. He launched the monthly with a few thousand dollars contributed in small amounts by supporters. Once he was forced to borrow money on his car to meet printers' bills.[50]

Although The Cross and the Flag did not earn a profit, it was successful in terms of circulation, influence, and longevity. It had the largest circulation of any extreme right periodical and more subscribers for most of its life than The Nation or The New Republic. It began with a modest paid circulation of 7,000; each member of Congress was mailed a free copy. By 1951 it had 13,500 subscribers and grew steadily. In the early 1940s The Cross and the Flag was hawked on the streets of Detroit by former peddlers of Social Justice, but for most of its life newsstand owners considered it too controversial to handle, fearing boycotts. Smith worked hard to increase circulation. In the 1950s he initiated a "prayer file," asking people to send him their mailing addresses so that he could pray for them. Everyone in the prayer file, of course, was added to the mailing list of the Christian Nationalist Crusade and received requests for money and subscription forms.[51]

In the late 1940s Smith began listing Don Lohbeck as editor of The Cross and the Flag, although Smith himself still wrote most of the copy and made editorial decisions. Lohbeck handled technical and mechanical tasks and wrote a one-page editorial for each issue. In 1953 Charles F. Robertson became editor, but he contributed even less content than Lohbeck. Smith never paid for articles; nevertheless, he received many unsolicited essays from novices, some of them crackpots, which he printed without checking their authenticity.

Articles appearing in The Cross and the Flag had titles like "Beasts in the Street" (about black crime) and "Persistent Poisoners" (about water fluoridation). Smith also included an essay on the Fourteenth Amendment (claiming that it had been illegally ratified) and one entitled "Abe Lincoln and the Rothschilds" (claiming that Jewish bankers precipitated the Civil War).[52] Smith explained the purpose of his monthly: "This is not a church periodical, although we support the church. This is not a doctrinal publication, although we believe in the great fundamental doctrines of Christianity. This is a political periodical which believes that the only redemption that can save America is a statesmanship based on the dynamic of man's faith in God as revealed through Jesus Christ."[53]

In addition to his magazine and his own tracts, Smith reprinted and sold cheaply many books and tracts written by other right-wingers. He did not ask their permission, but most of these authors were happy to have their works publicized. A sampling of the literature Smith sold and gave away includes: *The Plot to Abolish the United States* by Joseph P. Kamp; *Two-Party Treason* by Don Lohbeck; *Trial on Trial* by Lawrence Dennis and Maximilian St. George; *The Anti-Defamation League and Its Use in the World Communist Offensive* by Robert H. Williams; *The World Hoax* by Ernest Elmhurst; *The Third Zionist War* by George W. Armstrong; and *Alien Minorities and Mongrelization* by Marilyn Allen.[54] Smith saturated the extremist market. His Nationalist News Service, launched in 1945, provided free copy to some two hundred right-wing dailies and weeklies four times a week. Consisting of one-paragraph commentaries condensed from clippings and providing a nationalist slant on current events, it established the interpretive context for hundreds of small hate publications.[55] Other right-wing extremists mined Smith's pamphlets, press releases, and *The Cross and the Flag*, republishing their contents. Smith advertised his literature in their journals, including Gerald Winrod's *The Defender* and Conde McGinley's *The Broom*.[56]

It is not likely that many people who read Smith's literature for the first time were converted to his cause unless they were already prejudiced. Smith once wrote a young woman to whom he sent a dozen copies of *The Cross and the Flag* for distribution: "Please do not hand the magazines to people who need conversion. Our problem in America is rather to crystallize the people who already feel like we do."[57]

Smith identified a constituency and consistently played to it, but the shrillness of his voice limited his appeal. His support rose and fell from the isolationism of the 1940s through the McCarthyism of the 1950s, the civil rights movement of the 1960s, and the white backlash of the 1970s. All the while he continued to churn out propaganda and spin off conspiracy theories. His mastery of the art of public relations intensified his influence, but it is difficult to gauge the effects of Smith's emotional appeals. People are motivated by many things, often a combination of things, and to blame incidents such as the Detroit race riot of 1943 or the lynching of blacks in the South on Smith's tirades is speculation at best. Perhaps we can safely say that Smith helped create a climate that delayed the drive for racial equality and sometimes deflected well-meaning people into anti-Semitism.

Smith was essentially a "counter-reformer," opposing change and ferociously defending racist and fundamentalist values. If there was some inconsistency in his pilgrimage from fundamentalism through wealth sharing to the role of evangelical entrepreneur, one thing remained constant: his life was a process of ego gratification. He was never satisfied with praise; he felt compelled to sway the next audience, convert the next congregation, dazzle the next interviewer. His movement failed to survive after his death because he was unable to share power. Thus, for all of his oratorical gifts and his dedication to writing, he never defined a positive, tangible purpose in his work. For him, the power and the glory were in the crusade that consumed his life.

For most of his life Gerald Smith was not wealthy. He surrendered financial security when he left the ministry for politics, and for the twenty years following the death of Huey Long he needed to raise money to remain ahead of his creditors. When he left Louisiana for New York City, he made contacts with a few wealthy businessmen who financed his crusades against labor unions and Communism. But after Pearl Harbor Smith's position appeared unpatriotic and some of his backers deserted him under pressure from the government. After 1941, Smith relied upon small gifts, most under ten dollars. It was difficult for Smith's enemies to stem the flow of small, grassroots gifts, but it was also difficult for Smith to raise money quickly.

Smith's money-raising success lay in his direct mail solicitations. He pioneered money-by-mail long before the contemporary "New Right" entered the arena: doubtless he would have been a prodigious fundraiser by computer. Limited by technology and the number of staff he could afford, he nonetheless compiled one of the largest mailing lists of the far right, twenty thousand names by 1944, two hundred thousand by 1949, and three million by 1960.[58]

Smith began assembling his list from the list of Dr. Townsend's supporters. Later, he obtained Father Coughlin's mailing list, and through the years he received those of Carl Mote, George Deatherage, Congressman John E. Rankin, Myron Fagan, James True, William Kullgren, Frederick Kister, and Gerald Winrod. Some of these fellow crusaders freely gave their lists to Smith; others he obtained by planting supporters in their offices.[59]

Smith's lists of donors were categorized by city, state, region, occupation, amount contributed, and length of time since the last gift. Anyone who wrote to Smith, purchased literature, or subscribed to *The Cross and the Flag* wound up on his mailing list.

As his speaking career ebbed, Smith turned to the written word to win support and cash contributions. A prolific, meticulous, prompt letter-writer, he treasured his correspondence both because it brought him money and because it was his only contact with the masses who supported him. No matter where he was or what he was doing, he sent out three financial appeal letters every month. He begged for money, flattering the recipients by suggesting they were privy to sensitive, confidential information. Smith's form appeals were more personal than those that appeared in *The Cross and the Flag* or in his tracts. He used different letters for big, small, and new contributors. Sometimes he offered free books, tracts, certificates, calendars, and pictures of himself and his wife, asking for a "small donation" to cover mailing costs. Smith knew that true believers would donate more than he might charge and that this method gave them a personal stake in his movement.[60]

Smith's letters were hard sell and alarmist: the destiny of America hung in the balance; the only thing that could prevent a Communist dictatorship in America was the Christian Nationalist Crusade, and it needed more money to continue operating. Smith told his supporters that no financial sacrifice was too great—danger threatened, but he knew God and "patriots" such as the reader were on his side. The money was needed immediately—air mail. "You should not hesitate to give all you have, if need be," Smith wrote in 1949, "because if we lose this fight against Communism and this Christ-hating conspiracy, your money won't be any good anyway, and your life won't be worth two cents except in its relation to the great eternal values made possible by our Lord Jesus Christ."[61] Smith apparently had no qualms about frightening people into sending him money they needed themselves. He alienated some people with his alarmist messages, but he knew his readers well. Many had a limited education and read only sporadically, but they responded to his simplistic fundraising letters.[62]

Smith's work was not complete when he received money in the mail. A contribution qualified supporters to receive follow-up letters. Those who gave less than ten dollars were sent form letters and literature. Major contributors received form letters with postscripts designed to appear personal. Smith had individualized letters for different regions and states and for givers of more than a hundred dollars. The smaller the gift, the shorter the letter.[63]

In addition to direct mail solicitations, Smith received money from subscriptions to *The Cross and the Flag* and from the sale of tracts. He did not receive honorariums for his speeches, but he accepted reimbursements for travel and usually passed a collection plate, although he rarely grossed more than a few hundred dollars.

Smith's Christian Nationalist Crusade (CNC) was required by federal law to register and to file public financial reports quarterly with the Clerk of the U.S. House of Representatives. The law required that Smith furnish a list of all contributors of a hundred dollars or more. From these reports we can reconstruct a description of his gross income and how he used it.

In 1937, when he settled in Detroit, Smith paid $500 per week for a regular radio program and an additional $96,000 for a series of twenty special broadcasts. He spent $300–$500 a week for printed matter and about equal amounts for postage and for office expenses. He maintained a suite in the Detroit Leland Hotel ($150 per month) and rented a small home. By 1939, Smith had a staff of thirty-eight, broadcast on the radio twice weekly, and staged frequent mass rallies. He once paid $5,200 to use Detroit's Olympia Auditorium for a large rally.[64]

After his failure to win election to the U.S. Senate in 1942, Smith's income declined, but his expenditures remained high. Smith claimed that his major funding was provided by fifty thousand small contributors who gave from $.10 to $10 each. In 1942 his weekly expenses amounted to $500 for radio broadcasts and between $500 and $1,000 for payroll, printing, postage, and publishing. He had no source of income other than his contributors, who supported his wife, his son, and his elderly parents.[65]

In 1944, Smith ran for president as the candidate of his own America First Party. The party spent $10,953.00 to finance his campaign and continued to build for the future after his symbolic effort, reporting expenditures of $73,762.35 in 1945 and $77,980.10 in 1946, primarily for travel, hotel accommodations, rental of halls, printing, and postage. Smith's loose bookkeeping attracted the attention of the Internal Revenue Service, which billed him $1,789.23 for unpaid taxes in 1944 and 1945.[66] The America First Party loaned money to *The Cross and the Flag*, and Smith personally loaned money to the party.[67]

In 1947 Smith abolished the America First Party, replacing it with the Christian Nationalist Crusade. The following year his gross income increased substantially, reported at $110,527.85, with 104 donors giving more than $100 each (but most less than $200). The largest single donation was $650. He received $500 from Judge George W. Armstrong, a wealthy Texan and racist pamphleteer, and $500 from the publishing company owned by Rev. Harvey Springer.[68]

When Smith was hospitalized in 1949 for the removal of a large tumor on his back, his confinement prevented him from fundraising for several months. A major cash flow crisis resulted. When he returned to work he found that he was not receiving enough money to meet payrolls. Although he was still attracting about the same number of contributors, they were giving smaller amounts. Smith ordered Don Lohbeck to lay off some of the St. Louis staff, reduce the size of *The Cross and the Flag* by one-half, and discontinue the *Washington Newsletter*. He postponed payments to his printer, stopped sending letters by air mail, and instructed Lohbeck to make no purchases without his explicit authorization. Finally, he appealed to several rich supporters for emergency loans. By the end of 1949 he was back in the black. That year he took in $90,543.09 and spent $87,744.13.[69]

After Smith surmounted his money problems in 1949, his collections rose above the $100,000 level and never again dipped below it. He now rented two headquarters, one in St. Louis and one in Los Angeles, and commuted irregularly to each city from his home in Tulsa. He instructed his staff by mail and phone; his yearly telephone bills amounted to more than $2,000. He purchased hundreds of copies of extremist books and pamphlets from Joseph Kamp, Robert H. Williams, Ernest Elmhurst, Joseph Stoffel, Frederick Kister, Ron Gostick, and Judge Armstrong.[70]

Smith's best year of the decade was 1952, when he took in $202,359.71. The booming economy and the presidential election stimulated people to give. California contributors, many from the Los Angeles area, supplied the largest number of big gifts. Other major contributions came from the West and Midwest, with few from the South and none at all from the Northeast. Smith received four contributions over $1,000, two between $600 and $1,000, and six between $400 and $600. The only identifiable extremist on the list was Judge Armstrong, who gave $250.[71]

Smith never shared his wealth with his employees. The Labor Department filed suit against him for paying employees less than the minimum wage, for refusing to pay overtime, for hiring an underage person, and for keeping inadequate records.[72]

Smith's receipts declined after 1952 but remained relatively stable throughout the 1950s. He reported $185,369.77 in 1953; $155,135.82 in 1954; $165,254.77 in 1955; $173,967.12 in 1956; and $189,419.32 in 1957. For most of the period, contributions of $100 or more constituted about one-third of his gross income. He had a surplus at the end of each year. Smith paid himself a salary of $14,033.75 in 1957 and thereafter gave himself yearly wage increases averaging about $2,000.[73]

Smith grossed only $181,904.78 in 1960, but his contributions climbed steadily for the rest of the decade. During this period contributors from

California gave about one-half of the donations of more than $100. Smith received several dozen gifts of over $1,000 from Texas, and he also remained strong in the Midwest, especially in Michigan and Illinois.[74]

In 1965, a typical year, Smith took in $298,266.15, of which $101,673.48 was in amounts of over $100. He received forty-one contributions of over $400; eleven were from California. He expanded his field to the Pacific Northwest and continued to receive large amounts of money from Texas. He also received a few gifts from abroad, including three from Canada, two from Brazil, one from France, and one from South Africa.[75]

Smith paid himself $23,684.14 in 1965. For the first time his report showed expenditures in Eureka Springs, Arkansas, where he was beginning his *Christ of the Ozarks* and other Sacred Projects.[76] After he built his Sacred Projects and founded the nonprofit Elna M. Smith Foundation to handle donations, he began to mix funds from his religious and political movements. In 1966 the Christian Nationalist Crusade loaned $42,300.00 to the Smith Foundation; the loans continued for the next four years. Smith deliberately confused those who asked how his Sacred Projects in Eureka Springs were financed. He refused to divulge the cost of the *Christ of the Ozarks* and evaded questions about the specific source of its funding.[77]

In 1968, Smith paid himself $27,868.48, his highest salary to that date. His chief expenses were for mailing and handling ($76,454.84) and postage ($51,084.62). The CNC loaned $27,700.00 to the Elna M. Smith Foundation. Some of Smith's expenditures reflected changes in his movement. He gave $200 gifts to Mrs. Robert Hyde, wife of the director of his Passion Play in Eureka Springs, and to the wife of Roland Lee Morgan, his California office manager. He paid $1,500.00 for a gift for Charles W. Winegarner, whom he was grooming as his successor, and loaned $600.00 to Morgan. Smith donated $275.00 to the George Wallace for President Committee and gave an additional $500.00 to another Wallace committee. He purchased literature from the Palestine Arab Delegation in New York City ($52.00); the National States' Rights Party in Savannah, Georgia ($50.00); and Patriotic Publications out of Dallas, Texas ($314.34). His travel expense reports indicate that he traveled chiefly by car and stayed close to Los Angeles and Eureka Springs. The only major hall rental reported was for Embassy Auditorium in Los Angeles ($1,486.50).[78]

As Smith entered the last decade of his life he was financially independent and living comfortably. In 1970, he paid himself $27,975.95 and charged all of his expenses either to the Christian Nationalist Crusade or the Elna M. Smith Foundation. Total donations to the CNC set a record, $356,812.94, and at the end of the year he had his largest surplus on hand, $58,948.36. He had a record number of contributors of more than $100

Table 1. Smith Finances, as Reported to Congress

Year	Gross	Total Gifts over $100	No. of Gifts over $400	No. of Gifts over $1000	Smith's Salary
1952	$202,359.71	$ 61,874.70	14	3	$ 9,198.17
1953	183,369.77	36,874.70	0	0	—
1954	155,135.77	37,856.53	0	0	—
1955	165,254.77	50,834.54	0	0	—
1956	173,967.12	—	0	0	—
1957	189,419.32	39,386.08	10	1	14,033.74
1958	172,687.19	43,245.22	10	0	15,580.69
1959	168,743.57	52,143.12	13	1	17,798.11
1960	181,904.78	57,838.40	24	3	16,011.02
1961		Data missing from file			
1962	229,059.98	80,315.87	31	3	18,582.15
1963	246,730.27	91,445.06	—	—	—
1964	268,898.19	88,444.23	38	7	24,497.76
1965	298,266.15	101,673.48	41	9	23,684.14
1966	304,627.26	103,348.83	41	9	26,163.78
1967	287,233.73	103,773.51	41	10	24,643.06
1968	305,882.66	121,889.24	60	8	27,868.48
1969	276,414.22	113,649.94	61	11	27,601.00

— Figures not available
Source: Christian Nationalist Crusade annual reports to the Clerk of the U.S. House of Representatives, 1952–69

(519), of more than $400 (65), and of more than $1,000 (14), and he received his largest individual donation ever, $5,000 from a Cincinnati man. His international appeal increased as well: he received gifts of more than $100 from Canada (5), England (2), South Africa (1), the Virgin Islands (1), and Saudi Arabia (1).[79]

Smith's books reveal increasingly complex relations between the CNC and the Smith Foundation. Many of his cronies were officers in both organizations. In 1970 the Christian Nationalist Crusade loaned $14,095.52 to the Smith Foundation and $1,085.00 to Charles Robertson, now living in Eureka Springs and supervising the Sacred Projects. Elna Smith loaned $2,600.00 to the CNC and borrowed $3,100.00 from it. The CNC loaned money to the Smith Foundation while increasingly borrowing from individuals. Its report to Congress shows that it incurred ten loans above $1,000, one over $2,000, one above $3,000, and one of more than $4,000.[80]

In 1971 Smith mailed a record number of tracts and books. The CNC employed a dozen people in Los Angeles, and there were half a dozen on the payroll of the Smith Foundation in Eureka Springs. Total wages paid to employees averaged between $1,200.00 and $1,300.00 per week. Individual salaries were low, even for those who had worked for him for decades. His long-time secretary, Opal Tanner White, earned $238.85

weekly; his part-time secretary, Renata Legant Martz, earned $55.77. His "nephew," Roland Lee Morgan, earned only $105.56, while his chauffeur and bodyguard, Mike Mountjoy, a wounded Vietnam veteran, made $90.00.[81]

The affairs of the CNC continued to be entwined with the Smith Foundation. Smith listed loans from the CNC to the Smith Foundation of $7,250.90; $4,100.00 was loaned to Elna Smith personally. In turn, Elna loaned $1,500.00 to the CNC.[82]

Smith took in $242,253.64 in 1972 and $345,502.24 in 1973. In the latter year he received his largest donation ever from a single donor, $28,658.99 from a T. Kennedy of Long Beach, California; his second largest contribution ever, $10,018.00, came from a retiree, C. Yangvik of Yucaipa, California. The CNC also received its biggest public bequest, $56,412.89 from the estate of Eva O. Muhle.[83]

The CNC received $331,308.85 in 1974 and spent $355,064.77, thus recording a rare deficit, but it remained solvent because of money on hand at the beginning of the year. Among the expenditures was $100 for literature from the Rev. Buddy Tucker, Knoxville, Tennessee, who spoke at Smith's funeral in 1976. In 1975 the CNC disbanded as a political action group and reorganized as a nonprofit corporation that would not run or support candidates for public office; therefore, it no longer needed to report its income and expenditures.[84]

Because some of his most faithful supporters passed away during the 1960s, Smith was able to live quite comfortably on bequests. Some rich people who were reluctant to support him publicly while they were living gave him or his wife substantial sums in their wills. He used this money to buy his home in Eureka Springs and to construct his Sacred Projects in the Ozark community.[85]

Most of the people who gave generously to Smith were political zealots of moderate wealth. Thomas F. Cadwalader, a Baltimore attorney who donated $745.00 in 1964, was an anti-Semitic supporter of Senator Joe McCarthy; he believed that the Order of the Illuminati had invented Communism. Cadwalader also contributed money to We The People, Young Americans for Constitutional Action, Maryland Citizens for States' Rights, Democrats for Goldwater–Miller, and the National Economic Council.[86] W. G. Kerchner, a disciple of William Dudley Pelley who gave regularly to Smith and bought many copies of The International Jew and other books from him, was a businessman and realtor living in Lenhartsville, Pennsylvania. Seventy-nine and retired in 1963, he sent Smith small sums regularly. In 1965 he gave money despite hospitalization for a serious bladder infection.[87]

Ernest F. Elmhurst, of New York, who was not wealthy, donated money to Smith, Pelley, Elizabeth Dilling, Charles B. Hudson, Gerald Winrod, Lyrl Clark Van Hyning, George Edmondson, and Eugene Sanctuary. He was a defendent in the sedition trial of 1944. A friend of C. Daniel Kurts, Joe McWilliams, Wesley Swift, J. B. Stoner, George Deatherage, George Lincoln Rockwell, Major Robert H. Williams, and Conde McGinley, Elmhurst secretly entered East Germany in 1952 and 1956 to observe conditions there. He organized help for German refugees and wrote anti-Communist tracts.[88]

Mrs. Edith Essig, a housewife in Alameda, California, was a consistent contributor to Smith and a prodigious letter writer. Once an organizer for the America First Committee, she was active in the Daughters of the American Revolution and the auxiliary of the Veterans of Foreign Wars. She became interested in politics during the New Deal era, fanatically opposing Franklin Roosevelt; she believed that the president had killed himself in order to escape the consequences of his policies.[89]

Thousands of small, anonymous donors constituted the bedrock of Smith's movement. Most of them contributed from $1.00 to $10.00 two or three times a year. A few of them tithed 10 percent of their income to Smith because they believed he was doing the "Lord's work."[90] Many of the letters Smith received along with the contributions were from poor people sending him their last pennies because they were convinced America's survival was at stake. One widow with an income of $100.00 per month gave Smith $10.00;[91] another woman sent him $30.00 although her electricity had been turned off.[92] A man who had to borrow money to survive apologized to Smith for not giving more, explaining that in the past he had given money he should have spent on his wife and baby.[93] An eighty-eight-year-old woman did without food to send a few dollars to Smith.[94] The sister of an old man dying of cancer of the colon sent Smith $50.00, explaining that this would doubtless be her brother's final contribution.[95] The old and the ill, the lonely, the depressed, and the hungry sacrificed to send money to Smith. Seeking security, hopeful that Smith's prayers for them would bring better times, they mailed in their dollars.

Smith's lists of hundred-dollar donors for 1973 and 1974 identified contributors by occupation; the categories most often cited were "housewife" and "retired." Auto workers, farmers, maintenance workers, teachers, ministers, babysitters, and disabled persons also gave. A truckdriver donated $489.00, a housewife $940.00, a millwright $229.00, and a cooper $111.50. Some sent their money in installments; a few even borrowed money to give to Smith.[96]

Smith himself was not reciprocally generous to those in need. One Florida man, who wrote that he had lost his government job and that his father had been fired by a Jewish firm because of their support for Smith, begged for help. Smith sent him $5.00.[97]

Smith believed that his crusade was more important than food, shelter, and transportation, and encouraged his followers to sacrifice. Fiercely devoted to his movement, he rejected offers to work for rich men who admired him. He did, however, allow himself perks and spent lavishly for his hobbies. He dressed well, drove a big car, owned large homes, traveled first-class, and slept in expensive hotels. He had a housekeeper and a cook and owned expensive and pampered pets—dogs, goats, and miniature horses.

On the other hand, Smith owned no stocks, bonds, or other investments, never took vacations, and spent little on personal entertainment. For much of his life he and his wife lived like an ordinary middle-class family in which the husband worked at a white-collar job. Smith did not own a home of his own until he moved to Tulsa in 1949. He purchased a nine-room brick house there for $25,000.00, using as a down payment $5,000.00 he had won in a libel suit against the *Wichita Beacon*. The house had a large lawn and Smith paid a caretaker to mow, rake, and water it and to tend a flower garden. He also paid a housekeeper. When he was away Smith put his dogs in an expensive kennel.[98]

Smith bought a second home, a Victorian mansion, in Los Angeles in the early 1950s, and for almost twenty years he maintained dual residency in California and Tulsa. Located in an exclusive neighborhood, his Los Angeles home was protected by locks, fences, and electronic safeguards, and his address was unlisted. The house was built into the side of a hill. One entered through the third floor, which consisted of a living and dining area, then descended to the master bedroom and Smith's office. The house was crammed with an incredible collection of Victorian glassware, Persian rugs, sculpture, jewelry, paintings, and overstuffed antique furniture. Smith's office was a book-lined enclave containing a desk, a tape recorder, and a large American flag tacked to the wall. The lowest level consisted of a single large guest bedroom.[99]

When he established summer residency in Eureka Springs, Smith sold his Tulsa home and bought a mansion known as Penn Castle, much like his Los Angeles home, although it was impossible to conceal his address in the small town. He purchased a guest house nearby and furnished it with artwork and paintings. Smith's chief hobby was collecting antiques. He found it relaxing and he often made purchases while driving between cities. His house was so cluttered with art objects that he would not permit people to visit him with their small children. His antiques collection was insured for $500,000.[100]

Smith knew little about art or antiques; he only enjoyed the appearance of luxury it afforded. If it would help capture the attention of the rich and influential, if it would help elevate Smith in their eyes (and in his own), Smith would flaunt his possessions. His chief objective was adulation, not money. He was not a stereotypical televangelist who soaks his followers primarily to lavish riches on himself. Smith worked out of compulsion, not to make himself rich; and his followers were likewise compulsive in their giving.

nine

Crusades for the Presidency

‡

Gerald Smith was fascinated by the office of President of the United States and was most determined and energetic while campaigning for a candidate he liked—or, more frequently, against a candidate he detested. From Huey Long's death in 1935 to Franklin Roosevelt's in 1945, Smith was obsessed with removing President Roosevelt from office. His hatred for Roosevelt was deep and emotional, far beyond simply opposing his policies. Smith loathed the president and accused him of evil intentions, corrupt acts, and endless ambition. In 1940 Smith predicted that if Roosevelt were reelected he "will likely be the head of the American Fascist State."[1] Every lazy loafer who wanted something for nothing was for Roosevelt, Smith wrote, but "practically everybody that goes to church regular, is willing to work hard, and takes a bath once a week is against Roosevelt."[2]

Fearing that if Roosevelt were reelected in 1940 he would involve the United States in war, Smith urged Republicans to draft an antiwar platform and to nominate an isolationist candidate. He considered running himself, claiming that some "men of great wealth and influence" wanted to back him, but (according to Smith) these industrial millionaires withdrew their support when the Roosevelt administration threatened their businesses.[3]

Unable to run himself, Smith initially backed Governor John W. Bricker of Ohio, a fiscal conservative, but Bricker lost the nomination to Wendell Willkie. Smith hoped at the very least to persuade the Republicans to adopt an antiwar platform—he even offered to write their platform for them. The Republicans, however, refused to make preparedness an issue and nominated Willkie on an internationalist platform. Smith, plainly disappointed, reluctantly backed Willkie "since there is obvi-

152

ously no other course for old-fashioned, God-fearing, baby-having Americans."[4]

Smith was even more disappointed when Willkie continued to espouse internationalism after his defeat, became a traveling emissary for President Roosevelt, and published a book, *One World*, that supported American membership in a world organization. Smith came to hate Willkie and set out to keep him from winning the Republication nomination again in 1944. Smith accused Willkie of entering into a covert alliance with Roosevelt, warning an audience in St. Louis, "I wouldn't be surprised to see Willkie as the Vice President with Roosevelt, and then Roosevelt resign to become President of the World with Willkie becoming President of the United States."[5]

Willkie denied Smith's ridiculous fabrications and welcomed his opposition. "Any candidate of the Republican party who does not repudiate the America First party and Gerald L. K. Smith," Willkie asserted, "cannot possibly be elected President of the United States."[6] Smith boasted that this "rash" statement cost Willkie the Republican nomination, leading to his defeat in the Wisconsin primary, after which he withdrew from the race.[7]

After Willkie dropped out, Smith turned his attention to selecting a suitable alternative. His America First Party, based upon a constituency that included Roosevelt haters, Jew-baiters, Anglophobes, and Russophobes, vowed to run an independent candidate if neither major party nominated a "nationalist." Smith hoped to be able to support the Republican candidate because he thought the Democrats would nominate President Roosevelt for a fourth term. But he wanted to have in place the machinery to safeguard his interests. The America First Party was to be a flexible tool used as dictated by the actions of the nominees of the major parties.

Prior to the Republican convention, Smith jockeyed for position, switching from candidate to candidate, finding his overtures rejected, and warning of the consequences of offending him. He asked Charles A. Lindbergh to run as the America First candidate, but Lindbergh wanted nothing to do with Smith.[8] Smith said that the World War I hero Captain Eddie Rickenbacker was "presidential timber" and issued press releases proposing a Lindbergh–Rickenbacker ticket or one headed by Rickenbacker. He did not even consult Rickenbacker, and the ace pilot had done nothing to encourage him.[9]

Smith also wrote Senator Gerald P. Nye suggesting he run for president. Nye responded that no party should select its candidate from a small state like North Dakota. He even expressed concern about his own reelection to the senate in 1944.[10] Smith then urged Colonel Robert McCormick, isolationist publisher of the *Chicago Tribune*, to become a candidate, and he organized a Republican Nationalist Revival Committee to promote McCormick for the Republican nomination. William J. Grace and Earl Southard led the committee, which also received support from Joseph McWilliams, former Christian Mobilizer leader, Maximilian J. St. George, the Chicago attorney who had defended McWilliams from an indictment of sedition, and Michigan congressman Clare Hoffman. Mc-Cormick was flattered by the attention but declined to become a candidate.[11]

Smith, Father Coughlin, and William Dudley Pelley all encouraged General Douglas MacArthur to run for president, but he refused.[12] Smith was also attracted to the isolationist Robert R. Reynolds. Reynolds, who had retired from the U.S. Senate, said that he was "flattered and honored" by Smith's overtures and agreed that a third party might be necessary. He joined Smith to create a National Congressional Committee to support "nationalist" candidates for Congress—but he finally decided that his five failed marriages ruled out any presidential aspirations of his own.[13]

Smith hoped to be able to support a mainstream candidate such as New York governor Thomas E. Dewey or Ohio governor John W. Bricker, and he issued flattering statements about them to test their receptiveness. Bricker had never heard of Smith, and Dewey unequivocally rejected his support. "The Gerald L. K. Smiths and their ilk must not for one moment be permitted to pollute the stream of American political life," Dewey told the press. "Such would be a betrayal of the sacrifice now being made on the battlefields of the world by millions of Americans who fight for the basic principles which these rodents would undermine."[14] Smith responded angrily that his "ilk" included such prominent isolationists as Robert McCormick, Arthur Vandenberg, Henry Ford, and Charles A. Lindbergh—but Ford and Lindbergh denied any connection with Smith.[15] Smith admitted that he did not know the meaning of the word *rodents,* but after consulting a dictionary he determined that Dewey had called him a rat.[16]

Smith was more and more a pariah whose support was a liability, yet he could not understand why no one wanted his endorsement. At the Republican convention in Chicago in the last week of June, he held a rowdy press conference to offer Dewey "one last change" for his support. Dewey rejected Smith's support, but he was nominated anyway.[17]

Smith's efforts at the Democratic convention in July were equally futile. He checked into Chicago's Blackstone Hotel, summoned a press conference, ordered the Democrats to "dump Roosevelt" (calling Burton K. Wheeler an acceptable candidate), and threatened to create a third party if they did not. Smith was booed when he advocated an isolationist foreign policy before the platform committee. The Democrats ignored his threats; the press was amused.[18]

Despite Smith's threats, the Democrats renominated President Roosevelt. Smith concluded that his only remaining alternative was to run himself as the candidate of the America First Party in order to protest the internationalism of both major candidates. On June 31 in Detroit, he staged a convention of Michigan adherents to the America First Party. The convention nominated him for president and several of his assistants for state offices, including governor, lieutenant governor, and secretary of state. Because only delegates from Michigan attended the conference, Smith announced that he would hold a second America First Party convention later in August, including delegates representing a national constituency. He explained that he had been nominated prior to the national convention in order to secure a place on the Michigan ballot before the filing deadline. If the second convention nominated someone else, Smith promised to step aside.[19]

On August 30, the America First Party held its "national" nominating convention, also in Detroit. Not surprisingly, Smith was unanimously nominated for president with Harry O. Romer, a former Coughlin organizer from a small Ohio town, as his running mate. A platform was "suggested" by Smith and adopted without opposition. (In fact, Smith published the platform in *The Cross and the Flag* prior to the convention!) The platform advocated "food before whiskey" and an investigation of the war policies of President Roosevelt. It called for a stop to using "the poor man's taxes to save the British Empire" and demanded that money be given to "our servicemen before milk for Hottentots."[20] It also proposed that the United States absorb Canada, buy Greenland, and accept strategic islands in the Pacific in lieu of payment of the allies' war debts.[21] Smith's platform on race relations advocated the "Abraham Lincoln Plan" to provide American blacks with a homeland in Africa carved out of British and French territory. Young blacks would be paid to emigrate. "No one," he wrote, "should get the impression that this is an anti-Negro plank."[22]

The most controversial plank was proposed from the floor by delegate Homer Maertz, a former Bundist and Silver Shirt with a history of mental instability. Maertz suggested that the government deport Jews who refused to leave America voluntarily and sterilize any who for exceptional reasons had to remain. This was too much even for Smith, who referred the proposal to a committee for further "research." The platform did, however, recognize a "Jewish problem" and suggested an investigation of the role of Jews in Communism, the media, and the New Deal.[23]

Smith selected the American bison as the emblem of his America First Party and wrote Secretary of the Interior Harold Ickes to ask if he could purchase a buffalo from Yellowstone National Park. Ickes sardonically replied that he doubted any decent buffalo could "bear such a stigma."[24] Still in a jocular tone, Ickes concluded, "I can see that it might be a matter of great public interest as to whether you accepted the buffalo in behalf of the party or whether it accepted you and, if so, how and where."[25] One of Smith's own delegates objected to his choice of the bison because "everybody knows the buffalo is extinct."[26] but a journalist pointed out that the buffalo was appropriate because the word was also a verb meaning "to bewilder or bamboozle."[27]

Smith was incredibly industrious for one whose cause was so obviously hopeless. He conferred in New York, traveled to Washington, and held mass meetings throughout the Midwest. His theme was invariably hate Roosevelt, win the war, bring the boys home, and fight Communism and the New Deal. Smith orated, threatened, cajoled, and pleaded, although all he accomplished was gratification of his own ego. He warned that it would be political suicide for any candidate to reject him, but not a single one accepted his support.

On election day Smith polled only 1,530 votes in Michigan and 251 in Texas, the only states where he was on the ballot. This was a miserable showing for a man who had won more than 100,000 votes in Michigan for U.S. Senator two years earlier. He ran behind the Prohibition and Socialist candidates in Michigan and even behind his own party's candidates for state offices. Some of his allies in Congress were also defeated.[28]

After this vindictive, poorly planned campaign, Smith severed his already shaky ties with the Republican Party and with friends such as Senator Vandenberg. Rather than accept the result, he rationalized his defeat on the grounds that there was a Communist and Jewish conspiracy against him. He became increasingly strident, finding himself in a vicious circle: the more virulent he became, the more isolated, and in his isolation he grew increasingly bitter.

Smith gloated over the death of President Roosevelt in 1945, and initially supported President Truman, whom he described as a plain-spoken, humble American who had grown to manhood on a farm in the Midwest. But Truman's liberal policies on civil rights and labor soon alienated Smith, although he never hated Truman personally as he had Roosevelt. The chaos Smith predicted for the Truman presidency did not materialize and Smith's prospects of gaining political power in 1948 were even slimmer than they had been in 1944. Since "America First" was dated and identified with World War II, Smith renamed his party the Christian Nationalist Party.[29]

In the spring and summer of 1947 Smith began to search for a candidate he could back in the presidential election the following fall. He thought Truman was well-meaning but surrounded by Communists. He saw some hope for the Republican Party provided it would nominate a nationalist. He detested Tom Dewey, whom he called "a phony squirt, Tom Thumb and hypocrite." Taft and Bricker were good men, Smith said, but neither had a chance to win. The best candidate the Republicans could nominate was General Douglas MacArthur.[30]

Smith believed that MacArthur would run if nationalists "drafted" him. "Without doubt MacArthur is the most popular citizen of the United States as well as being our most able public servant," he wrote.[31] He found sympathy for the draft-MacArthur movement in Judge George W. Armstrong, a reactionary Texas millionaire in steel, banking, cattle, and petroleum. Armstrong, who wrote anti-Negro books and tracts and advocated repeal of the Fourteenth and Fifteenth amendments, had once offered a small Mississippi college fifty million dollars if it would teach white supremacy and limit enrollment to white Christians. Smith attempted to persuade the millionaire to finance a MacArthur campaign. Although Smith flattered Armstrong, and although Armstrong liked Mac-Arthur, the wealthy Texan was cool to Smith.[32]

The issue of race dominated the Democratic national convention, where Southern delegates walked out in protest after a strong civil rights plank was adopted with the support of President Truman. The dissident Southerners met at Birmingham and created the States' Rights Democratic Party, dubbed "Dixiecrats" by the press.

Smith attended the Birmingham meeting as a self-appointed "delegate" from Oklahoma, but he explained, "I kept myself deliberately in the background because I was anxious to do nothing that would introduce extraneous controversy into the wholesome and historic gathering."[33] He traveled incognito under the alias Stephen Goodyear. But a key Smith aide, Jonathan E. Perkins, helped plan the convention, escorted speakers to the platform, and was a personal guest of Mississippi governor Fielding L. Wright at the governor's mansion.[34]

Smith boasted in his autobiography that "many people, even students of political history, can scarcely realize that I did the pioneer work which later resulted in the formation of the Dixiecrat Party in the South."[35] Smith's blatant bigotry actually made his support a liability, and Dixiecrat presidential nominee J. Strom Thurmond attempted to take the high road by rejecting Smith's endorsement.[36] Smith was "stunned and amazed" at what he considered Thurmond's ingratitude.[37] "This soft-headed fool who calls himself Governor of the State of South Carolina is a villain of the first order," he wrote. He charged that Thurmond permitted blacks to vote in South Carolina and concluded, "These wretched Jews of New York and their compromising politicians are invading the South and I am not so sure but what they are using Thurmond as their fifth column."[38]

Smith fervently opposed Henry Wallace, the former vice president who ran for president as the candidate of his own Progressive Party, endorsing racial equality and friendship with the Soviet Union. Smith failed in his attempt to keep Wallace's name off the Oklahoma ballot by charging that Wallace was a Communist.[39]

After the Dixiecrats rejected Smith's support, he announced that he would hold his own convention on August 20–21 in St. Louis and would nominate an independent ticket. He rationalized this strategy by claiming that the Dixiecrats represented a "sectional movement," whereas his following was nationwide. Smith had had a "vision" which revealed that the Christian Nationalist Party would take over America.[40]

Don Lohbeck, who had attended the Democratic and Republican conventions as Smith's representative, chaired the Christian Nationalist Party Convention and delivered the opening address. Just in his late twenties, Lohbeck was an accomplished demagogue with a rich, sonorous voice and an imagination second only to Smith's when it came to manufacturing Jewish atrocities. A slender man with piercing eyes and a dark, scowling face, he seemed always engrossed in deep thought. He ejected his words with the cold precision of a machine gun. Lohbeck emphasized the urgency of creating a party to save America from Christ-hating Jews and their Communist pawns. "If the only way that we can repudiate the mad secret promises of the mad politicians is by organizing a new political party," he spat, "then by the grace of God let's organize tonight the fightingest and the shoutingest political party that the world has ever seen!"[41]

Gerald Smith himself was the keynote speaker, and he addressed for about eighty minutes an audience of three hundred, mainly elderly women. He denounced "international Jews," Communists, the Marshall Plan, the principles of the New Deal, the Roosevelt family, and advocates of racial equality. His listeners booed the names of the late President and Mrs. Roosevelt and applauded vigorously when Smith proposed that Supreme Court Justice Felix Frankfurter and former Secretary of the Treasury Henry W. Morgenthau be indicted as "war criminals."[42]

Smith announced the Christian Nationalist platform and after stating each plank he asked the audience to applaud if they approved. They responded enthusiastically, and when Smith called for a standing vote to endorse the entire platform the delegates rose. The platform advocated the deportation of blacks and Zionist Jews. Ghettoes would be constructed for Jews remaining in the United States, and the housing shortage would be resolved by giving the homes of deported Jews to veterans. Other planks advocated abrogation of secret international agreements made by the late President Roosevelt, support of the Chiang Kai-Shek government in China, and the rebuilding of Germany to prevent Communist domination.[43] The ticket of Smith for president and Harry O. Romer for vice president was also approved by acclamation. There were no debates, no motions from the floor, and no other nominations.[44]

Smith even had a surprise speaker, General George Van Horn Moseley, a retired army man and anti-Semite, viewed by some bigots as a charismatic leader. Moseley, who had not been present at the earlier sessions, stunned the assembly by announcing that he supported Thomas E. Dewey for president. Unaware that Smith had been nominated by the Christian Nationalists, he huddled with Smith on the platform and then withdrew his support of Dewey.[45]

Bedridden for several months by food poisoning, Smith had to curtail campaigning and fundraising for his 1948 campaign. He was further hampered by the defection of some of his closest allies. Elizabeth Dilling broke with him, issuing a pamphlet describing sordid details of Smith's movement. Gerald B. Winrod, Lawrence Reilly, Upton Close, Jonathan Perkins and Harvey Springer joined Dilling in repudiating Smith. The superficial issue was that Smith kept money ostensibly raised for the common cause; the real issue was that Smith's ego would not permit him to share power or acclaim with other nationalists.[46]

When he ran for president the first time, in 1944, Smith conceded that he could not win that year but predicted victory in 1948. In 1948, he said he would triumph in 1952.[47] It strains credibility to believe that Smith actually thought his party would come to power, but he apparently did delude himself. If he did not win, Smith said, Communists would take over: "Unless we win, you and I and others like us will die before Communist mobs or in the rubble of atom bomb destruction, or be driven into the slavery brought on by a Red dictatorship," a form letter to his followers threatened.[48]

When Smith's predictions failed to materialize and Truman won, he attributed the Democratic victory to the "hidden hand" of the Jews, who had inspired the Republicans to nominate an internationalist ticket that was merely a carbon copy of the Democrats. "The evil hand of Satan's providence has given us as President Harry Truman, the ghost of Franklin D. Roosevelt," he wrote.[49]

Smith's disenchantment with President Truman grew stronger during Truman's second term. He claimed that Truman was president in name only: the "hidden hand" machine of Frankfurter, Baruch, and Morgenthau actually made the key decisions.[50] Smith especially hated Justice Frankfurter. "The 'brain' is Frankfurter," he wrote. "The 'idea man' is Frankfurter. The adviser is Frankfurter. Acheson is his man and Truman does what Acheson says. The 'trained seals' in the White House have learned that it is unpleasant and uncomfortable to say 'No' to Frankfurter."[51] And as if this weren't bad enough, Smith revealed that "Harry and his wife Bess went over and enrolled for a special course in the study of the Talmud under the direction of Rabbi Finkelstein."[52] Truman might even be tainted with Jewish blood. Just as he called Roosevelt "Rosenfeldt" and characterized Eisenhower as a "Swedish Jew," Smith maligned Truman by falsely insisting that his middle initial stood for "Solomon."[53]

Throughout Truman's term Smith planned to elect a nationalist, segregationist president in 1952. Two of his representatives, Don Lohbeck and John W. Hamilton, attended the States' Rights Democratic Convention in Jackson, Mississippi, in 1950, where arch-bigot Leander H. Perez delivered the keynote address, attacking Truman's Fair Deal program as "socialism." Despite efforts by Perez and others to hold the Dixiecrat electoral machine together, the party dissolved before the 1952 presidential campaign.[54]

With the coming election in mind, Smith termed 1952 "the most important year in the life of our young Nation."[55] His objective was to win the Republican presidential nomination for General Douglas MacArthur by avoiding primaries and using Taft as his "stalking horse." Smith encouraged Taft to enter the primaries and line up delegates, but he wanted to keep Taft's delegates just below the number needed for nomination by spreading word that a Jew ran Taft's office. He collected photographs of the Jew, a Mr. Martin, and circulated them among nationalists. Smith planned a deadlock between Taft and Eisenhower on the first ballot; then Taft would release his delegates to MacArthur and the general would win the nomination. As a front for his operation, Smith created a Draft MacArthur Committee. He corresponded with delegates, businessmen, and politicians, using the pseudonym Stephen Goodyear, urging them to support MacArthur.[56]

Smith wanted desperately to prevent General Eisenhower from gaining the nomination. His objective, he said, was to "stop Eisenhower, the man who has been picked by the Jews to become the world dictator."[57] He had many reasons for opposing Eisenhower: all the Jews were for him; he was the candidate of Jimmie Roosevelt; he was as much an internationalist as

Dean Acheson; he "gave Berlin to the Russians and lied about it"; he was brought into politics by Harry Hopkins, who was a personal friend of Joe Stalin; and his speeches were written by his brother Milton, who was a New Dealer.[58]

Smith was completely uninhibited in his attempts to spread rumors and lies about Eisenhower. He distributed a photograph of Eisenhower hoisting a glass of wine with Russian Field Marshal Georgi K. Zhukov near the end of World War II. The caption read, "Zhukov, Communist General, decorates drinking partner Eisenhower at Frankfurt, Germany."[59] Later Smith was less restrained, writing that Eisenhower "fraternized in drunken brawls with Zhukov."[60] Actually the photograph depicted a group of American, British, and Russian generals toasting the end of the war when the allied forces met, but it had been cropped to exclude everyone but Eisenhower and Zhukov.[61]

Smith's most infamous smear of Eisenhower was his accusation that the general was a "Swedish Jew." This fantastic claim was based on a facetious caption in the *West Point Yearbook* of 1915, in which Ike's roommate described him as "the Terrible Swedish Jew" as well as "the handsomest man in the Corps."[62] The West Point librarian explained that the reference was a gag, taken out of context by Smith—Eisenhower was Swiss by ancestry and Episcopalian.[63] Smith, however, insisted that Eisenhower was Jewish, and he offered a free subscription to *The Cross and the Flag* to anyone who could prove otherwise.[64] He wrote in his monthly in 1951 that "a dispatch out of London reveals that the leading paper of that city now admits that Eisenhower is Jewish."[65] Smith charged, "that Swedish Jew was picked as a five-star general by Roosevelt because he knew how to say 'yes sir' even if it was treason."[66]

Nor did Smith have much good to say about Richard M. Nixon, Ike's running mate. Smith had backed Nixon's campaign for Congress in 1946 and for the Senate in 1950, but Nixon had repudiated Smith's endorsement in the senatorial campaign.[67] In 1952 Smith wrote that Nixon was a "phoney investigator" of Communists. "His striking resemblance to Gromyko merely emphasizes the obnoxious impressions that this young man has made upon some of us," he concluded.[68] Nixon retaliated by stating in a nationwide radio broadcast that the nation was endangered "from those on the right, for example, who advocate racist theories—and I mean people like Gerald L. K. Smith."[69]

Smith and a staff of nine went to Chicago for the Republican National Convention, establishing headquarters near the law office of his friend Maximilian St. George. Don Lohbeck staged a large Christian Nationalist rally for MacArthur that attracted several hundred people. Lohbeck handed out cards that depicted a caricature of Eisenhower over a Jewish star, the word "Ikie" beneath, along with a list of Jews who supported Eisenhower. Smith claimed that Eisenhower was nominated because Taft, who had promised to withdraw in favor of MacArthur on the first ballot, had been led to believe that he could win by remaining in the race and thus had prevented MacArthur's nomination. Smith also claimed that Jewish money had bought Eisenhower the nomination.[70]

Smith was equally disappointed by the Democratic Convention two weeks later, to which he sent Don Lohbeck as his surrogate. Although Smith devoted more time and space to criticizing Eisenhower than to denouncing the Democratic ticket of Adlai Stevenson and Estes Kefauver, he believed the Democrats were also tools of the Jews.[71] "Adlai Stevenson was a political abortion," Smith later wrote in his autobiography. "He was the result of a combination of the vote-stealing corrupt political machine of Chicago, headed by the Jew Jake Arvey, and the Alger Hiss treason committee in Washington, D.C. He had the support of every appeaser, left winger and traitor."[72] Stevenson's running mate, Estes Kefauver, was even worse. "We have no genealogical report that would indicate that there was any Jewish blood in Kefauver," Smith wrote, "but he has the Jewish mouth, the Jewish nose, and the Jewish profile. He obeys Jews, he runs with Jews, he collaborates with Jews, he allows Jews to form his strategy planning, and he performs like a Broadway actor under the direction of a Jewish nightclub operator."[73]

After both major parties nominated traitors, Smith said, his only alternative was to enter a third-party ticket. He admitted that his ticket had little chance to win but explained that "if I were to put an 'X' mark beside the name of Eisenhower, knowing what I know, I fully believe that God would punish me for dereliction."[74] Instead of running for president himself, Smith instructed his followers at the Christian Nationalist Party Convention to nominate General Douglas MacArthur. The delegates did what they were told, although MacArthur himself did not encourage them—in fact he never even acknowledged his nomination. For vice president, the Christian Nationalist Party nominated state senator Jack B. Tenney of California, chairman of the California Committee on Un-American Activities, who had been a harsh critic of Gerald Smith before converting to Christian Nationalism. Tenney campaigned without MacArthur.[75]

MacArthur appeared on the ballot only in Missouri, Arkansas, Texas, North Dakota, and Washington; his name could be written in only in California. In California and Texas General MacArthur was also the candidate of the Constitution Party organized by Mrs. Lyrl Clark Van Hyning.[76] General MacArthur polled fewer than eighteen hundred votes out of the sixty million cast.[77] Smith was bitter about the poor showing, but he claimed he was proud to stand on principle. Several days after the election he wrote a friend that "the Judas goat Republicans have led the Republican sheep into the Baruch-Winchell slaughter house. You and I can always be thankful that we didn't help the anti-Christ in the consummation of this villainy."[78]

Despite MacArthur's pathetic showing and his refusal to accept Smith's support, Smith never lost his affection for the general. He wrote MacArthur long, flattering personal letters, usually answered by brief notes from MacArthur's secretary.[79] After begging for years for a personal meeting without much encouragement from the general, Smith finally saw MacArthur for about three hours in 1954 in his hero's suite in the Waldorf-Astoria Hotel. Smith claimed that they agreed on practically everything, and that as he departed MacArthur placed his hand on Smith's shoulder and said, "Never weaken."[80]

We must, of course, consider this account with considerable skepticism. MacArthur and Smith did meet but, judging by Smith's penchant for hyperbole, his account of that meeting is likely to have been highly exaggerated. It is possible that MacArthur approved of Smith and may actually have said "Never weaken," but it is unlikely that MacArthur knew much about Smith.

Smith's hatred of General Eisenhower did not abate when Ike became president. Smith promised his followers that he would fight Eisenhower as strongly as he had fought Roosevelt. Eisenhower, he wrote, had "liquidated" the "fearless patriot," Senator Joseph R. McCarthy. The president "passed the word down the line to give McCarthy 'the works.' "[81] Eisenhower's entire career was tainted, Smith claimed. He had been promoted in the military for sleeping with Anna Rosenberg, an Austrian-born Jewish woman who held a high position in the Defense Department. While president of Columbia University, he had "accepted without reserve an endowment of money from Communist Poland for the establishment of a 'Chair of Polish Studies.' " Smith went all the way back to 1909, reporting that on November 9 of that year young Eisenhower had condemned the Republican Party in a speech to the Young Men's Democratic Club of Abilene, Kansas.[82] President Eisenhower was so clever that he did not appoint Jews to high positions in his administration, Smith said; rather, hidden hand manipulators like Bernard Baruch worked out of sight. According to Smith, the fact that Jews were not in high positions proved that they were in control.[83]

Smith's California friend Wesley Swift used Eisenhower's heart attacks as an excuse to call him "sick in the heart, sick in the stomach and sick in the head." Swift also claimed that "it was God's doing that he had his heart attack right after his appeasement meeting with the Russian leaders."[84] Through surrogates, Smith established a Knowland for President . . . If Committee to support California senator William F. Knowland in the event that President Eisenhower did not seek reelection. He promised to urge his "400,000 supporters" in California to back Knowland, but Knowland repudiated Smith's endorsement, stated that he had no intention of running for president, and voted for Eisenhower at the Republican National Convention.[85]

As much as he hated Eisenhower, Smith could not support the Democratic nominee, Adlai Stevenson. Stevenson would say or do anything to obtain the Zionist vote, he claimed.[86] Unable to support either major party candidate or to find a suitable candidate who would accept his support, Smith himself ran once again for president on the Christian Nationalist ticket. His running mate was his employee, former minister Charles F. Robertson of Los Angeles. The Christian Nationalist platform followed closely a Smith tract entitled "If I Were President." He presumed to outlaw interracial marriage, guarantee white supremacy, limit immigration, dismantle the federal bureaucracy, investigate the Anti-Defamation League, abolish the income tax, and withdraw the United States from the United Nations. Smith insisted that a majority of citizens supported these planks but were left ignorant and powerless by the "Jew manipulators" who prevented the truth from reaching them. If elected, he promised, he would defy the Jews by using a New Testament to swear his oath of office.[87]

Smith failed to get on the ballot in any state because he either applied after the filing deadline or could not obtain the requisite number of signatures on a nominating petition. The folly was embarrassing—only eight write-in votes, all in California. Dejected, he told an interviewer that at the age of fifty-eight he was in the "twilight years" of his career and vowed never to run for President again. Though he did not run again, he continued to be active in presidential politics for the next twenty years.[88]

Smith supported Eisenhower when the president opposed the Israeli invasion of Suez in 1956. "In spite of all President Eisenhower's weaknesses and in spite of the fact that he is perhaps the world's number one puppet," he wrote, "the fact still remains that he opposed Israel policy when the Jews attempted to invade Egypt."[89] But Smith never forgave the president for appointing Earl Warren chief justice of the United States Supreme Court. Smith abhorred the decisions of the Warren court, which he termed a "nine-headed tyrant" for its rulings on pornography, civil rights, state sovereignty, and school prayer.[90]

Some extremists wanted to impeach Chief Justice Warren, but that was not enough for Smith: he proposed to impeach all nine justices and send them to prison.[91] "In days when men were men," he claimed, "certain members of our Supreme Court might have been shot for treason."[92] Smith's employee, Opal Tanner White, took a fifteen-hundred-foot-long petition advocating the impeachment of all nine justices to Washington, where she was photographed with the unfurled document on the steps of the House Office Building. She also appeared on Dave Garroway's *Today* program to discuss the petition. Smith instructed White on what to say, telling her, "I doubt seriously if any task has ever been performed by an American woman more important than this. You could live in history like Betsy Ross."[93]

Angered by racial desegregation and the increasing influence of civil rights leaders such as Rev. Martin Luther King, Smith attempted to promote through surrogates Arkansas governor Orval Faubus, a segregationist, for president in 1960. He created Faubus for President committees to raise money for a campaign. But Faubus lost interest when he learned that Smith was behind the movement.[94]

Smith opposed the nomination of Senator John F. Kennedy by the Democrats but assured his followers that Kennedy could never be nominated or elected President. According to Smith, all of the Kennedys were whiskey-drinking whoremongers, fake Catholics "soft" on Communism, and puppets of international Jews.[95]

Smith disliked the Republican nominee, Richard Nixon, almost as much as he detested Kennedy. Nixon, he wrote, had committed "unpardonable" sins by stating that there was no place for Gerald Smith and his followers in the Republican Party, by supporting the "liquidation" of Senator McCarthy, and by praising Martin Luther King.[96] Smith predicted that Nixon, if elected, would persecute good nationalists like Gerald Smith in order to prove that he did not appreciate their support. To Smith, Nixon was a "super-beatnik who seems to be a cross between Elvis, the Pelvis, and Franklin D. Roosevelt."[97] After Nixon lost the close election, Smith wrote to him, explaining that he had lost because he had alienated Smith's supporters. Smith told Nixon that although Christian Nationalists opposed Kennedy, many had not voted at all, nor had they worked for Nixon or contributed money to him.[98]

Smith attacked the Kennedy administration mercilessly. He charged that JFK was his father's puppet, even after the elder Kennedy's stroke. He also attacked the president's leftist advisers such as Theodore Sorenson and John Kenneth Galbraith.[99] Kennedy should not have signed a nuclear test ban treaty with the Russians because they would cheat, Smith said. In 1963, he began to circulate a petition calling for Kennedy's impeachment.[100] Smith claimed that his assassination was a plot by Jews and Communists, who hoped to blame it on the right. This would be an excuse to "liquidate" right-wing "patriots."[101]

In 1964, Smith initially supported George Wallace for president, distributing thousands of tracts for Wallace in the early primaries while writing fawning letters to the Alabama governor. "There is no man in public life since the late Huey P. Long, who was shot down at my side, whose gifts and capacities have impressed me as have yours," he wrote Wallace. "You are in a position to become the 'white man's Martin Luther King.' "[102] Despite this lavish praise, Smith later asked Wallace to withdraw in order to avoid taking conservative votes away from Barry Goldwater.

Smith said that Goldwater was the first presidential candidate in his lifetime worthy of respect. He praised Goldwater for voting against the civil rights bill, for not abandoning Joe McCarthy, and for not rejecting the John Birch Society. The enemies of Barry Goldwater, he wrote, were the same pagan Communists who opposed Gerald Smith. He did not even object to Goldwater's Jewish blood because the Arizona senator was a practicing Christian.[103]

Smith loathed Lyndon Johnson's Great Society and civil rights legislation, and he expressed shock when the Democratic National Convention nominated Johnson. "I saw pimps in command," Smith wrote. "I witnessed the glorification of whoremongers . . . mealy-mouthed Southerners behaving like Judas Iscariot on the night of our Lord's betrayal . . . fine self-respecting white citizens of Mississippi kicked out, and the bloc of blacks manipulated from New York and Moscow permitted to sit in their places."[104] The Great Society was anathema to Smith: "It strikes me that Hitler had national socialism without Jews and LBJ has it with Jews."[105] Johnson was successful in passing legislation only because he plied Congressmen with whiskey and women.[106] "I think he's guilty of murder, homosexuality, a wide variety of perversions, thievery, treason, and corruption," Smith wrote. He saw Johnson's Vietnam policy as fainthearted and self-serving. "I have such a low estimation of his character," he wrote, "that I believe that he would actually promote a sustained unvictorious war in order that the helicopter company in which his wife is the controlling stockholder might sell more helicopters."[107]

Despite Johnson's landslide victory, Smith did not regret supporting Goldwater. Johnson won, he wrote, only because the public did not know the whole story of his villainy. Had the president been in office longer at the time of the election, the voters would have recognized Johnson for the knave he was. But Smith was gratified because he believed "the Republican Party has become the white man's party" and "the Christian party."[108]

Smith was glad that Johnson did not seek reelection in 1968, but no other Democratic candidate—with the exception of George Wallace—

came close to gaining his approval. He had earlier described Hubert Humphrey in the most uncomplimentary terms: "Senator Hubert Humphrey of Minnesota is a gabby, repulsive, aggressive, offensive, arrogant, egotistical, over-ambitious, radical and opportunistic individual."[109] He dismissed Senator Eugene McCarthy as an appeaser and a "bad man."[110] Senator Robert F. Kennedy was even worse. According to Smith, if Kennedy were elected he would turn the treasury over to welfare loafers, encourage Communists, Zionists, and mongrelizers, and persecute such patriots as Gerald Smith. "I get the impression," Smith wrote of Kennedy, "that he has deliberately groomed his hair in a goofy manner to strike the sex chord impulse stimulated by the disgraceful and scandalous Beatles."[111] Smith also disliked Republican candidate Richard Nixon, but he believed that George Wallace, running on a third party ticket, would win enough electoral votes to throw the election into the House of Representatives. In fact, Smith was a Wallace elector in Oklahoma.[112]

By 1970, however, Smith had become a lukewarm supporter of President Nixon. He praised Nixon for appointing conservatives to the Supreme Court and for opposing busing, and he endorsed the President's Vietnam policy. He also admired Spiro T. Agnew, Nixon's vice president, who regularly attacked liberals and the media.[113] Smith found the Nixon family "wholesome" in contrast to the libertine Kennedys, but he was horrified by a photograph of African blacks kissing Pat Nixon while topless dancers entertained the First Couple.[114]

Smith even supported Nixon's internationalist foreign policy. He now believed that China and Russia were established regimes and that the only sane policy was to accept them and prevent them from expanding their empires.[115] He endorsed trade with them—we did not have to become Communists to trade with Communists, he argued.[116] Smith had come full circle to favor a pragmatic foreign policy—actually coming to support the United Nations. No longer an isolationist, he saw value in pitting one Communist superpower against the other. He even had kind words for Henry Kissinger. "Although Kissinger is a Jew, he is one of the greatest diplomats that ever lived," Smith wrote.[117]

Smith initially supported George Wallace for president in 1972, but after Wallace was shot and crippled he shifted his support to President Nixon. "When I was faced with a situation in 1972 where I had to choose between President Nixon and George McGovern," he wrote, "I had to choose between the great self-respecting body of American citizens and a group of perverts, lesbians, women-Lib fakers, demagogues and downright traitors who kidnapped the Democratic Party, I had no difficulty in making a choice."[118] Smith claimed credit for engineering Nixon's overwhelming reelection and for influencing his policies: "I am convinced that the landslide that was brought about by people like George Wallace and myself and others, has greatly affected the thinking and the planning and the program of President Nixon."[119]

As Nixon became increasingly beleaguered by the Watergate scandal, Smith expressed his support for the president emphatically, terming Nixon "the greatest President we have had in this century."[120] He insisted that the Watergate burglars had been seeking evidence that George McGovern had received money from Fidel Castro.[121] Had their mission succeeded, the burglars would have been considered heroes. "This is one burglary that should have been justified," he wrote, "and I will go to my grave with only one regret concerning it—that it wasn't successful." "My one criticism of Nixon is that he didn't personally supervise the Watergate raid so that it would have been done right," he explained.[122]

Sometimes it was necessary for a good Christian like Nixon to lie. "If your little daughter or granddaughter were hiding from a ravisher in the closet of an upstairs bedroom and the rapist demanded that you tell him where she was, would you tell the truth or would you lie?" Smith asked.[123] According to him, "Mr. Nixon did not cover up enough. He did not hide enough diplomatic and military secrets from our enemies."[124] Smith also chose to overlook Nixon's profanity on the Watergate tapes and transcripts. Good men sometimes had minor vices, he argued; while those who would steal a home from a widow might never utter a profane word.[125] Nixon's language must be understood in context, Smith maintained, claiming that such famous men as Jefferson, Washington, and Lincoln were profane. Even King David and the Apostle Peter were profane. Truman's profanity was "unprintable," Lyndon Johnson's was "more than bad," and "the profanity of the Kennedy boys dips into a subversive and perversive vocabulary that would shock the keeper of a brothel," Smith expostulated.[126]

Smith blamed Nixon's resignation, as usual, upon a Zionist conspiracy. Nixon was really forced to resign not because of Watergate, but because he had been making friendly overtures to Arab nations.[127] Nixon resigned, Smith asserted, because "blackmailers" were "threatening to impeach him unless he gives Israel everything they want."[128] According to Smith, President Nixon was "railroaded" by the Jews, and many good men were sent to prison by barbaric blacks on juries in the District of Columbia. Judge John J. Sirica, who heard the cases, was a "sadist";[129] Samuel Dash was a "sadistic prosecutor who carried on the 'crucifixion' campaign in behalf of a so-called Watergate [Ervin] Committee" and "one of the greatest students of Talmudic law in the world." Senator Sam Ervin was "a watery-mouthed publicity hound and dishonest demagogue."[130] "Incidentally," Smith added, "I have a friend who is a minister of the Gospel who served as the pastor of a church in North Carolina about thirty years ago and he says that when he was there it was just assumed that Sam Ervin was a Jew." The clincher was that "the name Sam is a bit indicting."[131]

Smith's defense of Nixon during the Watergate scandal was his last major crusade. He died believing that Nixon was a great president who had been persecuted by Jews. Smith even sponsored a campaign to win for Nixon the Republican presidential nomination in 1976—on the grounds that Gerald Ford was incompetent. Smith, who hoped that George Wallace would run in 1976, was shocked by the prospect of Ted Kennedy's winning the Democratic nomination, and he complained that Jimmy Carter was not "presidential timber."

The chief constant in all of Smith's quixotic crusades for the presidency was that he backed losers—from himself to George Wallace. He claimed to uphold principle, but his stance can be more accurately described as inflexible stubbornness. He never admitted that he could misjudge candidates and issues like other politicians and journalists. Smith accomplished nothing constructive in his advocacy of lost causes. He campaigned for president himself and backed others out of his own egotism and his neurosis, not because he could realistically appraise men and issues.

Smith spent tens of thousands of dollars for campaigns that attracted very few votes; his return on these investments was therefore small. Moreover, as he became older his analysis of issues grew even weaker, and his appeal narrowed to the small number of people who accepted his views mindlessly. Smith's endorsements were shunned by serious candidates. Major party politicians repeatedly repudiated his support, and his endorsements were used against his favorites by their opponents. No person who had any chance of winning a major political contest even remotely considered implementing the planks of Smith's strident platforms, nor did anyone take his threats seriously.

Smith should not, however, be dismissed as a cheap bigot who was totally irrelevant to American politics. Despite his strident voice and often preposterous theories, despite his use of insult, innuendo, and outright lies, he spoke to an important segment of the electorate. He expressed views derived from frustration; and in the vast sea of the American population there were thousands of frustrated individuals. Although overt support for Smith dwindled after his unsuccessful senatorial bid, individuals continued secretly to donate money to his cause; far more people sympathized with him than would admit so publicly. It should also be remembered that some of Smith's views overlapped with those of responsible conservatives. Therefore, his support of a cause did not necessarily mean that its other supporters shared Smith's political perspective in toto.

The picture of Smith as a bitter old man advocating lost causes should not obscure the fact that he derived great personal satisfaction from campaigning and, vicariously, so did his followers. Of all the things Smith did during his lifetime, he most enjoyed campaigning. Unfortunately for him, but fortunately for our nation, his egotism, his profound stubbornness, and his tendency to alienate even those who agreed with him prevented him from spreading even more hatred than he did. Yet it should not be forgotten that his angry, bitter voice represented a small but significant portion of the electorate.

ten

Personality, Family, Friends,

and Followers

‡

"I have a tender heart, but a will of steel. Nothing can deter me," Gerald
L. K. Smith wrote of himself.[1] A man of great energy and forcefulness,
Smith chose to use his talents to spew hatred. Life was a battle of wills—
his will against the Jews, Communists, and atheists. Friends and enemies
alike described him as vigorous, tireless, and resilient, a gifted yet flawed
and ultimately tragic character.

Smith projected raw power and could, through his physical presence
alone, dominate a vast arena, a packed room, or a one-on-one conversation. Big-boned, bull-necked, and barrel-chested, he stood five feet,
eleven inches tall and weighed a muscular 210 pounds. With his piercing
blue eyes, his wavy brown unruly hair, his rugged beaked nose, and
sparkling white teeth, Smith looked like a hero in a Hollywood Western.
But his chief attribute was his powerful voice, which was as compelling
as it was dominating. When he spoke, he drew people the way a magnet
attracts metal.[2]

Despite his obvious gifts, Smith was a troubled individual, tortured by
guilt and by his own desire for importance. As to the sources of his guilt
we can only conjecture: perhaps it was the harsh discipline of his parents, the emphasis on sin in his religious beliefs, a sense in later life of the
wrongness of his parasitic existence on contributions from poor followers, or the absence of tangible accomplishments. Perhaps he suffered
a trauma as a child—we have no evidence. He did suffer from anxiety as a
student and young minister. As an adult, he became obsessed by guilt. He
once counseled a young man to seek solace from his guilt in religion:
"Tonight, kneel down beside your bed and summarize your inadequacies
like a grocery list, and if, in order to make it more graphic you need to use

171

a pen or pencil, take a piece of paper and number your sins and your senses of guilt—name them, number them."³

Doubting his worth, Smith needed reassurance. He actively sought praise and flattery and surrounded himself with sycophants in order to bolster his ego. His vanity and egotism could barely conceal his self-doubt and lack of confidence. He fed on friendships with persons who agreed with him, or pretended to, and he rarely questioned anyone who told him he was a great man. In an attempt to win sympathy and support, he bared his soul to people he hardly knew. When I visited him late in his life, Smith confided his most private thoughts in the hope of gaining my admiration and respect. The supreme irony of his career may have been that his bigoted crusading and hate-mongering were in fact a quest for love.

To give meaning to his life and to overcome the tremendous guilt he felt, Smith created out of his own imagination his mission to save civilization and gave it God's stamp of approval. He convinced himself that he had been chosen by God to save Christianity and America. But his hate-inspiring crusades against minorities fulfilled only his own needs. His battle, no less real because internal, was not really against flesh-and-blood foes but against imaginary ones. No evidence exists that he was ever wronged by Jews or Communists. Only their opposition to his activities confirmed his convictions and further fueled his insecurity until at last he lived fully in a world of fantasy in which every action and reaction had a hidden meaning.

By exaggerating the strength of his enemies and imagining conspiracies against himself, Smith elevated his own importance and that of his movement. He made of himself a martyr who was persecuted as Christ was. He liked to boast that Jews spent millions of dollars to destroy him and yet he remained strong. Stalin, Roosevelt, and the Jewish conspiracy could not defeat him because he was right, he believed. Smith twisted minor criticisms into assassination attempts, and he welcomed the thought of martyrdom: "There is nothing left for my enemies to do except kill me, and if they would kill me, I would expand into martyrdom."⁴ Jewish newspapers, he asserted, advocated putting him, Father Coughlin, and Charles Lindbergh against a brick wall and shooting them.⁵ Even more fantastic was his contention that California police had once warned him to remain at home because along the road ahead "representatives of the Mickey Cohen gang have been instructed to hide in the bushes and machine gun you as you go by."⁶ He claimed that in a single year, 1946, there were six attempts to assassinate him—yet there were no witnesses to the alleged attempts except Smith himself. Blacks in St. Louis plotted to kill him but were not prosecuted because white politicians there wanted black votes.[7] An even more complex plot was hatched in Chicago: "The conspiracy of my enemies in the City of Chicago was to lock me in the County Jail on some trumped up charge, and then hire some savage criminal, preferably a black, to slaughter me while I was waiting trial."[8] When that plot failed, his enemies had tried to burn down the hotel where he was living. "And," he explained, "anyone who has known me through the years knows that I do not have any symptoms of paranoia."[9]

Because he manipulated others, it was easy for Smith to believe that others plotted to manipulate him. He used the "ruthlessness" of his enemies to justify his own: "When you're right and know you're right you should now be ruthless." But he was not spoiling for a fight, he claimed— only acting in self-defense. Moreover, because the enemies of Christ sought to destroy him, he was obviously on the right side.[10]

To counter his adversaries and inflate his own sense of importance, Smith courted prominent figures. He was a habitual name-dropper, even identifying himself as a successor to the Founding Fathers because he preserved what they created.[11] He worshipped men of power, particularly "macho" types who were physically and verbally aggressive, and he relished any praise from them, however gratuitous. He claimed that General Douglas MacArthur had told him he was the greatest man since Jesus Christ.[12] When he could not get people to say good things about him he said them himself, boasting in his tracts and magazines, circulating praise of his orations by H. L. Mencken, even composing flattering introductions of himself to be read by others presiding at meetings. Smith once remarked that the Grand Canyon reminded him of his movement because it was impossible to exaggerate its greatness. He consoled friends who had lost loved ones with free subscriptions to *The Cross and the Flag* rather than flowers.[13]

Despite his pretensions to friendships with the powerful, Smith remained lonely and isolated all his life. He had to be isolated to get his work done, Smith rationalized. Moreover, he complained, when he talked to people they tried to tell him what to do, or even told him he was wrong. He believed others wanted something from him, wanted to use him. There were very few people worth knowing. Most were either ignorant of the great truths he knew or too cowardly to express them. Talking with such people was a waste of time, he believed; they would only deflect him from his great purpose. Smith's vanity and selfishness kept people at arm's length; most considered his pretensions repugnant and his self-serving conversations boring. Even some who fawned on him publicly recognized his vanity and joked about it behind his back.[14]

Smith isolated himself physically to avoid admirers and critics alike taking up his valuable time. His telephone was unlisted and calls to his private number were screened by his wife and his maid. He never permitted his home address to be published and always received mail in the name of his wife or his secretary. In Eureka Springs, where everyone in the tiny village knew him, he had an armed bodyguard, a watchdog, an iron fence encircling his home, and a prominent sign that read "Visitors by Appointment Only." Smith's self-imposed isolation meant that he rarely met Jews or blacks or other minorities he wrote about; they remained only symbols to him. The few blacks he knew were maids and gardeners; he never talked with any black person he considered his equal. And he personally knew only a very few Jews. All of the expertise he claimed about these people emanated either from instinct or from scattered reading of racist journals.

Smith blamed his loneliness on his dedication and, in a sense, he was right: even on vacation he was a constant, tireless, obsessive worker. When he retired to a weekend retreat he took along a tape recorder and dictated enough material to keep his secretary busy for a week.[15] When he visited friends he insisted on privacy in order to do his work. Once after visiting the Lohbecks in their home, he wrote an apologetic note: "I am fully aware of the fact that I do not make a very satisfactory guest. For fifteen years I have worked under a pressure which has consumed every waking moment, leaving no time even to consider the ordinary domestic details involved in a home. This is the price I have had to pay for my convictions."[16]

Smith used total immersion in work to shield himself from self-doubt and to feed his own hunger for fame. This was not without cost; he worried constantly and could not enjoy leisure or spontaneity. He took on more than he could do, worked himself to exhaustion, became lonely and depressed, then burst into another round of activity. Though not exactly a manic depressive, he was a compulsive worker. He arose each morning between five and six o'clock, shaved, drank a cup of strong coffee, then went into his study where for four or five hours he dictated to a tape recorder enough copy to keep two typists busy all day. Smith never typed or handwrote anything and never revised. His routine never varied, although for many years he dictated to a stenographer rather than to a recorder. Exhausting himself before noon, he ate lunch, took a brief nap, then resumed his paperwork. He worked every day, including Sundays and holidays, and spent entire days in his study.[17]

Work was Smith's only source of happiness. "I wish that I didn't have to work so hard," he once wrote, "but then I wouldn't be happy if I didn't."[18] Rather than feeling satisfied after completing a job, he immediately took up some new task. Smith literally never finished his work, and if he stayed away from it very long he suffered anxiety. His cause was his life.

Not that Smith's working hours were all productive. Because he was alone with his thoughts so much, he dissipated his energy in unnecessary activity. He meticulously answered every letter, no matter how trivial. Sometimes he wrote to journalists, ministers, and public personalities, who rarely replied to him. He also wrote complaints about car repairs, hotel service, and meals. All of this dictation had to be typed and mailed, which created work for others.

In the final analysis, Smith worked more to harness his relentless energy than to accomplish tangible results. Initially he directed his efforts toward finite goals, attracting a certain number of recruits or raising a given amount of money. Later, however, work became a habit, a compulsion, and finally work for its own sake. Even sleep was but a temporary respite. He went to bed by nine but sometimes arose in the wee hours of the morning to work on some idea, sleeping for only a few hours before arising again. An insomniac, he refused to accept evening telephone calls because worry about them prevented him from sleeping. If he overslept, he felt guilty.[19] "We get a little weary once in a while," he wrote to his mother, "—not with our work but the fact that it never ends. There is never a quitting place. Never any relief. No days off. Occasionally I take a day and then I am penalized by having to work day and night for the next day. So I am getting to the place where I prefer to just work all the time."[20]

Only when he was too anxious to work did Smith turn to hobbies or leisure activities, and even these he pursued with customary intensity. He explained that he could not understand how grown men could enjoy trivial pursuits like golf: "No, I don't play golf and I don't play tennis and I don't play cards. I don't condemn any of them. I just don't see how an intelligent man can walk around on green grass all afternoon just following one little ball. By the time I got to the second hole I'd think of so many things I ought to be back doing I'd lose control of myself."[21]

Smith had two diversions—raising pets and collecting antiques—both sporadic activities and both, to some degree, extensions of his search for love and reinforcement of his self-worth. During all his adult years Smith had pet dogs, primarily English Shepherds and bulldogs that also served as watchdogs. He liked these uncomplaining companions more than he did most people. He said he never trusted anyone who disliked dogs, believing that the relationship between men and dogs was one of God's most intriguing mysteries. He was certain that his dogs would be with him in heaven. "When God said that the lion and the lamb shall lie down together," he wrote, "He certainly was not limiting the Heavenly population to lions and sheep. Surely He included the cats and dogs."[22]

Smith also raised miniature horses, fifteen to thirty-four inches high, and even smaller pygmy goats. He had twenty-five of the docile little horses and kept some near him at all times, sometimes bringing them into his living room to pet. He compiled a picture book of himself with his horses and distributed it to friends and relatives. Most of the Lilliputian horses stayed at Eureka Springs, but he rented quarters for two of them in an expensive stable in Los Angeles. The goats he kept in a small fenced enclosure abutting Penn Castle in Eureka Springs.[23]

Smith's other hobby was collecting antiques. He devoted thousands of dollars to his collections of furniture, cut glass, Indian jewelry, and Victorian bric-a-brac, which he displayed in his homes in such profusion that they produced incredible clutter. He also collected Bibles and bought hundreds of works of art depicting Christ in every medium from clay to canvas. He displayed these in his Bible Museum and Christ Only Art Gallery in Eureka Springs. Although the antiques, Bibles, and artwork were valuable, Smith was no expert appraiser and often interspersed pieces of questionable taste with his most valuable treasures.

Smith did not have the time to see more than two or three movies a year—which was fine with him because he believed that the motion picture industry was dominated by degenerate Jews who produced sensational obscenities. His favorite genre was the religious epic—he enjoyed *Ben Hur*. Smith did not like television either. When he did watch an occasional show he preferred the comedy of Red Skelton and Jack Benny and religious songs performed by Kate Smith and Tennessee Ernie Ford.[24]

Smith enjoyed excellent health for most of his life but strained his strong constitution and occasionally aggravated minor illnesses by overworking, taking no regular exercise, and overeating. He abstained from alcohol and tobacco, for fear of weakening his resistance to Communism. His constitution was sufficiently robust that at the age of seventy-one he had not had to see a medical doctor for thirteen years.[25]

Smith did, however, have two serious health problems that confined him for months. While a minister in Shreveport, Smith developed a tumor on his back; and over the next decade it grew to a painful lump the size of a baseball, preventing him from sleeping on his back or even sitting comfortably in a chair or an automobile. All of his suits had to be altered to accommodate the growth. When he finally had it removed it weighed more than two pounds, but it was benign. He permitted no Jewish doctors or nurses to participate in his operation or care.[26]

In 1948, food poisoning confined Smith to bed for six months. At first he could hardly sit up in bed, sweated so profusely that he needed three changes of pajamas at night, and lost forty pounds. The slightest pressure from clothing was uncomfortable, and he was unable to wear a belt even after he left bed. He had bowel movements only with the help of enemas or liver pills. Smith did not speed his recovery any by relying on a doctor whom most physicians considered a "quack," a William F. Koch of Detroit, a homeopathic practitioner who claimed to cure cancer patients by injecting them with tissue from cattle. Koch had no license to practice in the United States, but because he shared Smith's anti-Jewish prejudices, Smith relied on him exclusively during the food poisoning affair. Smith believed that someone with access to his food, probably a Jewish Communist who had served him in a restaurant in Denver, had administered arsenic. At first he attempted to conceal the illness to avoid alarming his supporters, but later he liked to boast of cheating the Jew-Communist grim reaper.[27] Otherwise, an inflamed appendix and occasional bouts with hemorrhoids were his only ailments.[28]

Smith's worries about his health problems did not stem from pain and fear of death; rather, he was concerned because they took him from his messianic mission to save the world. His conscious comparison of himself to Christ bordered on sacrilege: "When I am cursed by a Jew, when I am hated by a Jew, when a Jew seeks to kill me, or smear me, or brand me as an evil force, then I have fellowship with Jesus Christ."[29] Just as Christ had risen from the dead, Smith said, so Gerald L. K. Smith would rise from the ashes of superficial defeat on this earth to an honored place in posterity. "I expect to live and die a smeared man," he wrote, "but in years to come, if America survives, patriots will decorate my grave with flowers because I dared to say things which were true but dangerous."[30]

Smith's personal religious beliefs were highly opinionated and unconventional. For example, he saw no possibility for life on other planets—the heavens had been created only to fill the sky for man.[31] Overpopulation was no problem because God could use atomic bombs to thin the population.[32] Nor should Christians hesitate to use force against their enemies. "Remember," he wrote, "Jesus was a man of strength and courage and resolution even to the point of taking a blacksnake whip and running the Jewish money-changers out of the Temple. Never allow yourself to be influenced by these lukewarm 'pantywaist' thinkers who call themselves Christian leaders."[33]

The work ethic that drove Smith was closely linked to his religious beliefs. Indeed, had he not been a believer, he would have despaired of finding any meaning in his work or value in his existence. He repeatedly stated that Christianity was the only thing which made his life worthwhile: "Nothing would be of interest to me if I did not have my Christian faith. All issues involving the nation and the world cease to be important without Jesus Christ. If He is not real, then what value does anything have?"[34] This bleak earthly life was not really meaningful to Smith without the hope of some reward for his Christlike suffering. "Man's belief in his own immortality defines the difference between everlasting values and discarded junk," he wrote.[35]

Despite his commitment to God, Smith mistrusted organized religion, citing the worldliness of many ministers and the Marxist influence in church organizations. Most preachers could not preach and many of them were atheists, he believed. There were "approximately 10,000 Communists who have become Priests in America and about 20,000 Protestant clergymen who are serving the propaganda purposes of Communism."[36] People wanted to hear the Gospel, but the renegade clergy preached sex education, pacifism, the psychiatric theories of Sigmund Freud, and atheism. "It is easy to understand why Elijah lost his patience and killed 400 preachers," he wrote.[37]

Smith particularly hated the National Council of Churches, which he accused of endorsing a distorted version of the New Testament, supporting the admission of Red China to the United Nations, and promoting "mongrelization." The ranks of this "enigmatic" organization included internationalists, integrationists, secularists, and financial racketeers.[38] These were the same agents of Satan who had given us the modernistic Revised Standard Version of the Bible, which did not even endorse the idea that the Mother of Christ had been a virgin.[39]

Smith believed it was not necessary to worship in a formal church, and for much of his life he worshiped at home. Raised in the denomination of the Disciples of Christ, he defected after it became modernist. When he lived in Detroit he attended the Pontiac Christian Church led by his old friend, Rev. Leland L. Marion. When he moved to Tulsa he joined the First Christian Church of his mentor from Valparaiso, Rev. Claude Hill. But after Hill retired Smith ceased attending because he no longer felt welcome—the new minister refused to permit him to teach Sunday School on the grounds that he was too controversial. The minister of a church Smith sometimes attended in Los Angeles asked him not to join it, which infuriated Smith. Afterward he ceased attending church altogether for almost twenty years. Finally, in 1970, he joined the small Eureka Springs Christian Church.[40] During the years that he remained at home on Sunday mornings, Smith refused to watch televised services because of his contempt for the electronic ministry.[41] Nor was he comfortable with demonstrative services and such outward manifestations of the spirit as shouting "Amen" and speaking in tongues. He liked services that were dignified and orderly.[42]

Smith believed enthusiastically in the power of prayer, particularly intercessory prayer. He and his wife prayed on their knees every night and he kept "prayed up" by asking for forgiveness of his sins shortly after he committed them. Smith also had a network of friends who prayed for him, including a convent of elderly nuns who devoted all of their time to prayer and helped him find solutions to his problems.[43]

Despite his appreciation for the praying nuns, Smith felt ambivalent toward the Catholic Church. As a young Protestant minister he had harbored some anti-Catholic prejudice and had even spoken out against Catholic presidential candidate Al Smith in 1928. Privately he continued to make anti-Catholic remarks for years afterward and sometimes he lamented that the Jews controlled the Church by manipulating the international investments of the Vatican. Many Catholic countries, like Poland and Cuba, had gone Communist because the Church was insufficiently vigilant. Some of Smith's friends and relatives, including his mother, were anti-Catholic. His assistant Wesley Swift was a Klan organizer in California; Smith's friend Harvey H. Springer, the cowboy evangelist of Denver, conducted an anti-Catholic crusade.[44]

Smith was sensitive to charges that he was anti-Catholic. He pointed that many of his friends, relatives, and supporters were Catholic, including his son and some of his staff, and that he had been a friend of Father Coughlin, Senator Joseph R. McCarthy, Dean Clarence Manion of the University of Notre Dame, and other Catholic anti-Communists. He helped Huey Long procure free textbooks for parochial schools and supported Franco in the Spanish Civil War. He also published a tract, "The Popes and the Jews," which listed purported anti-Jewish statements by Catholic pontiffs."[45]

Smith seethed in destructive anger rather than forgiving in Christian love, and his life was self-centered, not God-centered. He thrived on attention, even notoriety, and responding to it emotionally rather than refuting it logically. He found it so difficult to control his anger and settle down to work that he confessed, "In fact, no one except God can understand how many Niagara Falls and atom bombs explode within my soul every day. If you knew how many I harnessed and captured and curbed and suppressed, you would consider my occasional outbursts as a minimum deserving of a little congratulation."[46] It required great effort for Smith to focus his venom on activities even remotely constructive. His anger and frustration made every day, every hour, a struggle.

Smith saw adversity and "persecution" as tests from God. He became discouraged at times and confessed, "there are times as we come nearer to the sunset gate when the burden seems almost unbearable."[47] But God asked those chosen for special missions to prove themselves, and a trial by fire would purify him.[48] Smith believed he would reap celestial rewards while his enemies roasted in hell. He had no doubt that he would end up in heaven, although at times when he felt discouraged he wished to hurry the process along.

Smith found the thought of eternity comforting compared with the chaos and confusion on earth. He feared anarchy and even change. He disliked situations he could not control or manipulate; and the thought of strange laws, customs, and perhaps strange leaders made him fear a world state. He hated threats to such institutions as the family, the nation, and his religion; he despised such instruments of change as universities, liberal reformers, or laws to guarantee equality. He was also hostile to anyone who stated that America was imperfect.

There was no room in Smith's mind for doubt or ambiguity. He believed in absolutes, rejecting all evidence contrary to his prejudices or twisting the evidence to make it conform to his beliefs. He generalized without facts and accepted the most spurious "evidence" if it supported his ideas. One senses that Smith protested too loudly that he had no doubts—that he was trying desperately to convince himself that his mind was stable. Only by crusading for something that drained him of energy and doubt, something he considered bigger and better than himself, could he convince himself that life was worth living.

In the end, what Smith sought was not God or even meaning in life, but a respite from his inner turmoil. Particularly later in life, he longed for the respite of heaven. He had glimpsed it, he wrote, and it was a place "where there are no deadlines, no appeal letters, no Jews."[49] Except for the separation from his wife it entailed, death would be a welcome end to his discouraging fight. In the grave, perhaps, he would find the peace that he never experienced in life.

Living as he did in what amounted to a constant state of war, Smith relied heavily upon his small circle of relatives and friends. He also relied on his parents, even as an adult. His relationship with them was complex and ambiguous, his love for them born of fear. As a child he was disciplined harshly; consequently, he seemed unsure of his parents' love. Their love was conditional, so young Gerald had constantly to prove himself. He feared displeasing his parents; he feared punishment. The driving ambition he manifested in his adult life, fueled by his moralistic zeal, can perhaps be attributed to his need to prove himself worthy of his parents'—and, by extension, of God's—love.

Because his father was sickly, Gerald was thrust into the role of man of the family. In rural Wisconsin, physical prowess was a badge of manhood, but he was neither athletic nor particularly strong. He tried to act masculine, aggressive, and tough, but his was a compulsive, insecure masculinity. The young Smith perhaps decided that if he could not be physically tough he could at least talk tough and create for himself a sense of belonging by attacking outsiders.

The hatred Smith vented on Jews, blacks, Communists and liberals may have been meant for his parents. Although he never acknowledged this feeling, his hostility toward them surfaced from time to time, causing him guilt and anguish. As a grown man he confessed, "I want you to always know Mother dear and Father dear that I love you more than life itself and my one prayer is that I may be able to conquer that moping manner which I have around home. It seems to be the result of a desire to be alone and I am ashamed of it."[50]

Although he resented their mother's discipline, Smith pretended to appreciate it.[51] "One of the hard things of my life to bear a little bit when I was a boy," he wrote, "was the firmness and the lack of flattering emotion on the part of my mother. I mean, I'd go around to places and hear mothers brag on their sons and all that, but my mother was not the kind of a person who allowed her affection for me, which was deep and genuine, to blind her to my imperfections."[52] As an adult Smith was obsessed with proving to his mother that he was a success. After canceling his radio program in 1942, he became angry when she asked if he lacked the money to pay for the broadcasts. "It actually worries me for mother to assume every time I make a little adjustment in my program that I have failed," he told his sister, Barbara, imploring her, "If there is a way that you can impress upon mother the fact that my work is going well, I wish you would do it, although she nearly always seems to assume the worst."[53] He wrote Barbara, while his mother lay dying in the summer of 1955, "My nation will perhaps not realize what I have done for America until I am gone. I had hoped that my mother could understand before she left, but I have given up hope concerning this, one of the greatest desires of my life."[54]

Smith's mother, Sarah, was his only relative who followed politics. She took several newspapers, listened to his radio speeches, and read *The Cross and the Flag*. A former teacher, she was superficially informed about current events but rarely read a book other than the Bible. She never traveled and most of her immediate concerns were with her church and her family. Smith, rather than writing her long letters, sent her stacks of newspaper clippings about himself and copies of his magazines and tracts. Sarah wrote him two times a week, twice as often as he wrote her. She invariably began by describing the weather, then discussing the family farm and local political issues. She knew little about Communism except that she was against it.[55] She also fought fluoridation of her village's water supply, terming fluoride "dope" and "poison."[56]

Although prejudiced, Sarah Smith was not as hostile as her son, and she feared that sometimes he went too far. She cautioned Gerald to "be patient and just realize many are doing the best they know."[57] "Don't hate as hate only weakens us for our tasks," she implored him,[58] writing after reading some of his literature, "Sorry to see you're too bitter against folk that don't see things entirely as you do."[59]

Smith resented his mother's advice. He chided her, "Occasionally you write asking me to be careful about what I say. I don't want to preach to you, but I will answer by saying: 'Why should anyone who calls himself a crusader be cautious in speaking the truth?' "[60]

Despite possible inner hostility and disagreements, Smith financially supported his parents, paying their rent and medical expenses while his sister, Barbara, a farmer's wife, provided them with butter, cheese, milk, and meat. He did express some resentment, however, complaining that some people were able to purchase homes or ranches with the amount of money he gave to his parents.[61]

Gerald's father, L. Z. Smith, became senile ten years before his death, but he continued to shovel walks, cut lawns, sweep floors and wash dishes. Perhaps Gerald inherited his compulsion for hard work from his father. When L. Z. died in 1948, Smith did not attend his funeral because, he explained, he was feeling bad, the trip to Wisconsin would be expensive, and he was behind in his work. Nor did Smith attend his mother's funeral when she died in 1956. He said that the Wisconsin cold might affect his health and that Rose Bowl traffic made it difficult to leave Los Angeles. Instead, he placed a picture of his mother on his television set, Charles Robertson delivered a brief eulogy, and they sang gospel hymns.[62]

Barbara, ten years older than Gerald, lived only a few miles from their mother on a small farm near Delavan, Wisconsin. Her husband, H. J. Heals, was a quiet man who worked hard and rarely complained. He had no interest in Gerald's politics. Barbara worked all day at housework, cooking, and vegetable canning; their daughter, Mary Jane, helped in the house and in the fields. Barbara occasionally wrote to her brother, and once he published a simplistic essay she wrote against water fluoridation.

Gerald and Barbara clashed when they were together, and he believed she had prejudiced their mother against him.[63] After a visit from Barbara, he complained that she was a "tedious and impossible person" and an ingrate as well.[64] He had spent more than four hundred dollars when she visited him one Christmas, he said, but all she had given him was a tin cross worth twenty cents.[65] Gerald's bitterness increased with age. "I feel completely helpless in attempting to extend any expression of affection or consideration to my sister," he wrote, "because through the years she has increasingly accepted my gestures and then returned nothing but scorn and impudent disregard for my feelings."[66]

Only one close relative was perfect in Smith's mind: his wife, Elna. Although he had married her for her beauty, he found to his delight that they were compatible in many ways. He told an interviewer in 1968, as Elna sat beside him, "Mrs. Smith, as you can see even at seventy years of age, is a very beautiful woman. And when she was in her twenties and thirties, she was positively just stunning beyond imagination."[67]

As her husband evolved from country preacher to notorious bigot, Elna Smith remained loyal and supportive. She dutifully accepted his domination and never questioned him publicly. Although Elna lacked Gerald's intensity, she espoused his racism. However, her bigotry arose more from loyalty to her husband than from hatred of Jews and blacks. In 1958 she wrote, "For the benefit of any new friends who might wonder what my attitude has been through these years, I want it thoroughly understood, that through it all I have been and still am completely committed to this Cause to which both of us have given our lives."[68]

Smith said of his wife, "Next to my Christian faith and the deep convictions of my soul, the most important factor in my life has been the faithful, loyal, intelligent, valuable support of my wife, Elna."[69] They were compatible to such an extent that "when one itches, the other one scratches."[70] They were so attached, Smith claimed, that they prayed they would die together.[71]

Smith seemed to consider sex a relatively unimportant part of his marriage. He had no natural children and he and his wife slept in separate beds. He made no references to sex in his correspondence; even in his most intimate letters to his wife he did not express physical affection. His sexual drive seems rather to have been directed into his quest for power and dissipated in his emotional crusades. Because he was inhibited and associated sex with sin, he found release through oral aggression.

Gerald and Elna wanted children, however, preferably males to preserve the Smith name, preach the gospel, and carry on the crusade. After a few years of childlessness, they adopted an eight-month-old boy and named him Gerald L. K. Smith, Jr.[72] Gerry proved more a trial than a blessing. Because they could not make him study, the Smiths sent Gerry to military school. Gerry's principal interests were golf, parties, and girls, and his grades were poor.[73] He wrote only when he ran out of money.[74]

Gerry never graduated from high school. He dropped out in 1942, partly because of illness, but primarily because he did not like to study. His father used his influence with Henry Ford to get Gerry a job with the Ford Motor Company. Gerry got up every morning as if to go to work, but instead he spent the day playing golf. He deceived his parents for two months before his father found him out and ordered him either to work or go to school. Rebelling against the ultimatum, Gerry "turned on us with a bitterness and with an abuse that I have never experienced even in the most intense controversies in connection with my work," Smith wrote. "He even wound up by telling me how happy he was that I was defeated for the Senate." Gerry moved to the YMCA and took a job as a clerk at a sporting goods store.[75]

Smith claimed that his son was not a delinquent, just lazy. "He doesn't seem to do anything that is wrong or bad, except he absolutely refuses to improve himself—and when I attempt to help him, he resents it."[76]

Highly susceptible to the draft because he was unemployed, was not a student, and had no dependents, Gerry was called in 1942. His ship, on its way to India, was torpedoed; he spent four days in a life raft. Upon his rescue, he volunteered to serve with Merrill's Marauders in Burma. Gerry was wounded four times and suffered from dehydration and starvation, but he survived while many of his comrades died. He was hospitalized for a year then discharged from the army with honors.[77]

While stationed in Texas for training, Gerry had married a young Catholic woman named Mary, who gave birth to a baby girl while he fought in Burma. After his mustering out, Gerry refused to work at a steady job to support his family. Again Smith hired his son, this time as his driver and bodyguard, and Gerry even made a few speeches with his father in California, but the arrangement did not last. Gerry left the Crusade, claiming he could not stand the pressure, even though he was only working five hours a day.[78]

Gerry returned to his family in Tulsa. Smith procured a job for him at Sears-Roebuck, but he worked there only a few days. Gerry quarreled with his wife over money and sometimes used grocery money to buy golf equipment. He refused to support her and their two children. Although she loved him, she lost patience with his irresponsibility and they were divorced in 1950.[79]

Throughout the 1950s and 1960s Gerry continued to move from one city to another, working as a country club pro. He married again in 1953—his wife, Evelyn, managed restaurants. They had two children. Gerry wrote his parents when he and his wife needed money, but he evinced no enthusiasm for his father's movement. When Smith died, he left everything to his wife, nothing to Gerry.[80]

Gerald and Elna's relations with their other relatives were likewise unhappy. These relationships fell into a pattern of initial friendship, followed by personal visits and a deeper knowledge of Smith's work, and then, inevitably, an acrimonious break. Elna's sister, Nan, came to live and work with the Smiths in California after her husband died in 1956. Nan worked for the Crusade for a decade. When she became too old to work full-time, however, Smith reduced her salary and they quarreled. She broke bitterly with the Smiths and the Sorenson family sided with her.[81]

Smith's feuds with his relatives hurt because his social life was severely limited. His obsession with work caused him to decline dinner and party invitations. Because he felt guilty when not working, he could not enjoy a social life.[82] His work "robbed us of most of our home life, living in and out of suitcases, and meeting our friends on the run."[83] Of course, Gerald did not enjoy people whose viewpoints differed from his. "The only friends we have in this world are a part of this Movement," he confessed to a friend, "and we have no social life and we have no contacts outside of the people who are committed to the ideals to which we have given our lives."[84] Smith was close to only a select few who worked for him.

However, Smith was insensitive and overbearing to employees outside his inner circle. He insisted on being addressed as Mr. Smith, not Gerald. Most of his workers did not know his address or telephone number; and several of them worked for the Crusade for years without ever seeing him at the office. Yet they were expected to attend all of his meetings and rallies with their relatives. Smith even prescribed a reading course about the history of his movement for his employees and administered a test on it. He once fired a woman for smoking a cigarette after work.[85]

Smith bullied his employees, who worked a forty-three-hour week. Anyone who reported late had to remain after closing time. He wrote abusive memos to employees who took time off for personal reasons and refused to pay decent wages.[86] Smith expected his staff to put in the same long hours he did—he once complained about a secretary who did not want to work more than twelve hours a day.[87] An impulsive, mercurial man, he sometimes regretted later the demanding memos he wrote. He explained to Don Lohbeck and Opal Tanner, "I am sure that both of you can understand the circumstances which tempt me at times to impatience, but I do want you to know that these outbursts are followed by regrets, not for the substance of my criticism and not for having made constructive criticism, but the manner in which these criticisms are voiced."[88]

Lonely and moody, Smith was as effusive in gratitude as he was prone to anger. He craved human companionship. When the Lohbeck family sent him a card on his fiftieth birthday he wrote them, "Little demonstrations of thoughtfulness such as this card may seem like a small matter to some people, but not to me. Through the years I have been so tense, so occupied, and engaged in such aggressive activity that my personal friends and my relatives have usually assumed that these little rembrances [sic] did not mean much to me. Consequently, I am usually neglected on special days—Christmas, etc."[89]

After Don Lohbeck broke with Smith and resigned in 1953, he was replaced in Smith's affections by Charles F. Robertson, who became a surrogate son. Shortly after Lohbeck left, Smith wrote to Robertson: "You are the nearest to a son in my life that I have ever had, and I want you to know how very much I appreciate you."[90] Twenty-three years later Smith wrote, "I would to God that everyone who has a son could count on the tender consideration that we have received from Mr. Robertson year in and year out."[91] Although other Smith assistants dropped out of the movement or broke with their boss, Robertson remained a loyal subordinate and never criticized Smith.

Born in West Virginia, Robertson had grown up in California, where he became a licensed minister in Aimee Semple McPherson's Foursquare Gospel Church. After several years as an itinerant preacher, he quit evangelism because of his poor health and joined the family printing business, which did some work for Smith. Robertson joined Smith's staff in 1945 as an errand boy, fixing cars, loading luggage, mailing letters, and introducing Smith at meetings.[92] Robertson had none of Smith's zeal or intensity; he was more of a businessman than a crusader. After Smith's death he emerged from his diffidence to become heir to the Smith estate and manager of the Elna M. Smith Foundation.

Smith played matchmaker for Robertson's oldest daughter, Brittarose. Smith introduced his nephew, Roland Lee Morgan, to Brittarose shortly before Lee, an enlisted man in the Air Force, shipped out for duty in the Philippines. The young people corresponded for several years and were married when Lee returned. Lee than joined Smith's Los Angeles staff as a printer. A thin, nervous, abrasive man with only a high school education, he began to read Smith's tracts and after a few years the intensity of his anti-Semitism approached Smith's own. After the Sacred Projects in Eureka Springs were completed, Charles Robertson moved there to supervise them and Morgan became office manager in Los Angeles. Smith tried to groom Lee as his successor, but Morgan lacked the education, personality, and intelligence to lead the movement.[93]

One of Lee's friends, Charles W. ("Chuck") Winegarner, at one time seemed a promising candidate to carry on Smith's work. Winegarner, the son of Elna's sister Nan, was a brilliant young advertising executive who left a successful career to join Smith. He acted as executive secretary of the Citizens' Congressional Committee, fought the United Nations, and served as secretary-treasurer of the Christian Youth Against Communism. A polished speaker and skilled organizer, he held meetings, showed films, and raised money for these groups, gaining Smith's trust in the process. In 1969, however, without any warning, he quit Smith's movement to become a missionary in Indonesia, partly because of his zeal to preach, partly because he disliked being dominated by Smith.[94]

By the early 1970s Smith had broken with his own relatives as well as with other racist crusaders. Disappointed, disillusioned, and lonely, he channeled his frustration into intense activity. His single-mindedness and arrogance had taken its toll on his inner circle; now only Robertson and his beloved Elna remained. He never accepted the fact that his own personality, not plots by Communists and Jews, caused his isolation. In his own mind, he was a Christian martyr. This inevitable vindication of his life's mission was one of his few sources of peace in his last days.

eleven

The Sacred Projects

‡

In 1964 Gerald Smith, at the age of sixty-six, was no longer the formidable demagogue of the 1930s and 1940s. Paunchy and superficially affable, he seemed to have mellowed into an elder statesman of the far right. He still wrote bigoted books and essays, but he traveled little and conducted few public meetings, for the most part languishing in obscurity. Increasingly concerned about how history would view him, Smith did not want to die without leaving a suitable public monument.

Smith's first thought was to offer to posterity a pioneer farm complete with a log cabin and the furnishings and implements of the early frontier. Such a museum, he hoped, would lead young people to reflect upon their American heritage and would impart a sense of history to them. Smith instructed his trusted assistant, Charles F. Robertson, to find such a cabin for him. He search the country for several years, but his efforts were fruitless. Eventually he came to Eureka Springs, a charming hamlet nestled among the Ozark mountains of northern Arkansas. Robertson did not find a cabin in Eureka Springs, but he fell in love with an imposing Victorian mansion, known to local residents as Penn Castle, when a realtor showed it to him.

This once-resplendent structure was in disrepair and had been on the market for some time without attracting a buyer. Although he could not afford the house himself, Robertson thought he might interest the Smiths in it. Rather than trust his case to a mere verbal description, Robertson and his wife spent several days at the mansion, taking photographs from every angle, inside and outside. The Smiths were familiar with Eureka Springs: in fact, they had occasionally vacationed there and were quite fond of it. After viewing the pictures, Smith expressed some interest but was less enthusiastic than his chief aide. He instructed Robertson to offer half the asking price. To Robertson's surprise, the owner accepted.[1]

188

Smith thought of Penn Castle as a retirement home where he could spend a few weeks each year; after his death it could become a museum to house his memorabilia. Towering over the junction of Eureka and Mountain Streets, Penn Castle was a four-story, fourteen-room mansion of hand-carved gray stone, built in 1888 by Major William Penn, a Confederate officer, Southern Baptist evangelist, and businessman. Its walls were one-and-a-half to four feet thick and its windows were of Tiffany glass. It still contained much of Penn's original furniture, to which the Smiths added their own eclectic collection of antiques and curios. The Smiths completely renovated the house and furnished it richly if not always tastefully. Near the entrance hallway hung large portraits of Christ, Henry Ford, and Smith himself. A clutter of brightly colored religious artifacts, portraits, chandeliers, and Persian rugs filled the rooms. There was Mrs. Smith's collection of Navajo jewelry, a solid bronze, jewel-studded Oriental music box, a wooden table with tortoise-shell inlay, an ivory statuette, a Winchester chime clock, and Smith's own century-old bed with its hand-carved nine-foot headboard. The visitor's immediate impression—as intended—was that Smith was a wealthy man.[2]

The unusual village of Eureka Springs, which called itself "The Little Switzerland" and "The Stair-Step Town," seemed an ideal place to exhibit Smith's vanities. Scattered over two mountains and twenty hills, the town's main thoroughfares were all curves, twists, and inclines: 238 turns without a single stoplight, dead-end, or ninety-degree intersection. Sixty-three natural springs in town (and another twelve hundred within a seven-mile radius) were once the watering holes for such colorful figures of the American past as Frank and Jesse James and Carrie Nation, whose home, Hatchet Hall, could be seen on East Mountain. This rustic community claimed five mentions in Robert Ripley's *Believe It or Not*, one because its eight-story Basin Hotel had a ground-level opening on each floor. The town's multilevel Victorian homes were built on shallow lots that fell away so dramatically that front porches were at street level and back porches were on a line with the rooftops of the next street.

In the 1890s Eureka Springs had been a bustling spa of twelve thousand inhabitants which drew hundreds of vacationers to view its quaint architecture, drink its mineral waters, bathe in its warm medicinal springs, walk its winding streets, and shop for handicrafts. After World War I, however, modern medicine developed cures more effective than mineral water and baths, so the tourist trade, and with it the town, went into decline. By the early 1960s the population had dwindled to barely fourteen hundred. Most of them were elderly, but included as well were poets, painters, writers, and craftspeople drawn by the charming Ozark scenery, the spring water, and the cheap real estate. Eureka Springs' stores, boarded up and offered for sale, found few buyers. The once-thriving town had become a pocket of rural poverty.[3]

Then in 1964 Gerald Smith came to town, bought and remodeled Penn Castle, and made Eureka Springs his summer home. From the front of his "castle" Smith could admire the peak of Magnetic Mountain, looming above the horizon. According to his later account, one night he dreamed that he saw a huge statue of Christ, towering on a mountaintop, framed by the rising sun. The next day, without waiting to consider any of the details, Smith released to the *Eureka Springs Times-Echo* an announce-ment that he would build a giant Christ on 167 acres he had purchased. In this way he committed himself to the project publicly and left himself no room for later vacillation.[4] Smith explained his task as "a vision in my own heart of wanting to see a statue of Jesus Christ rise in monumental splendor."[5] The Smiths had often thought about such an undertaking, he explained, and now they felt divinely commissioned to execute it them-selves: "As devout believers in the diety and Lordship of Jesus Christ, my wife and I had been shocked down through the years that no one had ever lifted up a giant statue to our Savior and for many years we both had longed to see this happen."[6] "It struck us," he told a reporter, "that nothing could bring us more joy during the sunset days of our lives than to pay tribute to our Lord and Savior Jesus Christ."[7]

The initial account in the *Times-Echo* did not mention Smith; rather it attributed the announcement to Charles F. Robertson, Smith's advance man, who claimed to represent "a committee of citizens in various parts of the United States." Robertson vaguely referred to the principal parties only as "the personalities who are responsible for the development of this project." He cautioned against overly optimistic speculation but invited those with helpful ideas to write him in Los Angeles.[8]

It was several months before the Little Rock *Arkansas Gazette* revealed that Gerald Smith was behind the project.[9] By that time plans were well underway and the residents of Eureka Springs looked expectantly to the completion of the attraction, hoping that it would bring tourists back to their dying community. On June 11, 1965, a groundbreaking ceremony was held on Magnetic Mountain. Smith, although present, did not speak. Charles Robertson presided and Mrs. Smith delivered a few words writ-ten for her by her husband. But Smith did not maintain this low profile very long. Less than a week later he addressed the Eureka Springs Lions Club, his first appearance before any local civic group. He told the Lions that the Christ project was not commercial in nature, although he did hope that it would help the local economy. He admitted that he was a controversial figure, but he promised not to bring his political movement to Eureka Springs.[10]

Smith selected Charles Robertson to head the project. Neither Robertson nor Smith knew anything about sculpture or monument-building; they trusted their intuition to find a Christian artisan to do the work for them. Smith later claimed that, after a nationwide search for a sculptor, they found the best-qualified man right in Eureka Springs.[11] Perhaps, but it is more likely that they settled on the first person they met who impressed them; Smith was simply impatient to get on with the work.

The man chosen was Emmett Sullivan, a South Dakotan who had come to Eureka Springs to commemorate in stone a famous local Indian site, a scheme that had never materialized. Back in South Dakota, Sullivan, a cowboy and an attorney as well as an artist, had molded Indians of clay and had built a park of huge dinosaurs. An adopted son of the Sioux tribe and a protégé of Western painter Charles Russell, he had assisted Gutzon Borglum at Mount Rushmore.[12] Because Sullivan was seventy-four and in fragile health, Smith hired Adrian Forrette as his assistant. Forrette was expected to complete the project if Sullivan became incapacitated;[13] he would chisel the face and hands while Sullivan would handle the huge body and supervise the task. Smith also hired a local man as a "construction engineer." Although he had no engineering degree, he was, according to Smith, a "brilliant man who built the Berryville airport and who knows how to fix everything from a toaster to a truck."[14]

Smith professed great faith in his sculptor, who he believed worked by divine inspiration. Sullivan, for his part, never submitted models or sketches to Smith because, as he explained, he was inspired by God to construct the figure from the image in his mind. Although Smith claimed he never worried about the statue's completion, he was anxious that the work stay on schedule. Progress reports appeared weekly in the *Times-Echo*, at first in Robertson's name, then in that of the Elna M. Smith Foundation, which was formed to oversee what Smith began to call his "Sacred Project."

Sullivan supervised the work personally atop Magnetic Mountain. Progress was barely visible at first: Sullivan and a crew of workmen dug thirty feet to bedrock and laid a foundation of 340 tons of steel-reinforced concrete. Smith boasted that this would allow the statue to withstand five-hundred-mile-per-hour winds and predicted that it would last a thousand years, should God spare the earth so long. Next came a seven-story cruciform steel framework covered with wire mesh, followed by the application of twenty-four layers of mortar and cement glazed with silicon to produce a gleaming white surface. A specially constructed elevator allowed access to the top. Sullivan instructed his artisans from a miniature studio built on Christ's left arm.[15]

Smith's team chiseled the hands and face separately from blocks of concrete and mortar, trucked them to the site, and hoisted them into place. The face was fifteen feet long, the hands, from wrist to fingertip, a little over seven feet. The seventy-foot structure was twice the size of the better-known *Christ of the Andes* and half that of the Statue of Liberty.[16] Smith claimed that one could suspend an automobile from either outstretched arm without affecting the statue's stability, and he quoted an anonymous "brilliant and reputable engineer" as stating, "Only an act of God could affect this structure when it is complete. I could not imagine God permitting anything to happen to this sacred object."[17]

On June 15, 1966, although some folds in Christ's garments were incomplete and the scaffolding was still in place, some five hundred tourists and local people braved the summer heat to attend the formal dedication. In his remarks Mayor Jan Bullock departed from his prepared text to call for racial and religious tolerance in Eureka Springs. Smith, who spoke briefly, did not respond to this indirect criticism.[18]

Visible from four states (Arkansas, Oklahoma, Missouri, and Kansas), the completed statue appears from a distance as a tall cross. Blue, purple, and violet spotlights illuminate it at night, and the taped voices of Tennessee Ernie Ford and Kate Smith serenade it with Christian hymns.[19] The statue's aesthetic value remains a matter of individual taste. Its proportions are unnatural: in order to appear as a cross, the outstretched arms are much shorter than they should be. According to one less than charitable art critic, Smith's Christ is a monstrosity out of all anatomical proportion that calls to mind nothing more spiritual than a milk carton with a tennis ball stuck on top. From the side the arms are thin, attached like vertical flaps with no indication that they belong to a human figure. The only hint that Christ is clothed are folds in the drapery at the base of the statue. Completely inadequate to the monumentality of the likeness, the folds punctuate the surface with little sense of rhythm or integrated design. In short, the critic concluded, the statue is characterized by "ugliness and sham."[20]

Smith held a far different opinion. Sparing no adjectives in praising his creation, he claimed that people from all over the world had come to see it; some were inspired, he said, and others moved to tears. He claimed his statue was superior to any previous depiction of Christ, even those of Michelangelo. Sculptor Sullivan could have done no better had he had years to construct the statue. (His reward was immortality and a thousand-dollar bonus.) Smith refused to say how much the statue had cost; he did reveal, however, that it was three times Sullivan's original estimate. One journalist guessed $75,000; another put the figure at $120,000. A tax appraisal valued it at $72,000 in 1966 and $100,000 in 1969.[21]

The *Christ of the Ozarks*, as the statue came to be called, turned out to be only the first stage of Smith's plans for Eureka Springs. According to Smith himself, as he stood on Magnetic Mountain admiring his glistening, half-complete statue, he was struck by yet another inspiration, this time the staging of some sort of Easter tableau. He remembered that the tiny Bavarian village of Oberammergau had been staging a Passion Play at ten-year intervals since being spared from famine in 1634. The Passion Play depicted the last days of Christ's life on earth, beginning with Palm Sunday and culminating in the Ascension. Smith decided that the hollow between Magnetic Mountain and another peak (which he later renamed Mount Oberammergau) was topographically suited for an amphitheatre. He could build the stands right into the side of the mountain and the stage in the valley.[22]

One day, while standing at the foot of the statue watching the workmen, Smith mentioned his idea to associate sculptor Adrian Forrette. Forrette was immediately enthusiastic. He told Smith that his best friend, a writer and director named Robert Hyde, had wanted all his life to stage such a play. Hyde was a specialist in outdoor drama and would be the perfect person to undertake the project. A few weeks later, Forrette brought Hyde to Smith and introduced them.[23]

Hyde, another South Dakotan with a master's degree in fine arts, had written and directed *Crazy Horse*, the story of the great Indian chief's defeat of General Custer. In addition to staging *The Ghost of Fort Lowell* and supervising the construction of Old Tucson, a miniature village in Arizona, he had also written scripts for the television series *High Chaparral*.[24]

Hyde enthusiastically elaborated upon Smith's idea. Smith himself saw many difficulties ahead and told Hyde that financing would be a problem. Hyde replied that the actors could be local people and that he himself would ask only a modest fee until the play was successfully established, after which he would take a percentage of the profits. Smith authorized him to write a scenario. Some time later Hyde returned to Eureka Springs with a script. Smith read it and was favorably inclined, but he still would not commit himself. Two months later, Hyde brought him a recording of the script read by professional actors. To ensure audibility and uniform quality, he explained, the tape would be electronically projected through the amphitheater while the actors mimed their parts. Smith was convinced. He instructed Hyde to begin planning, stipulating only that he find actors with "Christian-sounding" voices for the speaking roles.[25]

Smith gave Hyde complete authority to organize the production. Hyde wrote the scenario, constructed the amphitheater, designed the set, directed the play, and played the role of Christ. Smith told a critic, who complained about Hyde's version of the voice of Jesus, that Hyde had had friends take him to a park where they tied his wrists and body to a cross and left him for four hours. When they returned, Smith concluded, he taped the voice of Christ on the cross.[26]

The set, a four-hundred-foot-long street of Old Jerusalem, constructed of stone and other fireproof materials and remarkably detailed, recalled Cecil B. deMille's biblical spectaculars with replicas of Pilate's court, the Temple, the Mount of Olives, the Garden of Gethsemane, Golgotha Hill, the tomb, and the Upper Room. The scenes were played on different levels, illuminated by a lighting technician in a control booth beneath the seating area, who received his cues by radiophone from an actor stationed out of sight on the set.[27]

Crowd scenes featuring colorfully costumed actors enhanced the physical set. These extras had no speaking parts but followed the action on the set as the lighting moved from scene to scene. Hyde signed about 200 actors, some 150 or 160 of whom appeared each night. They carefully rehearsed for two weeks before the production began, the second week in full costume. They reported an hour before the play to a huge dressing room, where they received makeup—and beards if they had none of their own. Hyde and his wife designed the costumes, and local people did the sewing.[28]

At first Smith did not pay the actors, instead allowing them to earmark their shares of the proceeds for local churches or charities. He did this, he explained, in order to attract Christian participants, rather than people who simply wanted to earn extra money. After several years, however, he discontinued the contributions to churches and allowed the cast members themselves to share a flat 20 percent of the profits. Pay varied from $.60 an hour for the smallest child to $3.40 per hour for the most important parts. In 1975 top actors who attended all ninety of the performances received $1,136.75 each. Regulars could pick up a little extra money, but certainly none of the bit players became wealthy from their acting. Skimping on salaries and using unpaid volunteers to mail out advertisements, as usual, enabled Smith to limit his payroll.[29]

Smith encouraged cast morale by sponsoring parties and awarding trophies. There were prizes for those who had appeared in the most performances, acted the greatest variety of parts, and traveled the longest distance to participate. A few college students even commuted nightly from the University of Arkansas at Fayetteville. Participation was frequently a family affair. Youngsters appeared as Hebrew children, their mothers as sellers of cloth and pottery, and their fathers as priests, soldiers, or elders. Most participants in the play seemed to enjoy it; few questioned either the play's content or the intent of its producer. However, there were some pranks. At one performance the woman who bathed Christ's feet put green dye in the water, and the actress who played Mary accompanied the line that she was shedding one last tear over her son's body by wringing out a wet sponge on Hyde.[30]

Complementing the human actors were sheep, goats, donkeys, Arabian horses, fan-tailed pigeons, and three camels. A trainer took them through the scenes at least fifty times before the actual performance, rewarding them with food when they performed correctly. Those who led or rode the animals also received special training. The animals added significantly to the realism of the performance. Smith kept them in Eureka Springs year-round and opened their quarters to visitors free of charge when they were not performing.[31]

The physical setting contributed to the overall effectiveness of the Passion Play. The audience sat in an amphitheater carved into the side of the mountain, provided with comfortable folding chairs arranged on tiered levels to facilitate viewing. Smith boasted that world travelers had "pronounced the amphitheatre as the most beautiful amphitheatre in the world."[32] When the play opened in 1968 seating capacity was about three thousand; Smith added another three thousand seats in 1973.[33]

As one took one's seat in the cavernous amphitheatre, a recorded voice introduced the production: "Ladies and gentlemen, you are about to witness a dramatic production unexcelled in the history of the Christian Era. As the story unfolds, in complete harmony with the scriptural account, you will become increasingly gripped to the point of silence."[34] Indeed, although the play ran two hours and ten minutes, with no intermission, the interest of the audience never flagged, even when rain interrupted the performance.[35]

The "acting" consisted of large numbers of "Israelites" moving from one place to another. The number of persons in the mob and street scenes varied from night to night, depending on the number of local citizens who could be induced to participate. No character was on stage continuously except Christ, played by Robert Hyde, or occasionally by stage manager Eugene Lyon, Hyde's understudy. The details were authentic, the timing exquisite. The play was no amateur production and the audience was generally appreciative. There was, as instructed, no applause because of the religious nature of the performance.[36]

The crowds grew each year. The 1969 attendance doubled that of the production's first, abbreviated season in 1968. It continued to grow each succeeding year, rising from 28,852 in 1968, to 129,720 in 1972, and to 188,218 in 1975—even improving in 1973, the year of the gasoline crisis, the only tourist attraction in Arkansas to do so. Attendance thereafter increased by about 25,000 each season. On August 21, 1976, several months after Smith's death, the Passion Play welcomed its millionth guest. By then it had become the largest outdoor pageant performed in the United States, surpassing its nearest competitor, Shepherd of the Hills at nearby Branson, Missouri, by nearly 20,000.[37]

All of the income, with the exception of that paid to Hyde and the cast, was placed in a trust fund to be used to maintain and improve the Sacred Projects. Smith attributed the high attendance not only to the quality of the production but also to the favor of God, who he said had blessed the Sacred Projects. Smith himself never tired of praising the play and repeating the compliments of those who had seen it, using the local newspaper as his mouthpiece and often buying full-page ads to publish favorable remarks. He told of a blind woman who had enjoyed the play and who wanted to return, of a minister whose grandchildren were moved to tears, and of spectators who had attended the original Passion Play in Bavaria and who now said the Eureka Springs production was superior. Smith modestly wrote that everyone who saw the Passion Play left "saying that the timing and direction and perfection of the Great Passion Play is so great that it must be viewed as a miracle."[38] He posed for pictures with contestants from the television program The Dating Game, who had won a trip to Eureka Springs to see the play, and with another couple who had come all the way from Australia.[39] Although he used mass mail circulars and bought advertisements in the local newspapers and other papers in the region,[40] he claimed that the most effective advertising for the play was word of mouth. He took such pride in the play that he refused to speak to interviewers until they had seen it.[41]

Smith eagerly exploited even the mildest praise. Leo P. Ribuffo, while a doctoral candidate at Yale University, had not been permitted to see Smith until he had first viewed the Passion Play. Afterward, Smith asked whether he had enjoyed it. Ribuffo, in order to avoid offending him, said that he had. The young graduate student was amused later to see an "Open Letter" from Smith to the Times-Echo stating, "Only a few days before this was written, a prominent historian from Yale University was our guest. He enthused by saying that it was worth the whole trip to see this presentation, and he would not rest until he had persuaded his best friends to come to Eureka Springs to see it."[42] Smith relished and embellished every scrap of praise for his Sacred Projects. In addition, he indirectly praised himself by glorifying his wife, who received numerous awards and special recognitions in her honor and attended banquets and receptions in the Eureka Springs area. Elna delivered to local civic groups many short speeches written by her husband.[43]

Conversely, Smith was hypersensitive to criticism of his production.

Once, believing the local community lacked sufficient enthusiasm, he threatened to close one of the two entrances to his Sacred Projects, the one that led tourists through the town.[44] He threatened to sue people who criticized the Passion Play, labeling them enemies of Christ. He even bought full-page advertisements in the *Arkansas Gazette* and *Times-Echo* to respond to criticism.[45]

Journalistic and academic critics wrote mixed reviews of the play. Robert Warner, director of the Bentley Historical Library at the University of Michigan, later archivist of the United States, saw the play as a quality production that reflected a substantial investment and a high degree of professionalism.[46] Erwin L. McDonald, *Arkansas Democrat* columnist, found the set, crowd scenes, and trained animals spectacular. However, he wrote that the "canned" nature of the performance (all the speaking parts are pretaped) eliminated the possibility of any spontaneity and relegated "the performance to an everlasting mediocrity."[47] Lester Kinsolving of the *Ann Arbor News* in Michigan, was more critical. He wrote that the production was "one of the worst massacres since the Holy Innocents," declaring that Robert Hyde played the role of Jesus more like an acrobat than a carpenter, "as if he were auditioning for lead ape in a Tarzan movie."[48] Without the taped soundtrack to which McDonald objected, however, the actors' voices would be inaudible in the back rows of the huge amphitheatre, and it would be impossible to include the background music and animal sounds. Kinsolving's critique was also perhaps excessively harsh when one considers the purpose of the play and the audience for which it was designed. Intended more as a Christian pageant than as a dramatic performance, its lack of subtlety was due to its panegyric intent.

More troubling were charges that the play was anti-Semitic. An objective evaluation of these charges is difficult because officials of the Smith Foundation have refused to make a copy of the script available to outsiders.[49] Jewish groups charged that the play accused the Jewish people of deicide and blamed them alone for the crucifixion. They noted that the play included a scene in which the crowd of Israelites, gathered before the governor's palace to call for the crucifixion of Jesus, shouted, "His blood be upon us and our children." (This line appears only in the Gospel according to Matthew, not in Mark, Luke, or John.)[50] Furthermore, some parts of the play seemed to deviate from the Scriptures. Jesus was flogged by order of Herod (who is Jewish) rather than Pilate (as in the Gospels). The production also included a death sentence in which Pilate attributed Jesus's execution to "the desire of the entire Jewish people."[51]

The director of the Anti-Defamation League's New Orleans office, A. I. Botnick, saw the Passion Play in 1968 and concluded, "The message

is clear; it is that the Jews as a people then and now are guilty of deicide. . . . Actors depicting bloodthirsty Jews hysterically chant Crucify
Him, Crucify Him. . . . The culpability of the whole Jewish people is the
theme of the play and it comes across loud and clear over the speakers."[52] Non-Jewish analysts were more temperate in their comments.
Erwin L. McDonald, the *Arkansas Democrat* columnist cited above, said
he found nothing even subtly anti-Semitic in it; Calvin Trillin, writing for
the *New Yorker* in 1969, found nothing overtly anti-Semitic.[53] There is in
fact an anti-Semitic undertone but it is not blatant. Smith, however,
hindered his own defense with his harsh responses to such criticisms.
His stock rebuttal was that he was adhering to the scriptural account and
would not change the Bible to satisfy his critics. He boasted that his
Passion Play was "the only presentation of this kind in the world which
has not diluted its contents to flatter the Christ-hating Jews."[54]

Criticism of Smith's Christ statue and of the Passion Play was not
limited to Jewish organizations. Some critics questioned the financing of
the Sacred Projects. From the beginning, there was no clear distinction
between Smith's Christian Nationalist Crusade and his Sacred Projects.
He solicited money for the Smith Foundation in the pages of *The Cross
and the Flag* and at anti-Jewish rallies, and he used the mailing list of the
Christian Nationalist Crusade to invite contributions to the Sacred Projects. The staffs of the crusade and the foundation also overlapped.[55]

As an incentive, Smith offered to reward donors to the Smith Foundation. Those giving a thousand dollars or more would be "immortalized
because of their loving contributions" on a giant plaque on the Passion
Play set. Smith seemed never to question the appropriateness of erecting
such a plaque of donors in an area created to resemble the Garden of
Gethsemane. The names of those who donated a hundred dollars or more
would be placed in the parchment "Golden Book" displayed in the Christ
Only Art Gallery. Those who sent five dollars or more would receive "a
beautiful art package" of material about the Sacred Projects. To prove that
contributions were tax deductible, the Smith Foundation would send "a
photostatic copy of the statement from the Internal Revenue Department."[56]

The Smith Foundation enjoyed tax-exempt status as a nonprofit corporation. However, in 1970 the county tax assessor questioned the foundation's exemption from local property taxes and requested a ruling from
state authorities. Arkansas Attorney General Joe Purcell, at that time a
candidate for the Democrat gubernatorial nomination, ruled that the
properties on which the Sacred Projects were located were taxable. Enraged, Smith vowed to carry his appeal to the United States Supreme
Court, predicting that by the time it reached the Court, a majority of

conservative justices appointed by President Nixon would replace the Christ-hating liberals who currently ruled in favor of pornography, crime, and Communism. Smith warned Purcell that he was flirting with political suicide by taxing holy shrines and predicted that the people would rise in rebellion against this pernicious decision. Nevertheless, the decision stood, and there was no rebellion.[57]

Less controversial than the Passion Play and the *Christ of the Ozarks* were two smaller projects of the Smith Foundation—the Christ Only Art Gallery and the Bible Museum. The Christ Only Art Gallery housed the Smiths' private collection, along with a few donated items, of depictions of Christ in numerous art forms from painting to pottery. The gallery had begun life in 1966 in a small shop on Spring Street, open only four hours a day, but in 1969 it moved to more commodious quarters, a white adobe structure designed by Robert Hyde, located near the Passion Play entrance. The museum subsisted on donations, a fifty-cent admission fee (raised to one dollar after Smith's death), and money generated by the Passion Play.[58]

The Bible Museum, opened in 1971 like the art gallery, was first housed in modest quarters and later moved to a larger building. Smith continued to add to it until his death. Like the art gallery, it houses some rare artifacts along with cheap imitations of valuable works. The sheer number of Bibles (seven thousand) and manuscripts (three thousand) is impressive. But they are not displayed in a meaningful way and Smith seems to have known little about the history of the objects he bought.[59]

The Bible Museum, art gallery, *Christ of the Ozarks*, and Passion Play transformed Eureka Springs from a dying town to a thriving tourist center. Five nights a week from May through October the Passion Play attracted over three thousand tourists—more than the resident population of the town. Motels filled to capacity and it was necessary to book reservations two years in advance for the fall foliage season. But during the winter months when there were no performances of the Passion Play, most motels closed down.[60]

The Sacred Projects made Eureka Springs the top tourism municipality in the state, pushing it ahead of Little Rock and Hot Springs. Restaurants proliferated and prospered and land once thought virtually worthless was sold at a premium. Gift shops lined the main streets, many of them selling miniature replicas of the Sacred Projects. Entrepreneurs built dozens of new motels and renovated the stately old Crescent Hotel. Assets of the town's only bank grew from four hundred thousand dollars when Smith arrived in 1964 to a million dollars in 1972. The town's gross municipal product rose from under a million to almost fifteen million dollars during the same period.[61]

Smith actively promoted tourism to help the local economy, advertising the town as well as the Passion Play in his brochures. He awarded certificates to townspeople who engaged in historic preservation, delivered talks to clubs, civic organizations, and groups of tourists, and sometimes preached guest sermons in the local Christian Church. When businesspeople asked him to begin the Passion Play a week early to boost tourism, Smith gladly complied. The old man's Sacred Projects were proving a bonanza for the local economy.[62]

Not everyone liked the new direction the town was taking. Some of the older residents objected to the traffic congestion and the increase in property taxes. Growth stretched water supplies and municipal services to the breaking point. A "back-to-earth" subculture began among young people who had come to escape city vices but now found local crime increasing. A few who knew a little about Smith disliked him for what he stood for. "His trip is hate," one hippie remarked.[63]

Although *The New York Times* published a glowing account of détente between Smith and the hippie subculture, Eureka Springs was no utopia.[64] In 1969, when the city council voted 10–2 to commend Smith for his local activities, Mrs. Georgia Ziffzer, one of the minority, objected and resigned her seat. The widowed fashion-shop proprietor soon found herself a minor celebrity and the subject of interviews by major dailies, but eventually she gave up fighting Smith and moved away.[65] Others who objected to Smith's growing influence in the community feared that he would transfer his racist California operations to Eureka Springs. Smith professed that his political activities were separate from the Sacred Projects. He would no more write about politics in the context of the Sacred Projects than he would profane his mother's grave, he swore. He made certain that no issues of *The Cross and the Flag* were mailed to Eureka Springs—only rarely did a local resident see a copy. This indicates a surprising consciousness on Smith's part regarding the embarrassing nature of his political activities.[66]

But Smith could not resist ridiculing his enemies in "Open Letters" to the *Times-Echo,* while boasting of his own accomplishments and his friendships with famous people during his long career. He disliked the long-haired artisans and back-to-nature advocates—even though some of them had grown their beards and hair to act in the Passion Play! After a newcomer to town, Ed Jeffords, scheduled a large outdoor rock, bluegrass, and folk concert on the same day as the Passion Play's yearly premiere, Smith became his bitter enemy. His distaste for Jeffords grew after Jeffords wrote a series of newspaper articles on the local environment, pointing out that some of the community's springs were becoming polluted and revealing that a few tourists had become ill after drinking contaminated water at the Passion Play. Smith forced the local publisher who employed Jeffords to fire the young journalist under threat of removing all his advertising from the paper. Jeffords sued and Smith was called to testify under oath. In his sworn deposition Smith claimed that he had never met Jeffords, nor read anything that he had written, nor contacted his boss about him. Smith swore that he did not even read the local newspapers. Technically, Smith could not be found guilty of lying: he had not mentioned Jeffords by name. However, on July 2, 1975, according to a photostat furnished by Jeffords, Smith had written to T. E. Larimer of the *Carroll County Tribune*, "I was greatly hurt when I discovered that you had on your payroll a man who is part of a subtle machine in the City of Eureka Springs to destroy me and to destroy the sacred projects. . . . I just couldn't believe that you had him on your payroll. . . . I must confess that I am writing this letter with tears in my eyes and a swelling in my throat."[67] Jeffords, present at the deposition, said, "He was lying and I knew he was lying and he knew I knew he was lying." The suit continued until Smith's death, when Jeffords settled for an apology and token payment of one dollar from the Smith Foundation.[68]

This incident makes clear that even within the relatively serene confines of the community he had adopted, Smith never lost his insecurity. He claimed that there had been two attempts to kill him as well as threats to blow up the *Christ of the Ozarks*, and that the Symbionese Liberation Army, captors of heiress Patricia Hearst, planned to kidnap Elna Smith. He complained of outsiders and anti-Christian agitators who debunked the town and his Sacred Projects. Smith hired a former deputy sheriff as a bodyguard; the busy man packed a pistol, protected Smith's home, and patrolled the area around the *Christ of the Ozarks*.[69]

Smith rarely descended into town from his palatial home on the hill. The iron fence that surrounded Penn Castle bore signs warning "Private Residence" and "Visitors by Appointment Only." He complained that local people hiked prices when they thought he wanted to buy something. Smith believed the local community was ungrateful. Once he mailed letters to 125 merchants asking for donations for a project called the "New Holy Land." Fewer than 30 of them replied. At best, the relationship between Smith and his fellow villagers was uneasy; frequently townspeople were suspicious of Smith's motives, and a few were even hostile.[70]

The Little Rock *Arkansas Gazette* opposed Smith from his first appearance in the state. Alerted by the Anti-Defamation League of Smith's intent to settle in Eureka Springs, the *Gazette* began crusading against him even before the *Christ of the Ozarks* was completed. Reporter Ginger Shiras published a number of exposés describing Smith's anti-Semitic history and the connections between his bigoted propaganda machine and his Arkansas projects. Smith responded in advertisements in the *Gazette* and in the *Eureka Springs Times-Echo,* and occasionally he threatened to sue. It was a standoff. The *Gazette* continued to oppose him, hoping to pressure him into leaving the state, but he refused to budge. Smith complained to a friend that he could not escape controversy: "The thought of retiring in Eureka Springs in the quiet of Ozark isolation is no longer a reality in our lives. We are destined to stand up and be counted as long as we live."[71]

Smith not only intended to remain in Eureka Springs but also planned an even greater extravaganza there: construction of a Christian amusement park in the form of a replica of the Holy Land shrines, a New Holy Land. Smith intended to add to it over a ten- or twenty-year period, at a cost he estimated at ten to twenty million dollars. It was intended to duplicate the Middle Eastern Holy Land which, he repeatedly said, was in the hands of Christ-hating Jews. "Even the lovers of Christ cannot look upon the birthplace of our Lord without paying cash to a Jew," Smith lamented.[72] Although war had destroyed the original holy shrines, he promised that Christians would be able to travel to Eureka Springs to observe the sites in their unspoiled, replicated grandeur. Tourists could walk from shrine to shrine to watch actors portraying scenes from the life of Jesus. Smith planned to tap local springs to create the Sea of Galilee and River Jordan, and he would reserve a spot on the river for ministers to baptize Christian converts.[73]

Robert Hyde, an artist and architect as well as the impresario of the Passion Play, left for the Middle East to make sketches. The first structure to be built was the Great Wall of Jerusalem. It was to be five stories high, with a gate wide enough for two buses to enter side by side, and constructed of concrete blocks weighing at least one ton each. By far the most ambition of Smith's projects, the New Holy Land was to be built on a pay-as-you-go basis; receipts from the increasingly lucrative Passion Play would be the chief source of funding. Smith also sought donations for the New Holy Land, using some of the same promotional gimmicks he had used to raise money for the Passion Play. Those who gave a thousand dollars or more would have their names inscribed on a plaque to be mounted on the Golden Gate entry to the shrines. Donors who financed a complete shrine would have a permanent plaque at the site of the shrine itself. Those who could not immediately afford a thousand dollars and who had no heirs, were asked to leave funds to the enterprise in their wills; they would be "immortalized" on a plaque. Lesser gifts were also welcome: everyone who gave at least a dollar would be rewarded with a certificate to display in the home.[74]

Smith realized that he would not live to see the New Holy Land completed, so he arranged through the Smith Foundation for Charles Robertson and Roland Lee Morgan to carry on after his death. Upon his death the Great Wall was the only finished structure.[75]

Smith's idea of rebuilding the Holy Land in Arkansas inspired imitators. In Alabama a promoter named Bill Caywood announced plans for a "Holyland U.S.A.," where a visitor who bought a six-dollar ticket could tour, among other things, Heaven, Hell, and the belly of Jonah's whale. Some "Christian" businessmen from Springfield, Missouri, bought a tract of land near Eureka Springs for six hundred thousand dollars and drew up a plan to reproduce the original design of Noah's Ark. They intended to build an auditorium and conference rooms inside, for religious meetings. Smith was happy about the ark project because he had heard that a young entrepreneur had planned to use the land to stage rock concerts.[76]

By 1968 it had become evident that the tourism promoted by Smith's projects was straining the resources of the little community. A better road to the site of the Passion Play and the *Christ of the Ozarks* was badly needed. Through a local judge, Smith promoted a plan to rebuild and asphalt county route 1226. A cost-sharing arrangement among the county, the Ozarks Regional Commission, and the United States Department of Transportation earmarked $182,000 in federal funds for the construction.[77]

When Jewish organizations learned of the plan to use federal money to improve access to Smith's shrine, they were outraged.[78] Federal officials claimed that they had not known that Smith was involved but, in any case, they could not have denied the funds on sectarian grounds. The *Arkansas Gazette*, using information supplied by the Jewish groups and some investigative work by Ginger Shiras, raised public consciousness, and the federal government came under increasing pressure to cancel the project. At first Arkansas governor Winthrop Rockefeller and most of Arkansas's congressional delegation supported the road. They argued that the existing road was unsafe, and even if a new one would aid Smith, it would help tourists and the community even more. Department of Transportation officials argued that the proposal had been approved with strict procedural correctness and that Smith's beliefs could not be grounds for cancellation.[79]

As the controversy continued, the road project attracted national headlines and there was growing hostility to it. Finally Transportation Secretary John Volpe canceled it on the ground that it was only marginally cost-efficient.[80] Smith threatened to sue, claiming that he was a victim of religious discrimination. If it was a sin to hate Jews, he argued, it was also a sin to hate him: "It's a sin to be a hatemonger. It's a sin to hate a man for his race. It's a sin to hate a man for his religion. . . . But there's one thing people don't realize. It's also a sin to hate Gerald L. K. Smith. I'm people."[81] Smith wondered how the controversy would have turned out if the road had been in front of a Jewish synagogue or a Baptist church. He hired an attorney and vowed to appeal all the way to the United States Supreme Court.[82] Eventually, however, he permitted the project to die. After he had conceived the New Holy Land, he claimed that cancellation of the road repairs had been God's will—the road would have damaged the environment and, more important, occupied property needed for the New Holy Land.[83]

Smith used such arguments to rationalize an embarrassing setback. He was not entirely vanquished, however, because the incident attracted far more national coverage for his Sacred Projects than could have been obtained by his efforts alone. He had escaped the quarantine that had successfully muzzled news about him since the early 1950s. Although he lost the battle, he nonetheless won a forum for his views, widespread publicity for his enterprises, and some sympathy for his claim that he was a victim of persecution.

Smith never found the peace he sought in Eureka Springs. His paternalism brought grudging acceptance, but many inhabitants of Eureka Springs were embarrassed to have Smith associated with their town. Although he loved the town, it only tolerated him. The real peace Smith sought, in vain, was internal. The massive Christ and the tons of stone used for the Great Wall of his Holy Land served perhaps as a ballast for his restless spirit. He wanted recognition—not only to feed his inordinate ego and unseemly pride, not only to honor his wife Elna and his God—but also as a cornerstone to affirm his self-worth. Desperate to ensure his work would survive him, he constructed for himself a memorial of mortar and stone.

In Smith's pilgrimage from Fundamentalist minister through wealth-sharing apostle to evangelical entrepreneur, one thing remained constant—his life as a process of ego-gratification. The Sacred Projects were built on a scale that dwarfed the enterprises of others. Anyone who criticized these shrines was an enemy of God, and an enemy of God's vicar, Gerald Smith. These sacred works were publicized and promoted in order that the entire world could appreciate their grandeur and the greatness of their creator. The profit motive was secondary: the money was poured into still more majestic works culminating in the New Holy Land—to make the name Gerald Smith inseparable from that of Jesus Christ.

In order to ensure that he would not be forgotten Smith built a crypt for his final resting place at the foot of the *Christ of the Ozarks*. This was ironically fitting. The gaudy, awkward statue had a tinsel garishness. Masquerading as a monument to Christ, Smith intended it in reality as a monument to himself.

twelve

Smith's Final Years

‡

Perhaps no American political figure in the twentieth century drew as much opposition—and as much hatred—as Gerald L. K. Smith. Smith's opponents were not limited to Jews, Communists, and radicals. President Roosevelt personally ordered the FBI to investigate him and the Federal Government ultimately produced more than ten thousand pages of reports on Smith, involving the State Department, the Post Office, the Department of Defense, Naval Intelligence, and Army Intelligence, as well as the FBI.[1]

Early in 1942, FBI director J. Edgar Hoover ordered his special agent in Detroit to submit weekly summaries of Smith's activities, including transcripts of all of his speeches and every copy of *The Cross and the Flag*. Agents interviewed people who knew Smith in New Orleans, Detroit, Chicago, Milwaukee, and Kansas City, investigated the Selective Service status of his son and key supporters, obtained copies of his income tax returns, and inspected monthly his account at a Detroit bank. The FBI also began to tap Smith's telephones. His phones were tapped for fifteen years as he moved his offices from Detroit to St. Louis, Tulsa, and Los Angeles. Smith died without knowing that many of his conversations had been monitored.[2]

While the government monitored Smith's activities, his more vociferous opponents took direct action. Some felt that militant and physical opposition to Smith could intimidate him and his followers, and dry up his contributions, more effectively than legal action. When Smith embarked on speaking tours he met militant opposition in many cities, led by labor unions, Jewish organizations, the Communist Party, and citizens' groups created specifically to oppose him.[3]

In 1946, violence broke out at a rally in Chicago at which Smith hosted reactionary Southern priest Arthur W. Terminiello. Picketers outside the auditorium hurled bricks and insults, but Terminiello and Smith were arrested, rather than the demonstrators, and charged with delivering inflammatory speeches. Convicted of disorderly conduct, they fought all the way to the United States Supreme Court, which overturned the convictions on the grounds that they had a right to speak, however odious their cause.[4]

Smith's success in stirring hatred and defying legal and journalistic efforts to stop him posed a dilemma for American Jewish leaders. Smith had been sued, picketed, physically ejected from auditoriums, and denounced in churches and synagogues, union halls, and the popular press. Yet some Jewish leaders believed that militant opposition would only aid Smith's movement by publicizing it and enabling him to pose as a martyr to his followers.[5] Smith himself desired the notoriety that came from militant opposition and privately gloated when he provoked opponents to excess. He attracted the biggest crowds where he encountered the most pickets.[6]

In the spring of 1947, the American Jewish Committee conducted a survey of Smith's meetings in order to determine the most effective means of combating him. It found that wherever Smith's meetings were unopposed and unpublicized, the attendance was invariably poor. Armed with this information, Rabbi S. A. Fineberg devised and promoted a strategy he called "dynamic silence"—in effect, a quarantine. He worked hard to convince other Jewish leaders that the best policy toward Smith was to ignore him. He did not win the point easily, and some dissenters never yielded; but the major Jewish groups—the American Jewish Committee, the American Jewish Congress, and the Anti-Defamation League of B'nai B'rith—agreed to implement a quarantine.[7]

Jewish officials approached publishers of major dailies and radio station owners to obtain their cooperation to smother Smith with silence. On some occasions they sought compliance by threatening boycotts of the media and advertisers. They asked labor, church, political, and civic groups to permit Smith to speak unopposed.[8]

Perusing clippings about Smith from major newspapers in the 1930s, 1940s, and 1950s, one cannot help but notice a dramatic decline in press coverage after the late 1940s. Prior to that time Smith had attracted more attention than almost any other American who was not a celebrity or a politician. After the late 1940s the articles were fewer, shorter, and confined to back pages. The confrontations also disappeared, and with them much of the controversy and its attendant publicity.

But Smith's decline as a public speaker was not due solely to the quarantine. Also involved were such factors as the growing popularity of television, the irrelevance of his bombastic oratory, the passing of arch-enemies in government and the press for him to attack, and his stubborn refusal to change his style or issues. His talks were no longer novel; they were outbursts of illogical invective that grew boring with their repetition. Smith's turning to the written word was an acknowledgment that he was no longer in demand as a speaker, as well as a natural evolution of age and temperament.

Until he moved to Eureka Springs in 1966 and created his Sacred Projects there, Smith's activities were rarely reported outside the cities where he lived. In the end, then, it was the quarantine that greatly limited Smith's influence in the 1950s, through 1970s.

Despite the press's indifference, Gerald Smith remained a stubborn crusader and compulsive worker all his life; his routine in his seventies varied little from his work habits in his fifties. He resolved never to retire and hoped that he would "die in my boots." People who "put themselves on the shelf at 60 and 65" wasted many productive years, Smith believed.[9] He pointed out that everything he had developed at Eureka Springs had been accomplished after he was sixty-five.[10]

Smith said that he did not envy the young; he was, however, frightened of senility, which had afflicted his father. "I have a horror of becoming one of those glass-eyed old men wandering around trying to figure out what to do," he wrote.[11] His work was his therapy, and his mission kept him going. He continued to rise early to dictate tracts and articles and he devoted much time to planning his New Holy Land and supervising work for a statue of Huey Long in Louisiana.

In his later years Smith alternated between despair and exhilaration. He felt depressed because America seemed morally depraved and headed toward socialism; the government and academe were riddled with Communists. Yet he found reasons to believe this tide was turning in his favor. The United Nations, which Smith once looked upon as an evil as threatening as Zionism and Communism, was no longer pro-Israel. The energy crisis had gained his Arab friends economic and political power.[12] There had been a civil rights backlash; it was becoming respectable to oppose busing of school children. Advocates of school prayer and opponents of abortion were riding a new wave of conservatism. Smith insisted that he was happy and some journalists had the impression that he had mellowed. An *Esquire* writer who interviewed him in 1968 termed him " a kindly old hatesmith," a friendly man who greeted children and handicapped persons at the entrance to the Passion Play, coexisting peacefully with the counterculture element in Eureka Springs.[13] This superficial geniality was deceptive. Beneath the surface there still boiled his hatred of Jews. He never shed this hatred, nor did he ever reconcile with his enemies, on the left or the right.

Near the end of his life Smith sat alone in the early hours of each morning, dictating messages to a world he seldom saw. He remained indoors except to attend the Passion Play and met visitors only at his invitation. He found it increasingly difficult to sustain the pace of the crusade, but to stop would be tantamount to dying. Lonely and isolated, he clung to his work like a life preserver. Insisting that victory was near, Smith's dictations became more and more repetitious and uninspired. What had once been a mission had deteriorated into a habit.

Smith feared death. A decade earlier he had become agitated when a woman wanted to leave him twenty-five dollars a month for the rest of his life: he refused to predict how long he might live.[14] Defensive about the subject of death, he tried to be optimistic. He wrote of Elna and him, "Our one ambition is to die penniless but rich, rich in the beautiful thought that we were able to consummate this life of ours in a tribute which cannot be destroyed until the trumpet of God sounds."[15]

For the last years of his life, Smith suffered from a variety of ailments. In 1971 he contracted a virus that caused pain in his neck, and the following year he developed a blockage in his left nostril that made breathing difficult. He had a bad case of influenza in 1974 and was unable to go outdoors. On New Year's Eve he began to suffer spasms in his back that he described as the most painful illness of his life. He underwent delicate surgery, followed by blood transfusions, and for nearly three months afterward, he required three nurses all day and all night. His doctor scolded him for not having reported immediately for an examination when the pain started. Smith replied that he had been too busy writing a tribute to Huey Long and planning the New Holy Land.[16]

Elna stayed with him in the hospital, suffering a mild breakdown followed by a prolonged period of depression. Smith was so concerned about his wife's condition that he summoned Charles Robertson to Los Angeles to care for her. He refused to let Robertson print news of his illnesses or hers, fearing that it would only alarm his friends and please his enemies.[17]

Smith's health worsened in 1975. In April he contracted phlebitis and his right foot became so swollen he could not walk. When he flew to Eureka Springs in June he had to be loaded aboard the plane in a wheelchair. A shut-in for the summer, he could not enjoy the mountains. Upon his return to Los Angeles in the fall, he became ill with intestinal influenza.[18]

Still in a weakened condition, Smith developed pneumonia in April 1976 and was admitted to the hospital on April 12. His body could not bear the strain of the complications that ensued, and on April 15 he suffered a heart attack and died. Elna later claimed that shortly before his

death her husband told her, "I have seen it—I have seen the new world—
it is beautiful."[19]

Smith's body was flown to Eureka Springs for burial on Magnetic
Mountain, according to his wishes, "because I don't know whether there
is a preacher who would preach my funeral sermon in church, and I don't
know whether there is a church which would permit my casket to be
rolled down the aisles—and I certainly am not going to be buried in a
cemetery where I am not wanted." He called himself an "outcast for
Christ."[20] His death was front-page news in Eureka Springs, and American flags at Penn Castle and at the Sacred Projects flew at half-staff.[21]

Some three hundred mourners attended the funeral ceremony beneath
the outstretched arms of Christ of the Ozarks. Most of the attendees were
local people. Smith's crusade had dwindled in influence, and he was
estranged from many of his racist allies. Former Arkansas governor Orval Faubus did attend, however, and Gerry Smith came to comfort his
mother.[22]

The funeral lasted an hour, opening with "The Old Rugged Cross" and
concluding with "Abide With Me." Eulogies were delivered by Rev.
Buddy Tucker of Knoxville and Father C. A. Altenbach, a Catholic priest
from Milwaukee. Tucker had known Smith for less than a year, but
Charles Robertson indicated that he had been chosen to speak because
"he knew the right issues."[23] His eulogy reeked of anti-Semitism: "All
issues sink into insignificance compared to the battle between Christ and
the anti-Christ Jew," he said.[24] In an interview after the service, Tucker
hinted that he might become Smith's successor, remarking, "Gerald L. K.
Smith's greatest hour is yet to be achieved. He will be one of the most
beloved men our nation has ever produced."[25]

Altenbach, who had known Smith for years and who visited him in Los
Angeles and Eureka Springs regularly, praised Smith as a man of great
courage who had been the victim of character assassination, concluding,
"Mr. Smith died during Holy Week. Was this just a coincidence? Hardly
dare we use the word coincidence. To me it is the result of divinely
providential planning in heaven above, and there will be that resurrection."[26]

A few days after the funeral Elna wrote a letter to supporters promising
to carry on her husband's work along with Charles Robertson and Lee
Morgan. Incredibly, she closed by requesting a donation: "Please do not
fail us! Give generously!"[27]

The following month, a memorial issue of The Cross and the Flag was
published, including short tributes by Robertson and Father Altenbach.
Robertson wrote, "Gerald L. K. Smith was the greatest man I have ever
known."[28] Altenbach added that Smith "loved his enemies but hated

their lies and exposed them."[29] Most of the articles were gleaned from Smith's previous writing, including "editorial briefs" attacking Jews and Communists that seemed inappropriate for a memorial issue. It was already becoming evident that no one could replace Smith.

The Cross and the Flag changed noticeably after Smith died and Roland Lee Morgan became editor. Morgan doubled the price from twenty-five to fifty cents per issue and reduced the length from thirty-two to twenty-four pages. He printed few original articles, relying instead on reprints of essays by Smith. In December 1977, Morgan terminated publication and moved the headquarters of the Christian Nationalist Crusade from Los Angeles to Eureka Springs. The CNC no longer endorsed political candidates, limiting its activities to mailing out tracts. All that remained of Smith's empire were the Sacred Projects.[30]

Charles Robertson, who directed the Sacred Projects, emerged as czar of Smith's truncated operations. Robertson did not attempt to emulate Smith. "His shoes just can't be filled," he said. "The Crusade has been reduced to just a small mailing. It will continue, but without the drive and the force he had." He explained that no new tracts would be published. "The Sacred Projects are set up as a corporation and they will go on perpetually," he promised. As for the New Holy Land, construction would proceed slowly because "there isn't the flow of cash as when he was here."[31]

Robertson emphasized good relations with the Eureka Springs community. He was elected mayor shortly after Smith's death. (Smith had followed a policy of staying out of local politics.) He commercialized the Sacred Projects by increasing admission fees to the Bible Museum and Passion Play and opening a gift shop, The Heavenly Shop, Inc., that sold slick photograph-packed souvenir programs, postcards, and memorabilia. Robertson expanded the Passion Play amphitheater and added a gospel singing group to the foundation's activities. He lived comfortably on the 35 percent of the gate proceeds he shared with his staff. The receipts exceeded $1.5 million in 1976 and have increased every year.[32]

Robertson consolidated his position by expelling Lee Morgan and his wife from the Smith Foundation's board of directors and replacing them with his own cronies. He arranged for Elna Smith to marry Donald Robe, an elderly friend of his who was employed by the foundation, explaining that Elna had become lonely after Gerald's death. He fired Robert Hyde, director, creator, and star of the Passion Play. Hyde sued Robertson for removing him and infringing on his copyright of the play, but he lost. He moved to Florida where he planned to construct a religious amusement park and stage his own Passion Play.[33]

Lee Morgan also rebelled against Robertson's high-handed tactics, filing a suit that claimed Robertson was running the Smith Foundation for his personal profit rather than in the interests of the foundation. Morgan resented the phasing-out of the anti-Semitic arm of the movement, complained that Robertson overcharged for the version of Smith's autobiography that he edited and sold, and claimed that he had no intention of proceeding with the New Holy Land. Morgan lost the suit, quit the movement, and moved away.[34]

Smith, very concerned about what posterity would say about him and his movement, would have been disturbed by this squabbling among his heirs. John Morton Blum wrote in 1976 that Smith was "the most infamous American fascist."[35] Indeed, many historians and journalists have speculated whether Smith was a fascist.

Raymond Gram Swing's perceptive account of fascism in America defined it as "a reorganization of society to maintain an unequal distribution of economic power by undemocratic means."[36] While one may quibble with any particular definition of fascism, clearly Smith shared some of the beliefs of European fascists: racism, anti-Semitism, xenophobia, extreme nationalism, red-baiting, authoritarianism, and glorification of war, force, and violence. Smith, however, consistently denied that he was a fascist. He wrote to an organizer of the American Fascist Union who sent him printed material, "I am not interested in your literature or any literature which glorifies Fascism. I am not a Fascist and I do not want to be a Fascist." He argued that fascism was un-American: "It is an [sic] European ideology and Christian Americans are devoted to Christian tradition—not European tradition."[37]

Perhaps the most important aspect of American fascism absent from the European variety is its emphasis on evangelical religion. Hitler and Mussolini were not religious men and did not rely primarily upon religious institutions or zealots for their support. But Smith's movement, and those of many of his allies, were interwoven with evangelical Christianity. Many, though not all, American extremists were religious zealots who used the Bible to justify their secular views. They believed it their Christian duty to purge society of infidels.

There is no doubt that Smith was influenced by the political and economic shift taking place during his early years. His family, rural and fundamentalist, saw their own fortunes being undercut by urbanism and industrialism; they were rock-ribbed LaFollette supporters. It is understandable that Smith might have tried to promote old-fashioned values. Yet most people who grew up in Smith's time and place did not manifest his bitter prejudice and perverted ideals. They reacted to change by accepting some new ideas. Smith, however, retreated inwardly and turned to hatred, because he could tolerate only absolutes. It was his personality and his degree of fanaticism, not simply the nature of his beliefs, that distinguished him from normal men and women. He was not merely an isolated bigot, but an extreme personification of attitudes shared by other Americans. His character dictated that he would strive to be the biggest and the best in whatever endeavor he undertook. It is tragic that he chose bigotry.

Epilogue

It is 7:00 A.M., January 6, 1988. I am sitting at my desk, drinking a steaming cup of coffee, trying to think of a way to sum up fifteen years of research on Gerald L. K. Smith. It's hard to believe that I have lived with Gerald Smith since 1972. During that time, from an indigent graduate student living on food stamps, I've become a professor of history, a homeowner, and a husband. My biography of Smith has taken me to Eureka Springs, Los Angeles, Detroit, Washington, St. Louis, Boston, Hyde Park, New York City, and Ann Arbor. The journey was fraught with obstacles: none of Smith's personal papers were available until 1983, and even though Smith himself was helpful, his associates were not.

More than once I felt like quitting. In 1973, when I drove to Eureka Springs to microfilm Smith's autobiographical collections, I discovered I had loaded the camera incorrectly and all the microfilm was ruined.

It was two years before I saw Smith again, spending two weeks at his headquarters in Los Angeles during the Christmas holidays of 1975. He agreed to let me return and microfilm his entire files the following summer. In May, a week before I was to travel to Los Angeles, his office manager, Lee Morgan, canceled my trip and told me that I could not see the papers. Finally, after Smith's death, I got access to the papers. But for eight years I was tormented by the thought that I might never complete the book.

There is something ironic about spending so much time and energy immersed in the life of someone I don't agree with. I never had any ambivalence toward Smith, never cheered him on, never hoped that he would be triumphant. I didn't fall in love with my subject.

And yet, my memories of Smith the man are all good. I found it difficult not to like him—superficially. He was hospitable, warm, and generous, and never made an attempt to conceal his views. Before publishing my first article about Smith, I offered to let him review it, but he declined, saying that he did not want to be a censor. He devoted four to five hours a day, for four days, to taping interviews with me. He put me up in his guest house and fed me a fried-chicken dinner. He paid my way to Disneyland and mailed me a copy of every tract he had written.

That is only part of the story, of course. I also received full cooperation from the Anti-Defamation League of B'nai B'rith and almost ten thousand pages of documents from the FBI under the Freedom of Information Act. I interviewed enemies as well as friends, Jewish investigators as well as Smith's cronies and bodyguards.

What emerged was the story of a remarkably complex man, sincere but bigoted, talented and industrious, but tragically flawed. The fact that he was forthright about his feelings did not make him any less a bigot. He was so guilelessly proud of his views that he spoke openly about them.

Smith's assistants were not so forthright. Charles Robertson, his successor in Eureka Springs, had an unlisted telephone number and refused to return my calls. Whenever I called the Passion Play headquarters, the secretary demanded my name before telling me whether Robertson was in. She would leave the telephone, obviously to consult with Robertson, returning to say that he could not be reached. These were not the actions of a man who had nothing to hide.

When I finally did interview Robertson in 1979, he concealed more than he told. He wrote down my requests for news clippings and copies of speeches, with no intentions of sending them to me. When I asked him for a copy of the script of the Passion Play, he said that it had never been transcribed. He would talk only about "safe" topics, such as improvements and additions to the Sacred Projects, evading questions about anti-Semitism. His bigotry was more opportunistic than Smith's: unlike Smith, he realized that admitting to such views would serve to discredit him.

If Robertson was evasive, Smith's other heir, Lee Morgan, was openly hostile. A high-strung, wiry man with darting eyes, he was suspicious of outsiders and defensive about the Christian Nationalist Crusade. Like Robertson he did not return telephone calls or answer mail. But he was more bitter than Robertson and more intense in his hatred of minorities.

When I last saw Morgan in Eureka Springs in 1979, the monolithic movement was splitting. Smith's son, Gerry, had filed suit to claim his father's estate, which had been left to the Smith Foundation. He lost, leaving Robertson and Morgan in control. Morgan and Robertson quarreled while trying to conceal their differences from the public. Morgan refused to tape an interview with me in the presence of Robertson, his father-in-law, and reacted defensively when I asked him about the future of the Christian Nationalist Crusade. Although I did not know it at the time, Morgan was angry about Robertson's unilateral decision to terminate the Christian Nationalist Crusade and cease publication of *The Cross and the Flag.* Frustrated with my unproductive interview, I finally arranged to interview Morgan privately the following day.

When I arrived at Morgan's home, I saw a "For Sale" sign in the front yard, my first clue that the movement was about to break up. Morgan explained why he had been reluctant to discuss the future of the movement the previous day. He said that Robertson knew nothing about organization and was incompetent without Smith's supervision. Worse yet, he had no plans to complete the New Holy Land, willing to let this last dream of Smith's die. Morgan asked me to accompany him to buy groceries, and we continued our conversation. We drove to a neighborhood shopping center, where Morgan bought meat, bread, and soft drinks, all the while complaining about being excluded from decisions by Robertson.

Because I had mentioned to Morgan that I had never heard Smith speak while in his prime, he brought along half a dozen tapes that he said he would have copied for me by a man who did taping for the Smith Foundation. When we arrived at this man's home after grocery shopping, he was watering his large lawn and garden. From their conversation, it was evident that Morgan's friend shared his antipathy toward Robertson. The man promised to make me copies of the six tapes and also some of the dozens of photographs of Smith Morgan showed me. I received neither the tapes nor the pictures, nor did I hear from the man again; letters and calls to him were unanswered. After I left, Morgan apparently changed his mind about cooperating with me and reinstructed his friend not to help me.

At the time he talked to me, Morgan was already looking for employment outside Eureka Springs. Shortly thereafter he moved away and filed a suit challenging Robertson for control of the Smith Foundation. He lost the suit and his plan to revive the Christian Nationalist Crusade faltered.

Robertson gradually eliminated all of his rivals in the foundation and now presides over the profitable Christian shrines unchallenged. Few people who go to see the Sacred Projects today know much about the sordid career of their creator. Smith is remembered in Eureka Springs as a somewhat eccentric real estate developer.

It would be tragic indeed if Gerald Smith were to be remembered chiefly as a purveyor of dimestore Christianity. Smith earned his niche in history by the force of his domineering personality, which he honed on hatred. In his heyday during the 1930s and 1940s, he was respected by friend and enemy alike as one of the most powerful speakers alive. In his declining years, he was an anachronism outliving his allies such as Huey Long, Father Coughlin, and Dr. Townsend, as well as most of his enemies—Roosevelt, Churchill, Stalin, and a host of New Dealers and internationalists. A thorn in politics, he provoked outbursts from prominent politicians rarely driven to danger. He served to unify his opponents and provoked Jewish organizations to develop strategies that later proved helpful in fighting other demagogues. He inspired essays, a motion picture, a documentary, and a novel. He raised false hopes in his followers, increased hatred for Franklin Roosevelt, impressed countless young people with his fanaticism, and hurt the anti-Communist movement by identifying it with extremism. He aroused hatred toward immigrants, Jews, and blacks, and sought false solutions to racial problems by perpetuating conspiracy theories. As a mass leader, he fed the paranoia and ego of his followers, oversimplified complex issues, created suspicion, and divided families. He raised expectations falsely by promoting unattainable objectives, and he inspired and nurtured lesser bigots.

Nonetheless, Smith was not as much a threat as he might have become. His forte was oratory, not organizing; winning headlines, not winning elections. Although he publicly boasted about electing candidates, his support alone never won anyone an election. Most of the people he reached were already prejudiced. He orated and threatened and traveled and sent out tons of junk mail, but he never won respectable adherents.

In another time and place, under different conditions, Smith might have caused great harm. Had the depression continued, or had a weak leader been president in the 1930s and 1940s, his agitation might have gotten results. Demagogues like Smith surface sporadically in America; perhaps they are always present but gain power in times of privation and turmoil. We can never rest assured that, should troubled times persist, "it can't happen here." Smith's decline was a matter of luck as well as deliberate policy.

Despite his professed belief in God and America, Smith was relentlessly negative. He criticized the government, the church, the labor movement, and countless individuals whom most Americans considered thoroughly loyal. He rarely said or wrote anything positive about America— only about what America used to be or could be. Most of the "patriots" he praised were critics and outsiders like himself. Nor did Smith ever define the kind of nation he wanted in any manner other than vague, syrupy platitudes. He had no idea how he would bring about such a society. What kind of nation did he want? A theocracy? A corporate state? A benevolent dictatorship? And what did he want for himself? To be president? To be an evangelical savior? Or did he just want recognition?

Smith once wrote to Mrs. George W. Armstrong," "If you and I and the rest of the patriots lose, God will know what we have done. If we win, our victorious accomplishments will be recorded in the history books of unborn generations."[1] Fortunately for posterity, Smith will not be remembered as a man of God. The monuments he left behind merely record his ego; and his true legacy is bigotry.

Notes

Prologue

1. Albert E. Kahn, "Dangerous Americans," *Reader's Scope* (Jan. 1945), 15.

2. Jules Archer, *Treason in America: Disloyalty Versus Dissent* (New York, 1971), 132.

3. H. L. Mencken, "Why Not Gerald?" *Baltimore Evening Sun*, Sept. 7, 1936.

4. Herbert Harris, "That Third Party," *Current History* 45, no. 1 (Oct. 1936), 85.

5. *Arkansas Gazette* [Little Rock], July 13, 1964.

6. Calvin Trillin, "U.S. Journal: Eureka Springs, Ark.," *New Yorker* 45 (July 26, 1969), 77.

7. James Graham Cook, *The Segregationists* (New York, 1962), 154; John Morton Blum, *V Was for Victory: Politics and American Culture During World War II* (New York, 1976), 204; Alfred McClung Lee, "The Press and Public Relations of Religious Bodies," *Annals of the American Academy of Political and Social Science* 146 (March 1948), 123.

8. Bert Cochran, *Harry Truman and the Crisis Presidency* (New York, 1971), 395.

9. See Richard Hofstadter, *The Paranoid Style in American Politics and Other Essays* (New York, 1965); and his *Anti-Intellectualism in American Life* (New York, 1962).

10. Obituary, *Arkansas Gazette* [Little Rock], April 24, 1976.

1. A Superabundance of Wind

1. Gerald L. K. Smith, *Besieged Patriot: Autobiographical Episodes Exposing Communism, Traitorism and Zionism from the Life of Gerald L. K. Smith*, ed. Elna M. Smith and Charles F. Robertson (Eureka Springs, Ark., 1978), 4.

2. Gerald L. K. Smith, taped interview with the author, Eureka Springs, Ark., Aug. 10, 1974; Smith, taped interview with J. Fraser Cocks III, Los

Angeles, Calif., March 26, 1968, Bentley Historical Library, University of Michigan, Ann Arbor, Mich.; Smith, taped interview with Leo P. Ribuffo, Eureka Springs, Ark., Aug. 25, 1969. Each of the above interviews was recorded over several days; I have cited the dates independently. I also recorded interviews with Smith on Aug. 11, 1974, Dec. 28, 1974, and Jan. 21, 1975. The Aug. 10 interview was primarily about his youth and early career. I wish to thank Professor Ribuffo for copies of his interviews.

3. L. Z. Smith diaries, Box (hereafter B) 97, Folder (hereafter F), L. Z. Smith, Pocket Diaries and Notebooks; and L. Z. Smith to Gerald Smith, Aug. 10, 1923, B 1, F Corr. with parents; both in Gerald L. K. Smith Papers, Bentley Historical Library, University of Michigan, Ann Arbor, Michigan. All subsequent references to documents by B and F are in the Bentley collection unless indicated otherwise. A portion of the collection was microfilmed; references to microfilmed documents are cited by reel (R) and file (F) and are from the Bentley collection unless indicated otherwise.

4. Ibid.

5. *The Cross and the Flag* 11, no. 9 (Dec. 1952), 2. *The Cross and the Flag*, published 1942–1976, was Smith's personal journal. All of the material cited from it was written by Smith himself unless indicated otherwise.

6. For a discussion of the various strains of populism see John D. Hicks, *The Populist Revolt* (Minneapolis, 1931); Richard Hofstadter, *The Age of Reform: From Bryan to F.D.R.* (New York, 1955); Norman Pollack, *The Populist Response to Industrial America* (Cambridge, Mass., 1962); and Lawrence Goodwyn, *The Populist Moment* (New York, 1978). Hofstadter interprets populism as a backward-looking political philosophy, while Pollack argues that it represented a progressive response to the problems of technology. For an excellent synthesis of the effect of populist thought on Smith, see Isabel B. Price, "Gerald L. K. Smith and Anti-Semitism (M.A. thesis, University of New Mexico, 1965), 11–20.

7. Hofstadter, *Age of Reform*, 232.

8. Smith interview with author, Aug. 10, 1974.

9. Ibid.

10. Ibid.

11. Ibid., Aug. 11, 1974; Smith interview with Ribuffo, Aug. 25, 1969.

12. Smith interview with author, Aug. 11, 1974.

13. Smith, *Besieged Patriot*, 141.

14. Smith interview with author, Aug. 10, 1974.

15. Smith, *Besieged Patriot*, 141.

16. Smith interview with Ribuffo, Aug. 25, 1969.

17. Smith interview with author, Aug. 10, 1974.

18. Smith interview with Ribuffo, Aug. 25, 1969.

19. Ibid.

20. *The Cross and the Flag* 11, no. 9 (Dec. 1952), 2.

21. Smith interview with the author, Aug. 10, 1974; Smith, *Besieged Patriot*, 141–42, 292.

22. *The Cross and the Flag* 10, no. 9 (Dec. 1951), 10.

23. Smith interview with the author, Aug. 10, 1974; Smith, *Besieged Patriot*, 141–42, 292.

24. Smith interview with the author, Aug. 10, 1974.

25. Ibid., Smith interview with Cocks, March 28, 1968; Smith, *Besieged Patriot*, 13; *Boston Globe*, Sept. 20, 1935.

26. *Capital Times* [Madison], Aug. 18, 1946.

27. Smith, *Besieged Patriot*, 12.

28. Smith to Ella May Nowlton, Nov. 1, 1960, B 87, F 1960, Nov. (9).

29. Smith, *Besieged Patriot*, 12.

30. Smith interview with Cocks, March 28, 1968.

31. The university later suffered a financial crisis and was purchased by the Lutheran Church, but while Smith attended it was a private institution. Needing money in the early 1920s, its trustees considered selling the university to Indiana's prospering Ku Klux Klan, which wanted to make it a "one-hundred-per-cent American Institution," envisioned as "a sort of Klan's Harvard." See David M. Chalmers, *Hooded Americanism: The History of the Ku Klux Klan*, 2d ed. (New York, 1981), 168.

32. Smith, *Besieged Patriot*, 5, 143–45; Smith interview with Cocks, March 28, 1969; Smith interview with the author, Aug. 10, 1974.

33. Gerald L. K. Smith, taped interview with Leo P. Ribuffo, Eureka Springs, Ark., Jan. 8, 1973; *Eureka Springs Times-Echo*, April 22, 1976.

34. Smith interview with the author, Aug. 10, 1974.

35. Ibid.

36. Ibid.; Smith interview with Cocks, March 28, 1968; unmarked clippings in B 97, F L. Z. Smith clippings (2); Smith, *Besieged Patriot*, 144–45.

37. Smith interview with Cocks, March 28, 1968.

38. Ibid.; Smith interview with the author, Aug. 11, 1974.

39. Hand tickets, photographs, and unmarked clippings for "Auto Sunday," B 97, F L. Z. Smith Miscellanea (2).

40. *Boston Globe*, Sept. 20, 1935.

41. Smith to parents, Aug. 14, 1922, B 1, F. Corr. with parents.

42. Smith, *Besieged Patriot*, 145.

43. Smith interview with the author, Aug. 11, 1974; Elna M. Smith to the author, Aug. 11, 1974. Elna refused to tape an interview with me, but she did handwrite for me a long account of her courtship and marriage.

44. Ibid.; *Besieged Patriot*, 145–46, 311.

45. Smith to parents, April 6, 1922, B 1, F Corr. with parents.

46. Ibid., April 24, 1922.

47. Smith, *Besieged Patriot*, 292.

48. Smith to parents, Sept. 12, 1922, B 1, F Corr. with parents.

49. Elna M. Smith to the author, Aug. 11, 1974.

50. Smith to parents, Sept. 30, 1922, B 1, F Corr. with parents.

51. Smith interview with the author, Aug. 11, 1974; Smith interview with Cocks, March 28, 1968.

52. Smith interview with the author, Aug. 11, 1974.

53. *Indianapolis Star*, Nov. 19, 1928.

54. David H. Bennett, *Demagogues in the Depression: American Radicals and the Union Party, 1932–1936* (New Brunswick, N.J., 1969), 115; Smith interview with the author, Aug. 11, 1974.

55. Smith interview with the author, Aug. 11, 1974.

56. Ibid.

57. Ibid.; Smith interview with Cocks, March 28, 1968.

58. Ibid.; Harnett T. Kane, *Louisiana Hayride: The American Rehearsal for Dictatorship, 1928–1940*, rev. ed. (Gretna, La., 1971), 151; W. A. Anderson to Mr. and Mrs. L. Z. Smith, Oct. 9, 1931, B 97, F L. Z. Smith Corr.

59. Price, "Gerald L. K. Smith and Anti-Semitism," 33, n. 8. A Bible given to Smith by Brill, with a complimentary inscription, is on display at the Smith Bible Museum in Eureka Springs, Ark. There was little overt anti-Semitism in Shreveport during the late 1920s and early 1930s. The Jewish community there was old, Reform, and assimilated. Jews intermarried with Gentiles, owned large tracts of land, held public offices, joined the country club, and taught at the local college. Shreveport had three Jewish mayors prior to 1921. See Beverly S. Williams, "Anti-Semitism and Shreveport, Louisiana: The Situation in the 1920s," *Louisiana History* 21, no. 4 (Fall 1980), 394–98.

60. Smith, *Besieged Patriot*, 6; Smith interview with Cocks, March 28, 1968; E. H. ("Lige") Williams, taped interview with T. Harry Williams, March 17, 1960. T. Harry Williams Papers, B 3, F 40, Louisiana State University, Baton Rouge.

61. Price, "Gerald L. K. Smith and Anti-Semitism," 34, n. 12. For an account of Smith's radio broadcasts see Bennett, *Demagogues in the Depression*, 116, and Kane, *Louisiana Hayride*, 150–51. Smith's relationship with W. K. Henderson is described in Earl Williamson, taped interview with Hubert Humphreys, Vivian, La., July 13, 1976, Oral History Collection, Louisiana State University–Shreveport.

62. Bennett, *Demagogues in the Depression*, 116; Smith, *Besieged Patriot*, 197; Smith interview with the author, Aug. 11, 1974. It was front-page news in the *Shreveport Journal* when Smith was appointed Shreveport sponsor of the National Recreation Association. His notification came in a personal letter from Mrs. Thomas A. Edison, a director. The *Journal* believed it was the first letter to a Shreveport resident from the wife of the famous inventor and reprinted the entire letter. The same story noted that Smith had recently made a series of talks in Tulsa for the national convention of the Recreation Association. See *Shreveport Journal*, April 21, 1931.

63. Bennett, *Demagogues in the Depression*, 116; Kane, *Louisiana Hayride*, 151; T. O. Harris, *The Kingfish* (New Orleans, 1938), 133–34.

64. Price, "Gerald L. K. Smith and Anti-Semitism," 33.

65. Mr. and Mrs. Marion Jouett and Mrs. K. A. Miller (Mrs. Jouett's sister), taped interview with the author, Shreveport, La., June 12, 1979. The remark quoted was made by Mrs. Miller.

66. Dr. Willis P. Butler (Coroner, Caddo Parish), taped interview with Dr. Dalton Cloud, Shreveport, La., March 21, 1977, Oral History Collection,

Louisiana State University–Shreveport. Dr. Cloud also interviewed Dr. Butler on March 15 and 23, 1977.

67. Confidential interview with the author, Shreveport, La., June 13, 1979. The subject, a member of the Kings Highway Christian Church, spoke on the condition that he remain anonymous.

68. Jouett and Miller, interview with the author. The quoted remark was made by Mrs. Miller.

69. Ibid.

70. Ibid. The remark quoted was made by Mr. Jouett.

71. Confidential interview with the author, Shreveport, La., June 11, 1979.

72. Ibid.

73. Smith interview with Ribuffo, Aug. 25, 1969.

74. Ibid., Jan. 8, 1973.

75. Butler interview with Cloud, March 21, 1977.

76. Ibid.

77. Price, "Gerald L. K. Smith and Anti-Semitism," 31, n. 1; Smith, *Besieged Patriot*, 6; "Gerald L. K. Smith," *Current Biography, 1943*, 707–08; Rita James Simon, ed., *As We Saw the Thirties* (Chicago, 1967), 50–51.

78. Smith, *Besieged Patriot*, 7.

79. Ibid.; Smith interview with the author, Aug. 11, 1974. Also see Williams, "Anti-Semitism and Shreveport," 387–98.

80. Smith, *Besieged Patriot*, 7–8; Smith interview with the author, Aug. 11, 1974; Smith interview with Cocks, March 28, 1968; "Gerald L. K. Smith," *Current Biography, 1943* 708; Studs Terkel, *Hard Times: An Oral History of the Great Depression* (New York, 1971), 369–70.

81. The most complete account of the *Washington Post* affair is "Statement by Gerald L. K. Smith," *Congressional Record—Senate*, 73d Cong., 2d Sess., vol. 78, pt. 2, Feb. 2, 1934, p. 1836. The incident was reported widely in the national press. See *Washington Post*, Feb. 4, 1934; *New Orleans Times-Picayune*, Feb. 4, 1934 and March 9, 1935; *New Orleans States*, Feb. 15, 1934; *Baton Rouge State-Times*, March 9, 1935.

82. Bennett, *Demagogues in the Depression*, 116; Smith interview with the author, Aug. 11, 1974; *Boston Globe*, Sept. 20, 1935; Harris, *Kingfish*, 134.

83. Smith, *Besieged Patriot*, 129.

84. Ibid. In his subsequent career Smith was sensitive to charges that he exploited Christianity for political ends and scrupulously refused to call himself *Reverend*, although many of his supporters continued to do so. He told an interviewer in 1968: "I think for a clergyman to stand up and deal with political issues is like a man that fights with his glasses on [who says] 'You can't hit me, I've got my glasses on.' Preachers that do that as much as say 'You can't attack me or they'll think you're attacking the church.' That's why I think Martin Luther King should not be known as Reverend Martin Luther King because he is nothing more or less than a pro-Communist black revolutionist that should never be honored with the term 'Reverend.' " Smith interview with Cocks, March 28, 1968.

85. Price, "Gerald L. K. Smith and Anti-Semitism," 35–38; George Thayer,

The Farther Shores of Politics (New York, 1968), 49; Jules Loh, *Yesterday's Crusaders Put Today's Militants in Focus," Detroit News,* June 23, 1961.

86. Quoted in Avedis Derounian, *Under Cover* (New York, 1943), 317.

87. Ibid.

88. Ibid., 318.

89. *Pelley's Weekly,* Oct. 28, 1936.

90. Ibid.

91. U.S. Congress, House, *Hearings Before the Committee on Un-American Activities,* 79th Congress, 1946, p. 20.

92. Gerald L. K. Smith to Robert R. Reynolds, April 21, 1942, author's microfilm collection of Smith documents, reel 2. In December 1974, Smith permitted me to microfilm a portion of his raw files, nine years before they were donated to the Bentley Library. These reels consist primarily of documents for 1942, the year Smith founded *The Cross and the Flag* and ran for the United States Senate. I cite them author's (auth.) microfilm (mic.) reel (r.). There are three such reels.

93. Smith to William Dudley Pelley, Feb. 20, 1950 and Pelley to Smith, Feb. 22, 1950, both in B 32, F 1950, Pelley, William Dudley.

94. "Gerald L. K. Schmidt" to Dr. Hugo R. Fack, July 8, 1933, File (hereafter F) 62–43818–939, Federal Bureau of Investigation (hereafter FBI). I obtained the FBI file on Smith through the Freedom of Information Act. The transcript of the Smith and Fack letters surfaced when the Committee on Un-American Activities called the FBI stating that it believed such letters existed. The FBI undertook a lengthy investigation of Fack, who published a paper entitled *The Way Out,* which became the official organ of the Free Economy League. The league strongly opposed Lend-Lease and aid to England. Fack was quoted as having said that Hitler was the greatest man on earth. Fack's house was searched and his correspondence, including Smith's letters, was seized in 1942. The papers were returned to Fack in 1945 after being microfilmed, but the microfilm was subsequently destroyed. However, a copy of the letters appeared in an FBI report dated July 29, 1942. The FBI intended to analyze the handwriting, but the letter was typewritten with only the signature in longhand, and the agency concluded that handwriting analysis was not feasible. See John S. Bugas, Special Agent in Charge (hereafter SAC), Detroit, to Director, FBI, May 23, 1943, F 62–43818–939.

95. Dr. Hugo R. Fack to "Reverend Gerald L. K. Schmidt," July 11, 1933, F 62–43818 [final digits illegible].

2. The Savonarola of the Swamps

1. Rita James Simon, ed., *As We Saw the Thirties* (Chicago, 1967), 49; Gerald L. K. Smith, "Or Superman,?" *New Republic,* 82 (Feb. 13, 1935), 14–15; Stan Opotowsky, *The Longs of Louisana* (New York, 1960), 87. Also see Smith's fawning biography of Long, *Huey P. Long: Summary of Greatness, Political Genius, American Martyr* (Eureka Springs, Ark., 1975).

2. Arthur M. Schlesinger, Jr. *The Politics of Upheaval*, vol. 3 of *The Age of Roosevelt* (Boston, 1960), 64.

3. Gerald L. K. Smith, *Besieged Patriot: Autobiographical Episodes Exposing Communism, Traitorism and Zionism from the Life of Gerald L. K. Smith*, ed. Elna M. Smith and Charles F. Robertson (Eureka Springs, Ark., 1978), 98.

4. Gerald L. K. Smith, taped interview with the author, Los Angeles, Calif., Dec. 28, 1974.

5. "Share-the-Wealth Wave," *Time* 25 (April 1, 1935), 16.

6. Schlesinger, *Politics of Upheaval*, 64.

7. Huey P. Long, *Every Man a King: The Autobiography of Huey P. Long* (Chicago, 1964), 290–94; T. Harry Williams, *Huey Long* (New York, 1969), 693; David H. Bennett, *Demagogues in the Depression: American Radicals and the Union Party, 1932–1936* (New Brunswick, N.J., 1969), pp. 120–21.

8. Smith, *Huey P. Long*, 37.

9. Gerald L. K. Smith, taped interview with J. Fraser Cocks III, Los Angeles, Calif., March 28, 1968.

10. *Augusta Chronicle*, April 23, 1935, Huey P. Long Scrapbook (hereafter Long Scrapbook), vol. 28, p. 76, Louisiana State University Archives, Baton Rouge (hereafter LSU Archives).

11. Smith interview with Cocks, March 28, 1968.

12. Ibid.

13. Simon, *As We Saw the Thirties*, 61.

14. Lillian B. Miller et al., *If Elected . . . : Unsuccessful Candidates for the Presidency, 1796–1968* (Washington, D.C., 1972), 408.

15. Ibid.

16. *New Orleans Times-Picayune*, May 6, 1934; Harnett T. Kane, *Louisiana Hayride: The American Rehearsal for Dictatorship, 1928–1940* (Gretna, La., 1971), 151–52.

17. *Baton Rouge State Times*, May 28, 1934; Kane, *Louisiana Hayride*, 152.

18. Smith interview with Cocks, March 29, 1968.

19. Studs Terkel, *Hard Times: An Oral History of the Great Depression* (New York, 1971), 370.

20. "Sheriff Faces Charges in Trouble Over Long Rally," unmarked clipping, Long Scrapbook, vol. 28, p. 38.

21. Smith, *Besieged Patriot*, 102.

22. Ibid., 64; Terkel, *Hard Times*, 376.

23. Smith, *Besieged Patriot*, 101–02.

24. Kane, *Louisiana Hayride*, 153.

25. Arthur M. Schlesinger, Jr., and Fred L. Israll, eds., *History of American Presidential Elections, 1789–1968* (New York, 1971), 3:2821.

26. Bennett, *Demagogues in the Depression*, 113.

27. William E. Leuchtenberg, *Franklin D. Roosevelt and the New Deal* (New York, 1963), 98.

28. Isabel B. Price, "Gerald L. K. Smith and Anti-Semitism," (M.A. thesis, University of New Mexico, 1965), 44.

29. *New York Times*, Sept. 22, 1935.

30. Bennett, *Demagogues in the Depression*, 125.

31. Schlesinger, *Politics of Upheaval*, 64; Hodding Carter, "How Come Huey Long?" *New Republic* 82 (Feb. 13, 1935), 11; Kane, *Louisiana Hayride*, 152.

32. Price, "Gerald L. K. Smith and Anti-Semitism," 47; Carter, "How Come Huey Long?" 11; Paul Y. Anderson, "Louisiana a Political Laboratory . . . ," *St. Louis Post-Dispatch*, March 3, 1935; Long Scrapbook, vol. 24, p. 150; "Facts That the Lying Newspapers Won't Print," unmarked clipping, Long Scrapbook, vol. 21, p. 3.

33. Price, "Gerald L. K. Smith and Anti-Semitism," 45; Carleton Beals, *The Inside Story of Huey P. Long* (Philadelphia, 1935), 292; Franklin Hope Carter, *American Messiahs* (New York, 1935), 22–24.

34. Bennett, *Demagogues in the Depression*, 111.

35. Kane, *Louisiana Hayride*, 224.

36. Leuchtenberg, *Franklin D. Roosevelt and the New Deal*, 100; Robert E. Snyder, "Huey Long and the Presidential Election of 1936," *Louisiana History* (Spring 1975), 131–35.

37. Snyder, "Huey Long and the Presidential Election of 1936," 127–28; Williams, *Huey Long*, 818; Simon, *As We Saw the Thirties*, 70–71; Terkel, *Hard Times*, 371.

38. Snyder, "Huey Long and the Presidential Election of 1936," 117–26.

39. Nathaniel Weyl, *The Jew in American Politics* (New Rochelle, N.Y., 1968), 129.

40. Martin, *Dynasty*, 146. Harnett T. Kane, *Louisiana Hayride*, 136, has a full account of the funeral. Smith's enemies charged that Smith plagiarized his funeral oration from an orator named Robert G. Ingersoll, and the charge has sometimes been repeated by scholars. Ingersoll was one of the greatest orators in America in the late nineteenth century and attracted as many as fifty thousand people to his speeches. A comparison of Smith's oration with all of the elegies included in Ingersoll's complete works leads me to the conclusion that Smith did not plagiarize. The only similarity to any of Ingersoll's elegies is in style—and Smith's is conspicuously inferior to Ingersoll's. There is another reason to believe that Smith never parroted Ingersoll. Ingersoll was known as "the great agnostic" and had no use for Christianity, God, or the Bible. It is doubtful that the strongly religious Smith would be attracted to such an agnostic. Smith may have read Ingersoll's "How to Become an Orator," but there were no books by Ingersoll in Smith's personal library. Robert G. Ingersoll, *Works* . . . , Dresden ed., 13 vols. (New York, 1902–12). "How to Become an Orator" is found in 8:594–99 (1902).

41. Seymour Weiss, interview with T. Harry Williams, New Orleans, La., July 3, 1957, Box 3, Folder 40, Williams Papers, LSU Archives.

42. Russell B. Long, interview with T. Harry Williams, Nov. 26, 1956 [no

place given], Box 3, Folder 34, Williams Papers; *New Orleans States,* Sept. 12, 1935, Long Scrapbook, vol. 37, p. 37; *New York Times,* Sept. 17, 1935; *St. Louis Post-Dispatch,* Sept. 16, 1935.

43. *New York Times,* Sept. 20, 1935; *Baton Rouge State Times,* Sept. 19, 1935, Long Scrapbook, vol. 35, p. 163; F. Raymond Daniell, "Preacher-Pupil Tries to Draw Long's Bow," *Christian Science Monitor* [Boston], Sept. 22, 1935; Kane, *Louisiana Hayride,* 196–97.

44. Kane, *Louisiana Hayride,* 154–55; *St. Louis Post-Dispatch,* Sept. 20, 1935; *New York Times,* Sept. 21, 1935.

45. Bennett, *Demagogues in the Depression,* 132; Kane, *Louisiana Hayride,* 156.

46. *Detroit Free Press,* Sept. 20, 1936; Bennett, *Demagogues in the Depression,* 132.

47. Smith, *Besieged Patriot,* 127–29; Terkel, *Hard Times,* 373; Bennett, *Demagogues in the Depression,* 133; Kane, *Louisiana Hayride,* 196.

48. Gerald L. K. Smith to Thomas Becnel, March 7, 1970, B 66, F 1970 "B" (5), Gerald L. K. Smith Papers; Gerald L. K. Smith to Robert Warner, Oct. 30, 1973, B 1, F Warner; Smith interview with Cocks, March 26, 1968.

49. Kane, *Louisiana Hayride,* 189–90.

50. Ibid., 141.

51. Elmer Irey, as told to William J. Slocum, *The Tax Dodgers* (New York, 1948), 96–97, 117.

3. Smith, Coughlin and Townsend: Three Merchants of Discontent

1. *New York Times,* Jan. 27, 1936.

2. Arthur M. Schlesinger, Jr., *The Politics of Upheaval,* vol. 3 of *The Age of Roosevelt* (Boston, 1950), 521–22.

3. *St. Louis Post-Dispatch,* April 15, 1936.

4. Schlesinger, *Politics of Upheaval,* 522.

5. "Goober Democrats," *Time* 27 (Feb. 10, 1936), 17.

6. *St. Louis Post-Dispatch,* April 15, 1936.

7. "Gerald L. K. Smith," *Current Biography,* 1943, 708.

8. *Detroit Free Press,* Feb. 5, 1936.

9. "Goober Democrats," 17.

10. George Wolfskill and John A. Hudson, *All But the People: Franklin D. Roosevelt and His Critics, 1933–1939* (New York, 1969), 105.

11. Edward Robb Ellis, *A Nation in Torment: The Great American Depression* (New York, 1971), 441; Isabel B. Price, "Gerald L. K. Smith and Anti-Semitism," (M.A. thesis, University of New Mexico, 1965), 56–57.

12. *St. Louis Post-Dispatch,* May 22, 1936; David H. Bennett, *Demagogues in the Depression: American Radicals and the Union Party, 1932–1936* (New Brunswick, N.J., 1969), 138; Studs Terkel, *Hard Times: An Oral History of the Great Depression* (New York, 1971), 374; Ellis, *Nation in Torment,* 440–41.

13. Schlesinger, *Politics of Upheaval*, 35–37.

14. Lloyd May Henderson, "The Political Activities of Gerald L. K. Smith" (M.A. thesis, University of California, 1955), 142.

15. *New York Times*, June 1 and 2, 1936.

16. Abraham Holtzman, *The Townsend Movement: A Political Study* (New York, 1963), 171–72.

17. FBI, Sec. 1, F 62–41602–28–20; Irving Kolodin, "Propaganda on the Air," *American Mercury* 35 (1935), 293–300; David Owen Powell, "The Union Party of 1936" (Ph.D. diss., Ohio State University, 1962), 6–8; Pat Riordin (son of Coughlin's chief fund raiser), interview with author, Milwaukee, Wis., Nov. 12, 1982; Alan Brinkley, *Voices of Protest: Huey Long, Father Coughlin, and the Great Depression* (New York, 1982), 91–94.

18. Ellis, *Nation in Torment*, 425; Arthur and Lila Weinberg, eds., *Passport to Utopia: Great Panaceas in American History* (Chicago, 1968), 271; Charles Herbert Stember et al., *Jews in the Mind of America* (New York, 1966), 113.

19. FBI, Sec. 1–5, F 62–41602–3–6, 72–64, 108, 216, 236.

20. J. Edgar Hoover to Attorney General [Francis Biddle], April 14, 1942, FBI, Sec. 2, F 62–41602–70.

21. Ellis, *Nation in Torment*, 423–24; Schlesinger, *Politics of Upheaval*, 64; Harold Brayman, "Long Seeks Unity of Radical Groups," *Evening Ledger* [Washington, D.C.], Feb. 16, 1935, Huey P. Long Scrapbook, Vol. 25, p. 90.

22. Powell, "Union Party," 73–77, 89–90, 98–99; Sheldon Marcus, *Father Coughlin: The Tumultuous Life of the Priest of the Little Flower* (Boston, 1973), 92.

23. Ibid., 102.

24. *New York Times*, June 28, July 14 and 15, 1936.

25. Schlesinger, *Politics of Upheaval*, 555.

26. Marcus, *Father Coughlin*, 113.

27. Schlesinger, *Politics of Upheaval*, 607.

28. Gerald L. K. Smith, "Barry Goldwater: An Appraisal," B 58, F 1964 "G" (misc.), Gerald L. K. Smith Papers.

29. Schlesinger, *Politics of Upheaval*, 526.

30. Hanson W. Baldwin and Shepard Stone, eds., *We Saw It Happen: The News Behind the News That's Fit to Print* (New York, 1938), 99; Hadley Cantril, *The Psychology of Social Movements* (New York, 1941), 184–86.

31. *Boston Globe*, July 16, 1936.

32. Terkel, *Hard Times*, 375; Schlesinger, *Politics of Upheaval*, 557; Herbert Harris, "That Third Party," *Current History* 45, no. 1 (Oct. 1936), 85.

33. Henderson, "Political Activities on Gerald L. K. Smith," 147.

34. Schlesinger, *Politics of Upheaval*, 558.

35. Ibid., 558–59.

36. Marcus, *Father Coughlin*, 118–19.

37. *St. Louis Post-Dispatch*, July 16, 1936.

38. Schlesinger, *Politics of Upheaval*, 558.

39. *St. Louis Post-Dispatch*, July 20, 1936.

40. Harris, "That Third Party," 85–86.

41. Marcus, *Father Coughlin*, 115.

42. Powell, "Union Party," 100; Victor C. Ferkiss, "The Political and Economic Philosophy of American Fascism" (Ph.D. diss., University of Chicago, 1954), 346.

43. Powell, "Union Party," 102–04; Schlesinger, *Politics of Upheaval*, 556.

44. Powell, "Union Party, 152–54; *New Orleans Times-Picayune*, June 23, 1936.

45. Schlesinger, *Politics of Upheaval*, 626.

46. Holtzman, *Townsend Movement*, 177.

47. Schlesinger, *Politics of Upheaveal*, 627.

48. *New York Times*, June 21, 1936.

49. Ibid., July 26, 1936; *New York Herald*, July 26, 1936.

50. Harris, "That Third Party," 83–84.

51. Schlesinger, *Politics of Upheaveal*, 627.

52. Harris, "That Third Party," 83.

53. Powell, "Union Party," 133–34.

54. Ibid., 143.

55. *Detroit News*, June 6, 1936.

56. Ibid., Oct. 20, 1936.

57. H. C. Garrison, "Who Is Gerald L. K. Smith?" *Detroit News*, May 3, 1942.

58. *New York Times*, Oct. 21, 1936.

59. Ibid.; *New York Tribune*, Oct. 21, 1936.

60. *St. Louis Post-Dispatch*, Oct. 21, 1936; *Indianapolis Star*, Oct. 21, 1936.

61. *New York Tribune*, Oct. 21, 1936; Schlesinger, *Politics of Upheaval*, 630.

62. *St. Louis Post-Dispatch*, and *Detroit News*, Oct. 23, 1936.

63. *St. Louis Post-Dispatch*, Nov. 3 and 5, 1936; *New York Times* and *New Orleans Times-Picayune*, Nov. 3, 1936.

64. Wolfskill and Hudson, *All But the People*, 85–87.

65. Basil Rauch, *The History of the New Deal* (New York, 1944), 263; Marcus, *Father Coughlin*, 136.

66. Donald R. McCoy, *Angry Voices: Left-of-Center Politics in the New Deal Era* (Lawrence, Kan., 1958), 131.

67. Powell, "Union Party," 203.

68. Schlesinger, *Politics of Upheaveal*, 627.

69. Marcus, *Father Coughlin*, 118.

70. Robert S. Gallagher, "The Radio Priest," *American Heritage* 23, No. 6 (1972), 104.

71. Smith to H. L. Mencken, Aug. 14, 1939, quoted in Leo P. Ribuffo, "Protestants on the Right: William Dudley Pelley, Gerald B. Winrod, and Gerald L. K. Smith" (Ph.D. diss., Yale University, 1976). The published version of Ribuffo's dissertation refers to the letter but does not quote it in

full. See Ribuffo, *The Old Christian Right: The Protestant Far Right From the Great Depression to the Cold War* (Philadelphia, 1983), 148.

4. A Run for the Senate

1. *New York Times*, May 9, 1937.

2. Campaign Expenditures, America First Party, Gerald L. K. Smith, Witness, *Hearings Before the Committee to Investigate Campaign Expenditures*, House of Representatives, 78th Cong., 2d Sess., on Res. 551, pt. 6 (Tues, Oct. 3, 1944), p. 359; FBI, Report on Gerald L. K. Smith, May 31, 1943, New York F 100–1907, 9–11.

3. *Christian Science Monitor* [Boston], March 2, 1937; "A Statement by the Editor," rough draft for *The Cross and the Flag* [1942], auth. mic. r. 2.

4. Ed., *Detroit News*, Jan. 2, 1937.

5. "Report on Gerald L. K. Smith," memorandum, n.d., American Jewish Committee Archives.

6. Isabel B. Price, "Gerald L. K. Smith and Anti-Semitism" (M.A. thesis, University of New Mexico, 1965), 67–70, 78.

7. Ibid., 70–71; *St. Louis Post-Dispatch*, Oct. 18, 1936.

8. Ibid.; Gerald L. K. Smith, taped interview with the author, Eureka Springs, Ark., Aug. 11, 1974; George Seldes, "Gerald L. K. Smith Backed by Economic Royalists," *In Fact* 5, no. 17 (Aug. 3, 1942), 2.

9. FBI, Report on Gerald L. K. Smith, New York, May 31, 1943, F 100–1097, pp. 9–11.

10. William Bradford Huie, "Gerald Smith's Bid for Power," *American Mercury* 55, no. 224 (Aug., 1942), 145–57.

11. FBI, Report on Gerald L. K. Smith.

12. Ibid.; J. Lacey Reynolds, "Gerald L. K. Smith Crusades Again with a New Cross for Our Flag to Bear," *Boston Globe*, April 30, 1942; "Gerald L. K. Smith," American Jewish Committee Archives; *New York Times*, Aug. 23, 1937. For the quotation see *New York Times*, Aug. 21, 1936.

13. FBI, Report on Gerald L. K. Smith; "Special Note," R. 15, F Prospectus, Gerald L. K. Smith Papers.

14. FBI, Report on Gerald L. K. Smith, Dec. 27, 1945, F 62–43818–398, pp. 1–6; FBI, Statement of Edward A. Powers, n.d., F 62–43818–398; *New York Times*, Aug. 20, 1937; *Christian Science Monitor* [Boston], Aug. 20, 1937; Gerald L. K. Smith, taped interview with J. Fraser Cocks III, Los Angeles, Calif., March 29, 1968.

15. Price, "Gerald L. K. Smith and Anti-Semitism," 77–78, 82; Smith interview with Cocks, March 29, 1968; *Campaign Expenditures*, 355–56; Smith to Commodore-Perry Hotel, May 23, 1939, B 1, F 1939–1942 (l. 1940–1942); Smith to John Pat Little, May 23, 1939, ibid.

16. *New York Times*, March 19, 1939; Leo P. Ribuffo, *The Old Christian Right: The Protestant Far Right from the Great Depression to the Cold War* (Philadelphia, 1983), 145; Gerald L. K. Smith, *Besieged Patriot: Autobio-*

graphical Episodes Exposing Communism, Traitorism and Zionism from the Life of Gerald L. K. Smith, ed. Elna M. Smith and Charles F. Robertson (Eureka Springs, Ark., 1978), 74–75.

17. *Detroit News,* May 3, 1942; Ribuffo, *Old Christian Right,* 146.

18. Price, "Gerald L. K. Smith and Anti-Semitism," 78.

19. "Who Is Gerald L. K. Smith?" B 2, F 1939–1942 (l. 1940–1942), Form letters: 1939; Form letter, Smith to "Fellow Patriot," Aug. 16, 1941, B 2, F 1939–1942 (l. 1940–1942), Form letters: 1941.

20. Price, "Gerald L. K. Smith and Anti-Semitism," 82–83; Gerald L. K. Smith, "Confidential Memo," n.d., B 4, F 1939–1942 (l. 1940–1942), Prospectuses and memoranda for meetings.

21. Tentative Program for Meeting, n.d., R 15, F Staff memos, 1939–1940; Memo to Management of Olympia, Oct. 30, 1939, R 15, ibid.; *Detroit News,* Nov. 3, 1939.

22. *Detroit Free Press,* Nov. 2, 1937.

23. *Campaign Expenditures,* 353–54.

24. FBI, Report on Gerald L. K. Smith by Special Agent, Detroit, Sept. 2, 1942, Detroit F 62–1126, p. 8.

25. *New York Times,* Aug. 23, 1937; *Detroit Free Press,* Nov. 2, 1937.

26. "Confidential memo [on organization of Committee of One Million]," n.d., R 15, F Staff memos, 1939–1940.

27. Memo, Nov. 26, 1939, B 4, F 1939–1942 (l. 1940–1942), Prospectuses and memoranda for meetings; Confidential memo [1940], ibid.; Confidential memos, R 16, F Prospectuses.

28. *New York Post,* Feb. 2, 1942; Topical Study Memorandum on America First Party, United States Naval Intelligence, Ninth Naval District, Sept. 6, 1942, p. 6; Smith to "My Dear Friend," Jan. 20, 1942, B 2, F 1939–1942 (l. 1940–1942), Inner Circle; Smith to Gerald B. Winrod, Feb. 12, 1942, B 7, F 1939–1942 (l. 1940–1942), Winrod, Gerald; George Seldes, "Hitlerites in Chicago," *In Fact* 4, no. 22 (March 9, 1942), p. 4.

29. Smith to J. Edward Jones, April 27, 1942, B 2, F 1939–1942 (l. 1940–1942), "J" (misc.); Smith to Nye Morehouse, July 17, 1939, B 1, F 1939–1942 (l. 1940–1942), Corr.: July 1939; Leo Lowenthal and Norbert Guterman, *Prophets of Deceit: A Study of the Techniques of the American Agitator* (Palo Alto, Calif., 1970), 91; Price, "Gerald L. K. Smith and Anti-Semitism," 85; "Gerald L. K. Smith," American Jewish Committee Archives, 1–2.

30. *Detroit News,* May 3, 1942; Smith memo, Dec. 3, 1942; Smith to Secretary of State of Michigan, Dec. 27, 1939; H. H. Lucker to Harold G. Groehn, Dec. 13, 1939; Lucker to Michigan Corporation and Securities Commission, May 7, 1940; Annual Non-Profit Report for 1940, Michigan Corporation and Securities Commission, March 3, 1941, all in auth. mic. r. 2.

31. "Technique for Interviewing G. L. K. Smith," n.d., American Jewish Committee Archives; Smith to Miss [Phyllis] Chandler, June 6, 1939, B 3, F 1939–1942 (l. 1940–1942), Memoranda: 1939; Friends of Democracy, "Pattern for Revolution," [1944], Kansas City, Mo., American Jewish Historical Society, Waltham, Mass.

32. Gerald L. K. Smith to staff [1939], B 3, F 1939–1942 (l. 1940–1942), Memoranda: 1939; *Detroit News,* July 16, 1945; Arthur Derounian [pseud. John Roy Carlson], *Under Cover* (New York, 1943), 316; Smith to George T. Eggleston, March 3, 1941, and Smith to Bernard Doman, Oct. 8, 1941, both in auth. mic. r. 2.

33. *Detroit News,* Feb. 19, 1939; Spencer R. McCulloch, "Gerald L. K. Smith—Rabble Rouser," *St. Louis Post-Dispatch,* Dec. 26, 1943; *Campaign Expenditures,* 316–17; Smith to Arthur Vandenberg, July 22, 1940, R 15, F Staff memos, 1939–1940.

34. Smith radio broadcast, Sept. 3, 1939, B 4, F 1939–1942 (l. 1940–1942), Radio broadcasts: 1939: Sept.

35. Smith radio broadcast, Aug. 20, 1939, B 4, F 1939–1942 (l. 1940–1942), Radio broadcasts: 1939: August.

36. *Detroit News,* March 6, 1939.

37. Smith, *Besieged Patriot,* 48.

38. Smith to Clare E. Hoffman, Feb. 24, 1942, B 2, F 1939–1942 (l. 1940–1942), "H."

39. Victor Reuther, *The Brothers Reuther and the Story of UAW: A Memoir* (Boston, 1976), 215. The dossiers compiled by the spies are summarized in R 15, F Staff Memos (misc.). The most ingenious piece of propaganda used against Walter Reuther was concocted by his rivals in the UAW: a forged letter that claimed Smith and Reuther were covert allies. The letter, allegedly written by Smith, stated, "As much as I appreciate his [Reuther's] value I am careful never to compliment Mr. Reuther in anything I write or speak. Inside informers tell me that Mr. Reuther is thoroughly alert to the Jewish issue." See Irving Howe and B. J. Widick, *The UAW and Walter Reuther* (New York, 1949), 169, and Reuther, *Brothers Reuther,* 263.

40. Price, "Gerald Smith and Anti-Semitism," 79–80.

41. Smith, *Besieged Patriot,* 26.

42. Smith radio address, Dec. 10, 1939, B 5, F 1939–1942 (l. 1940–1942), Radio broadcasts: 1939: Dec.

43. George Seldes, *In Fact* 12, no. 10 (Dec. 10, 1945), 3; "National Defense," Extension of Remarks by Hon. Clare E. Hoffman, Radio Address by Gerald L. K. Smith, Dec. 22, 1940, *Appendix to the Congressional Record,* 77th Cong., 1st Sess., vol. 87, pt. 10 (Jan. 3–March 14, 1941), pp. A28–A30.

44. Lucille B. Milner and Paul Brissenden, "Union Regulation by the States," *New Republic* 108 (June 14, 1943), 790; *St. Louis Post-Dispatch,* Aug. 4, 1938; *New York Times,* Aug. 5, 1938 and July 10, 1939; Henderson, "Political Activities of Gerald L. K. Smith," 33; George Seldes, *One Thousand Americans* (New York, 1947), 220; Smith to Don Lohbeck, Jan. 11, 1946, R 12, F The Don Lohbecks (personal); "Communists, Fascists, Gangsters," *Congressional Record—House,* 86th Cong., 2d sess., vol. 106, pt. 11 (June 27, 1960), p. 14634.

45. Albert Lee, *Henry Ford and the Jews* (New York, 1980), 3, 7, 162.

46. Gamaliel Bradford, "The Great American Enigma," *Harpers Magazine* 161 (Oct. 1930), 519.

47. Nathaniel Weyl, *The Jew in American Politics* (New Rochelle, N.Y., 1968), 103.

48. Harry Bennett, as told to Paul Marcus, *We Never Called Him Henry* (New York, 1951), 42.

49. Ibid., 47.

50. Ibid., 128–29.

51. Bradford, "Great American Enigma," 519–23.

52. Lee, *Henry Ford and the Jews*, 13–15.

53. Weyl, *Jew in American Politics*, 105.

54. Lee, *Henry Ford and the Jews*, 122.

55. Extension of Remarks of Hon. Clare E. Hoffman, Radio Address by Gerald L. K. Smith, Tues., April 19, 1941, *Appendix to the Congressional Record*, 77th Cong., 1st Sess., vol. 87, pt. 11 (March 17–May 20, 1941), pp. A1987–A1988.

56. Lee, *Henry Ford and the Jews*, 110–11; *The Cross and the Flag* 11, no. 9 (Dec. 1952), p. 5; Smith, *Besieged Patriot*, 44; Harold Levine, "Smith Is One-Man Night-Shirt Band," *PM Daily Picture Magazine* [New York], Sept. 7, 1942; Smith to Clara Ford, Jan. 10, 1942, B 2, F 1939–1942 (l. 1940–1942), "F" (misc.), and Clara Ford to Smith, July 26, 1942, ibid.

57. Smith, *Besieged Patriot*, 160–62. The quotations are from Gerald L. K. Smith, taped interview with the author, Los Angeles, Calif., Jan. 21, 1975.

58. *New York Times*, Oct. 5, 1944.

59. FBI, Report on Gerald L. K. Smith by Special Agent, Detroit, Sept. 2, 1942, Detroit F 62–1126, pp. 2–3.

60. Ibid.; *New York Times*, Oct. 5, 1944; Bennett, *We Never Called Him Henry*, 128–29; McCulloch, "Gerald L. K. Smith—Rabble Rouser"; Smith, *Besieged Patriot*, 69.

61. Gerald L. K. Smith, "Gerald L. K. Smith and the Jews: A Significant Summary," n.p., n.d.

62. Ibid.

63. "On Gerald L. K. Smith rally of Committee of One Million on Thursday, April 9, 1942, at Cass Technical High School Auditorium, Detroit," memorandum, n.d., American Jewish Committee Archives.

64. *The Cross and the Flag* 1, no. 2 (May 1942), 8.

65. Detached form, B 2, F 1939–1942 (l. 1940–1942), "G" (misc.).

66. Price, "Gerald L. K. Smith and Anti-Semitism," 100.

67. Nomination Petition, American Jewish Committee; Smith radio address reported by FBI, July 26, 1942, Detroit F 652–1126, pp. 16–19; [Name deleted] to FBI Director, July 17, 1942, F 62–43818–106.

68. Price, "Gerald L. K. Smith and Anti-Semitism," 100.

69. Ribuffo, *Old Christian Right*, 160; Smith interview with Cocks, March 29, 1968; Smith radio address, Aug. 2, 1942; FBI, Detroit F 62–1126, p. 23; John S. Bugas to Director, FBI, Aug. 20, 1942, F 62–43818–119; Smith, *Besieged Patriot*, 153–54.

70. Ribuffo, *Old Christian Right*, 161; *Detroit News*, June 14, Aug. 21, Sept. 4 and 9, 1942.

71. *Detroit News,* Sept. 30, 1942; *Detroit Free Press,* Oct. 1, 1942.
72. Dewey L. Fleming, "Gerald Smith Campaign Run on Tire Plan," *Baltimore Sun,* Sept. 13, 1942.
73. *Tulsa Daily World,* Sept. 15, 1942.
74. H. C. Garrison, "Who Is Gerald L. K. Smith?" *Detroit News,* May 3, 1942.
75. Fleming, "Gerald Smith Campaign Run on Tire Plan."
76. Garrison, "Who Is Gerald L. K. Smith?"
77. *Detroit Free Press,* Sept. 13, 1942.
78. W. A. Markland, "King of Rabble Rousers Smites His Bloomin' Lyre," *Detroit News,* July 18, 1942.
79. Editorial, *Detroit News,* Sept. 13 and 15, 1942.
80. W. A. Markland, "100,000 Smith Votes Mystify GOP," *Detroit News,* Sept. 20, 1942; *St. Louis Post-Dispatch,* Sept. 20, 1942.
81. John S. Bugas to Director, FBI, Sept. 24, 1942, F 62–43818–138.
82. Smith, *Besieged Patriot,* 153.
83. *Detroit News,* Sept. 28 and 30, 1942; Hub George, "GOP Assails Smith for Plan to Run," *Detroit Free Press,* Sept. 28, 1942; *Detroit Free Press,* Sept. 29, 1942.
84. *Official Election Return, United States Senator, Nov. 3, 1942* (gen. elec.), Michigan Department of State, Lansing, B 2, F 1939–1942 (l. 1940–1942), "K" (misc.). The totals have been rounded off.

5. War and Postwar Crusades

1. Gerald L. K. Smith to Mrs. L. Z. Smith, July 11, 1940, R 15, F Staff letters, 1939–1941, Gerald L. K. Smith Papers.
2. George Wolfskill and John A. Hudson, *All But the People: Franklin D. Roosevelt and His Critics, 1933–1939* (New York, 1969), 68, 75.
3. Gerald L. K. Smith, "Too Much and Too Many Roosevelts" (n.p., 1950), 63, copy in New York State Public Library, Albany, N.Y.
4. Margaret L. Coit, *Mr. Baruch* (Boston, 1957), 469.
5. Rough draft of editorial for *The Cross and the Flag* [1942], auth. mic. r. 2.
6. Smith radio broadcast, Aug. 27, 1939, B 4, F 1939–1942 (largely 1940–1942), Radio broadcasts: 1939: Aug.
7. Smith radio address, July 1, 1941, B 6, F 1939–1942 (l. 1940–1942), Radio broadcasts: 1941: July.
8. FBI, Report on Gerald L. K. Smith, September 24, 1945, F 62–43818, p. 3.
9. "Within the Gates," *The Nation* 151 (1940), 74.
10. Smith to parents, May 7, 1941, auth. mic. r. 2.
11. Remarks by Senator Robert R. Reynolds, *Congressional Record—Senate,* 76th Cong., 3d Sess., vol. 86, pt. 9 (July 9–Aug. 15, 1940, July 25, 1940), p. 9607. Vandenberg's comments on the petition appear in the same issue, p. 9597.

12. Memo submitted to House Foreign Affairs Committee, Sol Bloom, chair [1941], B 3, F 1939–1942 (l. 1940–1942), Lend Lease Bill 1776; *Detroit Free Press*, Feb. 6, 1941.

13. The quotations are from Raymond H. Dawson, *The Decision to Aid Russia, 1941: Foreign Politics and Domestic Politics* (Chapel Hill, 1959), p. 30. See also Warren F. Kimball, *The Most Unsordid Act: Lend-Lease, 1939–1941* (Baltimore, 1969), 162; and *St. Louis Post-Dispatch*, Feb. 5, 1941.

14. Isabel B. Price, "Gerald L. K. Smith and Anti-Semitism" (M.A. thesis, University of New Mexico, 1965), 104.

15. Smith to Gerald P. Nye, March 30 and May 7, 1941, both on auth. mic. r. 2; Price, "Gerald L. K. Smith and Anti-Semitism"; Wayne S. Cole, *America First: The Battle Against Intervention, 1940–1941* (Madison, Wis., 1953), 133–34.

16. *Los Angeles Times*, April 16, 1976; copy prepared for *The Cross and the Flag*, 1942, auth. mic. r. 3; Smith to Attorney General Francis J. Biddle, March 26, 1942, included in FBI, Report on Gerald L. K. Smith, July 22, 1942, Detroit, F 62–1126, pp. 10–14.

17. Smith to Carl H. Mote, Dec. 18, 1944, R 9, F Mote, Carl H.; FBI, Report on Gerald L. K. Smith, Oct. 26, 1944, F 62–43818–588, p. 3; *Detroit News*, Sept. 2, 1944, Jan. 4, 1945; *Washington Post*, Oct. 4, 1944.

18. Topical Study Memorandum on America First Party, United States Naval Intelligence Service, Ninth Naval District, Sept. 6, 1943, pp. 1–4.

19. FBI, John S. Bugas to the Director, Jan. 26, 1943, F 62–43818–192, pp. 1–2; Price, "Gerald L. K. Smith and Anti-Semitism," 112–13.

20. Topical Study Memorandum on America First Party, Naval Intelligence Service, Ninth Naval District, Sept. 6, 1943, p. 5; *Detroit Free Press*, Jan. 11, 1943.

21. *St. Louis Post-Dispatch*, Feb. 18, 1944.

22. Ibid.

23. Ibid., March 26, 1944.

24. Ibid.

25. Topical Study Memorandum on America First Party, Sept. 6, 1943, pp. 1–4.

26. Ibid., 94; Francis Biddle, *In Brief Authority* (Garden City, N.Y., 1962), 237–39; *St. Louis Post-Dispatch*, July 24, 1942.

27. Henry Hoke, *It's a Secret* (New York, 1946), 31–59; Richard Polenberg, *War and Society* (New York, 1972), 48. Polenberg erroneously includes Smith among those indicted.

28. Alfred McClung Lee, "Subversive Individuals of Minority Status," *Annals of the American Academy of Political and Social Science* 223 (Sept. 1942), 172.

29. *Detroit Free Press*, Aug. 6, 1945; Smith to Burdett W. Wakeman [his cousin], Feb. 20, 1942, and Smith to Dr. E. N. Sanderson, April 1, 1942, both in auth. mic. r. 2; *The Cross and the Flag* 11, no. 1 (April 1952), 23; Doman to Smith, Nov. 3, 1944, and Smith to Doman, Nov. 15, both in R 8, F B. A.

Doman; FBI, R. A. Guerin to Director, F 62–43818–568; FBI, Report on Gerald L. K. Smith, Dec. 9, 1944, F 62–43818, pp. 12–13.

30. FBI, Report on Smith, March 6, 1944, F 62–43818, p. 17; Ralph Lord Roy, *Apostles of Discord* (Boston, 1943), 75–76; *Detroit News*, Dec. 28, 1944.

31. Lohbeck to Smith, n.d., R 8, F Don Lohbeck. See also a series of letters from Lohbeck to Smith in the same file, and *Detroit News*, Dec. 28, 1944. An exchange of letters between Smith and General Louis B. Hershey in 1944 describes Lohbeck's health problems and attempts to obtain his release. See R 12, F The Don Lohbecks (personal).

32. Leon M. Birkhead, *Pattern for Revolution* (Girard, Kan. [1944]), R 9, F "Pattern for Revolution."

33. "A Public Statement by the United Mothers of America," n.d., R 9, F Mrs. David Stanley (United Mothers of America).

34. Mrs. Katherine M. Sutter to Smith, Nov. 31 and Dec. 16, 1941, March 19, April 28, May 12, and May 21, 1942, all in auth. mic. r. 2; Bertha Glebe to Smith, May 8, May 14, and June 3, 1943, and Smith to Glebe, May 11, 1943, all in B 8, F 1943, "Dayton Rally."

35. Smith to Winrod, Feb. 25, 1942 and Winrod to Smith, Feb. 26, 1942, both in B 7, F 1939–1942 (l. 1940–1942), Winrod, Gerald. The emphasis is in the original.

36. Ray Mitten, "Evangelist Suing for Libel, Guards Case," *Akron Beacon Journal*, Aug. 8, 1943.

37. Smith to Winrod, Feb. 16, 1942, B 7, F 1939–1942 (l. 1940–1942), Winrod, Gerald.

38. Smith to "Dear Patriotic Friend" [1943], auth. mic. r. 3.

39. Biddle, *In Brief Authority*, 119–20; Geoffrey Perrett, *Days of Sadness, Years of Triumph: The American People, 1939–1945* (Baltimore, 1973), 158–61; Nathaniel Weyl, *The Jew in American Politics* (New Rochelle, N.Y., 1968), 134–37.

40. Weyl, *Jew in American Politics*, 131.

41. Smith, *Besieged Patriot*, 269; Smith to Lindbergh, Oct. 9 and Nov. 26, 1941, March 28 and Nov. 19, 1942, and Lindbergh to Smith, Nov. 19, 1941, all in B 3, F 1939–1942 (l. 1940–1942), Lindbergh, Charles; Smith to Barbara, Herman and Mary Jane Heals, Dec. 9, 1942, B 6, F 1939–1942 (l. 1940–1942), Smith family (including son).

42. Jerome Davis, *Character Assassination* (New York, 1950), 46.

43. FBI, Report on Gerald L. K. Smith, March 6, 1944, F 62–43818–435, p. 21.

44. *Propaganda Battlefront*, Feb. 28, 1945, R 11, F "F."

45. Michael Sayers and Albert E. Kahn, *Sabotage: The Secret War Against America* (New York, 1942), 250.

46. Ibid.

47. Reynolds to Smith, March 23, 1942, B 6, F 1939–1942 (l. 1940–1942), "Reynolds, Robert R."

48. Reynolds to Mrs. J. Wistar Evans, June 10, 1944, R 9, F "U.S. Senator Robert Reynolds."

49. George Seldes, *In Fact* 11, no. 5 (May 7, 1945), 2, and 12, no. 10 (Dec. 10, 1945), 3.

50. Vandenberg to Smith, March 5, 1941, auth. mic. r. 3.

51. See Vandenberg to Smith, July 30, 1941, and Mrs. R. F. Thurman to Smith, July 16, 1941, both in auth. mic. r. 3. On April 16, 1941, Vandenberg wrote Smith: "I am always glad to exchange views with you and you are always welcome to any information or opinions which I may have." Auth. mic. r. 3.

52. Birkhead, *Pattern for Revolution,* 7.

53. Clare E. Hoffman to Smith, March 25, 1942, and Smith to Hoffman, April 7, 1942, both in B 2, F 1939–1942 (l. 1940–1942), Hoffman, Clare; *Washington Post,* April 14, 1942; Telegram, Hoffman to Smith, June 12, 1943, B 9, F 1943, Hoffman, Clare E.; *In Fact* 20, no. 3 (Oct. 17, 1949), 3.

54. Both quotations are from George Seldes, *In Fact* 10, no. 26 (April 2, 1945), 1.

55. Birkhead, *Pattern for Revolution,* 7. For the rubber issue see Woodruff speech in the House of Representatives, May 21, 1942, B 7, F 1939–1942 (l. 1940–1942), "Woodruff, Roy O."

56. Smith to Fish, June 28 and July 9, 1940, April 14, 1942, and Nov. 19, Dec. 21, and Dec. 24, 1942, and Fish to Smith, July 9, 1940, and Dec. 31, 1942, all in auth. mic. r. 2.

57. Gerald L. K. Smith, "Inside Post-War Europe" [1945], B 16, F 1945, Memos (confidential).

58. Thorp McClusky, "Huckster of Hatred," *Christian Herald* 73 (Feb. 1950), 65.

59. *The Cross and the Flag* 34, no. 1 (April 1975), 10.

60. Smith to Charles F. Robertson, Sept. 7, 1948, R 21, F "R."

61. *The Cross and the Flag* 10, no. 6 (Sept. 1951), 25.

62. Smith to Charles B. Hudson, April 11, 1961, B 54, F 1961, "H" (misc.).

63. "A Report on Unconditional Surrender," *Propaganda Battlefront,* Jan. 31, 1945, R 11, F "F."

64. Smith to "Dear Fellow American," April, 1948, R 19, F "B. A. Doman."

65. *American Jewish Year Book* 53 (1952), 135–36.

66. Gerald L. K. Smith, *Besieged Patriot: Autobiographical Episodes Exposing Communism, Traitorism and Zionism from the Life of Gerald L. K. Smith,* ed. Elna M. Smith and Charles F. Robertson (Eureka Springs, Ark., 1978), 248; Gerald L. K. Smith, "The Roosevelt Death: A Super Mystery" (n.p., n.d.).

67. Max Lerner, "Plot Psychosis," *New York Post,* June 5, 1950; R. A. Guerin, Special Agent in Charge, to Director, FBI, April 23, 1945, F 62–43818–701, p. 2.

68. FBI, on "Report of Gerald L. K. Smith," June 14, 1945, F 62–43818–757, p. 12.

69. Ralph Lord Roy, *Apostles of Discord: A Study of Organized Bigotry and Disruption on the Fringes of Protestantism* (Boston, 1953), 15.

70. Smith, "Roosevelt Death," 30.

71. FBI, Excerpts from a report on a meeting of the Postwar Recovery Commission held Sunday evening, Sept. 30, 1945, F 62–43818–805, p. 1.

72. Arthur Derounian (pseud., John Roy Carlson), *The Plotters* (New York, 1946), 103.

73. Smith press releases, Aug. 20 and 25, 1944, both in R 8, F Dumbarton Oaks.

74. Smith to Rev. M. Owen Kellison, June 4, 1945, R 12, F "W."

75. Victor Riesel, "Wheeler to Lead Fight against Security Plan," *New York Post*, May 5, 1945.

76. *Propaganda Battlefield*, April 30, 1945, R 11, F "F."

77. Victor Riesel, "Mr. Smith (That's G.L.K.) Goes to San Francisco," *New York Post*, April 6, 1945.

78. *The Cross and the Flag* 11, no. 9 (Dec. 1952), 6.

79. *New York Times*, May 16, 1945.

80. Smith, *Besieged Patriot*, 56–57; Gerald L. K. Smith, taped interview with J. Fraser Cocks III, Los Angeles, Calif., March 29, 1968; *New York Post*, May 12, 14, and 16, 1945; *New York Times*, May 15 and 16, 1945.

81. *New York Times*, May 15, 1945; *Denver Post*, Aug. 29, 1946; Smith to Senator Joseph R. McCarthy, March 2, 1953, B 39, F 1953. "Mc" (misc.); Smith interview with Cocks, March 29, 1968; Smith, *Besieged Patriot*, 60.

82. Smith, *Besieged Patriot*, 54.

83. *The Cross and the Flag* 12, no. 2 (May 1953), 5.

84. Ibid., no. 3 (June 1953), 6–8.

85. Ibid., 8.

86. Smith to G. F. Green, April 9, 1952, B 37, F 1952, Green, G. F.

87. Smith to "Dear Friend," Jan. 15, 1954, B 41, F 1954, *Herald Express* (L.A.).

88. Smith to Mr. and Mrs. Harry Clarke, Oct. 11, 1954, B 41, F 1954, Clarke, Harry.

89. Smith statement to supporters, Sept. 26, 1954, and "A Challenge and Ultimatum to Ambassador Henry Cabot Lodge" [1954], both in B 41, F 1954, "L."

90. *New York Daily Compass*, Aug. 22, 1950.

91. Smith, *Besieged Patriot*, 16.

92. *The Cross and the Flag* 11, no. 8 (Nov. 1952), 18.

93. Gerald L. K. Smith, "World Government Plan—Allied Troops to Police U.S.A.," n.p., n.d.

94. Tom O'Connor, "Nationalists Make Special Effort to Drag in Veterans," *PM* [New York], May 29, 1945.

95. *World-Telegram* [New York], Jan. 25, 1946.

96. Tom O'Connor, "'Nationalists' Take Over U.S. Fascist Drive," *PM* [New York], May 27, 1945.

97. *Philadephia Record*, Dec. 16, 1945.

98. *PM* [New York], May 28, 1945.

99. Gerald L. K. Smith, "Copy of Notes Made in Detroit Re Plans for Expansion," R 10, F "Ralph Baerman."

100. Gerald L. K. Smith, "A Postwar Challenge for Americans" [1945], R 11, F "Postwar Recovery Commission"; E[manuel] A. Piller, *Time Bomb* (New York, 1945), 126–30.

101. Gerald L. K. Smith, "The Plan," Detroit [1945], American Jewish Historical Society, Waltham, Mass.

102. Smith, "Postwar Challenge for Americans."

103. Report on Gerald L. K. Smith, March 27, 1944, FBI F 62–43818–467, p. 2; Eugene Segal, "Nationalists Hold Out Alluring Bait to Veterans," *World-Telegram* [New York], July 21, 1945.

104. Derounian, *Plotters,* 114.

105. Smith to Kenneth Goff, Aug. 29, 1947, R 14, F "Kenneth Goff"; Smith to Agnes T. Christian, July 17 and Aug. 25, 1956, and Christian to Smith, Aug. 21, 1956, all in B 45, F 1956, "C" (misc.); Elizabeth Dilling, "Gerald L. K. Smith" [1948], R 19, F "D."

106. Derounian, *Plotters,* 115.

107. Piller, *Time Bomb,* 124.

108. FBI, Special Agent in Charge, Detroit, to Director, Jan. 22, 1945, F 62–43818–644, p. 2; FBI, Report on Gerald L. K. Smith, Oct. 26, 1944, F 62–43818–588, p. 6; Archie H. Greenberg, National Commander, Jewish War Veterans, "Gerald L. K. Smith and the Veterans" [1945], American Jewish Committee Archives.

109. Lorence Asman to Franklin D. Roosevelt, quoted by Avedis Derounian in "Gerald L. K. Smith Gang at Work Again," *PM* [New York], April 14, 1946, R 12, F "Larry Asman."

110. *PM* [New York], Oct. 8, 1945; *New York Daily News,* Jan. 11, 1946.

111. Sam Stavisky, "Where Does the Veteran Stand Today?" *Annals of American Academy of Political and Social Science* 159 (Sept. 1948), 128–35.

112. Eugene Segal, "Nationalists Organize Youth on Hitler Plan," *World-Telegram* [New York], July 20, 1945.

113. Victor C. Ferkiss, *The Political and Economic Philosophy of American Fascism* (Chicago, 1954), 315.

114. *Washington Post,* Sept. 14, 1945.

115. Smith, *Besieged Patriot,* 316.

116. Ibid., 104.

117. Anti-Defamation League of B'nai B'rith, *Anti-Semitism in 1947* (New York, 1948), 81–82; Smith to Ralph Baerman, Dec. 15, 1947, R 14, F "Ralph Baerman"; Smith to Phil H. Davis, Jr., Oct. 22 and 25, Dec. 19, 1947, all in R 14, F "D"; Smith to John Daugherty, Oct. 24, 1947, and Daugherty to Smith, Oct. 28, 1947, all in R 14, F "D"; *National Jewish Post* [Indianapolis], Jan. 9, 1948; *Jewish Weekly Times* [Boston], Jan. 29, 1948; *St. Louis Globe-Democrat,* Feb. 20, 1948.

118. *St. Louis Post-Dispatch,* Feb. 20, 1948; *The Cross and the Flag* 11, no.

1 (April 1952), 14; FBI, Report on the Christian Nationalist Party of America, April 2, 1952, F 62–43818–1060, p. 27.

119. *St. Louis Post-Dispatch*, May 15, 1946.

120. Ibid., May 31, 1946.

121. Arnold Forster and Benjamin Epstein, *The Trouble Makers* (Garden City, N.Y., 1952), 244–45; *American Jewish Year Book* 51 (1950), 67, 111, and 53 (1952), 137–38; *St. Louis Post-Dispatch*, March 4, April 4 and 29, May 21, 1950, Jan. 29 and May 6, 1953; FBI, Report on Christian Nationalist Party of America, April 2, 1952, F 62–43818–1060, p. 22.

122. Smith interview with Cocks, March 29, 1968.

123. Smith to W. Henry MacFarland, Jr., Dec. 1, 1947, R 14, F "W. Henry MacFarland."

124. Citizens Congressional Committee press release, n.d., B 62, F 1968, "C" (2).

125. Smith to Mrs. Norma Coleman, June 23, 1951, B 34, F 1951, "Cm-Cz."

126. *PM* [New York], June 17, 1945; Carey McWilliams, "Ham 'n' Egg Bait Hook Suckers for G.L.K. Smith," ibid., Oct. 19, 1945; Rodney L. Brink, "Ham 'n' Eggers Renew Drive for $30 a Week," *Christian Science Monitor* [Boston], Feb. 23, 1946; Geoffrey Perrett, *Days of Sadness, Years of Triumph: The American People, 1939–1945* (Baltimore, 1973), 22.

127. FBI, Report on Gerald L. K. Smith, Dec. 19, 1945, F 62–43818–822, pp. 12, 14; Detroit *News*, July 21, 1945; Lloyd Ray Henderson, "The Political Activities of Gerald L. K. Smith," (M.A. thesis, University of California, 1955), 66–67, 79–86; *Los Angeles Times*, Oct. 16, and Nov. 2, 1945; Mary Hornaday, "Los Angeles Earns Feather: City 'Solves' Gerald L. K. Smith," *Christian Science Monitor* [Boston], Oct. 25, 1946.

128. *Detroit Free Press*, July 20, 1945.

129. Henderson, "Political Activities of Gerald L. K. Smith," 66–67, 79–86; Rodney L. Brink, "Los Angeles Recall Vote Repudiates Gerald Smith," *Christian Science Monitor* [Boston], March 21, 1946.

130. FBI, Report on Christian Nationalist Party of America, Jan. 5, 1954, F 62–43818–1135, pp. 1–2; FBI, Special Agent in Charge, Los Angeles, to Director, March 5, 1954, F 62–43818–1149, p. 1; *American Jewish Year Book* 55 (1954), 75; Price, "Gerald L. K. Smith and Anti-Semitism," 145–46; Smith interview with Cocks, March 29, 1968; *St. Louis Globe-Democrat*, April 17, 1953; *Christian Science Monitor* [Boston], March 10, 1951; "Minutes of National Committee of the Christian Nationalist Crusade, Reorganization," April 14, 1953, B 39, F 1953, "Christian Nationalist Crusade, Reorganization"; Smith to Gunda Robertson, April 17, 1953, B 40, F 1953, Robertson, Charles.

6. High Priest of Prejudice

1. Mrs. L. Z. Smith to Gerald Smith, May 1, 1950, B 33, F 1950, Smith, Mrs. L. Z., Gerald L. K. Smith Papers.

2. Mrs. L. Z. Smith to Smith, May 20, 1950, B 33, F 1950, Smith, Mrs. L. Z. The emphasis is in the original.

3. For example, see Mrs. L. Z. Smith to Smith, Dec. 19, 1949, B 29, F 1949, Smith, Mrs. L. Z.

4. *Westwood Hills Press* [Los Angeles], Nov. 9, 1945.

5. Isabel B. Price, "Gerald L. K. Smith and Anti-Semitism" (M.A. thesis, University of New Mexico, 1965), 124.

6. *The Cross and the Flag* 33, no. 2 (May 1974), 24.

7. Paul E. Grosser and Edwin G. Halperin, *The Causes and Effects of Anti-Semitism* (New York, 1978), p. 63.

8. Luke 23:34.

9. Thorp McClusky, "Huckster of Hatred," *Christian Herald* (Feb. 1950), 66.

10. Smith to G. F. Green, March 23, 1949, R 23, F G. F. Green.

11. *The Cross and the Flag* 17, no. 3 (June 1958), 2.

12. Benjamin Freedman, "Hidden Truth, Unrevealed Secrets Involving the National and International Crisis," pub. by Smith [c. 1973].

13. Smith to [Jim] Johnson, June 11, 1964, B 58, F 1964, "J."

14. Gerald L. K. Smith, *Besieged Patriot: Autobiographical Episodes Exposing Communism, Traitorism and Zionism from the Life of Gerald L. K. Smith*, ed. Elna M. Smith and Charles F. Robertson (Eureka Springs, Ark., 1978), 178.

15. FBI, Special Agent in Charge, Buffalo, to Director, Nov. 16, 1949, F 62–43818–991, p. 1.

16. Ralph Lord Roy, *Apostles of Discord* (Boston, 1953), 72.

17. McClusky, "Huckster of Hatred," 66.

18. Gerald L. K. Smith, taped interview with J. Fraser Cocks III, Los Angeles, Calif., March 28, 1968; "An Open Letter to Citizens of Eureka Springs and the World," *Eureka Springs Times-Echo*, Sept. 11, 1969.

19. Smith to George Sokolsky, July 3, 1942, auth. mic. r. 2.

20. U.S. Congress, House, *Hearings Before the Committee on Un-American Activities*, 79th Cong., 1945–46, p. 25.

21. Smith to Harvey H. Springer, Nov. 27, 1944, R 9, F Harvey Springer.

22. Smith to William Bradford Huie, June 25, 1942, B 2, F 1939–1942 (l. 1940–1942), "H" (misc.).

23. Allan A. Michie and Frank Rylic, *Dixie Demagogues* (New York, 1939), 118.

24. *The Cross and the Flag* 11, no. 9 (Dec. 1952), 3.

25. Ibid., 3–4.

26. Price, "Gerald L. K. Smith and Anti-Semitism," 135.

27. Ibid., 134; *The Cross and the Flag* 16, no. 2 (May 1957), 7, and 34, no. 10 (Jan. 1976), 2 [the latter published after Smith's death but written by him]; Smith, "Troubles! Why?" (n.p., Dec. 24, 1974).

28. Grosser and Halperin, *Causes and Effects of Anti-Semitism*, 352.

29. Ibid., 248–49: Morris Kominsky, *The Hoaxers: Plain Liars, Fancy*

Liars, and Damned Liars (Boston 1970), 206–11; James Parkes, *Antisemitism* (London, 1963), 46–51.

30. Kominsky, *Hoaxers*, 181–89; Harold E. Quinley and Charles Y. Glock, *Anti-Semitism in America* (New York, 1979), 165; George X. Johnson, *Architects of Fear: Conspiracy Theory and Paranoia in American Politics* (Boston, 1983), 26–27; Gerald L. K. Smith, "The Threat of Communism," rough draft of copy prepared for *The Cross and the Flag* [1942], auth. mic. r. 2.

31. Smith, "Abraham Lincoln and the Rothschilds" (n.p., n.d.).

32. Kominsky, *Hoaxers*, 15–17.

33. Gerald L. K. Smith, "The Civil War and the Jews" (n.p., n.d.).

34. *The Cross and the Flag* 34, no. 2 (May 1975), 3.

35. Ibid., 17, no. 3 (June 1958), 9.

36. Smith, "Truth Resurrected" (n.p., n.d.).

37. Smith, "Gerald L. K. Smith and the Jews: A Significant Summary" (n.p., n.d.).

38. Smith to Don Lohbeck, Feb. 3, 1948, R 20, F Don Lohbeck.

39. Smith, *Besieged Patriot*, 181.

40. Smith, "Franklin the Prophet" (n.p., n.d.), R 23, F Benjamin Franklin.

41. *The Cross and the Flag* 10, no. 8 (Nov. 1951), 20–21.

42. Ibid., 17, no. 1 (April 1958), 8.

43. *New York Times*, April 22, 1955.

44. Smith, "If the Crusader Quits, What Happens?" [1972].

45. Smith, "Super Secret: A White paper," B 92, F Israel.

46. For an excellent brief account of fundamentalists and the radical right see David Danzig, "The Radical Right and the Rise of the Fundamentalist Minority," *Commentary* 33 (1962), 291–98.

47. For a general discussion see Gordon Allport, *The Nature of Prejudice* (Reading, Pa., 1980), 418.

48. The conclusions are mine, but see Fred J. Cook, "The Right Has Nine Lives," *Nation* 204 (March 13, 1967), 330.

49. According to reports of FBI agents who attended Smith's meetings, women outnumbered men and the elderly outnumbered the young. See FBI, Report on Gerald L. K. Smith, Sept. 27, 1944, F 62–43818–570, p. 12. For a general discussion of the kinds of people attracted to "native fascism," see Reinhold Niebuhr, "Pawns for Fascism—Our Lower Middle Classes," *The American Scholar* 6, no. 2 (Spring 1937), 145–52.

50. See Gertrude J. Selznick and Stephen Steinberg, *The Tenacity of Prejudice: Anti-Semitism in Contemporary America* (New York, 1969), 79–93, 160–61.

51. Smith to Jack B. Tenney, July 13, 1945, and Smith to Earl Craig, July 12, 1945, both in R 16, F Los Angeles Meetings.

52. Smith to Don Lohbeck, Feb. 3, 1948, R 20, F Don Lohbeck.

53. Smith, "The Dangerous and Glorious Search for Truth" (n.p., n.d.), 5.

54. Ibid., 6.

7. Fighting Reds and Blacks—and Every Shade in Between

1. *The Cross and the Flag* 12, no. 3 (June 1953), 17.

2. Morris Kominsky, *The Hoaxers: Plain Liars, Fancy Liars, and Damned Liars* (Boston, 1970), 105.

3. Smith to "Dear Loved Ones" [Roland Lee Morgan and family], March 9, 1953, B 39, F 1953, "M" (misc.).

4. Smith, "Is Communism Jewish?" (St. Louis, n.d.), American Jewish Historical Society, Waltham, Mass.

5. *The Cross and the Flag* 16, no. 7 (Oct. 1957), 23.

6. Ibid., 17, no. 6 (Sept. 1958), 11.

7. Ibid.

8. *American Jewish Year Book* 69 (1968), 263.

9. *Madison Capital Times* [Wisconsin], Sept. 17, 1947.

10. Smith to Timothy Trumbull, Aug. 3, 1965, B 60, F 1965, "G" (misc.).

11. Smith, "Dangerous Enemies" (n.p., n.d.), 27–28, 50–51, 73.

12. Smith, "Twenty Surrenders!! What is the Answer? Read-Weep-Resolve: A Summary," n.p. [1969].

13. Michael Parenti, *The Anti-Communist Impulse* (New York, 1969), 40.

14. Mark Sherwin, *The Extremists* (New York, 1963), 216–17.

15. *The Cross and the Flag* 10, no. 8 (Nov. 1951), 23.

16. Copy of petition to outlaw Communism in B 2, F 1939–1942 (l. 1940–1942), Form Letters: 1941.

17. Gerald L. K. Smith, *Besieged Patriot: Autobiographical Episodes Exposing Communism, Traitorism and Zionism from the Life of Gerald L. K. Smith*, ed. Elna M. Smith and Charles F. Robertson (Eureka Springs, Ark., 1978), 209.

18. *The Cross and the Flag* 17, no. 9 (Dec. 1958), 3.

19. Ibid., 12, no. 3 (June 1953), 11.

20. Smith, "Matters of Life and Death" (n.p., n.d.), American Jewish Historical Society, Waltham, Mass.

21. Erling Jorstad, *The Politics of Doomsday: Fundamentalists of the Far Right* (Nashville, 1970), 63–64.

22. Smith petition "Against Communism: For Christian America," B 32, F 1950, Memos (2).

23. Flyer for Erie, Penn., meeting, B 1, F 1939–1942 (l. 1940–1942), Comm. of 1,000,000: Erie rally, April 15, 1940; *St. Louis Post-Dispatch*, April 19, 1949; Michael Sayers and Albert E. Kahn, *The Great Conspiracy: The Secret War Against Russia* (Boston, 1946), 361.

24. Nathan Perlmutter, "Evangelist Demagogues, 1952 Model; Both Sides of the Coin," *Commentary* 14 (1952), 336.

25. Kenneth Goff to "Dear Christian Friend," R 14, F Kenneth Goff.

26. *American Jewish Year Book* 63 (1962), 196–97; R. E. Legant to Circuit Riders, Feb. 27, 1960; M. G. Lowman to Walter L. Phillips [pseud. for Smith],

March 11, 1960; Phillips to Lowman, March 16, 1960; Lowman to Phillips, March 22, 1960, all in B 51, F 1960, "C" (misc.); Smith to John Frank, April 13, and May 18, 1960, B 52, F 1960, "F" (misc.).

27. Smith to Robert Welch, Sept. 9 and Dec. 14, 1959; Welch to Smith, Sept. 16, 1959, all in B 51, F 1959, "W" (misc.); Welch to Hal W. Russell, Jan. 3, 1962, B 55, F 1962.

28. Smith to Jim Reagan, June 11, 1974, B 78, F 1974, "R" (1).

29. *The Cross and the Flag* 11, no. 3 (June 1952), 19, 24.

30. Smith, "Mysterious Facts Behind the Death of Senator Joseph McCarthy" (n.p., n.d.), 11.

31. Joe McCarthy to Smith, Nov. 1, 1951, B 35, F 1951, McCarthy, Joseph.

32. Smith, "Mysterious Facts Behind the Death of McCarthy," 11.

33. *New York Daily News*, Dec. 10, 1954.

34. Drew Pearson, "Pro-McCarthy Pressure Group Borrows Technique of Reds," *St. Louis Post-Dispatch*, Nov. 17, 1954; *Jewish Examiner* [Brooklyn], Jan. 28, 1955.

35. *New York Post*, Dec. 17, 1954.

36. Petition, "Apologize to McCarthy," B 44, F 1955, "P" (misc.); Smith to Senator Ralph Flanders, May 24, 1957, B 47, F 1957, "F" (misc.).

37. Smith, "An Interview with Mr. X" (n.p., n.d.), 4.

38. Smith to Joe McCarthy, Sept. 9, 1955, R 17, F "Mc."

39. Smith to Edith Essig, July 23, 1956, B 45, F 1956, "E" (misc.).

40. Smith, "Lest We Forget: A Tribute to the Late U.S. Senator Joseph McCarthy," B 49, F 1958, "Mc" (misc.).

41. Smith, "Mysterious Facts Behind the Death of McCarthy," 9.

42. Ibid., 8. The emphasis is in the original.

43. *The Cross and the Flag* 17, no. 1 (April 1958), 10.

44. *Baltimore Sun*, Aug. 21, 1948.

45. Will Chasan, "Whose Trojan Horse?" *The Nation* 155 (1942), 322.

46. *Jewish Voice* [California], June 15, 1951, B 41, F 1954, Circulars.

47. Mike Newberry, *The Yahoos* (New York, 1964), 104.

48. S. A. Fineberg, memorandum, Oct. 6, 1944, American Jewish Committee Files.

49. *Washington Post*, Jan. 31, 1946.

50. Walter Goodman, *The Committee: The Extraordinary Career of the House Un-American Activities Committee* (New York, 1968), 182.

51. Oliver Pilat, "G. L. K. Smith Slams F. D. R., New Deal, 'Jewish Gestapo,'" *New York Post*, Jan. 30, 1946.

52. *Tulsa Tribune*, Jan. 7, 1948.

53. *The Cross and the Flag* 16, no. 3 (June 1957), 17.

54. The meeting is described in Smith to Lohbeck, Nov. 28, 1948 and the final quotation is from Smith to Lohbeck, Dec. 12, 1948, both in R 20, F Don Lohbeck.

55. Myron C. Fagan to Smith, March 12, 13, and 20, April 6 and 18, 1949, and Smith to Fagan, March 17, April 18 and 25, 1949, all in R 23, F Myron C. Fagan; Fagan to Smith, Oct. 30, 1950, B 36, F 1950, Fagan, Myron C.

56. Smith to Mr. and Mrs. L. Z. Smith, Feb. 14, 1947, R 15, F Rev. and Mrs. L. Z. Smith.

57. Smith to Mrs. L. Z. Smith, Oct. 27, 1949, B 29, F Washington Newsletter; Smith to Ed and Mildred Sorenson, Sept. 30, 1963, B 58, F 1963, "S" (misc.); *The Cross and the Flag* 16, no. 3 (June 1957), 4.

58. Smith to William Stephenson, March 11, 1957, B 48, F 1957, "S" (misc.).

59. *The Cross and the Flag* 17, no. 5 (Aug. 1958), 10.

60. Smith to Rev. Donald W. Holly, Oct. 24, 1960, B 52, F 1960, "H" (misc.).

61. Arnold Forster and Benjamin R. Epstein, *The New Anti-Semitism* (New York, 1974), 20.

62. Smith, taped interview with J. Fraser Cocks III, Los Angeles, Calif., March 28, 1968.

63. Smith, *Besieged Patriot*, 24.

64. Smith to Gerry Smith, Oct. 30, 1944, R 9, F Gerald L. K. Smith, Personal Correspondence.

65. Mrs. L. Z. Smith to Smith, July 15, 1946, R 13, F Smith Family.

66. Smith to Ed and Mildred Sorenson, June 3, 1955, B 44, F 1955, Sorenson family.

67. Smith to [Pat] Weston, Dec. 14, 1962, B 56, F 1962, "W" (misc.).

68. Mr. and Mrs. Gerald L. K. Smith "To Whom It May Concern," Dec. 21, 1947, R 14, F "J."

69. Smith to Theodore G. Bilbo, March 15, 1947, R 14, F Theodore G. Bilbo.

70. *The Cross and the Flag* 17, no. 7 (Oct. 1958), 13; Bertrand Comparet to Smith, Feb. 24, 1956, R 17, F Bertrand Comparet.

71. *The Cross and the Flag* 17, no. 5 (Aug. 1958), 11.

72. Ralph Lord Roy, *Apostles of Discord* (Boston, 1953), 66–67.

73. Smith press release, April 12, 1947, R 15, F Press Releases, 1947.

74. Smith, *Besieged Patriot*, 289; Smith to Rear Admiral John G. Crommelin, Sept. 17, 1957, R 18, F Admiral John G. Crommelin.

75. *The Cross and the Flag* 17, no. 6 (Sept. 1958), 24; Smith to A. X. Clark, June 11, 1959, B 50, F 1959, "C" (misc.); Newberry, *Yahoos*, 188.

76. Smith, *Besieged Patriot*, 93.

77. Smith, "I Love the Church" (n.p., n.d.), 4.

78. Smith to Mrs. Claud B. Jordan, April 2, 1970, B 67, F 1970, "J."

79. Smith, "America Kidnapped" (n.p., n.d.), 14.

80. Thorp McClusky, "Huckster of Hatred," *Christian Herald* (Feb. 1950), 64; *St. Louis Post-Dispatch*, Jan. 3, March 26, Sept. 27, and Dec. 13, 1949; *St. Louis Globe-Democrat*, Dec. 30, 1948, Jan. 4, March 26, April 4, and Dec. 14, 1949.

81. *St. Louis Post-Dispatch*, June 27, 1948.

82. Smith to Opal Tanner White, May 11, 1959, B 51, F 1959, Memos.

83. Smith, "Prepare for a Shock," May 23, 1966, Anti-Defamation League files.

84. Smith to Mrs. L. Z. Smith, May 25, 1954, R 16, F Mrs. L. Z. Smith.

85. Smith, "Matters of Life and Death."

86. Smith, "Poison Water Red Plot" (n.p., n.d.); Smith to Walter Westenberg, May 21, 1975, B 81, F 1975, "W" (2).

87. *The Cross and the Flag* 17, no. 6 (Sept. 1958), 9.

88. Smith, "Jews on the Wrong Side of Every Major Life and Death Issue" (n.p., n.d.), 4.

89. Smith, "A Prophetic White Paper," n.p. [1973].

90. *The Cross and the Flag* 34, no. 10 (Jan. 1976), 25.

91. Smith, "Principles Worth Living and Dying For" (n.p., n.d.), 9.

92. Smith, "Twenty Surrenders!!", 3.

93. Smith to T. R. Burke, March 24, 1965, B 59, F 1965, "Bp-Bz" (misc.).

94. Smith, "Sex 'Education' (?)" (n.p., n.d.), 3.

95. Smith, "America Kidnapped," 8–9.

96. Smith, "Jews on the Wrong Side," 4.

97. Smith to Fred Kurtz, March 17, 1970, B 67, F "R" (2).

98. "Outlaw the Slaughter of the Infants," petition to Congress [1973], my copy.

99. Smith to A. Bachleda, April 28, 1972, B 71, F 1972, "B" (1).

100. *The Cross and the Flag* 33, no. 8 (Nov. 1974), 36.

101. Ibid., 17, no. 4 (July 1958), 17.

102. Ibid., 33, no. 11 (Feb. 1975), 11.

103. Smith, "Don't Forget the Big Issue: Law and Order" (n.p., n.d.).

104. Smith, "Twenty Surrenders!!", 4.

105. Smith to H. Myers, Dec. 17, 1974, B 78, F 1974, "M" (4).

106. Smith to National Rifle Association of America, June 2, 1975, B 80, F 1975, "N."

107. Smith, *Besieged Patriot*, 17.

108. Ibid., 23.

109. Smith to Clifton M. Jones, Oct. 27, 1972, B 70, F 1972, "J."

110. *The Cross and the Flag* 34, no. 11 (Feb. 1976), 15.

111. Ibid., 34, no. 5 (Aug. 1975), 18.

112. Ibid., 15.

113. Ibid., 16.

114. Ibid., 33, no. 2 (May 1974), 14.

115. Ibid., 34, no. 12 (March 1976), 11.

116. Smith, "Lieutenant Calley, Martyr" (n.p., n.d.).

117. Smith, "Troubles! Why?" (n.p., Dec. 24, 1974).

118. Smith, "A Secret Interview" (n.p., n.d.), 13.

8. A Glib Tongue, Acid Pen, and Hard Cash

1. *Shreveport Times*, "Biographical Information Furnished by United Press Associations."

2. Robert Goldston, *The Great Depression: The United States in the Thirties* (Indianapolis, 1968), 1949.

3. Raleigh G. Hoover, "America First Ropes Bison for Symbol," *Detroit News*, Aug. 31, 1944.

4. H. C. Garrison, "Who Is Gerald L. K. Smith?" *Detroit News*, May 3, 1942.

5. "Gerald L. K. Smith," *Current Biography*, 1943, 707.

6. Mark Sullivan, untitled reprint from *New York Herald Tribune*, Aug. 16, 1936.

7. William Bradford Huie, "Gerald Smith's Bid for Power," *American Mercury* 55 (Aug. 1942), 145.

8. Smith, "My Fight for the Right" (St. Louis, n.d.), American Jewish Historical Society, Waltham, Mass.

9. Gerald L. K. Smith, taped interview with J. Fraser Cocks III, Los Angeles, Calif., March 28, 1968.

10. Arthur Derounian (pseud., John Roy Carlson), *The Plotters* (New York, 1946), 109.

11. "The Life of Christ," Lecture No. 1, by Gerald L. K. Smith, reported by Margaret Lucky and Evelyn Chadock, B 1, F 1922–1938, Lectures, Gerald L. K. Smith Papers.

12. *Detroit News*, May 3, 1942.

13. Brenda Ueland, "What Goes On Here?" *Minneapolis Daily Times*, Oct. 15, 1943.

14. Ibid.

15. Spencer R. McCulloch, "Gerald L. K. Smith—Rabble Rouser," *St. Louis Post-Dispatch*, Dec. 26, 1943; Gerald L. K. Smith, *Besieged Patriot: Autobiographical Episodes Exposing Communism, Traitorism and Zionism from the Life of Gerald L. K. Smith*, ed. Elna M. Smith and Charles F. Robertson (Eureka Springs, Ark., 1978), 83, 100.

16. Smith to Phyllis Liebig, Dec. 2, 1940, R 15, F Applications.

17. Gertrude Newman to Smith [1945], R 10, F Chicago File, Special; Ernest Elmhurst to Smith, Oct. 30, 1949, R 23, F "E"; "A friend and supporter" to Smith, Feb. 25, 1959, B 60, F 1959, "A" (misc.).

18. Herbert Harris, "That Third Party," *Current History* 45, no. 1 (Oct. 1936), 84.

19. Lee Casey, "Snake Oil—or Poison?" *Rocky Mountain News* [Denver], Oct. 12, 1948.

20. S. A. Fineberg to St. Thomas Friedman, June 23, 1952, American Jewish Committee Files.

21. Smith, *Besieged Patriot*, 321.

22. Smith to Mrs. L. Z. Smith, Aug. 30, 1955, R 17, F Mrs. L. Z. Smith.

23. Smith to Brother [Leland L.] and Mrs. Marion, April 1, 1957, B 47, F 1957, "M" (misc.).

24. Smith, *Besieged Patriot*, 4.

25. Thorp McClusky, "Huckster of Hatred," *Christian Herald* (Feb. 1950), 64.

26. *The Cross and the Flag* 16, no. 5 (Aug. 1957), 3.

27. Ibid., 17, no. 6 (Sept. 1958), 22.

28. Ibid., no. 7 (Oct. 1958), 11.

29. Smith, "Confidential: Only for those who can understand," Oct. 1948, New York State Library, Albany.

30. Smith to Ed and Mildred [Sorenson], July 25, 1969, B 65, F 1969, "S" (3). Warner, of course, was an archivist, not "chair of the historical department." As director of the University of Michigan's Bentley Historical Library, Warner negotiated the donation of Smith's papers, given to the Bentley after Smith's death. Warner subsequently became archivist of the United States and in 1984 returned to the University of Michigan as dean of the School of Library Science.

31. Smith to Mrs. Isabelle S. Brown, Jan. 27, 1965, B 59, F 1965, "Bp-Bz" (misc.).

32. FBI, R. A. Guerin to Director, Feb. 10, 1945, F 62–43818–659.

33. Erling Jorstad, *The Politics of Doomsday: Fundamentalists of the Far Right* (Nashville, 1970), 105.

34. Smith to Larry L. Legge, March 28, 1974, B 78 "L" (1).

35. Smith to Joseph Kamp, May 30, 1962, B 55, F 1962, "K" (misc.).

36. Smith to Noel N. Hamdan, Nov. 13, 1970, B 67, F 1970, "H" (4).

37. Smith to Ralph Baerman, Feb. 15, 1947, R 14, F Ralph Baerman.

38. Smith to Don Lohbeck, Sept. 30, 1947, R 14, F "Lohbeck."

39. This and the discussion of Smith's reading that follows are based upon a survey of books taken from Smith's personal library included in B 95.

40. Smith to Charles E. Mills, April 15, 1969, B 64, F 1969, "M" (2).

41. Gerald L. K. Smith, taped interview with the author, Aug. 10, 1974, Eureka Springs, Ark.

42. Smith to Josef Czumbil, Nov. 17, 1970, B 66, F 1970, "C" (2).

43. Smith to Sen. Rush D. Holt, Feb. 12, 1942, auth. mic. r. 2.

44. *The Cross and the Flag* 11, no. 1 (April 1952), 2.

45. Ibid., 1, no. 1 (April 1942), 2.

46. Smith, Memo on *The Cross and the Flag* [1942], auth. mic. r. 2.

47. *The Cross and the Flag* 1, no. 1 (April 1942).

48. Smith interview with Cocks, March 29, 1968.

49. Ibid.; Smith to Don Lohbeck, March 21, 1953, B 39, F 1953, Lohbeck, Don; Smith to Edith Morgan, Aug. 24, 1962, B 55, F 1962, "M" (misc.); Smith to Don Lohbeck, Opal M. Tanner, and Joel D. Sugg, Jan. 17, May 4, and May 31, 1951, all in B 34, F 1951, Christian Publishers; Smith to Lohbeck and Tanner, Sept. 14, 1951, B 35, F 1951, Memos (3); Smith, *Besieged Patriot*, 227, 314; *The Cross and the Flag* 11, no. 1 (April 1952), 22.

50. *The Cross and the Flag* 10, no. 1 (April 1951), 26; 11, no. 1 (April 1952), 22; 34, no. 4 (July 1965), 18; Smith to Edwin Bischoff, Jan. 30, 1974, B 76, F 1974, "B" (3); Smith to Congressman Adolph J. Sabath, April 2, 1942, auth. mic. r. 2.

51. FBI, Report on Gerald L. K. Smith, April 9, 1942, Detroit F 62–1126, 1, 12; *American Jewish Year Book* 60–67 (1959–66); Group Research, Inc., Report, June 24, 1963, B 61, F 1966, Memoirs and Corres.; Smith to U.S.

Senator Elmer Thomas, Feb. 18, 1950, B 33, F 1950, "T" (misc.); *The Cross and the Flag* 34, no. 7 (Oct. 1975), 19.

52. These appeared in a sample year, 1958.

53. Quoted in Ralph Lord Roy, *Apostles of Discord* (Boston, 1953), 66.

54. Isabel B. Price, "Gerald L. K. Smith and Anti-Semitism" (M.A. thesis, University of New Mexico, 1965), 143.

55. "Gerald Lyman Kenneth Smith," *Timely Biographies* (Aug. 1948), American Jewish Committee Archives; *Detroit Free Press*, March 22, 1945; *In Fact* 14, no. 2 (Oct. 14, 1946), 1; *American Jewish Year Book* 51 (1950), 67; FBI, Report on Christian Nationalist Party of America, Dec. 16, 1952, F 62–43818–1086, p. 1.

56. Memo to Opal Tanner and Renata Legant, undated, B 31, F 1950, Los Angeles meeting.

57. Smith to Patrice Schuette, Aug. 3, 1943, auth. mic. r. 3.

58. These estimates are derived from a study of Smith's list of contributors and personal correspondence. This figure for 1949 is from Arnold Forster, *A Measure of Freedom* (Garden City, N.Y., 1950), 38.

59. Mailing list with notation "Kister List," B 2, F 1939–1942 l. 1940–1942), "K" (misc.); Smith to Don Lohbeck, May 30, 1947, and Renata E. Legant to Lohbeck, Telegram, June 2, 1947, both in B 21, F 1947, Memos: interoffice (1); Lohbeck to Smith [1948], R 20, F Don Lohbeck; Smith to Lohbeck, Nov. 28, 1949, B 28, F 1949, Memos, Sept.–Dec.

60. Smith interview with Cocks, March 29, 1968. Many solicitation letters are included in the Smith Collection at the Bentley Historical Library.

61. Smith to "My dear good friend," March 10, 1949, B 28, F 1949, Response form letters.

62. See, for example, Mrs. H. A. Clipton to Smith, Sept. 3, 1970, B 91, F Notes.

63. See Smith's office mail, B 83–90. This is a large collection of Smith's incoming correspondence.

64. J. Lacey Reynolds, "Gerald L. K. Smith Crusades Again with a New Cross for Our Flag to Bear," *Boston Globe*, April 30, 1942; "Gerald L. K. Smith," memorandum [1939], American Jewish Committee Archives; Smith memo, n.d., R 15, F Staff Memos, 1929–1940.

65. Smith to George Sokolsky, July 3, 1942, B 6 F 1939–1942 (l. 1940–1942), Sokolsky, George; Questions put to Smith by William Bradford Huie of *American Mercury*, June 4, 1942, B 2, F 1939–1942 (l. 1940–1942), "H" (misc.).

66. America First Party, Reports to Congress, 1945 and 1946; Hugh Daly, "Gerald L. K. Smith Under House Fire," *Detroit Times*, Jan. 7, 1948; *Detroit Free Press*, April 2, 1947; *New York Daily Mirror*, Jan. 21, 1946.

67. America First Party, Report to Congress, 1947; Smith, "Must It Be Chain Gangs, Firing Squads and Prison Camps for the Lovers of Jesus Christ?" (Oct. 1947), American Jewish Historical Society, Waltham, Mass.

68. Christian Nationalist Crusade, Report to Congress, 1948 (hereafter

Report to Congress); U.S. Individual Income Tax Return, 1948, B 28, F 1949, Smith, Gerald L. K. (re income tax).

69. Report to Congress, 1949; Arnold Forster, *A Measure of Freedom* (Garden City, New York, 1950), 37; Smith to Don Lohbeck and Opal Tanner, Jan. 18, 1949, and Smith to Lohbeck, April 4 and 11, 1949, all in R 24, F Don Lohbeck; Smith to Mr. and Mrs. E. E. Manney, R 24, F E. E. Manney; Smith to Mr. and Mrs. L. L. Marion, April 16, 1949, R 24, F Leland L. Marion. For loans see correspondence with many of Smith's best supporters in R 24, F Loans.

70. Report to Congress, 1950.

71. Ibid.

72. *St. Louis Post-Dispatch*, May 21, 1952.

73. Reports to Congress, 1953–1957.

74. Ibid., 1960–1969.

75. Ibid., 1965.

76. Ibid.

77. Ibid., 1966–69.

78. Ibid.

79. Ibid., 1970.

80. Ibid.

81. Ibid.; Smith to Devin Garrity, Jan. 21, 1972, B 72, F "G" (3).

82. Report to Congress, 1971.

83. Ibid., 1972 and 1973.

84. Ibid., 1974; Charles F. Robertson to Pat Jennings, Jan. 22, 1975, included with the financial statement.

85. See, for example, In re: Estate of Millard M. Wagner, Deceased, Estate No. 44–72–114, In the Court of Common Pleas of Mifflin County, Pa., April 1973.

86. Thomas F. Cadwalader to Smith, Jan. 12, Feb. 19, June 24, and Sept. 14, 1965, and Smith to Cadwalader, Feb. 25 and Aug. 11, 1965, all in B 59, F 1965, "Ca-Cm" (misc.).

87. Don Lohbeck to Smith, n.d., Smith to Lohbeck, June 6, 1947, and Smith to Kerchner, Sept. 8, 1947, all in R 14, F W. G. Kerchner; Kerchner to Smith, Jan. 12, Jan. 18, Jan. 29, Feb. 20, and Aug. 24, 1948, and Smith to Kerchner, Jan. 14 and 19, 1948, all in R 20, F "K"; Kerchner to Smith, Dec. 27, 1963, B 57, F 1963, "K" (misc.); Kerchner to Smith, June 3, 1965, and Smith to Kerchner, June 11, 1965, both in B 60, F 1965, "K" (misc.).

88. Ernest F. Elmhurst to Smith, Nov. 5, 1948, R 19, F Ernest F. Elmhurst; Elmhurst to Smith, Dec. 14, and Aug. 22, and 28, all in R 23, F "F"; Elmhurst to Smith, Sept. 12, 1956, B 45, F 1956, "E" (misc.).

89. "Autobiographical Sketch of Mrs. Edith Essig," B 45, F 1956, "E" (misc.); B 36, F 1952, Essig, Mrs. Edith; Essig to Smith, March 23 and April 16, 1945, R 11, F "E"; FBI, Special Agent in Charge, Detroit, to Director, April 3, 1945, F 62–43818–697; B 39, F 1953, Essig, Edith; B 43, F 1955, Essig, Edith.

90. Mrs. Louis Rasmussen to Smith, n.d., B 40, F 1953, Special Letters.

91. Helen M. Schott to Smith, Feb. 21, 1968, B 62, F 1968, Large Donors.

92. Hester Victornine to Smith, March 6, 1968, B 62, F 1968, Large Donors.

93. Daniel Boone to Smith, July 3, 1958, B 48, F 1958 Appeal.

94. Mrs. L. R. Doyle to Smith, March 26, 1968, B 62, F 1968, "D."

95. Esther Kellander to Smith, Jan. 3, 1968, B 62, F 1968, "K."

96. Reports to Congress, 1973 and 1974.

97. Arthur D'Angelo to Smith, Sept. 7, 1950, Smith to D'Angelo, Aug. 31 and Oct. 13, 1950, all in B 30, F 1950, "D" (misc.).

98. E. H. Shepler to Smith, Jan. 30, 1949, B 28, F 1949, "Sa-Sh" (misc.); Smith to Herrin Transfer, Feb. 24, 1949, R 24, F "H"; Smith to Mark Spear, May 7, 1949, B 28, F 1949, "Sp-Sz" (misc.); Smith to American Legion *Reveille,* Sept. 17, 1949, B 28, F 1949, "R" (misc.).

99. Based upon personal observation and the description by Cocks, included with the transcript of his interview with Smith.

100. Smith to John D. Boyd, July 16, 1957, B 55, F 1962, Antiques; Smith to Ed and Mildred [Sorenson], Nov. 25, 1968, B 63, F 1968, "S" (4).

9. Crusades for the Presidency

1. "Gerald L. K. Smith," memorandum, March 31, 1941, p. 3, American Jewish Committee Archives.

2. Gerald L. K. Smith to mother, July 11, 1940, B 1, F 1939–1942 (l. 1940–1942), Corr.: 1942, Gerald L. K. Smith Papers.

3. Gerald L. K. Smith, *Besieged Patriot: Autobiographical Episodes Exposing Communism, Traitorism and Zionism from the Life of Gerald L. K. Smith,* ed. Elna M. Smith and Charles F. Robertson (Eureka Springs, Ark., 1978), 36.

4. William Bradford Huie, "Gerald Smith's Bid for Power," *American Mercury* 55 (Aug. 1942), 152.

5. FBI, Report on Gerald L. K. Smith, March 6, 1944, F 62–43818–481, p. 3.

6. Ibid., March 22, 1944.

7. Neal Stanford, "America First Nominee Testifies on Funds," *Christian Science Monitor* [Boston], Oct. 3, 1944.

8. *Detroit News,* Oct. 9, 1942; *New York Times,* March 25, 1944; *Detroit Free Press,* Sept. 3, 1944.

9. Smith press release, n.d., R 15, F Press Releases, 1943.

10. Gerald P. Nye to Smith, Dec. 29, 1942, auth. mic. r. 3.

11. Victor Riesel, "Fascist GOP Block Maps Raid on New York," *New York Post,* July 8, 1943; *Detroit Free Press,* July 3, 1943.

12. John McCarten, "General MacArthur: Fact and Legend," *American Mercury* 58 (Jan. 1944), 7–8, 11.

13. FBI, Report on Gerald L. K. Smith, Sept. 27, 1944, F 62–43818–570, p. 17; *Christian Science Monitor* [Boston], *St. Louis Post-Dispatch,* and *Wash-*

ington Times-Herald, Nov. 16, 1943; *American Jewish Year Book* 47 (1945–46), 271–73.

14. *New York Times*, May 27, 1944.

15. *Detroit News*, April 9, 1944.

16. "A Personal Message About Chicago–Dewey America First," July 1944, R 9, F Mimeographed Forms.

17. *New York Post*, June 26, 1944; *Besieged Patriot*, 157–158.

18. *Chicago Sun*, July 17, 1944; *New York PM*, July 19, 1944; *New York Times*, July 22, 1944; Smith to "Dear Fellow American," July 1944, R 8, F Chicago Meeting.

19. America First Party Press releases, Aug. 1 and 5, 1944, B 94, F "Duplicates"; Smith to parents, Aug. 9, 1944, R 9, F Gerald L. K. Smith, Personal Correspondence.

20. Richard Mathison, *God Is a Millionaire* (Indianapolis, 1950), 351.

21. "America First Party Platform Highlight," and Smith press releases, Aug. 7 and 11, 1944, all in R 15, F Smith Press Releases, 1944.

22. Raleigh G. Hoover, "America First Ropes Bison for Symbol," *Detroit News*, Aug. 31, 1944; New York *Herald-Tribune*, Aug. 8, 1944.

23. Hoover, "Smith on the First Ballot Hinted at Smith Convention," *Detroit News*, Aug. 30, 1944, and Hoover, "America First Ropes Bison."

24. *New York Times*, Aug. 17, 1944.

25. *PM* [New York], Aug. 17, 1944.

26. *Detroit News*, Sept. 4, 1944.

27. Hoover, "America First Ropes Bison."

28. For the above statistics see Leo P. Ribuffo, *The Old Christian Right: The Protestant Far Right From the Depression to the Cold War* (Philadelphia, 1983), 175; *PM* [New York], Dec. 14, 1944; Earl Southard to Smith, Nov. 17, 1944, R 9, F Captain Earl Southard; FBI, Special Agent in Charge to Director, Dec. 9 and 12, 1944; FBI F 62–43818–624, pp. 1–2.

29. *Christian Science Monitor* [Boston], July 30, 1947.

30. *Boston Journal-American*, July 30, 1947.

31. Smith press release, Sept. 25, 1947, R 15, F Press Releases, 1947.

32. Judge George W. Armstrong to Smith, Dec. 23, 1946, Jan. 25 and June 27, 1947, and Smith to Armstrong, Jan. 21, 1947, all in R 13, F George W. Armstrong.

33. *Detroit News*, July 19, 1948.

34. *In Fact* 17, no. 19 (Aug. 9, 1948), 1.

35. Smith, *Besieged Patriot*, 37.

36. *Detroit News*, July 20, 1948.

37. *Christian Science Monitor* [Boston], July 20, 1948.

38. Smith to Judge George W. Armstrong, Aug. 11, 1948, R 19, F Armstrong Foundation.

39. *Daily Oklahoman* [Oklahoma City], April 5, 1948; Smith press releases, April 11 and May 11, 1948, R 21, F Press Releases.

40. Lloyd Ray Henderson, "The Political Activities of Gerald L. K. Smith" (M.A. thesis, University of California, 1955), 116.

41. Transcript of first Christian Nationalist Party Convention, 1948, St. Louis, Mo., provided by Gordon D. Hall.

42. *Baltimore Sun*, Aug. 21, 1948.

43. Ibid.

44. *Tulsa Daily World*, Aug. 22, 1948.

45. *St. Louis Post-Dispatch*, Aug. 22, 1948; *Washington Post*, Aug. 23, 1948.

46. *National Jewish Post* [Indianapolis], Sept. 24, 1948.

47. Smith press release, Aug. 10, 1948, R 19, F Christian Nationalist Party convention.

48. Smith letter to "Dear Crusader Friend," Sept. 1948, cited in Henderson, "Political Activities of Gerald L. K. Smith," 118.

49. Gerald L. K. Smith, "The Darkness Falls—Only the Courageous Can Survive" (Nov. 1948), cited in Henderson, "Political Activities of Gerald L. K. Smith," 121.

50. *The Cross and the Flag* 10, no. 6 (Sept. 1951), 24.

51. Ibid., 10, no. 10 (Jan. 1952), 11.

52. Ibid., 16, no. 3 (June 1958), 8.

53. Arnold Forster and Benjamin R. Epstein, *Cross-Currents* (Westport, Conn., 1975), 29.

54. *New York Times*, May 11, 1950.

55. *The Cross and the Flag* 10, no. 10 (Jan. 1952), 2.

56. Smith to Don Lohbeck, Oct. 23, 1951, B 34, F 1951, Lohbeck, Don; Smith to H. L. Hunt, June 21, 1952, B 37, F 1952, MacArthur, Douglas.

57. Smith to "Dear Friend," March 11, 1952, B 36, F 1952, Appeal letters.

58. *The Cross and the Flag* 11, no. 5 (Aug. 1952), 7–8.

59. *Christian Science Monitor* [Boston], April 11, 1952.

60. Smith to Rev. Bob Shuler, Oct. 30, 1952, B 38, F "S" (misc.).

61. Ralph McGill, "Vendors of Hate and Lies," *Atlanta Constitution*, reprinted in *Bee* [Fresno, Calif.], July 15, 1952, B 36, F 1952, "F" (misc.).

62. *The Cross and the Flag* 10, no. 1 (April 1951), 12–13.

63. *New York Times*, May 22, 1952.

64. *The Cross and the Flag* 12, no. 2 (May 1953), 16.

65. Ibid., 10, no. 1 (April 1951), 12.

66. Forster and Epstein, *Cross-Currents*, 310.

67. Kirkpatrick Sale, *Power Shift: The Rise of the Southern Rim and Its Challenge to the Eastern Establishment* (New York, 1975), 215–16; Frank Mankiewicz, *Perfectly Clear: Nixon from Whittier to Watergate* (New York, 1973), pp. 56–57.

68. *The Cross and the Flag* 11, no. 6 (Sept. 1952), p. 6.

69. *Washington Post*, Oct. 31, 1952.

70. FBI, Report on Christian Nationalist Party of America, June 16, 1952, F 62–43818–1071, pp. 7–9; Ralph Lord Roy, *Apostles of Discord* (Boston, 1953), 15–19; *Jewish Voice* [California], July 18, 1952, B 38, F 1952, Republican National Convention, Chicago; *The Cross and the Flag* 11, no. 4 (July 1952), 2.

71. *The Cross and the Flag* 11, no. 5 (Aug. 1952), 17.

72. Smith, *Besieged Patriot*, 214.

73. Roy, *Apostles of Discord*, 20.

74. *The Cross and the Flag* 11, no. 5 (Aug. 1952), 12.

75. Smith, *Besieged Patriot*, 202; *Christian Science Monitor* [Boston], Oct. 8, 1952.

76. *New York Times*, Nov. 7, 1952.

77. Forster and Epstein, *Cross-Currents*, 61.

78. Smith to Bertrand L. Comparet, Nov. 5, 1952, B 36, F 1952, Comparet, Bertrand.

79. Smith to Gen. Douglas MacArthur, Oct. 6, 1954, B 42, F 1954, "M" (misc.).

80. *The Cross and the Flag* 16, no. 3 (June 1957), 18.

81. Gerald L. K. Smith, "Is Eisenhower a Communist? No! But—" (n.p., n.d.), 19.

82. Ibid., 44.

83. Forster and Epstein, *Cross-Currents*, 62.

84. *California Heritage*, June 21, 1956, B 46, F 1956, Newspaper clippings.

85. *Christian Science Monitor* [Boston], June 18, 1956.

86. *American Jewish Year Book*, 58 (1957), 147–48.

87. Gerald L. K. Smith, "If I Were President" (n.p., 1956).

88. *Christian Science Monitor* [Boston], May 17, 1957.

89. *The Cross and the Flag* 17, no. 5 (Aug. 1958), 15.

90. Gerald L. K. Smith, "End Supreme Court Tyranny" (n.p., n.d.).

91. Smith, *Besieged Patriot*, 15.

92. Gerald L. K. Smith, "Twenty Surrenders!! What Is the Answer? Read-Weep-Resolve: A Summary," n.p. [1969].

93. Smith to Opal Tanner White [1959] and White to Smith, Feb. 4, 5, and 6, 1959, all in B 51, F 1959, "W" (misc.); *Herald Express*, (L.A.) Feb. 4, 1959, B 51, F 1959, Petitions, *The Cross and the Flag* 17, no. 12 (March 1959), 5.

94. Smith to Rev. James P. Dees, April 22, 1960, B 52, F 1960 "D" (misc.); Smith, "Formula for Political Power" (n.p., n.d.); Report, Faubus-for-President Club, Jan. 1–May 31, 1960; Press release, April 22, 1960, and Press statement of Governor Orval E. Faubus, March 25, 1960, all in B 52, F 1960, Faubus for President Correspondence.

95. Gerald L. K. Smith to Virgil Davis, March 22, 1960, F 1960, March; Smith to Paul J. Hines, April 27, 1960, F 1960, April (9); *San Francisco New Call Bulletin* [1960], B 52, F 1960, "N" (misc.); Smith, "John F. Kennedy: What Is His Background? Who Is This Man? Who Are His Advisers? What About His Radical Associates? Is He Jew Controlled?" n.p. [1960].

96. *The Cross and the Flag* 16, no. 4 (July 1958), 14.

97. Smith to Benjamin Freedman, Oct. 31, 1960, B 52, F 1960 "F" (misc.).

98. Smith to Richard M. Nixon, March 21, 1961, B 54, F 1961 "N" (misc.).

99. Smith to Harold Arrowsmith, March 28, 1961, B 53, F 1961, "A"

(misc.); *The Cross and the Flag* 33, no. 2 (May 1974), 12; Smith, "Barry Goldwater: An Appraisal," 1964, B 58, F 1964, "G" (misc.).

100. "A Petition to Impeach President John F. Kennedy," B 57, F 1963, Fields, Edward R.

101. Smith letter to supporters, Dec. 4, 1963, Milwaukee Anti-Defamation League.

102. Smith to George C. Wallace, July 14, 1964, B 59, F Wallace, George.

103. Smith, "Barry Goldwater: An Appraisal" (n.p., 1964), 2–4.

104. *Washington Post*, Oct. 12, 1964.

105. Smith to Thomas F. Cadwalader, Sept. 30, 1965, B 59, F 1965, "Ca-Cm" (misc.).

106. Gerald L. K. Smith, "The Ultimate in Corruption," Feb. 10, 1964, Anti-Defamation League files.

107. Gerald L. K. Smith, taped interview with Leo P. Ribuffo, Eureka Springs, Ark., Aug. 25, 1969.

108. Gerald L. K. Smith, "Goldwater's Victory" (n.p., Dec. 1964).

109. *The Cross and the Flag* 17, no. 11 (Feb. 1959), 11.

110. Smith to Harvey Griffin, April 12, 1968, B 62, F 1968, "G."

111. Gerald L. K. Smith, "A Beatle for President" (n.p., 1968).

112. Smith to Ella Graham, April 5, 1968, B 88, F 1968, May; William F. Buckley, Jr., *The Governor Listeth: A Book of Inspired Political Revelations* (New York, 1970), 60.

113. Smith to Mrs. Lena McCarty, April 30, 1970, B 67, F 1970, "M" (1).

114. Smith to Mrs. Edna G. Gainer, Feb. 2, 1972, B 72, F 1972, "G" (3).

115. Smith to Ermine G. Wesenick, Dec. 12, 1973, B 76, F 1973, "W" (1).

116. *The Cross and the Flag* 33, no. 8 (Nov. 1974), 21.

117. Smith to Editor, *Carroll County Tribune*, May 3, 1974, B 77, F 1974, "C" (1).

118. Smith, *Besieged Patriot*, 92.

119. Gerald L. K. Smith, "Who Are the Enemies of President Nixon?" n.p. [1973].

120. Smith to James L. Buckley, March 21, 1974, B 75, F 1974, "B" (5).

121. Smith to T. Migliorati, May 9, 1975, B 80, F 1975.

122. Smith, taped interview with the author, Eureka Springs, Ark., Aug. 10, 1974.

123. *The Cross and the Flag* 34, no. 3 (June 1975), 14.

124. Ibid., 33, no. 12 (March 1975), 11.

125. Smith to George D. Bohlen, May 12, 1974, B 76, F 1974, "B" (6).

126. *The Cross and the Flag* 33, no. 9 (Dec. 1974), 9–10.

127. Smith interview with author, Aug. 10, 1974.

128. Gerald L. K. Smith, "The President Must Not Be Impeached: Why?" n.p. [1974].

129. Gerald L. K. Smith, "Names! Names! Names!" n.p. [1974].

130. *The Cross and the Flag* 33, no. 4 (July 1974), 8.

131. Smith, "Names!"

10. Personality, Family, Friends, and Followers

1. Smith to Issa Nakhleh, Feb. 21, 1968, B 63, F 1968, "N," Gerald L. K. Smith Papers.

2. FBI, Report on the Christian Nationalist Party of America, April 2, 1952, F 62–43818–1060–29; "Confidential Memos," B 4, F 1939–1942 (l. 1940–1942), Prospectuses and memoranda for meetings.

3. Gerald L. K. Smith, "Open Letter to the Lost" (n.p., n.d.).

4. Gerald L. K. Smith, "Gerald L. K. Smith and the Jews: A Significant Summary" (n.p., n.d.).

5. Gerald L. K. Smith, "Mysterious Facts Behind Terrible Realities" (March 1, 1963), American Jewish Historical Society, Waltham, Mass.

6. Gerald L. K. Smith, *Besieged Patriot: Autobiographical Episodes Exposing Communism, Traitorism and Zionism from the Life of Gerald L. K. Smith*, ed. Elna M. Smith and Charles F. Robertson (Eureka Springs, Ark., 1978), 65.

7. Lloyd Ray Henderson, "The Political Activities of Gerald L. K. Smith" (M.A. thesis, University of California, 1955), p. 123.

8. Smith, *Besieged Patriot*, 113.

9. Ibid., 119. Smith reported to the FBI that the killer of Huey Long had tried to murder him and that Jews in Detroit planned to "frame" him, but both claims were groundless. See FBI, Report on Gerald L. K. Smith, July 22, 1942, Detroit, F 62–1126, pp. 4–12.

10. Gerold Frank, "Huey Long the Second," *The Nation* 143 (July 25, 1936). 93.

11. Smith to Jack B. Tenney, Oct. 1, 1952, B 38, F "Tenney, Jack B."

12. Gerald L. K. Smith, taped interview with Leo P. Ribuffo, Eureka Springs, Ark., Aug. 25, 1974.

13. Smith to Mrs. Hallie H. Burns, Feb. 11, 1970, B 66, F 1970, "B" (3); Smith to Don Lohbeck, Oct. 21, 1948, R 20, F "Don Lohbeck."

14. Smith to G. F. Green, May 2, 1950, B 30, F 1950, "Green, G. F."

15. Smith to Edith [Morgan], Nov. 2, 1962, B 55, F 1962, "M" (misc.).

16. Smith to Virginia Lohbeck, Feb. 15, 1949, R 14, F "Don Lohbeck."

17. Smith to Edith [Morgan], Sept. 22, 1965, B 61, F 1965, "Sm-Sz" (misc.); Smith to Roland and Edith Morgan, Aug. 26, 1957, B 47, F 1957, "M" (misc.); Smith to Harrold C. Voyle, Feb. 22, 1973, B 76, F 1973, "V."

18. Smith to Mrs. L. Z. Smith, June 1, 1950, B 33, F 1950, "Smith, Mrs. L. Z."

19. Smith to Jim Johnson, May 29, 1968, B 62, F 1968, "J."

20. Smith to Mrs. L. Z. Smith, July 16, 1949, B 29, F 1949, "Smith, Mrs. L. Z."

21. Gerald L. K. Smith, taped interview with the author, Eureka Springs, Ark., Aug. 11, 1974.

22. Smith to Virginia Gillas, Jan. 8, 1971, B 70, F 1971, "G" (4).

23. When I visited Smith in Eureka Springs in 1974, he proudly showed me his goats and asked me to return and photograph him with them. When I

was unable to return he wrote me an angry letter, telling me that I was young enough to learn good manners. For an account of Smith's horses and goats see Smith, *Besieged Patriot*, 237; Smith to Mr. and Mrs. A. L. Caldwell, Dec. 30, 1974, B 77, F 1974, "C" (5); Smith to Henry and Belva Tall, Jan. 31, 1974, B 79, F 1974, "T" (1); Smith to Henry and Belva [Tall] and Ed and Mildred [Sorenson], March 22, 1974, B 78, F 1974, "T" (1).

24. Smith to B. J. Hadley, Sept. 12, 1960, B 86, F 1960, "Sept." (1); John Fergus Ryan, "Twilight Years of a Kindly Old Hatesmith," *Esquire* 70 (Aug. 1968), 91; Smith to Tom Duggan, May 1, 1956, B 50, F 1959, "Duggan, Tom."

25. Smith to Mrs. Ira Bronson, May 12, 1949, R 22, F "B"; Smith to Mildred [Sorenson], May 11, 1949, B 28, F 1949, "Si-So" (misc.); Leo P. Ribuffo, "Protestants on the Right: William Dudley Pelley, Gerald B. Winrod, and Gerald L. K. Smith," 2 vols. (Ph.D. diss., Yale University, 1976), 538; Gerald L. K. Smith, taped interview with J. Fraser Cocks III, Los Angeles, Calif., Sept. 12, 1967; Smith to Dr. William Hornaday, n.d., B 62, F 1968, "H."

26. Smith, *Besieged Patriot*, 157; Smith to Don Lohbeck, March 28 and April 4, 1949, R 24, F "Don Lohbeck"; Smith to Mrs. L. Z. Smith, April 2, 1949, B 29, F 1949, "Smith, Mrs. L. Z."; Smith to Maximilian J. St. George, April 18, 1949, B 28, F 1949, "St. George, Maximilian."

27. Smith to "Dear Loyal Supporter," Feb. 15, 1948, R 19, F "Emergency Letters"; Smith to Mrs. L. Z. Smith, March 24, 1948, R 21, F "Mrs. L. Z. Smith"; Smith newsletter, "Confidential: Only for those who can understand" (Oct. 1948), New York State Library, Albany; Smith to Dr. William Frederick Koch, Feb. 5, Feb. 16, March 22, May 19 and 24, and June 3, 1948, R 20, F "K"; Smith letter to supporters, "Prison Avoided—Saved from Death—We Carry On" (March 1948), American Jewish Historical Society, Waltham, Mass.; Smith to Mrs. Ira Bronson, May 12, 1949, R 22, F "B"; Smith to Bessie Beam, Feb. 10, 1948, R 19, F "B"; Leo P. Ribuffo, *The Old Christian Right: The Protestant Right From the Great Depression to the Cold War* (Philadelphia, 1983), 231; "Resolution of the Ministerial Federation of America to the Senate Judiciary Committee Regarding the Koch Treatment," Acted Upon at Detroit, Oct. 2, 1947, R 14, F "W"; "The Koch Treatment," Extension of Remarks by Hon. William Langer of North Dakota in the Senate of the United States, *Congressional Record*, 80th Cong., 2d sess., Monday, June 7, 1948, pp. 1–2, in R 20, F "K."

28. Smith to Bertrand L. Comparet, March, 7 and 13, 1956, B 45, F 1956, "Comparet, Bertrand"; Smith to Charles B. Hudson, April 17 and July 5, 1956, B 45, "H" (misc.), and Smith to Barbara Heals, March 24, 1956, same F; Smith to Miss [Opal] Tanner and Miss [Renata] Legant, July 10, 1956, B 45, "V" (misc.).

29. Gerald L. K. Smith, "Jesus vs. the Jews" (n.p., n.d.).

30. Smith to Logan Billingsley, April 30, 1954, 1954, B 41, F 1954, "B" (misc.).

31. *The Cross and the Flag* 33, no. 5 (Aug. 1974), 22, and no. 8 (Nov. 1974), 8.

32. Smith to Dr. L. E. Marshall, Dec. 5, 1968, B 62, F 1968, "M" (4).

33. Smith to Bill Stephenson, June 19, 1958, B 48, F 1957, "S" (misc.).

34. *The Cross and the Flag* 34, no. 7 (Oct. 1975), 20.

35. Smith to Walter and Stella Van Winter, Sept. 9, 1955, B 44, F 1955, "V" (misc.).

36. Gerald L. K. Smith, "Bread vs. Stones" (n.p., n.d.).

37. Smith to Edith Essig, July 23, 1956, B 45, F 1956, "E" (misc.).

38. Gerald L. K. Smith, "I Love the Church," B 59, F 1965, "Bp-Bz" (misc.).

39. Gerald L. K. Smith, "Jews Boast That New Bible Translation Proves Christ Imposter" (n.p., n.d.).

40. Ribuffo, *Old Christian Right*, 233; Smith to Dr. Jesse Kellems, April 27, 1951, B 34, F 1951, "K" (misc.); Smith to Rev. and Mrs. Roy F. Horton, March 24, 1970, B 67, F 1970, "H," and Smith to Virginia Hoover-Melville, April 23, 1970, same F; Smith to Billy James Hargis, Oct. 22, 1970, same F.

41. Smith, "I Love the Church."

42. Gerald L. K. Smith, taped interview with J. Fraser Cocks III, Los Angeles, Calif., March 23, 1968.

43. Smith to Benjamin Freedman, Oct. 31, 1960, B 52, F 1960, "F" (misc.); Gerald L. K. Smith, "My Fight for the Right," B 93, F "Personal Experiences."

44. Ribuffo, *Old Christian Right*, 147; Smith to Mrs. L. Z. Smith, Jan. 20 and March 13, 1950, B 33, 1950, "Smith, Mrs. L. Z."; Smith to Rev. James A. Haggart, Aug. 8, 1961, B 54, F 1961, "H" (misc.); Extension of Remarks of Hon. Clyde Doyle of Calif., Report of Subversive Activities by Legion of Illinois Commission, *Appendix to the Congressional Record*, 82d Cong., 1st sess., vol. 97, pt. 14 (July 12–Sept. 17, 1951), July 30, 1951, p. A4771.

45. Smith to Most Rev. Edward Mooney, June 14, 1939, B 1, F 1939–1942 (l. 1940–1942), "Corr."; Smith to Rev. B. H. Ginther, July 5, 1956, B 45, F 1960, "G" (misc.); Smith to J. Sullivan, Aug. 24, 1960, B 85, F 1960, "Aug." (5); Smith to Tom Schott, Aug. 15, 1960, B 86, F 1960, "Aug." (7); *Christian Science Monitor* [Boston], May 14, 1947; *Detroit Free Press*, Jan. 31, 1946; Ralph Lord Roy, *Apostles of Discord* (Boston, 1953), 71.

46. Smith to Renata Legant, Aug. 3, 1950, B 31, F 1950, "Legant."

47. Smith to Sister Cecilia M. Hall, S.P., Jan. 16, 1970, B 68, F 1970, "S" (1).

48. Smith to Paul Curtiss, Sept. 1, 1950, B 30, F 1950, "C" (misc.).

49. Smith to Mrs. Smith, Miss Legant, Miss Tanner, the Lohbecks and the Robertsons, Oct. 10, 1952, B 38, F 1952, "Smith, Gerald L. K. (introspective letter to family and staff)." The emphasis is in the original.

50. Smith to parents, Jan. 28–30, 1930, B 1, F Corres. with parents.

51. Smith, *Besieged Patriot*, 12.

52. Smith interview with Cocks, March 28, 1968.

53. Gerald L. K. Smith to Barbara Heals, Dec. 9, 1942, auth. mic. r. 3.

54. Ibid., June 15, 1955, B 43, F 1955, "H" (misc.).

55. Mrs. L. Z. Smith to Gerald L. K. Smith, Jan. 9, 1941, auth. mic. r. 3.

56. Ibid., April 9, 1954, B 42, F 1954, Smith, Mrs. L. Z.

57. Ibid., Oct. 18, 1948, R 22, F Mrs. L. Z. Smith.

58. Ibid., July 18, 1946, R 13, F Smith family.

59. Ibid., May 4, 1953, B 40, F 1953, Smith, Mrs. L. Z.

60. Smith to Mrs. L. Z. Smith, Feb. 4, 1954, B 42, F 1954, Smith, Mrs. L. Z.

61. Smith to Mrs. Bernard Doman, March 25, 1959, B 30, F 1950, Doman.

62. Gerald L. K. Smith to Mrs. L. Z. Smith, Feb. 27, 1948, R 21, Mrs. L. Z. Smith; Smith to Barbara Heals [1948], R 20, F H. J. Heals, Smith to Mr. and Mrs. Bertrand Comparet, Jan. 4, 1956, R. 17, F Bertrand Comparet; Smith to Barbara and Herman Heals, Jan. 9, 1956, B 45, F 1956, Heals, Barbara.

63. Smith to Mary Jane [Birdsall], April 10, 1963, B 57, F 1963, "B" (misc.). Mary Jane's married name was Birdsall.

64. Smith to Edith Morgan, Dec. 10, 1962, B 55, F 1962, "M" (misc.).

65. Smith to Mary Jane Birdsall, Feb. 5, 1963, B 57, F 1963, "B" (misc.).

66. Smith to Mary Jane Birdsall, Aug. 10, 1964, B 58, F 1964, "B" (misc.).

67. Smith interview with Cocks, March 28, 1968.

68. *The Cross and the Flag* 17, no. 8 (Nov. 1958), 15.

69. Smith to Mr. [first name omitted] Gawthorpe, Aug. 4, 1960, B 52, F "G" (misc.).

70. Smith to Mrs. E. G. Whitacre, Sept. 12, 1960, B 86, F 1960, Sept. (3).

71. Smith, *Besieged Patriot*, 133.

72. Smith to Mr. and Mrs. L. Z. Smith, Oct. 24–25, 1924, B 1, F Corres. with parents; Smith to Mrs. L. Z. Smith, Sept. 21, 1951, B 36, F 1951, Smith, Mrs. L. Z.; Smith to Sylvia Davis, Jan. 16, 1956, B 45, F 1956, "D" (misc.).

73. Gerry Smith to parents, Jan. [n.d.], Dec. 19 and 26, 1940, auth. mic. r. 3; Jefferson Military College, Principal's office, report of Cadet Gerry Smith, week ending Dec. 6, 1940, auth. mic. r. 3.

74. Gerald L. K. Smith to Gerry Smith, June 30, 1941, auth. mic. r. 3.

75. Smith to Barbara, Herman, and Mary Jane Heals, Dec. 9, 1942, B 6, F 1939–1942 (l. 1940–1942), Smith family (including son).

76. Ibid., Nov. 13, 1942.

77. Smith, *Besieged Patriot*, 147; Smith interview with Cocks, March 29, 1968.

78. Gerald L. K. Smith to parents, Jan. 11, 1946, R 13, F "Smith Family"; Smith to Don Lohbeck, June 28, 1949, R 24, F Don Lohbeck.

79. Bernard A. Doman to Smith [1948], R 19, F B. A. Doman; Smith to Gerry Smith, Aug. 2, 1948, Smith to Mary Smith, Aug. 2, 1948, R 21, F Gerald Smith, Jr.; Mary Smith to Gerald L. K. Smith, July 3, 1949, B 29, F Smith, Gerry; Gerald L. K. Smith to Mrs. L. Z. Smith, Nov. 29, 1949, B 29, F 1949, Smith, Mrs. L. Z.; Mary Smith to Gerald L. K. Smith, July 27, 1959, B 33, F 1950, Smith, Gerry; Gerald L. K. Smith to Mary Smith, July 28, to Don Lohbeck, Sept. 27, and Gerry Smith to Gerald L. K. Smith [n.d.], all 1950, in B 33, F 1950, Smith, Gerry.

80. Gerald L. K. Smith to Barbara Heals, Aug. 24, 1953, B 39, F 1953, "He-Hz" (misc.); Gerry Smith to Mother and Father, Aug. 10 and Oct. 4, 1953, and Gerald L. K. Smith to Gerry, Oct. 9, 1953, all in B 40, F 1953, "S" (misc.); Gerry to Mother and Father, Oct. 15, 1959, B 51, F 1959, "S" (misc.); *Eureka Springs Times-Echo*, April 1, 1982.

81. Smith to Ed and Mildred Sorenson, April 14, 1956, B 46, F 1956, Sorenson Family; Smith to Edith and Roland Morgan, Aug. 26, 1957, B 47,

F 1957, "M" (misc.); Smith to Donna and Emmagene [last name omitted], July 12, 1965, B 59, F 1965, "Ca-Cm" (misc.); Smith to Henry and Belva Tall, April 16, 1968, B 63, F 1968, "T"; Smith to the Sorensons and Talls, Feb. 10, 1969, B 65, F 1969, "S" (1).

82. Smith to Bertrand Comparet, Feb. 2, 1955, R 16, F Bertrand L. Comparet.

83. Smith to "Dear Friend" [1950], B 30, F 1950, "D" (misc.).

84. Smith to A. T. Hagstrom, Jan. 15, 1960, B 52, F 1960, "H" (misc.).

85. Smith to C. F. Robertson, Aug. 20, 1958, B 49, F 1958, "R" (misc.).

86. Smith to "Miss Cook," Dec. 22, 1939, B 3, F 1939–1942 (l. 1940–1942), Memoranda: 1939; Smith to Mrs. [Virginia] Lohbeck, March 13, 1945, B 16, F 1945, Memos (2); *St. Louis Post-Dispatch,* May 21, 1952.

87. Smith to Mrs. [Virginia] Lohbeck, Sept. 7, 1946, B 18, F 1946 Memos (interoffice) (2).

88. Smith to Don Lohbeck and Opal Tanner, Sept. 11, 1951, B 35, F 1951, Memos (3).

89. Smith to Don, Virginia, Kurt, and Michelle Lohbeck, Feb. 27, 1948, R 20, F Don Lohbeck.

90. Smith to Charles F. Robertson, July 14, 1953, B 40, F 1953, Robertson, Charles.

91. Leroy Donald, "Long-time Smith Follower Takes Reins at Eureka Springs," *Arkansas Gazette* [Little Rock], Nov. 14, 1976.

92. Ibid.; *The Cross and the Flag* 17, no. 8 (Nov. 1958), 3.

93. Smith, *Besieged Patriot,* 290–91; Smith to Edith and Roland Morgan, Feb. 10, 1961, B 54, F 1961, "M" (misc.); Smith to Lee [Morgan], Oct. 6, 1969, B 64, F 1969, "M" (1).

94. Smith to Henry and Belva [Tall], Jan. 22, 1971, B 71, F 1971, "T" (2). See also Smith to Roland and Edith [Morgan], B 67, F 1970, "H" (2); Résumé, Charles Wesley Winegarner, B 53, F 1960, "W"; and Smith to Chuck [Winegarner] and C. B. [Robertson], June 6, 1961, B 53, F 1961, Christian Youth Against Communism.

11. The Sacred Projects

1. Leroy Donald, "Long-time Smith Follower Takes Reins at Eureka Springs," *Arkansas Gazette* [Little Rock], Nov. 14, 1976.

2. *Eureka Springs Times-Echo,* Aug. 10, 1972; July 19, 1973; Robert M. Warner, B 94, F "Impressions recorded by J. Fraser Cocks (Sept. 12, 1972) and Dr. Robert M. Warner (June 28, 1969)" (hereafter cited as "Impressions"), Gerald L. K. Smith Papers; John Fergus Ryan, "Twilight Years of a Kindly Old Hatesmith," *Esquire* 70 (Aug. 1968), 88–91; "An Open Letter from Gerald L. K. Smith," Eureka Springs, Ark., Elna M. Smith Foundation (hereafter Smith Fdn.), 1973; *Arkansas Democrat* [Little Rock], July 9, 1964; *Arkansas Gazette* [Little Rock], Jan. 20, 1966, Oct. 22, 1969; Studs Terkel, *Hard Times:*

An Oral History of the Great Depression (New York 1970), 369; Smith to Mr. and Mrs. Peter P. Betchner, Nov. 29, 1974, B 76, F 1974, "B" (2).

3. Arnold Forster and Benjamin R. Epstein, *The New Anti-Semitism* (New York, 1974), 21; *St. Louis Post-Dispatch*, June 25, 1972; Calvin Trillin, "U.S. Journal: Eureka Springs, Ark.," *New Yorker*, 45 (July 26, 1969), 69; John R. Starr, "Gerald L. K. Smith: From Politics to Passion," *Tulsa Daily World*, Nov. 7, 1971.

4. *Eureka Springs Times-Echo*, Jan. 7, 1965; Gerald L. K. Smith, *The Story of the Statue of the Christ of the Ozarks* (Smith Fdn., n.d.), 12.

5. "A Monument to Himself," *Time* 88 (July 22, 1966), 23.

6. Ryan, "Twilight Years of a Kindly Old Hatesmith," 88.

7. Forster and Epstein, *The New Anti-Semitism*, 22.

8. *Eureka Springs Times-Echo*, Jan. 7, 1965.

9. Forster and Epstein, *The New Anti-Semitism*, 22.

10. *Eureka Springs Times-Echo*, June 17, 1965.

11. Ibid., May 20, 1965; Gerald L. K. Smith, taped interview with the author, Eureka Springs, Ark., Aug. 11, 1974.

12. *Eureka Springs Times-Echo*, May 20, 1965, Jan. 13, 1966; Ryan, "Twilight Years of a Kindly Old Hatesmith," 88; Watson Crews, Jr., "Christ Over Arkansas," *Detroit News*, June 26, 1966; William Thomas, "Christ of the Ozarks," *Mid-South Magazine* in *Memphis Commercial Appeal*, June 5, 1966.

13. Smith, *Story of the Statue*, 29.

14. *Eureka Springs Times-Echo*, Jan. 27, 1966.

15. Smith, *Story of the Statue*, 25, 31–34; Bill Lewis, "Smith's Statue Is Dedicated as Mayor Opposes Bigotry," *Arkansas Gazette* [Little Rock], June 26, 1966; Oct. 22, 1969; *Eureka Springs Times-Echo*, May 20 and 27, June 10 and 17, 1965; Crews, "Christ Over Arkansas."

16. Crews, "Christ Over Arkansas"; Thomas, "Christ of the Ozarks."

17. *Eureka Springs Times-Echo*, Dec. 9, 1965.

18. Ibid., June 30, 1966; Lewis, "Smith's Statue Is Dedicated as Mayor Opposes Bigotry."

19. Terkel, *Hard Times*, 368.

20. Edgar A. Albin, "The Colossal Ungainly Christ of Arkansas's Magnetic Mountain," *St. Louis Post-Dispatch*, June 20, 1971.

21. *Eureka Springs Times-Echo*, Aug. 4, 18 and 25, 1966; Gerald L. K. Smith, "Christ of the Ozarks" (flyer, n.d.); Smith, "God Bless Eureka Springs and Her People: An Open Letter from the Smiths," *Eureka Springs Times-Echo*, Nov. 9, 1967; Ernest Dumas, "Woman Leads Fight Against Gerald L. K. Smith," *St. Louis Post-Dispatch*, Dec. 18, 1969; "A Monument to Himself," 23.

22. Trillin, "U.S. Journal," 75; *Eureka Springs Times-Echo*, Nov. 17, 1966; Feb. 16, March 9, April 6, May 11 and 25, Oct. 7, 1967; Gerald L. K. Smith, "The Passion Play: An Open Letter by Gerald L. K. Smith," *Eureka Springs Times-Echo*, Feb. 1, 1968.

23. Smith, "Passion Play."

24. "Who Is Mr. Hyde? An Open Letter by Gerald L. K. Smith," *Eureka Springs Times-Echo*, Feb. 1, 1968; "Man Who Initiated Passion Play Is Also Director and Principal Actor," and "Key Employees of Play Perform Many Duties," *Eureka Springs Times-Echo*, May 22, 1975.

25. Smith, "Passion Play"; Ryan, "Twilight Years of a Kindly Old Hatesmith," 91.

26. Smith to Mrs. M. O. Moore, Nov. 10, 1971, B 70, F 1971, "M" (3).

27. "Man Who Initiated Passion Play"; Ryan, "Twilight Years of a Kindly Old Hatesmith," 91; Forster and Epstein, *The New Anti-Semitism*, 23; "Set of Passion Play was Designed for Authenticity, Maximum Use of Surroundings," *Eureka Springs Times-Echo*, May 22, 1975.

28. "Careful Planning, Expert Guidance of Actors, Insure Smooth Production," and "Cast, Staff, Make Ready for Eighth Season of Great Passion Play," *Eureka Springs Times-Echo*, May 22, 1975.

29. John R. Starr, "Gerald L. K. Smith Draws Tourists to Ozark Town," *Baton Rouge Morning Advocate*, Nov. 26, 1971; *Eureka Springs Times-Echo*, June 13 and 20, July 18, Aug. 1, 1968, April 22 and 29, 1976.

30. *Eureka Springs Times-Echo*, April 29, July 29, Oct. 14 and 28, 1971, Nov. 1, 1973; *Eureka Springs Flashlight* (monthly supplement to the *Times-Echo*), May 1976; Trillin, "U.S. Journal," 79.

31. *Eureka Springs Times-Echo*, Aug. 7 and Dec. 4, 1975; *Eureka Springs Flashlight*, May, June 1976.

32. Gerald L. K. Smith, "The Great Passion Play" (Eureka Springs, Ark., n.d.).

33. *Eureka Springs Times-Echo*, Aug. 1, 1968; *Arkansas Gazette* [Little Rock], May 19, 1973; Smith to Stephen D. Chyrchel, Jan. 18, 1973, B 74, F 1973, "C" (2).

34. Trillin, "U.S. Journal," 76.

35. The first night I saw the Passion Play in 1974, the amphitheater was packed. About halfway through the production it began to rain; it soon became torrential. However, few of the spectators left, and the actors seemed undaunted. I was torn between a desire for a warm, dry blanket and a cup of hot coffee, on the one hand, and my concern that I would offend Smith by leaving his play, on the other. I stayed. Smith himself attended nightly, occupying a box unprotected from the elements in the first row, where he mingled with spectators and signed autographs.

36. *Eureka Springs Times-Echo*, Nov. 27, 1969 and Nov. 6, 1975.

37. Ibid., Sept. 6, 1973, Aug. 26, 1976, Nov. 27, 1969, and Nov. 6, 1975. The play runs five nights a week from May 21 through Oct. 30.

38. Editorial, *Eureka Springs Times-Echo*, Sept. 6, 1973; Sept. 12, 1974; May 18, 1972; Rev. J. Harold Smith to Gerald L. K. Smith, *Eureka Springs Times-Echo*, Aug. 5, 1971, Gerald L. K. Smith, "Miracle on the Mountains" (broadside, n.d.).

39. *Eureka Springs Times-Echo*, June 29 and Aug. 3, 1972.

40. See, for example, *Rogers Daily News* [Ark.], Oct. 16, 1975.

41. Smith interview with author, Aug. 11, 1974.

42. Conversation with Leo P. Ribuffo; Gerald L. K. Smith, "An Open Letter to the Citizens of Eureka Springs and the World," *Eureka Springs Times-Echo,* Sept. 11, 1969.

43. For example, Elna, but not her husband, spoke at the groundbreaking for the *Christ of the Ozarks,* and the foundation is in her name. The Passion Play received national attention in *The New York Times* and *New York Daily News, St. Louis Post-Dispatch, Los Angeles Times, Memphis Commercial Appeal, New Yorker,* and *Esquire.*

44. Smith interview with author, Aug. 11, 1974.

45. Smith announced in a large ad in the *Times-Echo* that "certain individuals have come to Eureka Springs and are on the payroll of outside anti-Christian elements." He claimed that they were "being paid to downgrade Eureka Springs and its sacred projects" by "anti-Christian personalities and anti-Christian organizations." He charged that the same thing had happened at Oberammergau, Germany. *Eureka Springs Times-Echo,* July 17, 1975.

46. Warner, "Impressions."

47. Erwin L. McDonald, "The Great Smith Play," *Arkansas Democrat* [Little Rock] (date illegible), 1973.

48. Lester Kinsolving, "Mecca for Tourists," *Ann Arbor News,* Aug. 5, 1972.

49. Charles F. Robertson told me that there was no written script: "Some day we may get around to having it written down." This was an obvious falsehood. Charles F. Robertson, taped interview with the author, Eureka Springs, Ark., June 1, 1979. Opponents of the play also have been guilty of exaggeration. Many writers who have condemned the play as anti-Semitic have never seen it.

50. Forster and Epstein, *The New Anti-Semitism,* 24.

51. *Ann Arbor News,* Aug. 5, 1972.

52. Botnick's observation was reported by Jack Anderson, "Anti-Semite Smith Gets U.S. Windfall," *Washington Post,* Jan. 17, 1970.

53. McDonald, "Great Smith Play"; Trillin, "U.S. Journal," 77.

54. *The Cross and the Flag* 34, no. 9 (Dec. 1975), 30.

55. Report to Congress, Christian Nationalist Crusade, Jan. 1–Dec. 31, 1966. In a June 17, 1965, article on the groundbreaking ceremony for the *Christ of the Ozarks,* Charles F. Robertson listed the officers and directors of the Elna M. Smith Foundation. Elna M. Smith [Mrs. Gerald L. K. Smith] was president and Robertson [also editor of *The Cross and the Flag*] was secretary-treasurer. Included on the board of directors were Wesley Sorenson of Baton Rouge, La. [Mrs. Smith's nephew]; Opal Tanner White of Los Angeles [Smith's private secretary]; Dr. Edmund Sorenson of Elkhorn, Wis. [Mrs. Smith's father]; Darlene Robertson of Los Angeles [Mrs. Charles F. Robertson]; and Mrs. Victor Nearhoof [Mrs. Smith's sister]. The names are listed in the *Eureka Springs Times-Echo,* June 17, 1965. I have supplied the information in brackets. Later listed as vice president of the Foundation was Roland Lee Morgan, son-in-law of Charles F. Robertson. He was director of the

Citizens Congressional Committee, a Smith front group, and later became office director of the Christian Nationalist Crusade headquarters in Los Angeles. Morgan became editor of *The Cross and the Flag* after Smith's death. For information on Morgan see Press Release, Dec. 12, 1970, Milwaukee Anti-Defamation League.

56. Charles F. Robertson, "Open and Informative Letter," in Roland Lee Morgan, *The Christ Only Art Gallery* (Smith Fdn., 1971), 28–29.

57. *Arkansas Democrat* [Little Rock], June 30, 1970; *Eureka Springs Times-Echo*, July 2, 1970; *Arkansas Gazette* [Little Rock], July 14 and 15, 1970; *Tulsa Daily World*, July 18, 1970.

58. *Eureka Springs Times-Echo*, Nov. 4, Dec. 2 and 9, 1965, Feb. 17, June 30, July 14, Oct. 20, and Nov. 24, 1966; Trillin, "U.S. Journal," 77; Morgan, *Christ Only Art Gallery*, 4, 7, 10, 26; *Eureka Springs Flashlight*, May 1976; Starr, "G. L. K. Smith Draws Tourists."

59. *Eureka Springs Times-Echo*, Sept. 14, 1970, May 6, 13, 20, 1971; "A Tribute to a Great Lady: Elna M. Smith," *Eureka Springs Times-Echo*, May 22, 1975; *Eureka Springs Flashlight*, April, May, and Aug. 1976; Gerald L. K. Smith, "An Open Letter from Gerald L. K. Smith" (Smith Fdn., 1973); Gerald L. K. Smith, *Bible Museum* (Smith Fdn., n.d.). In 1966 Smith added to his complex in northern Arkansas a pioneer cabin in Norfolk called Wolf House, which he restored, furnished, and operated. In 1976 the vollage of Norfolk took it over. See *Arkansas Gazette* [Little Rock], Jan. 20, 1966, Jan. 15, 17, and 20, 1976; *Eureka Springs Times-Echo*, Jan. 22, 1976; Gerald L. K. Smith, *Besieged Patriot: Autobiographical Episodes Exposing Communism, Traitorism and Zionism from the Life of Gerald L. K. Smith*, ed. Elna M. Smith and Charles F. Robertson (Eureka Springs, Ark., 1978), 252–53.

60. Starr, "G. L. K. Smith Draws Tourists"; Phillip Bullock, taped interview with the author, Eureka Springs, Ark., June 3, 1979.

61. Bullock interview with author; Smith to *Arkansas Gazette* [Little Rock], July 16, 1975; James E. Adams, "Planning a 'New Holy Land,'" *St. Louis Post-Dispatch*, Jan. 30, 1972.

62. Bullock interview with author; *Eureka Springs Times-Echo*, Nov. 3, 1966; Forster and Epstein, *New Anti-Semitism*, 22, 26; Starr, "G. L. K. Smith Draws Tourists."

63. Ed Jeffords, taped interview with the author, Eureka Springs, Ark., June 1, 1979; John R. Starr, "Gerald L. K. Smith Puts Eureka Springs on Map," *Daily Town Talk* [Alexandria], Nov. 4, 1971. The hippie spoke to me in a local coffee house on my visit to Eureka Springs in 1974.

64. *New York Times*, July 27, 1972.

65. Georgia Stratton Ziffzer to *Arkansas Gazette* [Little Rock], Oct. 29, 1969; Bobbie Forster, "Action Praising Smith Foundation Draws Protest," *Arkansas Democrat* [Little Rock], Oct. 22, 1969. News stories about Mrs. Ziffzer are numerous. See, for example: Steve Darst, "Ozark Town New Anti-Semite Base," *National Catholic Reporter* [Kansas City, Mo.], Oct. 30, 1970; Ernest Dumas, "Woman Leads Fight Against Gerald L. K. Smith," *St. Louis*

Post-Dispatch, Dec. 18, 1969; *New York Times*, Nov. 28, 1969; *Tulsa Tribune*, Dec. 3, 1970.

66. Trillin, "U.S. Journal," 78–79; Starr, "G. L. K. Smith Draws Tourists"; Ginger Shiras, telephone conversation with the author, Nov. 10, 1976; Jeffords interview with author.

67. Gerald L. K. Smith to T. E. Larimer, Sr., July 2, 1975. A photostat of the letter was given to me by Ed Jeffords.

68. Ibid. Jeffords said that his argument was with Smith, not his heirs. Jeffords interview with author; Jeffords to the author, March 2, 1983; *Eureka Springs Times-Echo*, Oct. 23, 1975; *Carroll County Tribune*, Oct. 17, 1975; *Springfield News Leader*, Oct. 20, 1975; *Tulsa World*, Oct. 16, 1975; Deposition of Gerald L. K. Smith in *Ed Jeffords et al. vs. Gerald L. K. Smith et al.* before *Notary Public Martha Brown*, Eureka Springs, Ark., Nov. 19, 1975.

69. Smith, *Besieged Patriot*, 239–40; *Arkansas Gazette* [Little Rock], Sept. 20, 1975; *Eureka Springs Times-Echo*, Nov. 3, 1966.

70. Smith interview with author, Aug. 11, 1974; Smith to Robert O. Baker, Dec. 12, 1974, B 76, F 1974 "B" (2).

71. Trillin, "U.S. Journal," 69–70; *Arkansas Gazette* [Little Rock], Oct. 4, 1972; *Arkansas Democrat* [Little Rock], Sept. 20, 1975. The quotation is from Smith to John Frank, Dec. 23, 1969, B 64, F 1969, "F."

72. *The Cross and the Flag* 33, no. 12 (March 1975), 11; Smith interview with author, Aug. 11, 1974.

73. Smith interview with author, Aug. 11, 1974; *The Cross and the Flag* 34, no. 12 (March 1976), 15; Gerald L. K. Smith, "An Open Letter from Gerald L. K. Smith," *Eureka Springs Times-Echo*, Sept. 13, 1973, May 2 and June 20, 1974.

74. *The Cross and the Flag* 34, no. 12 (March 1976), 12; *Arkansas Gazette* [Little Rock], May 8, 1971; *Eureka Springs Times-Echo*, June 8 and Aug. 10, 1972; Gerald L. K. Smith, "An Open Letter from Gerald L. K. Smith," *Eureka Springs Times-Echo*, July 6, 1972; Smith interview with author, Aug. 11, 1974; Gerald L. K. Smith, "The New Holy Land: The Most Sensational Project of the Century" (flyer, Smith Fdn., n.d.).

75. *Eureka Springs Times-Echo*, Sept. 30, 1971.

76. *Ann Arbor News*, Aug. 5, 1972; Smith to John Frank, Dec. 8, 1972, B 72, F 1972, "F" (2).

77. Forster and Epstein, *New Anti-Semitism*, 21, 27–28.

78. Justin Finger to ADL Regional Offices, Dec. 10, 1969, Milwaukee Anti-Defamation League files; *American Jewish Year Book* 71 (1970), 335, and 72 (1971), 254. Jack Anderson broke the story in a syndicated column entitled "Anti-Semite Smith Gets U.S. Windfall," *Washington Post*, Jan. 17, 1970.

79. Justin Finger to ADL Regional Offices, Dec. 10, 1969; Ginger Shiras, "Look at 'Smith's Road' Plan Raises Question by Some: Is It for Flatlanders?" *Arkansas Gazette* [Little Rock], March 8, 1970; Forster and Epstein, *New Anti-Semitism*, 27–36; *Washington Post*, Jan. 10, 1970.

80. Extension of Remarks by Mr. Edward I. Koch of New York, "More on

Gerald L. K. Smith," *Congressional Record—House*, 91st Cong., 2d sess., vol. 116, pt. 1, Jan. 19, 1970, pp. 236–237; Forster and Epstein, *New Anti-Semitism*, 33–36; Jack Anderson, "Penn Central Retains Ex-Nixon Firm," *Washington Post*, June 20, 1970; *Tulsa Daily World*, June 23, 1970.

81. *Arkansas Democrat* [Little Rock], May 22, 1970.

82. Leroy Donald, " 'Conspiracy' Killed Road, Smith Says; Plans Action," *Arkansas Gazette* [Little Rock], May 22, 1970; *Eureka Springs Times-Echo*, July 9, 1970.

83. Smith, *Besieged Patriot*, 261–62; *Arkansas Gazette* [Little Rock], May 8, 1971.

12. Smith's Final Years

1. FBI, Franklin D. Roosevelt to J. Edgar Hoover, March 25, 1943, F 62–43818–257; FBI, Francis Biddle to J. Edgar Hoover, May 28, 1943, F 62–43818–257; George Seldes, *In Fact* 5, no. 2 (April 20, 1942), 4.

2. FBI, J. Edgar Hoover to Special Agent in Charge (S.A.), Detroit, April 23 and May 18, 1942, F 62–43818–56 to 59; Hoover to S.A., May 18, 1942, F 62–43818–58; "Undeveloped Leads" [1942], Detroit F 62–1126; "Undeveloped Leads" [1942], F 62–43818.

3. Isabel B. Price, "Gerald L. K. Smith and Anti-Semitism," (M.A. thesis, University of New Mexico, 1965), 115.

4. *Propaganda Battlefront* 3, no. 2 (March 31, 1945), R 11, F "F," Gerald L. K. Smith Papers; Eugene Segal, "Nationalists Organize Youth on Hitler Plan," *New York World-Telegram*, July 20, 1945; *PM* [New York], Nov. 29, 1945; *Birmingham News*, Dec. 17, 1945; *Christian Science Monitor* [Boston], Jan. 5, 1946; Avedis Derounian (pseud. John Ray Carlson), *The Plotters* (New York, 1946), 126–27; *Chicago Sun*, Feb. 8, 1946; *Chicago Tribune*, Feb. 14, 1946; Ralph C. Cessna, "America First 'Gag' Case Poses Free Speech Tests," *Christian Science Monitor*, May 22, 1946; *Terminiello v. Chicago*, 337 U.S. (1949), 4–5.

5. Quoted in Solomon Andhil Fineberg, "Checkmate for Rabble-Rousers," *Commentary* 2 (Nov. 1946), 223.

6. Solomon A. Fineberg, Irwin Lee Glaustein, and Irving Howe, "How Fight Rabble-Rousers?" *Commentary* 2 (Nov. 1946), 465–66.

7. Price, "Gerald L. K. Smith and Anti-Semitism," 143–44; George Kellman to Isaiah Termin, "An Appraisal of the Silent Treatment," May 27, 1947, American Jewish Committee Archives; Smith, "Quarantined by the Anti-Christ" (n.p., n.d.).

8. Kellman to Termin, "Appraisal of the Silent Treatment"; Editor, *Jewish Advocate* [Boston], July 17, 1947; *Denver Post*, Aug. 11, 1949; Editor, *Milwaukee Journal*, Oct. 12, 1949.

9. Smith to George S. Schuyler, Feb. 1, 1968, B 63, F 1968, "S" (1).

10. Smith to John Frank, March 6, 1970, B 66, F 1970, "F" (2).

11. Smith to Renata [Martz], Jan. 6, 1972, B 78, F 1974, "M" (3) [misfiled].

12. Smith to George F. Miller, Nov. 26, 1974, B 78, F 1974, "M" (4).

13. John Fergus Ryan, "Twilight Years of a Kindly Old Hatesmith," *Esquire* 70 (Aug. 1968), 88–91.

14. Smith to Bertrand L. Comparet, Oct. 26, 1959, B 50, F 1959, Comparet.

15. *Arkansas Gazette* [Little Rock], May 6, 1970.

16. Smith to Renata Martz, Dec. 15, 1971 [misfiled], and Jan. 19, 1973, both in B 78, F 1974, "M" (3); Roland L. Morgan to Inamullah Khan, Feb. 21, 1975, B 80, F 1975, "K" (2); Smith to the Sorensons and Talls, March 8, 1974, B 78, F 1974, "S" (1).

17. Smith to Mrs. George Armstrong, May 3, 1974, B 76, F 1974, "A" (2); Smith to Edith and Roland Morgan, April 25, 1974, B 78, F 1974, "M" (1).

18. Smith to Dr. Dante B. Marinelli, April 7, 1975, B 80, F 1975, "M" (2); Smith to Mr. [first name omitted] McQueeny, June 13, 1975, same F; Smith to Bob Arteaga, Dec. 26, 1975, B 79, F 1975, "A" (2).

19. Mrs. Gerald L. K. Smith to Loyal Friend, April 19, 1976, Milwaukee Anti-Defamation League files.

20. Smith to John [Frank], n.d., B 60, F 1965, F "F" (misc.).

21. *Eureka Springs Times-Echo*, April 22, 1976.

22. James Scudder, "Smith Buried in Shadow of Statue," *Arkansas Democrat* [Little Rock], April 24, 1976; Ginger Shiras, "Gerald L. K. Smith Buried at Foot of Christ Statue," *Arkansas Gazette* [Little Rock], April 24, 1976.

23. Charles F. Robertson, taped interview with the author, Eureka Springs, Ark., June 1, 1979.

24. Shiras, "Smith Buried."

25. Scudder, "Smith Buried."

26. Ibid.

27. Mrs. Smith to Loyal Friend, April 19, 1976.

28. *The Cross and the Flag* 35, no. 3 (June 1976), 3.

29. Ibid., 17.

30. Ibid., 36, no. 3 (June 1977), 2; *Arkansas Gazette* [Little Rock], Dec. 24, 1977; Charles F. Robertson to W. Pat Jennings, U.S. House of Representatives, Office of the Clerk, Report of Receipts and Expenditures, Christian Nationalist Crusade, Jan. 31, 1975.

31. Robertson, interview with author.

32. Leroy Donald, "Long-Time Smith Follower Takes Reins at Eureka Springs," *Arkansas Gazette* [Little Rock], Nov. 14, 1976; "The Great Passion Play," souvenir program (Eureka Springs, Ark., 1978); *Eureka Springs Times-Echo*, April 6, 1978.

33. "A Call for Help," Charles F. Robertson to Smith supporters [1982], author's copy. Ginger Shiras, telephone conversation with author, Eureka Springs, Ark., 1984.

34. *Carroll County Tribune*, Aug. 17, 1979; *Eureka Springs Times-Echo*, Sept. 6, 1979.

35. John Morton Blum, *V Was for Victory: Politics and American Culture During World War II* (New York, 1976), 204.

36. Raymond Gram Swing, *Forerunners of American Fascism* (New York, 1969), 14 (first published in 1935).

37. Smith to Richard Hamel, Aug. 9, 1950, B 30, F 1950, "Ha" (misc.).

Epilogue

1. Smith to Mrs. George W. Armstrong, July 25, 1952, Gerald L. K. Smith Papers, B 36, F 1952, Armstrong, George W.

Essay on Sources

Archives

The most significant collection of Smith documents is the Gerald L. K. Smith Papers at the Bentley Historical Library, University of Michigan. Donated by the Smith estate in 1982, the 100 linear feet include correspondence, memoranda for staff, clippings, published and unpublished speeches, pamphlets, and articles. Because Smith worked at home rather than at his office, he instructed his staff by memo and rarely telephoned. Memos to and from him were meticulously filed and are included in their entirety. Smith was a voluminous correspondent with major political figures, obscure individuals, and almost every person of the political and religious far right.

There are also newspaper clippings, a few tape recordings of speeches, articles about Smith, and a portion of Smith's personal library. There are only a few papers from before 1939; these include some letters to and from his parents, notations he made as a student, and his father's account books. From the later period there are hundreds of letters between Smith and his parents, some of which reveal a highly introspective individual. I spent fifteen months, ten full-time, working in the collection in 1984–85. The papers not only document Smith's life; they are useful for anyone studying the extreme right in America since the 1930s.

The Huey P. Long Papers, T. Harry Williams Papers, and Huey P. Long Scrapbooks at the Louisiana State University Special Collections are an under-utilized collection valuable for people interested in Huey P. Long and his associates. The papers were not available to Professor T. Harry Williams for his lengthy biography of Long. The Williams Papers include transcripts of nearly three hundred interviews conducted by Williams, as well as some of his notes. They are most useful for Long's early career and contain little relating specifically to Smith. The many volumes of clippings scrapbooks, however, contain substantial information about Smith's work with the Share-Our-Wealth Society.

Several extensive taped interviews with friends and opponents of Smith and Huey Long conducted by Hubert Humphreys are housed in the Oral History Collection of the Louisiana State University–Shreveport Archives

and Special Collections. The most useful are interviews with Cecil Morgan
and Harney Bogan.

Jewish organizations collected clippings, reports, and published material
by and about Smith. The Anti-Defamation League of B'nai B'rith, the American Jewish Committee, and the American Jewish Congress in New York City
furnished substantial documents, as did the American Jewish Historical
Society in Waltham, Massachusetts. Two presidential libraries also hold
some documents relating to Smith: the Franklin D. Roosevelt Library in Hyde
Park, New York, and the Herbert Hoover Library in West Branch, Iowa.

Several libraries contain clippings files on Smith, including the Detroit
Public Library, the New Orleans Public Library, the Louisiana State Library at
Baton Rouge, and the New York State Public Library at Albany. I also had
access to Smith documents, mainly from 1942–43, which I microfilmed at
Smith's headquarters in Glendale, California, in December 1974–January
1975. Smith also gave me a copy of every book, pamphlet, and tract still in
print at that time.

Federal Bureau of Investigation

I utilized the Freedom of Information Act to obtain the FBI files of Smith,
Huey P. Long, Father Charles E. Coughlin, and Elizabeth Dilling. The FBI
furnished ten thousand pages of reports on Smith, including information
from telephone taps, informants, and persons who infiltrated Smith's staff.
The material on Long and Couglin amounts to approximately five hundred
pages each; it is interesting but reveals little new information. Dilling's file is
about a thousand pages long; some of it pertains to her initial alliance and
later break with Smith.

Government Documents

The most revealing government documents were the annual financial statements Smith submitted to the Clerk of the House of Representatives, beginning in 1948. Smith was compelled by the Corrupt Practices Act to furnish
lists of people who donated a hundred dollars or more to his organizations, as
well as total income and disbursements. Of the government reports dealing
with Smith, the most helpful is *Investigation of Un-American Propaganda
Activities in the U.S.* (Gerald L. K. Smith), January 30, 1946, 79th Cong., 2d
sess. This includes sixty pages on the America First Party, *The Cross and the
Flag*, and the leadership of Smith's organizations. After Smith ran for the U.S.
Senate in 1942 his campaign finances were investigated and reported in U.S.
Congress, House, *Hearings Before the Committee to Investigate Campaign
Expenditures*, 78th Cong., 2d sess., 1944.

Oral Interviews

I taped interviews with Smith on August 10 and 11, 1974, in Eureka Springs, Ark., and on Dec. 28, 1974 and Jan. 21, 1975 in Glendale, Calif. I also used interviews taped by Leo P. Ribuffo at Eureka Springs, Ark., Aug. 25, 1969 (furnished to me by Ribuffo) and by J. Fraser Cocks III, on March 28, 1968, in Los Angeles. The Cocks interview is included in the Smith Papers at the Bentley Historical Library of the University of Michigan. It is the most comprehensive; Smith's memory was best then.

I also taped interviews with people who knew Smith: Charles F. Robertson, Robert Hyde, Ed Jeffords, Roland Lee Morgan, Phillip Bullock, Mr. and Mrs. Marion Jouett, Mrs. K. A. Miller, Cecil Morgan, Mrs. Bland Bruns, and Harney Bogan. I conducted four additional interviews with individuals who requested that I not mention their names.

Newspapers and Magazines

Hundreds of newspaper and magazine articles were written about Smith. I examined complete runs of the following: *The Cross and the Flag*, *In Fact*, Boston *Christian Science Monitor*, *New Orleans Times-Picayune*, *Baton Rouge Morning Advocate*, *Shreveport Times*, *Shreveport Journal*, *New York PM*, *St. Louis Globe-Democrat*, *St. Louis Post-Dispatch*, *Detroit Free Press*, *Detroit News*, *Washington Post*, *New York Times*, *Tulsa Daily World*, *Tulsa Tribune*, *Eureka Springs Times-Echo*, *Arkansas Gazette*, *Arkansas Democrat*, and *Los Angeles Times*.

The following articles were most important: H. L. Mencken, "Why Not Gerald?" *Baltimore Evening Sun*, Sept. 7, 1936; Hodding Carter, "How Come Huey Long?" *New Republic* 82 (Feb. 13, 1935), 11–13, and in the same issue a reply by Gerald L. K. Smith, "Or Superman?" 14–15; Herbert Harris, "That Third Party," *Current History* 45, no. 1 (Oct. 1936), 77–92; "Gerald L. K. Smith," *Current Biography, 1943*; Solomon Andhil Fineberg, "Checkmate for Rabble-Rousers: What to Do When the Demagogue Comes," *Commentary* 2 (Sept. 1946), 220–26. Fineberg and others debated the tactics for combating Smith in "How Fight Rabble Rousers? A Discussion": pt. 1, "Against 'Silent Treatment,'" by Irwin Lee Glaustein; pt. 2, "The Value of Mass Action," by Irving Howe; pt. 3, "Fight on the Real Battle-Line," by Solomon Andhil Fineberg, *Commentary* 2 (Nov. 1946), 460–66. For the period Smith spent in Eureka Springs see John Fergus Ryan, "Twilight Years of a Kindly Old Hatesmith," *Esquire* 70 (Aug. 1968), 88–91; and Calvin Trillin, "U.S. Journal: Eureka Springs, Arkansas," *New Yorker* 45 (July 26, 1969), 69–70, 75–79.

Books by Smith

Smith wrote dozens of short books and hundreds of pamphlets and tracts. He gave me a copy of each of his publications available in 1974 and I obtained some out-of-print works from the Bentley Library, the American Jewish Historical Society, the American Jewish Committee, the American Jewish Congress, the Anti-Defamation League of B'nai B'rith, and the New York State Library.

Smith wrote a series of biographical episodes published after his death under the title *Besieged Patriot: Autobiographical Episodes Exposing Communism, Traitorism and Zionism from the Life of Gerald L. K. Smith*, ed. Elna M. Smith and Charles F. Robertson (Eureka Springs, Ark., 1978). *Besieged Patriot* is not an autobiography in the conventional sense but rather a series of anecdotes in no particular order revealing Smith's arrogant egotism. However they do clarify some events in his life and provide insights into how he felt about himself. The episodes on his childhood and his relationship with his wife are particularly helpful.

Smith wrote a fawning biography of Huey Long which purports to describe his relationship with the Louisiana Kingfish, *Huey P. Long: Summary of Greatness, Political Genius, American Martyr* (Eureka Springs, Ark., 1978). The book is unreliable but provides a glimpse of Smith's hero worship and an exaggerated view of his role in the Long organization.

The most complete account of Smith's *Christ of the Ozarks* is his seventy-page handbook, *The Story of the Statue of the Christ of the Ozarks* (Eureka Springs, Ark., 1967), which discusses the conception, planning, and construction of the statue. Smith's conspiratorial views are elaborated in *Is Communism Jewish?* (St. Louis, Mo., n.d.). His hatred of President Franklin D. Roosevelt and FDR's family is described in *Too Much and Too Many Roosevelts* (St. Louis, Mo., 1950), and his obsession to destroy the United Nations is explained in *Abolish the United Nations: A Handbook for Patriots* (St. Louis, Mo., 1953).

Theses and Dissertations

The most useful unpublished study of Smith is Isabel B. Price, "Gerald L. K. Smith and Anti-Semitism" (M.A. thesis, University of New Mexico, 1965). Unpublished accounts of Smith's political and religious crusades include Lloyd Ray Henderson, "The Political Activities of Gerald L. K. Smith" (M.A. thesis, University of California, 1955); and Stanley R. Miles, "The Anti-Semitism of William Dudley Pelley, Father Charles E. Coughlin, and Gerald L. K. Smith: 1933 to 1941" (Ordination thesis, Hebrew Union College–Jewish Institute of Religion, 1975). Michael Wickham Bouton, "Depression Era Extremists: A Study of Three Demagogues and Their Tactics" (Ph.D. diss., Illinois State University, 1978), discusses the oratory and organizing tactics of Smith, Coughlin, and Eugene Talmadge in the context of teaching the history of the Depression era to high school American History classes. Fred S. Bodker, "Gerald L. K. Smith: The Evolution of an Anti-Semite" (Senior Honors thesis, University of Michigan, 1986), draws upon a limited portion of the Smith papers at Ann Arbor. Bodker argues that Smith did not evolve into anti-Semitism during the 1940s but that he was actually anti-Semitic all along. The best unpublished study of Huey P. Long is Albert Edward Cowdrey, "Huey Long in National Politics" (M.A. thesis, Johns Hopkins University, 1957). There are several additional unpublished studies on Long, but they are superseded by the published literature.

Books

By far the most useful study of Smith is Leo P. Ribuffo, *The Old Christian Right: The Protestant Far Right From the Great Depression to the Cold War* (Philadelphia, 1983). Ribuffo examines Smith, Gerald P. Winrod, and William Dudley Pelley in separate chapters and analyzes their ideology. Unfortunately he did not have access to the Smith papers at the University of Michigan.

Other than Ribuffo's, this is the first study of Smith. A few books include chapters on Smith, or discuss him in a few pages with other far right advocates. There is substantial literature on Huey Long and some studies of the Depression era are relevant to the study of Smith. In addition, works on anti-Semitism in America help put Smith in context. I discuss only a fraction of this literature here; during the course of my research I examined over 150 volumes.

There are no published accounts of Smith prior to his alliance with Huey Long. Most depict Smith during the Great Depression as an ally of Long, Father Charles E. Coughlin, and Dr. Francis E. Townsend. T. Harry Williams, *Huey Long* (New York, 1969), is exhaustive but excessively pro-Long and does not utilize the Long papers at Louisiana State University. Alan Brinkley, *Voices of Protest: Huey Long, Father Coughlin, and the Great Depression* (New York, 1982), is more balanced, placing Long and Coughlin in a national context.

David H. Bennett, *Demagogues in the Depression, American Radicals and the Union Party, 1932–1936* (New Brunswick, N.J., 1969) is indispensable for a study of the alliance between Smith, Coughlin, Townsend, and William Lemke in their third-party crusade against Franklin D. Roosevelt in 1936.

Several books dealing with the Great Depression and the World War II and postwar eras include chapters on Smith and Long or discuss them in the context of other demagogues. The most useful are Reinhard H. Luthin, *American Demagogues* (Boston, 1954); Ralph Lord Roy, *Apostles of Discord: A Study of Organized Bigotry and Disruption on the Fringes of Protestantism* (Boston, 1953); Allan A. Michie and Frank Rylic, *Dixie Demagogues* (New York, 1939); Raymond Gram Swing, *Forerunners of American Fascism* (New York, 1935); Studs Terkel, *Hard Times* (New York, 1971); Rita James Simon, ed., *As We Saw the Thirties* (Chicago, 1967); Thomas L. Stokes, *Chip Off My Shoulder* (Princeton, N.J., 1940); and Unofficial Observer [John Carter Franklin], *American Messiahs* (New York, 1935). Biographies of other figures of the Great Depression, biographies of Franklin D. Roosevelt, and studies of the

New Deal include scattered references to Smith, but none discusses him separately. Victor C. Ferkiss, *The Political and Economic Philosophy of American Fascism* (Chicago, 1954), helps place Smith in perspective.

For the period of Smith's involvement in prewar isolationism the most useful accounts are Wayne S. Cole, *America First: The Battle Against Intervention, 1940–1941* (Madison, Wis., 1953), and Cole, *Roosevelt and the Isolationists, 1932–1945* (Lincoln, Neb., 1983). George Wolfskill and John A. Hudson, *All But the People: Franklin D. Roosevelt and His Critics, 1933–1939* (New York, 1969), focuses on some of Smith's isolationist allies.

A number of "exposés" written during the war era discuss Smith and his allies. The best known are Avedis Derounian [pseud., John Roy Carlson], *Under Cover: My Four Years in the Nazi Underworld of America* (New York, 1943), and Derounian, *The Plotters* (New York, 1946). Henry Hoke's *Black Mail* (New York, 1944) and *It's a Secret* (New York, 1946); and Emanuel A. Piller, *Time Bomb* (New York, 1945), also have material on Smith. Nathaniel Weyl, *Treason: The Story of Disloyalty and Betrayal in American History* (Washington, D.C., 1950), has a chapter on "Pro-Nazis in World War II."

More general accounts of the far right include Seymour Martin Lipset and Earl Raab, *The Politics of Unreason: Right-Wing Extremism in America, 1790–1970* (New York, 1970); Ronald Radosh, *Prophets on the Right: Profiles of Conservative Critics of American Globalism* (New York, 1975); David Caute, *The Great Fear: The Anti-Communist Purge Under Truman and Eisenhower* (New York, 1978); and Richard O. Curry and Thomas M. Brown, eds., *Conspiracy: The Fear of Subversion in American History* (New York, 1972). Albert Lee, *Henry Ford and the Jews* (New York, 1980), discusses the beliefs of the auto magnate whom Smith claimed as a friend. Richard Mathison, *God Is a Millionaire* (Indianapolis, 1960), discusses religious charlatans and includes a chapter on Smith. Morris Kominsky, *The Hoaxers: Plain Liars, Fancy Liars, and Damned Liars* (Boston, 1970), discusses several conspiracy theories propagated by Smith, including *The Protocols of the Learned Elders of Zion*. George X. Johnson, *Architects of Fear: Conspiracy Theory and Paranoia in American Politics* (Boston, 1983), includes a history of the Illuminati conspiracy.

Smith is discussed in several books dealing with aspects of the far right. Books written by officials of the Anti-Defamation League are among the most important and have extensive accounts of Smith's activities. These include Arnold Forster, *Anti-Semitism—1947* (New York, 1948), and *A Measure of Freedom* (New York, 1950); and Arnold Forster and Benjamin R. Epstein, *The Troublemakers* (Garden City, New York, 1952); *Cross-Currents* (New York, 1956); and *Danger on the Right* (New York, 1964). George Thayer, *The Farther Shores of Politics: The American Political Fringe Today* (New York, 1967), has an excellent chapter on Smith. Daniel Bell, ed., *The Radical Right* (Garden City, New York, 1963), is a useful point of reference.

If material on the far right is extensive, books on anti-Semitism and racism are innumerable. Gordon Allport's classic, *The Nature of Prejudice* (Reading, Penn., rev. ed., 1980) is still useful after several decades. Solomon Andhil

Fineberg, *Overcoming Anti-Semitism* (New York, 1943), describes effective means of combating bigotry. More recent useful books include James Parkes, *Antisemitism* (London, 1963); Charles Herbert Stember and others, *Jews in the Mind of America* (New York, 1966); Gertrude J. Selznick and Stephen Steinberg, *The Tenacity of Prejudice: Anti-Semitism in Contemporary America* (New York, 1969); Stephen D. Isaacs, *Jews and American Politics* (Garden City, New York, 1974); Paul E. Grosser and Edwin G. Halperin, *The Causes and Effects of Anti-Semitism* (New York, 1978); and Harold E. Quinley and Charles Y. Glock, *Anti-Semitism in America* (New York, 1979). Nathaniel Weyl, *The Jew in American Politics* (New York, 1968), places the subject in context. Arnold Forster and Benjamin R. Epstein, *The New Anti-Semitism* (New York, 1974), includes a chapter on Smith's attempt to obtain government money to build a road leading to his Sacred Projects.

The 1980s have produced a fresh wave of books dealing with anti-Semitism. Nathan Perlmutter and Ruth Ann Perlmutter, *The Real Anti-Semitism in America* (New York, 1982), describes the moderate right's role in protecting Jewish interests. Ernest Volman, *A Legacy of Hate: Anti-Semitism in America* (New York, 1982), is a synthesis of recent research. David A. Gerber, ed., *Anti-Semitism in American History* (Urbana and Chicago, 1986), includes several essays on the recent period, including one by this writer.

Some anti-Semites were anti-Communists and racists and a few were fundamentalists. Books dealing with extremism of the far right include Mark Sherwin, *The Extremists* (New York, 1963); Michael Parenti, *The Anti-Communist Impulse* (New York, 1969); and Erling Jorstad, *The Politics of Doomsday: Fundamentalists of the Far Right* (Nashville, 1970).

Index